CRITICAL ESSAYS ON
British South Asian Theatre

British South Asian theatre has formed one of the most significant features of British and diaspora culture over the last thirty years. Despite remarkable achievements and high levels of popular recognition, it has not received the diversity of critical attention it requires.

This collection brings together a wide range of critical voices to offer significant insights into the social and historical contexts, processes of production and audience reception of British South Asian theatre.

The book is a companion volume to *British South Asian Theatres: A Documented History,* which is accompanied by a complimentary DVD including photographs, articles and clips from play recordings. The documented history volume is also edited by Graham Ley and Sarah Dadswell and published by University of Exeter Press.

Graham Ley is Professor of Drama and Theory at the University of Exeter. He has written and published widely, including *From Mimesis to Interculturalism: Readings of Theatrical Theory before and after 'Modernism'* (University of Exeter Press, 1999), *A Short Introduction to Ancient Greek Theater* (2nd revised edition University of Chicago Press, 2006) and *The Theatricality of Greek Tragedy* (University of Chicago Press, 2007), and is also the author of articles on British Asian theatre.

Sarah Dadswell is a cultural historian specialising in performance and Honorary Research Fellow in the Department of Drama at the University of Exeter. She co-edited *Victory over the Sun: The World's First Futurist Opera* (University of Exeter Press, 2012) with Rosamund Bartlett and is also the author of articles on British Asian theatre.

Exeter Performance Studies

Series editors: Peter Thomson, Professor of Drama at the University of Exeter; Graham Ley, Professor of Drama and Theory at the University of Exeter; Steve Nicholson, Professor of Twentieth-Century and Contemporary Theatre at the University of Sheffield.

From Mimesis to Interculturalism: Readings of Theatrical Theory Before and After 'Modernism'
Graham Ley (1999)

British Theatre and the Red Peril: The Portrayal of Communism 1917–1945
Steve Nicholson (1999)

On Actors and Acting
Peter Thomson (2000)

Grand-Guignol: The French Theatre of Horror
Richard J. Hand and Michael Wilson (2002)

The Censorship of British Drama 1900–1968: Volume One 1900–1932
Steve Nicholson (2003)

The Censorship of British Drama 1900–1968: Volume Two 1933–1952
Steve Nicholson (2005)

Freedom's Pioneer: John McGrath's Work in Theatre, Film and Television
edited by David Bradby and Susanna Capon (2005)

John McGrath: Plays for England
selected and introduced by Nadine Holdsworth (2005)

Theatre Workshop: Joan Littlewood and the Making of Modern British Theatre
Robert Leach (2006)

Making Theatre in Northern Ireland: Through and Beyond the Troubles
Tom Maguire (2006)

"In Comes I": Performance, Memory and Landscape
Mike Pearson (2006)

London's Grand Guignol and the Theatre of Horror
Richard J. Hand and Michael Wilson (2007)

Theatres of the Troubles: Theatre, Resistance and Liberation in Ireland
Bill McDonnell (2008)

The Censorship of British Drama, 1900–1968: Volume Three, The Fifties
Steve Nicholson (2011)

British South Asian Theatres: A Documented History
edited by Graham Ley and Sarah Dadswell (2011)

Victory over the Sun: The World's First Futurist Opera
edited by Rosamund Bartlett and Sarah Dadswell (2012)

CRITICAL ESSAYS ON
British South Asian Theatre

edited by

Graham Ley and Sarah Dadswell

UNIVERSITY
of
EXETER
PRESS

Cover image: Scene from *Rafta, Rafta* ... at the National Theatre, photographed by Catherine Ashmore (reproduced with kind permission of the photographer).

First published in 2012 by
University of Exeter Press
Reed Hall, Streatham Drive
Exeter EX4 4QR
UK
www.exeterpress.co.uk

British Library Cataloguing in Publication Data
A catalogue record for this book is available
from the British Library.

Paperback ISBN 978 0 85989 835 5

Web addresses were correct as the book went to press, except where a date in
parentheses is used to indicate the last time a page was accessed.

Typeset in Sabon, 10 on 12 by
Carnegie Book Production, Lancaster
Printed in Great Britain by
TJ International Ltd, Padstow

Contents

Illustrations

Contributors

Rukhsana Ahmad co-founded Kali Theatre Company (with Rita Wolf) and led it into revenue funding. Her theatre credits include *Song for a Sanctuary*, *River on Fire* (finalist for the Susan Smith-Blackburn International Prize), *The Gate-Keeper's Wife* and *Mistaken ... Annie Besant in India*. Radio adaptations include *Wide Sargasso Sea, Maps for Lost Lovers, Midnight's Children* and *The Far Pavilions*.

Chris Banfield has worked as a drama lecturer, freelance theatre director, and teacher with an interest in Indian theatre for over twenty years. He has run a range of theatre practice workshops during that time for students in India—Allahabad, Chennai and Madurai—as well as in the UK. He is co-author, with Brian Crow, of *An Introduction to Post-colonial Theatre* (1996) in which he discusses the plays of Badal Sircar and Girish Karnad. He currently teaches at Ibstock Place School, Roehampton, and lives in Battersea, south-west London.

Suman Bhuchar has a long career in PR, marketing and arts production. Highlights include award winning documentaries: *The Journalist & The Jihadi: The Murder of Daniel Pearl* (HBO, nominated for 2 Emmys); *Dead Man Talking*: *A Forensic Murder Investigation by Hampshire Police* (Channel 4) and *Alone Together*: *Portrait of the Singh Twins*, winner 'Best film on Art', Asolo Film Festival 2001. She writes for numerous publications and is a speaker/curator of seminars on Asian arts and Bollywood cinema. She is a regular contributor to www.theatrevoice.com and a Fellow of the Royal Society of Arts.

Giovanna Buonanno lectures in English at the University of Modena and Reggio Emilia. She is the author of *International Actresses on the Victorian Stage* (2002) and has published articles on modern and contemporary British and Italian theatre, intercultural drama, black British culture, and black and Asian British women's writing. She is currently working on a monograph on British Asian women writers.

Colin Chambers is Professor of Drama at Kingston University. Formerly a journalist and theatre critic, he was Literary Manager of the Royal Shakespeare Company from 1981 to 1997. His books include *The Story of Unity Theatre* (1989); the award-winning *Peggy: the Life of Margaret Ramsay, Play Agent* (1997); *The Continuum Companion to Twentieth Century Theatre* (editor and contributor, 2002); *Inside the Royal Shakespeare Company: Creativity and the Institution* (2004); *Here We Stand: Politics, Performers and Performance—Paul Robeson, Isadora Duncan and Charlie Chaplin* (2006); and *Black and Asian Theatre in Britain: A History* (2011).

Claire Cochrane is Senior Lecturer in Drama and Performance at Worcester University. As the author of *Birmingham Rep: A City's Theatre 1962–2002* (2003) she explored the theatre's record in the development of British Asian and Black British actors and playwrights. Other recent essays have widened the exploration to other venues in Birmingham and at Nottingham Playhouse. Her latest book, *Twentieth Century British Theatre Industry, Art and Empire* (2011) incorporates the black British experience of theatre into the landscape of UK theatre as a whole, across the century.

Susan Croft is Co-Director of the project *Unfinished Histories: Recording the History of Alternative Theatre* (www.unfinishedhistories.com) and Clive Barker Research Fellow at Rose Bruford College of Theatre and Performance. She was Senior Curator (Contemporary Performance) at the V&A Theatre Museum from 1997 to 2005, where she initiated a range of projects foregrounding black and Asian materials in the collections, including web resources, exhibitions and edited *Black and Asian Performance at the Theatre Museum: A Users' Guide* (2001). Formerly an academic and Director of New Playwrights' Trust, she has published widely on women playwrights, black playwrights in Britain and live art (see www.susan.croft.btinternet.co.uk).

Jerri Daboo is a Principal Investigator in Drama at the University of Exeter. She has worked professionally for many years as a performer and director in theatre, dance and music. Her research focuses on performance and culture, as well as embodiment and performer training. She was a member of the research team of the AHRC-funded project on British Asian Theatre in the Department of Drama at the University of Exeter, and expanding on contacts from this project, is now the Principal Investigator on a new AHRC-funded project researching the cultural history of Southall.

Stephen Hodge is Senior Lecturer in Drama and a member of the Centre for Intermedia at the University of Exeter. He curates the Theatre, Dance and Live Art programme at Exeter Phoenix, and is a member of the UK's New Theatre Architects. He is a practicing live artist and a core member of Wrights & Sites, a group of artist-researchers with a special relationship to site, city/landscape and walking. He is co-author, with Cathy Turner, of the chapter on 'Site' in D. Heddon and J. Klein (eds) *Histories and Practices of Live Art in the UK* (due 2012).

Naseem Khan OBE has been at the forefront of cultural policy for much of her working life, having written the seminal *The Arts Britain Ignores* in 1976. Her involvement in Asian arts has been as both practitioner and critic. She trained in Indian classical dance and was co-director of the Academy of Indian Dance. As a writer, she has followed Asian theatre in Britain as Theatre Editor of *Time Out* in the 1970s, theatre critic for *The Evening Standard* and weekly columnist in *The New Statesman* in the 1980s. Head of Diversity for the Arts Council for six years, she currently works freelance.

Chandrika Patel works freelance as a researcher, writer and facilitator of arts-led projects. She has extensive experience of working in South Asian communities and has worked on three heritage-related projects. Her essay contains examples of analysis drawn from her thesis, which was concerned with the study of signs used in British South Asian theatres, and the extent to which they determine British Asian work.

Victoria Sams holds a PhD in Comparative Literature from University of California, Los Angeles (UCLA). She taught in the Humanities Program at UCLA and subsequently in the English Department at Dickinson College in Carlisle, Pennsylvania. She is the editor of *The Random House Treasury of Poems about Cities Around the World* (2004), and is completing a book on postwar immigration and contemporary British theatre.

Christiane Schlote teaches drama and postcolonial literatures and cultures at the University of Zurich. She has published extensively on postcolonial literatures and cityscapes, British Asian theatre, Anglophone Arab writing and Latina/o and Asian-American culture. She is the author of *Bridging Cultures: Latino-und asiatisch-amerikanisches Theater in New York* (1997) and co-editor of *New Beginnings in Twentieth-Century Theatre and Drama* (2003) and *Constructing Media Reality: The New Documentarism* (2008). She is currently editing the manuscript for a book on transnationalism in British Asian and South Asian American drama and fiction and co-editing a study on literature from the Middle East and its diasporas as well as a volume on literary and linguistic representations of war and refugeehood.

Rajni Shah is an artist working in performance and live art. Whether online, in a public space or in a theatre, her work aims to open up new spaces for conversation and the meeting of diverse voices. From 2006 to 2010 she conducted a three-year enquiry into the relationship between gift and conversation in public space called Small Gifts. From 2005 to 2012 she produced a trilogy of large-scale performances (*Mr Quiver, Dinner with America* and *Glorious*) addressing the complexities of cultural identity in the twenty-first century (see www.rajnishah.com).

Introduction

This collection of essays forms a companion to *British South Asian Theatres: A Documented History*, and the overarching emphasis in both volumes is on the performance of live theatre.[1] The scope of the essays is also similar, ranging from the theatrical representation of South Asians in Britain in the three centuries before the modern period to the emergence of a strong accent on self-representation in the second half of the last century, which continues to the present. These essays have been commissioned from independent scholars in the field in Britain, Europe and the USA, and British Asian practitioners who are offering reflections on their work. In this respect, the collection gathers together a wide range of critical voices with divergent interests and approaches, who offer significant insights into the context, process, production and reception of British South Asian theatre.

If the premise of the first volume is that British South Asian theatre has been inadequately documented, then the premise of this volume is that it has not received the critical attention it requires. These two considerations are obviously closely related, and both point to a failure of academic responsibility that has begun to be repaired only in the last few years by a number of valuable publications. The fact is that, despite its forty years of burgeoning activity, Asian-led theatre in Britain has not figured at all in prominent and supposedly authoritative accounts of the contemporary British theatre. What is remarkable about this absence is that several Asian-led companies and their leading practitioners have been well known to theatre-goers for the last twenty years, not least because 'the sector' (as it is currently known) has been required by the conditions of its funding to tour widely throughout Britain.[2] If theatre-goers and reviewers in the national and regional press, and on-line, are thoroughly familiar with the vitality and diversity of the work, its absence from the academic or critical record seems inexplicable. To put that in more formal terms, the primary reception of British South Asian theatre in all its varieties by audiences and reviewers has not been matched by an appropriate level of secondary reception by those who might review achievements at a greater distance, from an academic or critical standpoint.

To accept this situation is to condemn British South Asian practitioners and the movement as a whole to a constant state of hazardous ephemerality, of existing without the history that is allowed to others. It would suggest the worst of an academic and intellectual culture, which would through neglect be mirroring the underlying refusal of a society to recognise the belonging-over-time that is the reality of any diaspora or postcolonial community.[3] To produce a history is, in the first instance, a recognition of a reality, in whatever field of activity, artistic or otherwise. In the presentation of that detailed record, more will be suggested and required than can be answered by any single voice or overarching interpretation. The general moral clearly applies here: if through the increasing documentation of the achievements of British South Asian theatre we appear to know more, what kind of sense do we make of our greater knowledge? How would we best approach the understanding of something we know is important without quite knowing the ways in which it registers its importance?

That is the function of this collection of essays, which comes at a particular point in the evolution of critical writing on British Asian theatre. In the last few years there has been a marked increase in publication which has brought varieties of insight to bear. In the first phase, two leading publications from a theatrical perspective combined elements of documentation with theoretical and critical assessments in a generous but not altogether coherent manner, while a third promoted theatre writing by women in the context of literary and gender studies.[4] Dimple Godiwala's edited volume embraced longer documentary studies of Black and Asian theatre with shorter theoretical reflections on the theatre and identity by the editor. Critically, more than a third of the book was devoted to studies of plays, with the emphasis for British Asian writers lying on plays by women writers; performance analysis featured strongly only in one contribution on British Asian theatre, by Dominic Hingorani on selected work by Tara Arts and Tamasha.[5] The volume edited by Geoffrey Davis and Anne Fuchs was divided between studies of Black and South Asian British theatre and interviews with practitioners, with the greater length given to the essays. Of the essays on British Asian theatre, Christiane Schlote argued for the importance of women playwrights in maintaining an emphasis on the British Asian experience, while Anne Fuchs traced the importance of the idea of heritage in the work and profile of Tamasha.[6] Underpinning the critical emphasis in both volumes on plays by women writers was the precedent set by Gabriele Griffin, who published her monograph on Black and Asian women playwrights in Britain slightly earlier. Griffin's approach came from diaspora and gender studies, and was predominantly thematic and literary, with playtexts viewed as authorial representations of lived experience largely unmediated by performance or production circumstances.

Taken together, and with the previously published essays on which some of their contributions depend and to which they refer, these books constituted a major breakthrough in scholarly attention to a neglected field, complementing an expanding critical interest in diasporic fiction in Britain.[7] More recently, two further books have broadened perspectives on the subject, adding greater historical depth and attention to performance and production. Colin Chambers has conjoined black and Asian in what amounts to an alternative, long view of British theatre history, while Dominic Hingorani has reviewed a selection of significant productions by leading British Asian theatre companies from the last thirty-five years.[8] The essays collected here maintain that emphasis on the primacy of performance and production.[9]

The collection is opened by an overview from Naseem Khan, a distinguished critic and consultant on diversity in the arts, and author of the ground-breaking study *The Arts Britain Ignores*.[10] Khan remains concerned about the status of South Asian performing arts in Britain, and her meditations on this subject are informed by her close acquaintance with policies pursued by the Arts Council and national funding bodies over the last thirty years.[11] She discusses the shifting terms of the debate on diversity in British culture, considering the impact of multiculturalism in British society and the place of Asian arts within that conceptual framework. Her essay looks back to the 1970s, registering the early confusion between ethnic and community arts and the subsequent tension between the need to present ethnicity and a desire not to be confined exclusively to its representation. Her essay concludes with an accent on contemporary concerns about employment in the creative industries and training.

The background to the modern activities and role of British South Asian theatre within British culture is the subject of a historical essay by Colin Chambers, who traces stage representations of the 'other' from Renaissance times to the twentieth century. Chambers records that South Asia was often confused with the Middle East and China in an orientalising attitude, but argues that images of the 'other' have been central to the development of British drama. Despite some criticism of colonialism, the superiority of the British was generally promoted, with South Asians presented as figures of mystery and the objects of linguistic mockery. In the later nineteenth century, oriental themes proved to be commercial box-office successes, in a counterpoint to the occasional appearances of South Asians in pageants and as street entertainers. Chambers concludes his essay with a number of the initiatives taken by South Asians in Britain during the first half of the twentieth century. An additional and detailed sketch of the initiatives undertaken with and by the Bangladeshi community in the inner London borough of Tower Hamlets is provided by Susan Croft, with a focus on the 1980s and the role of the Half Moon Young People's Theatre.

In the first of the contributions from practitioners, the playwright and co-founder of Kali Theatre, Rukhsana Ahmad, reflects on her initial encounters with playwriting with Tara Arts and subsequently in the company that she co-founded with Rita Wolf. For Ahmad, after an educational background studying plays as literature in Pakistan, her move to London brought her into regular contact with professional live theatre production. She traces her practice as it evolved in the commissions for Tara Arts, her contact with Monstrous Regiment, and her involvement with the Asian Women Writers Workshop and the Writers Guild. Radio proved to be a welcoming medium, but in this essay Ahmad keeps the accent on live theatre, discussing her relationship with the directors Debbie Bestwick and Helena Bell and her close involvement with Vayu Naidu, which led to the script for *Mistaken ... Annie Besant in India*. Ahmad's first play for Kali Theatre, directed by Rita Wolf, was *Song for a Sanctuary*, and in her critical essay Christiane Schlote compares its treatment of the themes of the refugee and the refuge with that in the play by Tanika Gupta, *Sanctuary*. Drawing on theories originating in refugee and diaspora studies, Schlote builds on Gabriele Griffin's earlier discussion in her monograph to emphasise agency and the break from documentary realism in Ahmad's play, an aspect that connects with Ahmad's concern for the evocative powers of poetry. Schlote is particularly drawn by the fact that both Ahmad and Gupta dramatise and problematise the idea of 'refuge', highlighting the sacrilege of violence committed in the place of sanctuary.

Ahmad's involvement as a script-writer in the process that led to the production of *Mistaken ... Annie Besant in India* is viewed by Chris Banfield from the perspective of a director of the relatively novel form of story-telling theatre. In his capacity as director, Banfield has been associated with Vayu Naidu Company over several projects, and he reflects on the interaction of storytelling with music, movement and drama as modes integral to the form, but in need of artistic reconciliation. His reflections cover three productions, *Nine Nights: Stories from the Ramayana* and *South* in addition to *Annie Besant*, examining the processes and practical working methods involved. He concludes by suggesting that a storyteller may undergo a progressive loss of creative freedom and autonomy as the role is theatricalised, or accommodated within a dramatic framework established by an authored script.

From 1999 Vayu Naidu played an influential role in the formation of policy and repertoire at the Leicester Haymarket Theatre, at which *Nine Nights: Stories from the Ramayana* was staged. In her essay, Claire Cochrane looks closely at the evolution of policies for the development of British South Asian audiences at the Haymarket in Leicester and the Birmingham Rep. She distinguishes sharply between the South Asian demographics of both cities and assesses the aims and achievements of productions conceived and promoted to foster interest in what might be perceived as 'white spaces'. It is clear from her account that at the Leicester Haymarket leading figures such as Paul Kerryson and Kully Thiarai, Sita Ramamurthy, Dipak Joshi and Vayu Naidu were influential, but that in both theatres stakeholders were expecting these initiatives to pull them out of larger financial holes. Cochrane also sketches the background of British Asian new writing for The Door at the Rep in Birmingham, noting work by Ray Grewal, Amber Lane and Yasmin Khan and providing the context for the events surrounding Gurpreet Kaur Bhatti's play *Behzti*, which was withdrawn during violent protests at the Rep in December 2004.

During the 1990s Tamasha was repeatedly engaged by the Birmingham Rep as a part of those evolving policies, as Cochrane outlines in her essay, in what was a formative period for the company. In her essay on the 'kitchen-sink drama' of Tamasha, Victoria Sams is implicitly asking what it was in this period that made Tamasha so appealing to audiences and to theatre managements. She selects two productions from the later 1990s for close analysis: Ayub Khan Din's *East Is East* and *Balti Kings*, a script developed by Sudha Bhuchar and Naushaba Shaheen Khan from research conducted in Birmingham's Asian restaurants. Both plays feature the workplace and its claustrophobia as part of the environment of British Asian family life alongside the home itself, and both consider the flawed position of the leading male within that environment. In particular, Sams highlights the diasporic qualities of the plays, examining how Britain functions in the expectations constructed within the families. Tamasha's success with theatre managements is also the starting point for the comparative study by Suman Bhuchar of the marketing of British South Asian shows in the subsidised and commercial sectors. Bhuchar was associated with Tamasha from the outset, and developed her approach to outreach and selling largely during Tamasha's years in Birmingham. Bhuchar reflects on aspects of her role and of a general strategy for working the press and marketing in relation to two productions, Tamasha's *Fourteen Songs, Two Weddings and a Funeral* of 1998 and 2001, and Andrew Lloyd Webber's enterprising *Bombay Dreams* of 2002. Despite the differences between the ventures, she concludes that the commercial production was able successfully to borrow methods that had been elaborated in the subsidised sector, although there was no subsequent attempt to consolidate that commercial achievement in expanding audiences.

Bombay Dreams is also representative for Jerri Daboo of a movement that has seen, in the new millennium, large-scale productions of South Asian or British South Asian material being staged in mainstream spaces. Daboo employs ideas drawn from cultural geography to consider how far these productions represent a movement from the margins to the centre, and the degree to which they can claim to be making a community culturally visible. Space is a central concept here, and Daboo looks at the work of Hardish Virk, who has concentrated professionally on building British South Asian audiences by making the theatre buildings seem more familiar, more integral to a diasporic culture. Running through Daboo's essay is the theme of power, the power that mainstream theatres can wield over what is seen in their spaces, and so over what is considered 'mainstream' and how it is constructed aesthetically. Meera Syal was the script-writer for *Bombay Dreams*, and her rise to the celebrity she held at this point is charted by Giovanna Buonanno in an essay that looks back to the mid-1980s and the variety of roles exercised by Syal. Buonanno considers how far Syal, as she herself claimed, was able to enlarge the scope of the representation of British Asian women on stage and screen through both comic performance and scripting. What becomes clear from Buonanno's analysis is that the transformative quality of acting has influenced Syal's writing, and that both have been instrumental to the self-fashioning process on which Syal embarked.

In the central period of the three decades of its activity (since 1977) Tara Arts became closely identified with a process and style of production known as 'Binglish'. One of the more recent Binglish productions, *The Marriage of Figaro*, is the subject of an analysis by Chandrika Patel alongside Tamasha's *A Fine Balance* of the same year, 2006, which was adapted from the novel by Rohinton Mistry. Patel's leading question is how major British Asian theatre companies have created representations of an 'Indian' identity on the British stage, since both productions were overtly located in the sub-continent. She draws on the signifying theories of the Sanskrit treatise of the performing arts, the *Natyasastra*, of semiotics and of Bertolt Brecht to suggest the meanings of signs registered through the design and production of both plays, and of the role played by the evocation of 'India' in the profiles of both Asian-led companies.

The final contributions to the volume introduce a shift of emphasis in theatre-making, with the new approaches to performance led by Keith Khan and Ali Zaidi in the work of their company, **moti**roti. Stephen Hodge tracks the productions by **moti**roti from the company's earliest days to the production of *Alladeen* in 2003, while the performance artist Rajni Shah charts the development of her four-hour installation *Mr Quiver* from its conception to later realisations. Her piece started as a short autobiographical solo and grew over the years into a complex examination of image and identity from a female British Asian performer. Shah reflects on the experience of making a piece over time, tracing ideas, situations and connections that were influential in its composition.

The publication of this collection of essays was assisted by an award from the Society for Theatre Research, for which the editors are very grateful. Most of the essays collected here were first presented as papers at the conference 'British Asian Theatre: from Past to Present', held at the University of Exeter in April 2008, at which the Rajni Shah Theatre gave its final performance of *Mr Quiver*.

1

British Asian Theatre

The Long Road to Now, and the Barriers in-between

Naseem Khan

It is impossible to even start to consider British Asian theatre without engaging with the wider cultural context of race, representation and integration. Virtually since its inception, the genre (if genre it is) has based itself in a controversial area—hard to define, difficult to place and impossible to simplify. Both its existence and its struggles to find a foothold have said more about the British social scene than they have about the intrinsic quality and merits of British Asian theatre itself.

There is a commonly held myth about the British capacity to absorb. Part of Britain's virtue is held to be its tolerance, seen in the way that it can take in difference and make it its own. But the last half century has demonstrated nothing of the sort. It has seen struggle, disappointment and confusion, lit up by several bright sky-rockets in the dark and trackless night.

To be fair, the theory of absorption held water in times when change was slow and gradual. Dissecting the English language, for instance, reveals layers of vocabulary laid down by conquests, trade routes, religious practice and empire. I have always been struck by the experience of visiting London's Museum of Garden History. You might think that little could be more quintessentially English than an English country garden. But you must think again. The Museum's sample garden has all the usual suspects (roses, hollyhocks, irises, geraniums and the like). But closer examination reveals that they are all incomers. Notices by each one give the date at which it was first recorded. It transpires that truly 'British' native species are few and far between, and that those few consist of green and undifferentiated foliage. The familiar colour of 'traditional' English flowerbeds came in through trade routes, colonisation and plant collectors such as the Tradescants and Joseph Banks.

The slow change of outline that took place horticulturally no longer holds good. The pace of change has quickened and international tensions have made accommodation a far more troubled affair. Nowadays the description of cultural diversity expounded by the then Home Secretary, Roy Jenkins, in the 1960s, which stressed tolerance and laissez-faire, can seem sadly old-fashioned.[1] More recently the ground of the debate has shifted and tangled up with it British Asian theatre and culturally diverse expression at large. Attitudes to difference have taken a sharp turn, to focus on the threats of mixed societies rather than—as in earlier times—on the advantages. Anxiety over the development of a fragmented society with no central allegiance has meant that diversity policy is beginning to be questioned. The doubt has been reinforced by a number of artists of black or Asian origin who publicly reject any identification of themselves in racial terms as stereotyping, constraining and racist.

Behind it all lies an uneasy new malaise that ponders wider fundamentals. What *is* 'Britishness' and 'British culture'? Is it in danger of dilution, as some claim? What relevance do new cultural voices, springing from different ethnic roots and experiences, have? Or old non-indigenous traditions kept up by diverse ethic communities?

Looking at this concern from the standpoint of culture is a curious experience. It is hard to see the dangers in cultural diversity that are now increasingly cited in broader society. How has this panic arisen or where has it come from, we might wonder? It differs from confusion. Confusion over the true nature of other cultures or cultural voices has been present as an element ever since those voices were officially recognised some forty years ago and, when they had become openly acknowledged, it then increasingly underpinned policy. The turns and shifts reflect policy's constant search for the 'right' solution. What seems curious in the current climate, however, is the way in which general (and legitimate) concern over a socially unified Britain has apparently come to mean a similarly homogeneous cultural life. How this conflation has arisen is hard to understand. It is well known that culture has always grown by accretion, and that its influences observe no territorial boundaries. Rather than creating exclusion and incomprehension it enables connection and makes for empathy. But we seem to be in danger of losing that perception in anxiety over national security.

This is not to say that today's more complex societies do not pose profound issues. But it is disappointing that the terms of the debate have been dictated so largely by a different agenda and that so few voices are raised to challenge what is fast becoming received wisdom: that 'multiculturalism has failed'.

The impact of multiculturalism

How has 'multiculturalism' affected Asian arts? A seemingly simple question becomes more complex the more we look at it—what is 'multiculturalism', firstly? And, secondly, what are 'Asian arts'? The first term is taken to imply official approval—if not a downright encouragement—for people of different ethnic origin to cut themselves off and define themselves solely in terms of their once mother culture. Is this reading correct? A look back at the history of cultural policy—with its regular attempts to build bridges—will tell us that it is certainly not the case. The second term is, of course, so broad as to be meaningless, leading to yet another one of the many problems in this highly complex arena.

Terminology has been an issue throughout the history of this country's varied ethnic engagement. It signifies more than a confusion over what to call various manifestations of the arts. For, unpacked, it can be an extraordinarily revealing guide to unarticulated attitudes. The long chain of title and counter-title started in the 1970s, with the first research into the nature and scale of activity, when the term 'ethnic minority communities' arts' was coined. It was generally considered reasonable, by artists as well as what was still then called 'the host country'; at that time, with communities still fragilely settling in, it was not disputed. The bulk of the (considerable) arts work that emerged was very locally based and community-focused. Overwhelmingly, it took the form of activities promulgated by community associations or held together by highly motivated individuals. Very few people could aspire to earn their living via the arts and they were technically 'amateur', which should not be taken to mean poor quality. Interestingly, strong feelings towards rejecting professionalism and official support made themselves known in the conferences that followed the publication of the research I undertook at that time as *The Arts Britain Ignores*.[2] Partly this was an act of shrewd protectionism. People—and especially community leaders—realised that official funding would bring in other criteria and lead to a loss of control. In this they were correct. But partly it was a reflection of the role that the arts played in their communities' lives—from Poles to Pakistanis, Cypriots to Sri Lankans. Nationally there was an impressive record of community endeavour and support—community halls of varying status and stature (Derby's Poles, Manchester's Indians and Ukrainians, Cardiff's Pakistanis) and a flowering of celebratory events around Chinese New Year, Eid, Baisakhi and Diwali. Largely invisible to the mainstream, this work entered the public arena mainly in the form of Multicultural Evenings frequently organised by the active network of community relations councils that was at that time a force across the country.

The 1970s and the publication of *The Arts Britain Ignores* brought a wealth of creative work out of the closet and challenged funding systems to define their attitude and response. Typically they did so in terms of their own perspectives and frameworks, first of all linking the new work that had appeared on the scene with the then emerging Community Arts movement. This linkage failed to appreciate the distinctiveness of the work itself—the difference between, for instance, classical music training with its strict adherence to tradition, and moves towards South Asian contemporary dance.[3] Again, from the viewpoint of the funding system, because very few 'diverse' artists earned their living in the arts it followed that they were not professionals and therefore could be funded only via Community Arts. At a local level, the youth services started to take a hand, funding, for instance, the energetic National Association for Asian Youth and the Southall Youth Movement, which, in their turn, gave rise to a quantity of energetic profile-raising competitions, activities and festivals, from bhangra to pop music to amateur theatre.

The social work and community arts connection turned out to have longer-lasting implications. It was responsible for persistent suspicions about 'quality' and motivation. What was the apparently hidden aim of the policy? Was it instrumentalist in nature, concerned more with building community than with the arts and artistic quality? A feeling persisted that official approval of 'ethnic arts' was really part of a tacit plan to create racial harmony or—as we would put it now—'community cohesion'. And good old racism surely played its quiet part in questioning whether 'ethnic arts'—as they then became more snappily called—were really on a par with native indigenous Western arts. It could be argued that, despite progress, this incipient sense still colours reactions.

But there was another element that helped to shape the stance and perception of 'ethnic arts'. This came about through the alliance that the arts at that time made with the rights movement. The 1960s and 1970s saw significant popular protests, across the board, around discrimination and inequality. Statistics showed clear disparity—fewer and less good jobs, fewer economic opportunities, worse housing, worse schooling: the list could go on. The fight for equality had, of course, to include a fight for the individual creative voices of people who were oppressed, and whose inner lives had a value that had not been recognised officially. But that sense of special pleading has also marked the perception of the 'diverse' arts, and it may be that we need to look more closely at the connection nowadays between equal opportunities and artistic practice.

Right from the start, the contradictions in assuming a homogeneity became apparent. 'Ethnic arts' were not 'community arts', or only occasionally so. New arrivals on the cultural scene felt no identification with that siting and insisted on the wider relevance of their work. Tara Rajkumar, for example, started the Academy of Indian Dance in the 1970s—renamed the Akademi and one of the major forces now in South Asian arts development—not as a suburbs-based enterprise but with clear aspirations to the mainstream. Classically trained in India, Tara had been appalled at the amateurish opportunities she had found for her work when she had arrived. She had found herself put on stage, she said with some alarm, in a mixed variety show to promote 'intercultural understanding', sandwiched between a limbo dancer and an Armenian poet. A generation that had largely or entirely grown up in Britain wanted to escape the backward gaze of the community-focused work but its close coupling with community and equality in terms of funding at that stage did not help.

The attempts to get out of the box have involved a process of negotiation and have involved a raft of conflicting expectations. Young Punjabi-based theatre work in the Midlands in the 1970s used techniques similar to the style of Hindi movies, but struggled to find an audience since the older Asian community generally preferred—understandably—to go to real Hindi movies.[4] The funders (namely, the Arts Council) remembered ethnic roots and still tended to believe that non-white work needed to speak to non-white audiences. This was not confined to Asian work. Frank Cousins, founder of the Dark and Light Theatre, is categorical about the way in which he believes funding stipulations cramped and finally destroyed his pioneering company.[5] The Arts Council had made its grant dependent on tours that were black community-based. And given that no theatres existed that fitted that bill, it meant the company had to find, book and play in adapted community or school halls for one- or two-night stands. The theatrical experience was of course diminished and the expense of hiring in equipment in itself was prohibitive. And a newly black British audience that had little theatrical tradition behind it was predictably slow to come forward.

What was the work? Who was it for? Who were the main movers and players? None of these questions was easy to answer for South Asian arts practitioners at that stage. As with the burgeoning Fringe theatre of the 1970s, there were varying models and aspirations. Anti-racism gave fuel to a number of young theatre groups such as the Bangladeshi Youth Movement in East London. Now a venerable thirty years old, the company was formed in 1977 in sympathy with demonstrations in Southall and the death of activist Blair Peach. But it equally took its energy from outrage at the invisibility of an Asian presence and Asian issues on the main stage. Early productions acknowledged the lack of contemporary material that reflected them adequately and took the very simple step of making their own. In the way of Joint Stock and other radical theatre groups of the time, the group set out to research specific issues and brought material back to base where it was crafted into plays.

Material was one thing, aesthetic another. New performance work had provided a problem for the Arts Council in early days because the work rejected the art-form differentiation that constituted the historic basis of its grants. This new work could wander across boundaries, taking in music, dance and theatre all in one production: so where would it go for funding? Even large-scale events such as the Notting Hill Carnival needed a new department—named, rather weakly, Special Applications—since it could legitimately claim to come under Music and Visual Arts.

The terminology was changing, however, showing that the exclusive linkage to communities was being modified by experience. The phrase 'ethnic minorities' communities' arts' had implied openly that the arts in question were by communities and for communities, and that they were 'minority' in scope. But time was bringing change in both the so-called mainstream and the area of diversity arts itself. World music (the start of Womad, for example, in the 1980s) opened ethnicity out, and 'ethnic arts' came to accompany 'ethnic dress' and 'ethnic food' as a marketable commodity. But the sobriquet 'ethnic' became rightly troubling to practitioners, with its connotations of distance, exoticism, orientalism and glamour. Claims were even made that the dictionary definition of 'ethnic' was 'primitive'. But the real issue was that the title had been applied by the outside world, not by practitioners themselves. One particular segment of the diverse theatre movement adopted the term 'Black Arts', which provided an umbrella that they themselves felt was respectful and appropriate. But not everyone agreed.

Diversity policy and the arts: evolution

In general, when there is no easy answer to a question, the question itself needs to be re-examined. This is the case here too. For the anxiety over terminology actually reflects something wider—a deep-seated confusion over the relative place of new arts and new peoples in the whole pantheon of British arts and society. Previously it had been relatively simple—newcomers were absorbed over time and always had been. But the scale and speed of migration and the fluidity of migration patterns in recent times necessitated other responses. They involved a fundamental reassessment of internal relationships and of the rights and duties of contemporary citizenship. The notorious *Behzti* story, where a playwright's right to offend seemingly came into conflict with a community's right not to be given offence (though the story in fact was more complicated) illustrates the fault-lines that can appear.[6] Critics took it to be proof that a pusillanimous attitude towards other cultural traditions and mores had led to the undermining of Britishness and its treasured free speech.

The function of a diversity policy has to be re-examined. Was it or is it helpful? How has it affected the arts, and in particular Asian arts? Certainly, when a diversity policy took off significantly in the 1980s with the Greater London Council (GLC) weighing in powerfully, the arts got a valuable leg-up. A number of initiatives were established then that started to provide the sort of infrastructure that the arts need if they are to be sustained. The first moves towards what became Iniva[7] were made at this time. The umbrella grouping Black Theatre Forum began, and productions in London's West End at the Arts Theatre as part of its annual festivals gave Tara Arts, Asian Cooperative Theatre and others useful mainstream exposure.[8]

The early Arts Council policy had faults—very much ones of its time—but it can be seen to have achieved three extremely important things that laid the foundations for the future. Firstly, it induced community-nurtured work to look outward, and as time went by gave it the oxygen of new impulses, inputs and outlets. A number of local groups found themselves for the first time on Arts Council mailing lists and began to look at their practice in a new way. The idea of professionalism—rarely considered as a career option—began to seem not such an alien idea. A greater mainstream awareness of diversity encouraged incoming arts, and they too brought energy and inspiration to locally based artists. Programmes such as Lift (London International Festival of Theatre) developed and cross-continental partnerships were formed.[9] Early grant-giving policies had helped Tara Arts establish itself and director Jatinder Verma is categorical about the value he found in working with the Indian theatre director Anuradha Kapur as Tara developed its own aesthetic. The stimulus provided by new work from India itself—Vijay Tendulkar's *Ghashiram Kotwal* from Pune and Habib Tanvir's Naya Company—not only inspired groups such as Tara but also helped to stretch and internationalise the perspective of British theatre and its audiences.

Secondly, policy has helped to create a stepping stone from ethnic specificity to a mainstream statement. It motivated practitioners into finding ways in which to open out their work and their thinking. South Asian dance provides immediately visible evidence as it is so grounded in traditional formulation and religious myth. The work that has slowly emerged from Britain's Asian dancers has worked from its solid base to impressive contemporary experiments. Drama at large has made a similar journey (albeit different in type), with local concerns becoming broader issues, as in Hanif Kureishi's *Borderline* for Joint Stock and Ayub Khan-Din's *East Is East* for Tamasha. Both have personal community affairs at their core, which are then located—as each work unfolds—within the broader context of contemporary politics, posing questions (however tangentially) about integration, discrimination and the often painful choices that come with multicultural societies.

Thirdly, a diversity policy has nudged Britain into seeing itself as a multicultural society. To say that multiculturalism has failed is a case of shutting the stable door; Britain *is* multicultural. We export without a second thought Tara Arts, Tamasha, Shobana Jeyasingh and Akram Khan. The work is of high quality—challenging, observant, innovative and committed. Nor has it gone unremarked in other countries. When I went on official visits in 1997 for the Council of Europe's diversity policy, time and again I was told how admirable people found our work: how much it spoke for a new and diverse Britain.[10]

Intervention works. It is a tricky tool and should be used circumspectly, but there are times when it is needed if all the voices in society are to be heard. However, it requires a difficult and subtle balancing act. A series of apparently contradictory imperatives exists. There is the need, on the one hand, to establish equality of opportunity and yet, on the other, to establish a society where unity (and hence some homogeneity) takes precedence over fragmentation. There is the need to take new cultural perspectives into the 'mainstream', but also to recognise that a proportion of people (whose identity changes as migration patterns change) will want passionately to retain their cultural roots, seeing them as their prime source of value and identity. There is the need to acknowledge diversity, but also to see that it is not the single most defining factor: he was a writer, Hanif Kureishi has frequently said, and not an ethnic minority writer. There is, finally, the need to build in stability but also flexibility, since if any one thing is certain it is that the agenda will change.

Professor Jasbir Jain, in her essay in the collection *In Diaspora: Theories, Histories, Texts*—a study of Indian diasporic culture—lays out a ladder of progression that she sees rolling out over time.[11] At first, she claims, Indian (or for our purposes, South Asian) work consciously exoticises itself in order to find a place where it can 'encash its marketability'. A defensive phase, it is left behind when individuals begin to feel more established and to want to redefine themselves in terms of where they are. Jain elides this phase with a subsequent one that she terms 'Fantasy', in which individuals (and especially writers) feel able to manipulate past and present, very often into myth-making and perhaps magic realism. 'Collision' follows, when artists become all too aware of the conflict between their root values and those of society at large. Finally comes the 'third space', which locates itself between worlds but adheres totally to none. This is the territory so cogently laid out and analysed by Professor Homi Bhabha, in which creativity is a prime factor. Stimulated by a sense of internationalism and rootlessness, it is free from ties or tradition and lends itself superbly to innovation. It is in those third and neutral spaces, wrote playwright David Edgar in 2005, that 'different people can share a similar experience of discovery ... It is in such spaces ... that some of the most imaginative and successful forms of community healing have taken place.'[12]

Like all schemas, Jain's cannot be taken too literally. All or several phases, for instance, might be impulses at any one time in the working psyche of a writer or artist. That tension could even be a source of creativity. And because Jain is concentrating on writers and their relationship with the mainstream she omits that other layer of South Asian culture—the community-oriented work. It is particularly strong where the performing arts are concerned, and the story of its relationship with so-called mainstream South Asian work is telling.

While classical musicians play at the South Bank Centre or the Leeds School of Music, others are performing in semi-formal gatherings in private homes to *rasikas*, or aficionados. While Tara Arts plays at the National, Gujarati-language plays tour the country for sell-out Sunday dates. While Shobana Jeyasingh and Akram Khan and others take their choreographies to Sadler's Wells and The Place and their regional counterparts, there are quantities of other dancers performing in South Indian temples up and down the land, learning dance in local 'garage schools' and showing their paces in the demanding debut performances called *arangetrams*.

The relationship with roots, ethnic identity and 'the community' is a fascinating one. How much do artists become de-ethnicised? Or can the two states co-exist simultaneously? I was interested in exploring that area for 'The Road to Interculturalism: tracking the arts in a changing world' in Comedia's overall Intercultural City project, for which I interviewed a number of artists (Chinese, Caribbean, Asian).[13] Behind much contemporary work lies the shadow of tradition, they all claimed. 'There's no way you'll have a tree with good leaves and fruit without a tap root,' said Peter Badejo firmly, about his own Africa-rooted choreographic work.[14] Shobana Jeyasingh described the moment when working purely within her tradition became invalid. She had been kitted up in the ornate garb of the classical dancer—jewellery, flowers, silk and gold costume, reddened palms—and been making her way through the dark and cluttered backstage of a theatre on her way to the stage. At that moment, she said, she had been struck by the disconnection between what she was about to portray and the circumstances in which she was portraying it. This experience helped to start a train of thought that eventually led her work far away from overt roots, but she would not deny the presence of their shadow. Jatinder Verma has always asserted the importance of roots: no-one comes to Britain minus baggage, he has said, and Tara's 2002 trilogy *Journey to the West*, exploring the layers of Asian diasporic movements, served to remind people of that old base. Both Tamasha and Man Mela have seen the value of keeping the history in mind, whether of the First World War or of Partition, and they are not alone in this. Reflecting back has been part of Asian theatre's function.

Ethnicity need not be overt. British-based sculptor Avtarjeet Dhanjal has a story that has a decidedly dramatic edge and that neatly encapsulates the idea of an essence. He had been on a trip back to his native Punjab in India, looking for support for an exhibition in Britain of Punjabi art. Village elders had been dubious. 'Will your work tell people', they had asked, 'about our Sikh gods and heroes?' Dhanjal is an abstract sculptor and knew that his work would not fit into the villagers' framework, so he launched into a story instead. A friend who was a farmer, he said, had an orchard and one day set out to market with a load of oranges. On the way he met another person who asked him where he was bound, and then said how foolish he was to lumber himself with actual oranges; he should go home and pulp his oranges and make juice. He had done so and set off once more. On the way he met another friend who asked him where he was bound, and then said he was foolish to lumber himself with all those heavy vats and barrels of juice. Townspeople didn't like whole juice, he stated: the fashion there was to dilute an essence of oranges. Make a concentrate, he said, and then take that to market. The farmer could see the strength of this advice, and went home and did just that. And his sculptures, concluded Dhanjal, laying out pictures of his own work as he took his story to its conclusion, were the essence of Sikh gods and heroes; they had all the character and the virtues of their originals.

Shifting terms and shifting policies

We have now arrived at—and are perhaps about to depart from—'cultural diversity', so what does this sequence of terms and attitudes have to say about Asian arts and the context in which they have struggled to make their way? The term 'cultural diversity' can be read as signalling an urge to blur and soften the lines of race; it sees a more complex society. This version of 'diversity' sets out to be a broad church, an umbrella that gives shelter to differences in age, sexuality, class and ability as well as race. In theory the term should benefit Asian theatre, if Dhanjal's claim of a constant 'essence' is correct. But there are dangers. First is the breadth of the term and resulting policy: how can it reflect the specificities of each member group adequately? Secondly, it could nudge policy itself into the area of compensation. Its tendency could be to concentrate on marginalised work rather than work *per se*, thereby encouraging both artists and funders to see themselves and their work in that light. If these two points seem contradictory, it is because the fields to which they refer are also complex and contradictory. And perhaps there is no way round it? The fight against inequality always carries within it the seeds of separateness. Its agenda and nature is to struggle for entry—into an institution, culture, country or whatever—and so it automatically divides the world into excluders and excluded. The trick has to be, once having gained entrance, to drop the garb of victim, protestor or excluded and resume one's true lineaments as a full human being.

The mechanisms for gaining entry have multiplied in recent years, and with good reason. Diversity policy has trained a spotlight on unequal representation—fewer directors, designers, technicians and so on of 'diverse' origin. The knock-on effect of their absence at the core of a cultural endeavour is clear—it affects what work is commissioned, how it is directed, how audiences are approached and what staff are appointed. Hence we have had useful initiatives such as the Independent Theatre Companies' Fast Track scheme for black and Asian administrators and Gain's programme to develop black and Asian board members.[15] Arts Council England's broad Eclipse agenda and the Sustained Theatre initiative aim to develop infrastructure and new work. Its extended Decibel programme promoted diversity as a whole—visual arts, publishing, music, theatre, performance art and dance—acting on the theory that both infrastructure and profile are needed.[16]

There is a new spirit in the air, without doubt. At times a look backwards illuminates. I happened to chance on an old press photograph the other day

1. Abdul Wasi Khan, Naseem Khan's father, caught by a random photographer
at a cricket match, Edgbaston *c.* 1952.

and found my attention held. Taken at some point in the 1950s at a cricket
match in Edgbaston, it was a random shot of the crowd. The spectators
were generally an informal lot, and they were—bar a handful—oblivious
of the camera lens. Except for one man. Right in the centre of the group
sat a solitary Indian man, dressed, by contrast, extremely formally, in a
three-piece suit, and gazing directly and assessingly at the camera. The
picture struck me for two reasons—firstly because the man was my own
father, Abdul Wasi Khan, and secondly for the eloquent messages that
the picture embodies. Firstly they speak visually of a time when a random
shot of the crowd at a sporting event in Britain's second city would show
spectators who were all—except for one—white. That in itself is striking.
But it was the quality of my father's regard that really held me. There was,
by contrast to that of the locals, a watchfulness and an alertness about
it. It seemed the watchfulness of the outsider, of a person whose survival
depended on keeping his eyes peeled and his wits about him. And his formal
suit—so different to the casual dress of so many of the others all around
him—seemed to have the protective quality of armour.

I wondered how that quality might have expressed itself artistically. I
was delighted by Tara Arts' *Playing the Flame* in 1979, for instance, with
its passionate documentary-style attack on hypocrisy; but strong as it was, it
had a quality of self-consciousness about it, of bringing news from a foreign
country, that would not be present today. In question is that indefinable

quality of naturally claiming one's own space, in the same way that an actor may be said to have 'stage presence'.

The young woman who became the emblem for the Akademi's 2003 mega dance spectacular, *Escapade*, had it in spades. A feisty young woman dressed in a sari printed in a military camouflage pattern, and sporting combat boots and a bandolier, stands planted foursquare with the sky behind her. She is clutching a skateboard to her side, and clearly sees no limits as to where it could take her. The piece itself drew heavily on vivid large-scale devices and was directed by Keith Khan, with a nod to his own broad-ranging and eclectic theatre and performance work for **moti**roti. Set in and around London's South Bank Centre, *Escapade* took a cheesy Bollywood theme and then proceeded to play with it joyfully with the help of 137 performers, bits of film, club-culture and skateboarding—to the delight of hundreds.[17]

The siting of the work at the heart of iconic London culture had a cheekiness that is engaging, but also a confidence that was certainly not present at the time of the cricket match picture. It speaks for a progression that has taken South Asian arts out of small backrooms and community centres into the mainstream. Both policy and time have played a part in that progression. But, at the same time, it is worth looking briefly under the counterpane.

Akademi's confidence comes very much from a sector that has determinedly done its groundwork. It has, as a whole, looked for ways in which to position its art form in the main cultural framework, considering training, accreditation and educational key stages as well as exploring the issues that arise when cultures evolve and collide. Akademi has brought substantial thought and experience to bear on the whole problem of relocation, and the results are there to be seen. They also bear witness to the advantages of a long run-in. Indian classical dance first impinged in a significant way on the British cultural scene with Uday Shankar's experiments in the 1920s, after which Ram Gopal's season in London's Aldwych Theatre in 1939 drew high praise from critics and sell-out houses. The terms in which the work was discussed privileged the exotic, even though Ram Gopal himself strove to find devices in which to frame his traditional dance so that it became more comprehensible. Both dancers came from India and the work was seen very much as a foreign import, even though Ram Gopal, again, tried hard to establish a British school and British-based company.

Since then, generations of dancers have addressed the same problem of translation. Akademi and others have benefited from that long history of exploration and trial and error. In contrast, Asian theatre overall has not had such a cohesive past, and there are certainly not the numbers of young Asians wanting to be actors as there are wanting to learn dance. Dance has been written into the Indian cultural canon since time immemorial, while theatre has had a far more haphazard profile in India. And the acquisition of dance skills is considered an irreproachable gain for young women of Hindu background. But, despite these disadvantages, the theatrical profession has developed an attitude towards training its own that is younger than but not dissimilar to the discoveries made by Asian dance.

Tamasha's Developing Artists Programme, which started in 2002, is a particularly interesting example. The TDA alternates two basic and well-thought-out annual workshops, one focused on designers and directors and the following one on new writers. It is a broad system that takes young talent in hand and mentors it carefully through to professionalism via workshops, master-classes, courses and traineeships. Partnerships with mainstream institutions such as Goldsmiths' College and—currently—the Conservatoire for Dance and Drama mean that students have a foothold in the broader theatre world, as well as developing a peer network through their fellow-trainees. All in all, it gives the impression of a carefully considered and integrated structure that promises to satisfy Tamasha's own aims for a system that can offer career-long support and escape from the all-too-common 'develop and drop' syndrome. But it is not cheap. Recently Tamasha staged the first production to have grown out of the TDA. *Sweet Cider* was by a young woman, Emtiaz Hussain, who came out of club-culture into theatre. Her piece had been workshopped with her for eighteen months before it reached the stage—a luxury that few outfits could afford.

The very fact of a TDA—and other initiatives within the Asian theatre world—could have pertinent things to say about the state of theatre, given that neither Tamasha nor Tara nor anyone in the field wants to corral themselves into an area marked out 'British Asian Theatre'. But the take-up in itself—sixty people applied for eight places on Tamasha's 2008 writers' course—indicates a perceived need. There is work that only Asian organisations, with their specific knowledge, shared history and local presence, can do. It is not a glamorous job or a high-profile one, but it is, it seems, a necessary one.

There is no question—however strong the backlash against 'multiculturalism' might be—that this country's historic diversity focus and policy has released new energies and resulted in an expanded and more representative form of British culture. The task has to be to make sure that society comes to deliver in a more integrated and thoroughgoing way than has so far been the case, so that the Tamasha grassroots schemes lead to opportunities and the presence of a company such as Tara at the National comes to seem not a matter for remark but a matter of course.[18]

2

Images on Stage

A Historical Survey of South Asians in British Theatre before 1975

Colin Chambers

Long-accumulated perceptions of the Other, as well as the need to present countervailing images, played crucial roles in shaping the environment in which post-1975 British South Asian theatre became a distinctive reality, however unstable and disputed. This essay sets out to contextualise post-1975 achievements and problems firstly by tracing in very broad outline the trajectory of illustrative stage representations of the Other from Renaissance times to the twentieth century and secondly by recording and exploring briefly the initial, fragmented strands of South Asian theatre practice, which became discernible from the end of the Victorian period.

The definition 'South Asian' appears late in this process of becoming, and what it attempts to describe is often subsumed in a bundle of non-geographically and non-historically specific images of the Other, a bundle sometimes collectively and loosely dubbed the Orient or the East. Definitions change over time and place, depending on context, and are problematic across culture, religion, skin colour, notions of race and ethnicity. 'South Asian' loosely embraces people from the Indian sub-continent and its diaspora, or those who have noteworthy associations with either. Given the nature of this history, individuals are included in this essay regardless of the degree to which they identified with any particular version of South Asian identity, itself a changing, contradictory and complex reality. All labels tend to obscure individuality and lose the specificity of the thing they are meant to describe, but discourse cannot do without them.

Images of South Asia and related presumptions of the 'host' community are not created in one genre alone or in isolation from other cultural and social phenomena; this survey, however, will necessarily focus on drama, but without intending to deny or downplay any overlap and mutual influence between theatre and other artistic and social categories. For most of the period under review theatre was a significant, popular and powerful medium. Stage images of the Other, therefore, are of considerable cultural importance. They helped mould over time the set of preconceptions about the Other that forms both the context in which Asian theatre practitioners have had to work as well as the wider social context with which all peoples perceived as the Other have had to contend. In the theatre, this meant conforming to notions of Asia that were defined by the imperial host country and not by Asian practitioners themselves. The struggle to define and assert autonomous identities shapes not only the earliest and isolated manifestations of Asian theatre in Britain but also the post-1975 endeavours that form the core of this book.

Representation of the Other has always been central not only to British drama since the sixteenth century but also to the formation of notions of British national identity. Whilst the strands that comprise this representation follow the contours of the expansion of British capital and culture into colonialism, imperialism and post-colonialism, it would be wrong to read these images in simple terms, particularly using the binary of victim and oppressor. These strands of representation were intricate and interlacing, and formed part of a complex ideological matrix in which gender, class, nationality, ethnicity and colour were intermixed. They were not homogenised and were frequently contested, containing much that was subversive. Nevertheless, the overwhelming ideas of control and containment of the Other and of the superiority of British civilisation were rarely challenged with any determination or thoroughness.

It has become a familiar observation since the salience in the latter part of the twentieth century of postcolonial studies and deconstructive, postmodern philosophy that identity is created in relation to the Other, and that the Other has to be created through familiarity in a *process* of representation rather than the mere replication. Yet many difficulties remain in interpreting images of the Other from the past and their role. This is especially true in theatre (which can be both transgressive and conservative) because it carries multiple meanings and is read in multiple ways through performance as well as through texts and associated commentary. There is not space here to explore the complexities of the impact of performance— the contribution of make-up, gesture, costume and music, for example, the factors that give rise to differentiated reception or performance strategies that undermine or counteract text—but such elements need to be borne in mind when attempting to make judgements about theatrical influence.

Caveats are also necessary regarding the transposition of contemporary attitudes when interpreting history; just because the first Elizabethans, for instance, did not think of race or skin colour in ways that became common in the nineteenth or twentieth centuries does not mean that prejudices or discriminatory practices were not active. Nor should the difficulties in unpicking meanings, and the recognition that this involves inevitable shortcomings, prevent the attempt. Indeed, it is striking how constant the chief anxieties regarding the Other—sex, religion, morality, status—remain throughout their different historical manifestations.

Early British theatre

Scholarship is uncertain about the extent and nature of the representation of the eastern Other in the British drama of the medieval period. The picture becomes a little clearer, even though many texts have been lost, in the sixteenth and early seventeenth centuries, the beginning of modern British theatre. Terms such as Turk and blackamoor were widely used as catch-all labels, applied regardless of culture, faith or geographical origin, combining and confusing peoples from Asia with those from Africa and the Americas. The term Indian, despite the celebrity of the Indian boy in Shakespeare's *A Midsummer Night's Dream* who conjures up images of spice as well as servitude and barter, seems to have been used mostly for people of the 'New World'. Representation of the eastern Other in this period is also linked to the use of the colour black. Black carried several connotations, from signifying sorrow, mourning or constant and unrequited love to confirming Christian iconography (though it is not exclusive to Christianity) as the colour of evil. At a time when the Ottoman Empire was the most powerful in the world, the dominant sense in the early modern repertoire soon became this negative one.

Although geography was more a matter of imagination than science, and drama was not intended to be ethnographically authoritative, theatrical creations were a means to handle actual engagements with a rapidly changing and intensely contested multicultural world. As travellers increasingly made knowledge available—often highly inaccurate and feeding stereotypes—notions of the racialised Other inherited from the Crusades were reassembled through, and in turn were transmitted back into, trade, war, politics and cultural exchange. With London the dynamo of the expanding economy as well as of the newly emerging professional theatre that spread out from the capital, it is not surprising that plays of the period were full of 'foreigners', both contemporary and historical, from near and far. Alongside Irish, Scots, Welsh, Spaniards, French, Italians, Scandinavians and Jews can be found Moroccans, Moors, Turks, Persians and a host of Others. Louis Wann lists forty-seven plays from the period 1579–1642 (closure of theatres) in which at least one Oriental character (i.e. from Turkey, North Africa, Malta, Arabia, Persia or Tartary) appears in the cast list.[1]

The societies from which such characters came were often used metaphorically as a useful way to bypass censorship or to indulge in (male) fantasies of travel, intrigue and sex, unfettered by the straitjacket of fact. The exotic, therefore, was a significant factor in the theatre's appeal as well as a convenient means of addressing topical issues, a combination that was to endure. In Marlowe's version of the central Asian conqueror Timur the

Lame, a.k.a. Tamerlaine or Tamburlaine, for example, both the dramaturgy and the narrative epitomise certain ascendant qualities of the period set against a backdrop of the European tussle between England and Spain, Protestant and Catholic Christianity, and the wider battle between papal Christendom and Islam.

Amid the plethora of stage images of the infidel Turk and the vengeful Moor that linked lust and irreligion to darker skins of both sexes, there was very little specific to South Asia, a reflection of the differences in contact between the cultures at the time. The main conduit for exchange was the East India Company (EIC), which, in competition with the Dutch, began to bring Indians to England at the beginning of the seventeenth century. Those who came were often used as servants, and a few made appearances as civic pageant performers in displays that extolled the virtues of mercantile expansion (e.g. Thomas Dekker's 1629 mayoral pageant, *London's Tempe, or the Fields of Happiness*, commissioned by the ironmongers society, which has an Indian youth sporting a long tobacco pipe and dart).

As the power of the EIC grew, so did interest in the lands it was exploiting. India, along with other distant locations and cultures, came to figure in plays of the late seventeenth century, such as John Dryden's invocation of Mughal India in *Aureng-Zebe; or the Great Mogul* (Drury Lane, 1675), as a metaphor for the vicissitudes of the Stuart court and its preoccupations. Plays also began to include characters and plots that reflected the new economic reality, ranging, for example, from the nabob (a Briton who makes fortunes in India) in John Crowne's *Sir Courtly Nice; or, It Cannot Be* (Drury Lane, 1685) and Samuel Foote's *The Nabob* (Haymarket, 1772) to the young Indian in love with a white woman in Robert Jephson's *The Campaign; or, Love in the East Indies* (Covent Garden, 1784).[2]

After the Restoration into the eighteenth century

Following the Restoration, the dominant theatrical tropes that represented the Other were increasingly shaped by the rise and consequences of trading slaves: the Noble Savage, the black comic servant and the vengeful slave (all gendered as well as racialised). These ran alongside the common Oriental stereotype of the East as inherently theatrical because both exotic and enigmatic, with its central figures of the tyrant and the harem. Terminology remained loose, and depictions of the colonies generally reproduced the imperial attitude of disdain or indifference that underlined such imprecision, or contained a critique of those (as had happened in India) who had 'gone native'. EIC employee James Cobb's *Love in the East, or Adventures of Twelve Hours* (Drury Lane, 1788) confuses those of East Indian and African origin; travel writer and playwright Mariana Starke, who grew up in Madras (Chennai) and who uses Indian settings, echoes in her comedy of manners *The Sword of Peace, or a Voyage of Love* (Haymarket, 1788) the common unconcern toward distinctions between indigenous African, North American and South Asian peoples while at the same time reproducing a meticulous hierarchy of colour, a hierarchy that maps white anxiety against degrees of blackness and problematises the abiding topic of 'mixed' marriages and their issue.

Encounters with the eastern Other in the usual conflation of cultures fed vigorously into popular hybrid forms of the eighteenth century, such as burlesque or pantomime. A premium on authenticity spurred by advances in seafaring and a new taste for science, paradoxically, made the illusion all the more plausible. Reviews of plays with exotic settings often commented on supposed verisimilitude. *Omai, or A Trip round the World* (Drury Lane, 1785) by William Shield, John O'Keefe and Philip de Loutherbourg, for instance, not only capitalised on the presence and celebrity in London of the Tahitian Mai who had sailed with Captain Cook, but was also noted for its spectacular scenic effects, which were directly influenced by John Webster, chief illustrator on Cook's final voyage to the Central and South Pacific. Starke's *The Widow of Malabar* (Covent Garden, 1790) was commended for its recreation of a suttee, a funeral practice among some Hindu communities in which a recently widowed woman immolates herself on her husband's funeral pyre. Notwithstanding its inaccuracies, Cobb's *Love in the East*, set in Calcutta, was applauded for the designs based on drawings of the city, and likewise the scenery for his *Ramah Droog, or, Wine Does Wonders* (Covent Garden, 1798) and James Messink's *The Choice of Harlequin, or, the Indian Chief* (Covent Garden, 1781), which were inspired by watercolours, drawings and engravings of India. William Thomas Moncrieff's melodrama *The Cataract of the Ganges! Or, the Rajah's Daughter* (Drury Lane, 1823) featured real horses and cascading water, as if to emphasise the theatrical nature of Britain's subjugation of both nature and India.[3]

The theatre itself (its structures, financing and social position) was closely connected to the profits of transnational commodity trade, at the heart of which was slavery; yet the theatre could still feature criticism of the system that sustained both it and the social milieu of its audiences (a significant proportion of whom were female, being entertained by the new phenomenon of the female playwright). At a time when the anti-slavery campaign in Britain was gaining considerable momentum, Starke, in *The Widow of Malabar*, a tragedy set in Southern India, questions human trafficking while simultaneously trumpeting Britain, the dynamo of the abhorrent practice, as the cradle of liberty, an increasingly familiar trope in the succeeding century. Starke's play may carry a humanist, anti-slave-trade message, but it is also concerned with establishing a new middle-class sensibility and defining what it is to be British; the Other might be human, but being British is another thing altogether. As Daniel O'Quinn points out, anti-EIC discourse and abolitionism often blended together at this time.[4]

Elizabeth Inchbald, playwright, actress and novelist, likewise draws on South Asian settings, but, while using them to compare the values of Europe and the East, directs her audience's attention to dilemmas at home rather than to those of Mughal India. Her farcical afterpiece *The Mogul Tale, or, the Descent of the Balloon* (Haymarket, 1784) satirises in an allegory of a runaway balloon which descends into a harem the defeat of Prime Minister Fox's India Bill the year before; her *Such Things Are* (Covent Garden, 1787), which finds the English in Sumatra, prefigures *The Sword of Peace* in its criticism of the extravagances of EIC leaders such as Robert Clive and Warren Hastings, who had been impeached for corruption two years earlier.[5] Aspects of colonialism, such as the mercantilist mentality of the slavers, the decadence of the nabobs and the repression of the EIC, were challenged on the British stage, even if the underlying ideological thrust of British superiority that promoted and sustained colonialism and imperialism was seldom questioned. An embrace and even enjoyment of the Other seems possible but only at the expense of historical specificity; the theatrical effect comes to mask the oppression it might be criticising, thereby mitigating any discomfort the audience might feel at complicity with that oppression.

Validation (where it existed) of the indigenous culture of the colonised peoples was confined to the study. Sir William Jones, for example, in 1789 translated the Sanskrit classic drama *Sakuntala* into Latin and then into English, but the play was not performed in Britain for more than a century afterwards. Taken from the *Mahabharata* by Kalidasa, the story of King Dushyanta and a young woman raised by birds was the first Sanskrit drama to be made available to the European reader. It was reprinted at least five times in England in the next two decades, as well as being translated and published many times across Europe. Such enthusiasm has subsequently been attacked by postcolonial writers such as Edward Said as part of an Orientalist discourse that venerated Sanskrit because it validated the European enlightenment project.[6]

Nineteenth-century fantasies

All the productions cited thus far were first seen in England at a patent theatre, licensed under a system introduced at the Restoration of the monarchy to control theatrical output. Some of the plays were taken up elsewhere in the 'illegitimate' theatres that grew in number and geographical spread towards the end of the eighteenth century and increasingly in the early decades of the nineteenth, when the failure of the patent system came to be acknowledged by the authorities. Several 'illegitimate' theatres in London, such as the Royal Coburg or the Surrey, were located in river areas linked to East and West trade; the opening in 1803 of the West India Dock and in 1806 of the East India Dock further altered the local demographic.

A section of the East End with a high proportion of Indian lascars (seamen) as well as Chinese sailors who had arrived with the EIC became known by the 1830s as the Oriental quarter, or the black hole of the East End, echoing a derogatory (and historically inaccurate) phrase that had entered popular usage from the EIC campaign to subjugate India; unsurprisingly, the quarter gained a reputation for danger and exoticism, the staples of Asian representation in British drama.[7]

Trade with India had increased the South Asian population in Britain, some of whom are recorded in contemporary drawings and prints trying to make a living in the world of travelling fairs and street entertainment as dancers, jugglers and magicians. There are records of an Indian 'gentoo' (Hindu) conjuror at Bartholomew Fair back in 1790, an East Indian conjuror doing card tricks and thought reading, and stranded lascars working as entertainers in the Victorian period. It is possible that some may have appeared at theatres like the Coburg or the Surrey, where audiences would be drawn from this multi-ethnic population. They might even have seen plays that countered the dominant imperial view and, as David Worrall says, gave space to Islamic Indian pride and protest at the British invasion, in plays such as William Barrymore's *El Hyder; or the Chief of the Ghaut Mountains* (Royal Coburg, 1818) or H.M. Milner's *Tippoo Saib; or, The Storming of Seringapatam* (Royal Coburg, 1823).[8]

They might also, as Heidi J. Holder suggests, have seen plays that showed images of ethnicity in the modern city that were disconcerting to certain sections of the indigenous population: in *How We Live, or, London Labour and London Poor* (author unknown, Surrey Theatre, 1856) the figure who acts as guide through the urban jungle no longer comes from the privileged class: he is not only a coster (someone who sells fruit and vegetables) but also a 'Hindoo', called Araxa.[9] In James Willing and Frank Staniforth's *Glad Tidings* (Standard Theatre, Shoreditch, 1883), the plot's pivotal figure is a female Indian beggar Juanna (who is later discovered to be related to the main character). Holder says the play asserts the significance of the working-class roles but does this by having them appear in West End settings. Both Juanna and Araxa criticise the cruel treatment of the poor by the ruling class, a staple of working-class drama, and, instead of passively carrying notions of race, class and gender, they are the active agents of social restoration and humane values, even if they renovate the existing social order by eventually being sacrificed. Both achieve their dynamic role in deathbed confessions and then are required no more, a device also seen typically in Noble Savage plays. As Holder says, the two characters are not 'fully incorporated' into society; they are used symbolically as well as realistically, and may have been cast as Indians rather than been given darker skins to allow a blurring fluidity of colour.[10] Generally, however, Indians and other Asians were merely decorative, or limited to the minor or background roles of servants, entertainers and beggars (often deployed in crowd scenes), such as the Chinese Ah Luck, a comic servant in Paul Merritt and George F. Rowe's *New Babylon* (Duke's, 1879), or Rampunkah, a 'hindoo' servant in Joseph Derrick's *Twins* (Olympic, 1884). Holder points out that Wilkie Collins, in his own 1877 adaptation of *The Moonstone* (Olympic), missed the opportunity to put on stage the Indians, who—even if portrayed as menacing—are crucial to the story, and thereby lost the novel's use of them as scrutinisers of the English.[11]

When South Asians did figure prominently it was usually at the wrong end of a British bayonet. A series of shows presented at Philip Astley's theatre, for example, acted like a tabloid Living Newspaper following the British campaigns in the south-west of India against Tipu Sultan (albeit some months afterwards): *Tippoo Saib, or British Valour in India* (1791), *Tippoo Sultan, or the Siege of Bangalore* (1792), *Tippoo Saib, or, East India Campaigning* (1792), *Tippoo Saib's Two Sons* (1792) and the last, *The Siege and Storming of Seringapatam* (1800), which saw the final defeat of Tipu.[12] Birmingham in the late 1840s hosted panoramas and dioramas on the recent Indian wars from a British perspective, and the plays and other spectacles produced in the aftermath of the 1857 Uprising reinforced notions of British liberty.[13] A new sense of being British was being fashioned, underpinned by an apparently science-based racism that was fuelled by supremacist Christianity, even as—and to some extent because—images of the colonised and the dramaturgy that presented them increasingly bore the imprint of new scientific disciplines such as geography and anthropology, or wished to appear to do so. The need to create the human subject, as Edward Ziter says, organised the nineteenth-century theatre as much as it did the nineteenth-century prison and clinic.[14]

Bolstered by increased travel opportunities and greater newspaper readership, ethnography was mixed with fiction right across theatrical life. Display sanctioned by trade and science became highly theatricalised at the height of empire and demonstrated in a range of spectacles— melodramas, optical and mechanical shows, and touring exhibitions, for instance—mastery over the colonial body. The British Museum opened an ethnographical gallery in 1845; the Great Exhibition at Crystal Palace in 1851 boasted all manner of exotica, including an Arabian Nights apartment transposed to India. The 1895 Empire of India Exhibition had the Empress Theatre, Earl's Court decorated like a Mughal temple; Imre Kiralfy's *India*, a 90-minute spectacle looking at nearly 2,000 years of Indian history in order to justify the British Raj (by, among other things, ignoring discordant episodes such as the 1857 Uprising), employed a cast of 1,000 (not Indian) and, it is estimated, was seen over the summers of 1895 and 1896 by at least one and a half million people.[15]

In the last decades of the Victorian period and up to World War I, this broad appeal of Orientalism echoed across drama and the other arts and could be found in fashion, interior design and architecture too. (The auditoria of late Victorian and Edwardian theatres such as the Hackney Empire display a dazzling array of 'Eastern' references) In the field of musical comedy and light operetta, which reinforced the stock characteristics found in pantomime, fantasy collations of China and the Middle East as well as South Asia proved extremely popular. Aside from *The Mikado*, a title that has survived, successful shows included *The Geisha* (1896, which ran for 760 performances), *A Chinese Honeymoon* (1901, 1,075 performances), the musical play *The Cingalee* (1904, 365 performances), set in what was then called Ceylon, and *Chu-Chin-Chow* (1916, 2,238 performances during the war, then a record for the longest stage run). The presumed box office appeal of specifically South Asian titles also appears to have grown, as the breadth of a selection of titles suggests: *The Nautch Girl*, *My Friend from India*, *Indian Prince*, *The Prince of India*, *The Great Mogul*, *The Nabob's Fortune*, *The Saucy Nabob*, *Carlyon Sahib*, *Carnac Sahib*, *The Mahatma*, *The Star of India*.

A constant theme was inter-racial relationships, in which women (often in a generalised 'eastern' sense) tended either to be chaste innocents or titillating yet dangerous sirens. They might be part of a harem, or an Oriental chorus or procession symbolising the East (e.g. in *Aladdin* at Drury Lane, 1885 or *The Crown of India* at the Coliseum, 1912, which had major cities personified by women who were virtuous but in need of protection). Alternatively, they might appear as individuals with particular metaphorical weight: Cleopatra, Scheherazade, the Queen of Sheba or Salome. In 1913, however, the India Office banned an Earl's Court spectacle, *The Romance of India*, not because of the eroticism of the 'nautch girls' (dancers) but because the piece portrayed human sacrifice in lurid terms, and this was deemed to cause offence to religious feeling.[16]

Transcultural exchange

Theatre in the colonies played its part in the imperial project, too, and helped sustain the connections between the various constituent parts of the empire. Military and civilian EIC officials acted in plays such as *The School for Scandal* by Richard Brinsley Sheridan (himself a leading Whig MP for three decades and actively engaged in parliamentary debates on India). Such activities were part of the insistent export of British culture that was symbolised by the dissemination of Shakespeare as the pre-eminent universal poet. This transcultural exchange, nonetheless, had positive as well as negative effects. Indigenous cultures may have been denigrated but in India play production was revived in the nineteenth century because of the British presence. Playwright Girish Karnad argues that, because the British did not possess the quality of music of the Germans but did have Shakespeare, it was theatre that made the greatest cultural impact.[17] When Indian playwrights portrayed the white sahib critically, however, stage censorship was introduced in India, an intervention, which, argues Claire Pamment, had repercussions for post-1975 British South Asian theatre.[18]

A curious example of influence flowing in both directions comes from 1885,when the Parsee Victoria Dramatic Company from Bombay appeared as a novelty act at the Gaiety and Opera Comique theatres in London. The company performed four items. The first two were *Solomon's Sword*, the story of the capture of a nobleman's wife by a ne'er-do-well in league with the devil and of her release by a youth with an enchanted sword, played in Hindustani with songs of English or American provenance, and a sketch of American origin prepared for performance by 'nigger troupes'—minstrelsy was a powerful genre in Britain and had been granted respectability in 1846 by a royal performance. Britain sent minstrel troupes to India, in keeping with its 'divide and rule' strategy of making the colonised Asian feel superior to the colonised black, and here the Parsee company was returning the favour. It was announced that this sketch (about black servants being duped to let uninvited guests into the master's ball) would be performed in English, but *The Times* said the 'chief character struggled, the remainder proved unequal to the task and the result was a confusion of languages'. Following these came scenes from Kalidasa's *Sakuntala* and a Hindustani version of Bulwer Lytton's popular play *The Lady of Lyons*. According to *The Times*, this latter simply evoked derision instead of sympathy because the audience could not understand it, an attitude that apparently summed up the whole programme and revealed a condescension, especially towards the use of English and its pronunciation, that was to persist.[19]

Also towards the end of the nineteenth century, in the face of burgeoning urban bustle and Victorian materialism, a different kind of Orientalism looked East for aestheticism, asceticism and a spirituality that often embraced mysticism and the occult. In contradiction to the political situation in South Asia, the Indian sub-continent, like the rest of the East, was seen as unchanging and therefore a source of transcendental balm. The pioneering actor and director William Poel, who believed in universalism, turned to *Sakuntala* for inspiration and produced an open-air performance in the Conservatory of London's Royal Botanical Gardens in 1899 for the Elizabethan Stage Society, which he had founded to explore continuous and ensemble methods of staging and acting. Giyani Singh Giyani, a law student at Gray's Inn, coached the cast in posture and gesture. He and a Capt. Nath lent costumes, there were Indian performers, although not in leading roles, an Indian singer was used, and music was played on Elizabethan instruments by Indian musicians.[20] Poel says that 'Oriental notabilities' were present in the audience at what appears to be the first British production of *Sakuntala*. His inclusion of a stuffed tiger and antelope provoked hilarity, however, and *The Times* reviewer, who found the performance 'very inadequate', decided that the 'imperfect English' of the Indians 'hardly added to the dignity of the production'.[21] Poel says that in 1911 Indian students mounted a series of 'very beautiful' tableaux illustrating the incidents in *Sakuntala* but gives no details, and none has so far come to light.

The next year, Poel was involved as a producer in performances at the Court Theatre, Sloane Square, of *Buddha*, an adaptation by S.C. Bose of Edward Arnold's narrative poem *The Light of Asia*, presented 'under Indian management' (which was, in fact, Kedar Nath Das Gupta). The production featured six episodes from the life of the spiritual leader, who was played by the white English actor Clarence Derwent alongside a 'company of Indian actors, mainly composed of students of law and medicine'.[22] According to Poel, as a result of *Buddha* a group of Indian students formed the Hindusthan Dramatic Society and presented in 1912 at the Whitney Theatre, Aldwych, a dramatisation by H.N. Maitra and N. Pal of the romantic nineteenth-century Indian novel *Durgeshnandini* by B.C. Chatterjee, which they named after the story's Bengali heroine *Ayesha*.[23] Poel said it did not reach the level of *Buddha*, and was without merit or distinction. *The Times* reported it as a new Indian play, and said proceeds were to go to St Bartholomew's Hospital and Indian charities.[24]

Poel, meanwhile, wanted to revive *Sakuntala* in order to improve on the previous production. As a scholar keen on authenticity, he was aware of issues of translation and the suitability of using English actors, and was in correspondence with a body called the Council of the Oriental Guide, for which he prepared a performance in 1912. A public production was held indoors (because of bad weather) in Cambridge, with Derwent in the lead and Indian students playing non-speaking parts. Poel had enlisted the help of Mrs P.K. Ray and Mrs P.L. Roy, who attended rehearsals and showed the women how to wear saris and the men how to fold turbans.[25] The following year, the Indian Art, Dramatic and Friendly Society, with which Poel was in contact, presented *Sakuntala* at the Royal Albert Hall (five performances) and the Cosmopolis Theatre (three performances), using Indian performers, though still not in the lead roles.[26]

According to Poel, 'perhaps the most valuable object-lesson as regards Indian dramatic art that the English public and English actors have ever received' was seen at the Court in March 1912 for two performances; it was the story of Kalidasa's poem *Kumarsambhava* presented as *The Birth of the War-God* in eighteen tableaux. Proceeds went to the Indian Women's Education Association, to train women to be teachers in India, which suggests that the motivation behind mounting the production was charitable as well as artistic. Mrs P.L. Roy arranged the tableaux, costumes were copied from antique Indian prints lent by the librarian of the India Office, and it was acted anonymously by some thirty Indian women and children. *The Times* said the cast showed some faults common to the amateur, the chants were weird to western ears but 'full of atmosphere', and there was a 'curious exotic fascination' about the whole production. This last comment encapsulates a continuing imperial attitude to the Other despite 300 years of Anglo-Indian encounters and the presence in Britain of well-established though small and disparate South Asian communities.[27]

First collective experience

Although the bias of the archive in favour of mainstream events makes discovering amateur or semi-professional activity a patchy and problematic process (and even more so for activity outside London), it seems likely that in the events cited above can be found the first stirrings of a South Asian theatre in Britain. At this point, the essay therefore changes perspective and concentrates more on the journey of South Asian performers and artists than on the representation of South Asia in the dominant theatrical culture. The weight of empirical recording in the following pages, beyond the extent that the wider impact of the productions listed below might otherwise suggest, derives from their importance as early stepping stones in this journey, and also from the lack of readily available information about them elsewhere.

The journey remains mostly disjointed, as South Asian migration and settlement continued to be relatively minor (for example, compared to Caribbean immigration) until the 1950s and 1960s, and brought to Britain people whose cultural background generally did not predispose them to the particularities of the British theatre. As well as the lascars and nannies (ayahs), there were students and professionals (teachers, doctors, lawyers) living in Britain, but they did not form a unified community and, apart from a concentration in London, they were spread out and relatively few in number. It is not surprising that in the years from Poel's time to 1975, with some important exceptions, there is little evidence of concerted South Asian theatrical activity, though much desire to 'correct' the distortions offered by prevailing dramaturgy. While Poel sought South Asian involvement in order to refine his production values, when South Asians began to organise themselves theatrically their desire was to reclaim authenticity, celebrate their own culture and change perceptions of the 'host' audiences. Although the political background was the growing demand for Indian independence, the strategy in the theatre did not lead to an emphasis on difference but an insistence on parity, that the 'real' India had a culture that could be judged in 'western' terms as being as rich as the West's.

Central to the early presence and attempt at collective activity was the Indian Art, Dramatic and Friendly Society, founded by its key and indefatigable figure, Kedar Nath Das Gupta, who arrived in England from India in 1908. In order to increase understanding between the two cultures he founded the Union of East and West, which was supported by H.G. Wells and which staged a number of Indian plays, mostly in the afternoons or when theatres were not being used for commercial productions.[28] The Society (a.k.a. the Indian Art and Dramatic Society) often appeared under the auspices of the Union. Das Gupta, who was manager of the *Buddha* production, adapted *Sakuntala* for the performances at the Cosmopolis Theatre and Albert Hall where, in 1912, the Society also presented a programme comprising a short play, *The Maharani of Arakan*, adapted by playwright George Calderon from the Bengali writer Rabindranath Tagore, along with a recitation of poems by Tagore. Later that year, *Sakuntala* was revived at the Albert Hall with *The Maharani of Arakan*.[29] Tagore was a vital figure in South Asian culture, and the following year he became the first Indian, and the first Asian, to win the Nobel Prize for Literature. He was knighted in 1915.

In 1913 the Society presented at the Cosmopolis Theatre another Sanskrit historical play, *Ratnavali*, or *the Necklace* (attributed to the emperor Harsha), together with a revival of *The Maharani of Arakan*. A Society meeting in Cromwell Road was presided over by the leading actor-manager Sir Herbert Beerbohm Tree, and Tagore read an English adaptation of his play *Chitra*. In 1915 at Chiswick Town Hall, West London, four pieces were presented as a 'Grand Performance in Aid of the Wounded Indian Troops', with a cast of both Indian and white British performers: *Caliph for a Day* by Das Gupta, *Savitri, or, Love Conquers Death*, an adaptation from *The Mahabharata* by Das Gupta, *The Gardener* by Tagore, and *The Maharani of Arakan*. In 1916 Das Gupta's adaptation of Kalidasa's *Vikramorvasie*, under the title *The Hero and the Nymph*, was performed by the Society at the Grafton Galleries, London. It was Kalidasa's last play, and Das Gupta claimed it had never been performed before anywhere.[30] Other wartime activities included a staging of Tagore's play *Malini*, a reading of *The Little Clay Cart*, the première of Das Gupta's own musical play *Bharata* (India), and a production of Bhavabhuti's *Malati and Madhava*. After the war, the Union and the Society continued their activities with even greater intensity: in 1919 they presented the British première of Tagore's *The King and Queen*, paired with *Savitri*, at the Comedy Theatre. This was followed, at the Hill, Hampstead and then at the Prince of Wales, by *The Ordeal* (a.k.a. *King Harischandra*) by Das Gupta and K.C. Chunder, a play based on a legend about priestly domination taken from the Puranas, an ancient Indian genre of literature.

At the end of the year came a major event, a production of *Sakuntala* at the Winter Garden, Drury Lane and Apollo Theatre. A twenty-two-strong committee of mainly Indian and a few white British notables was formed to oversee it.[31] Using an English version by Laurence Binyon based on a text prepared by Das Gupta for an English audience, and with a prologue specially written for the production, it was directed by Lewis Casson with Sybil Thorndike playing Sakuntala.[32] *The Times* declared that it was the first 'worthy' production of the Indian 'masterpiece', a 'panegyric to love'.[33] Despite the main roles still being performed by white actors, the production had cultural importance and was attended by a bevy of British aristocrats as well as the Aga Khan and Maharaja of Baroda. The Union revived the play in 1920, with two open-air performances in Lord Leverhulme's Hampstead garden. Such connections with the elite, both artistically and socially, were in keeping with the general intention of validating Indian culture as worthy of respect and the assimilationist strategy associated with this project.

In 1920, at the Wigmore Hall, the Union presented two more Tagore plays: *The Autumn Festival* and *The Post Office*, followed two months later by five short Tagore plays at the same venue: the first time, it was said, they had been performed in English.[34] This year also saw a return to the Prince of Wales with *Chitra* and Tagore's *Sacrifice*, while Das Gupta accompanied Tagore to the United States and decided to remain there, founding an American branch of the Union of East and West. He became involved in attempts to bring religions together and merged the Union with an integrationist body called the League of Neighbours to form the Fellowship of Faiths. The London Union of East and West continued its activities: in 1921, in Lord Leverhulme's garden again, it presented three Indian plays—*The Farewell Curse*, *Kunala* and *Savitri*; at the Prince of Wales a play about mysticism, *Affinities*, by Zula Maud Woodhull; at Wigmore Hall, a revival of the ancient Hindu play *Malati and Madhava* along with the première of Tagore's *Trial by Luck*; and, in Cambridge's Guildhall under the patronage of the University's vice-chancellor and the town's mayor, performances of Indian plays, ancient and modern; in 1924, at Wigmore Hall, an English adaptation of the Bengali drama *Vilwamangal*, which had enjoyed a long run in Calcutta, was presented.

Tagore, a supporter of Indian independence, who, following a British massacre at Jalianwalabagh, Amritsar, renounced his knighthood, remained a link through the subsequent years of Asian theatre practice. *Sacrifice* was seen with an all-Indian cast during the international theatre season at the Little Theatre in 1928, and again in 1952 paired with *The Post Office*, in another festival of international plays at another small theatre, the Irving, which was managed by D.P. Chaudhuri. The following year, the Irving presented Tagore's *Red Oleanders*. In 1963, Bristol University Drama Department invited Ram Gopal to dance in and choreograph *The King of the Dark Chamber* by Tagore. The first play performed by Tara Arts in 1977 was *Sacrifice*, adapted by its founder Jatinder Verma from Tagore's *Balidaan*, which he had written in support of World War I pacifists and translated into English in 1917.

Student activity

It is likely there is more autonomous South Asian activity to be uncovered from the late nineteenth and early twentieth century because Indian students, who played an important role in the beginnings of British South Asian theatre, were well organised and ran their own cultural events in their hostels, but this phenomenon, along with the amateur work of groups such as the India Office Drama Society, has not been adequately researched. For example, little is known about the Indian Students' Union Play-Reading Circle. There may also be more to discover about Cornelia Sorabji, a Christianised Parsi from Western India who came to England to study at Oxford in 1889 and was asked to provide Mrs Patrick Campbell with a play. Sorabji turned to an ancient Sanskrit drama, Shudraka's *The Clay Cart*, but Mrs Campbell, whose role turned out not to be the lead, wanted changes that Sorabji refused to make. Her text was sent to Bernard Shaw, who made what Sorabji took to be a disparaging comment, and she abandoned the play.[35] It is possible that Sorabji was active in one of the many amateur dramatic societies that flourished at the turn of the century, or was involved with student cultural activity. Her play *Gold Mohur Time: 'To Remember'* was published in Britain in 1930, but there is no record of its having been performed. Another example is that of S.P. Khambatta, who came to London from India to study law and appeared in a production of Una Marson's *At What a Price* presented by members of the League of Coloured Peoples, which was first seen at the YWCA in Holborn in 1933 and then played at the Scala Theatre in early 1934.

It did look, briefly, as if a former medical student, Niranjan Pal, who had appeared in *Buddha* and co-wrote the adaptation *Ayesha*, might carry on Das Gupta's pioneering work, bringing a South Asian presence to British audiences as well as asserting cultural pride for Indians in Britain. Pal began writing whilst a student in London and formed the Indian Players to direct his play *The Goddess* in 1922 at the Duke of York's Theatre.[36] Importantly, it had an all-Indian cast and Indian stage management'. *The Times* reviewer, nevertheless, praised the 'remarkably good' diction of the cast. The play deals with the life of a Brahmin priest who rejects his faith for rationalism and pronounces a beggar woman with whom he is in love as the incarnation of the goddess Kali. Despite being unhappy with the deception, she agrees to appear as Kali in order to please him, but she then commits suicide to atone for her sacrilege. While the *Era*, which thought the principal recommendation of the production was its 'picturesqueness', found the pronunciation of English 'a little precarious', and the *Sunday Times* said the production was acted in the 'quaintest of English', *The Times* praised the 'remarkably good' diction of the cast, and the *Stage* found the production was 'acted admirably'.[37] *The Goddess* also played at the Ambassadors and transferred to the Aldwych for 66 performances. At the end of the run rehearsals were due to begin for the next production by the Indian Players, for an Indian Repertory season, but nothing seems to have come of this.[38]

Pal next wrote a farce with an English setting called *The Magic Crystal* (a.k.a. *What a Change!* and also *The Blue Bottle*), which was performed on tour for two months and then at the Scala Theatre, London, in 1924. In the play, a visionary Indian with the gift of a box appears to the bankrupt

Englishman Reggie when he has nothing left. As Reggie takes the box, his personality is transported into his butler and the comedy unfolds, but, in the end, it turns out that Reggie has only been dreaming.[39] The opportunity to satirise the English through humour has to be unmistakably unreal. Pal also wrote *Shiraz*, which was due to appear in the West End in 1926, but there is no record of a production. Instead, it became a film, with members of the Indian Players in the cast, including Himansu Rai, who had come to London to train as a lawyer and had played the lead in *The Goddess*. Pal wrote the successful film *The Light of Asia* (*Prem Sanyas*), which Rai, a pioneer of Indian film, acted in and directed. Pal and Rai moved back to India to work in films and the Indian Players were no more. They and Pal, like Das Gupta's Society, had worked within conventional, liberal British–Indian discourse. The challenge they offered British audiences was not so much what they were presenting (which was not provoking) but the ways in which they performed and the fact that they were able to perform at all. However slight it may seem, to gain a measure of acceptance in the Britain of the early twentieth century and to demonstrate a capacity for self-organisation and artistic expertise in an unreceptive environment were notable achievements.

South Asian presence in the 'mainstream'

Despite the massive, though at the time under-recorded, influence of the East on western theatre (e.g. Artaud, Brecht, Copeau, Craig, Stanislasvky, Yeats), the Asian presence in British drama in the first half of the twentieth century was generally much less than that of the African American. After World War I there were no South Asian stars like the African Americans Paul Robeson or Elizabeth Welch and no drama equivalent of the influential dancers Uday Shankar and Ram Gopal, who changed the traditional British–Indian discourse while appearing within, and reinforcing, its terms.

South Asia still tended to be represented in the 'mainstream' culture as an extension of the fantasy exotic East that had been highly popular and lucrative in the years leading up to and during World War I. Mirroring the world of fashion, Oriental settings (still loosely defined) remained in vogue in the 1920s in, for example, 'sheikh' shows such as *Prince Fazil* (1926) or the musical *The Desert Song* (1927), although cinema was already taking over this niche. Scarborough, Blackpool and Battersea's Festival Gardens had their exotic Indian Theatres, which featured novelty acts and various types of variety performance that were a standard of the popular imagination. The latter two theatres were run by Amir Bux, a royal Indian magician who came to Britain in 1924, the year of the British Empire Exhibition at Wembley, which boasted an Indian Pavilion with a full set of clichés: snake charmers, jugglers and a Madras Chow Chow, described by the *Stage* as a sort of Indian variety show with novelty 'girl' dancers.[40] Sometimes performers in such shows were of South Asian origin and sometimes they assumed the role as a passport to entertainment acceptance, just as black performers often assumed African identities to further a professional career.

South Asia did feature occasionally in Britain's art theatre repertoire: Shudraka's Sanskrit play *The Toy Cart* (a.k.a. *The Little Clay Cart*) appeared in 1916 at the Queen's, in 1930 at the Lyric, Hammersmith, and on tour, and in 1964 at Hampstead Theatre. Lena Ashwell and her company appeared in *The Maharani of Arakan* at the Coliseum in 1916 alongside Arthur Bourchier and his company in J.B. Fagan's *The Fourth of August*, which dramatised German plans to induce the Maharaja of Mulpur to revolt against the British Raj at the outbreak of World War I; *Sakuntala*, as well as being broadcast on BBC Radio in 1929, was revived by the Norwich Players under Nugent Monck in 1931, accompanied by a series of tableaux drawn from the poetry of Omar Khayyam. In the political sphere, the Workers' Theatre Movement of the early 1930s produced *Meerut*, an agitational piece about an Indian railway workers' strike and imprisoned union leaders in which class was more important than nationality or race.

A few South Asian individuals, such as Indira, Princess of Kapurthala (from the Punjab), and Devika Rani, often referred to as India's first film star, studied at the Royal Academy of Dramatic Art (RADA) but made no impact in the absence of either an outstanding individual profile (in the manner of a Robeson or a Welch) or a collective presence. Indira apparently aroused much gossip in India when she spurned her parents' wishes, saved her allowance in secret and escaped to enrol at RADA. She appeared in films in the 1920s, made her stage debut in 1938 as a Turkish slave in *The Heart Was Not Burned* (Gate Theatre), a forgotten play about Keats, Byron and Shelley, and also appeared in a children's revue *Let's Pretend* (St James's, 1938–9). She gave up acting but became a theatrical backer and long-serving BBC news reader.[41]

A fascinating individual who briefly succeeded in challenging the norms of western theatre was the Indo-Irish author Aubrey Menon (or Menen). While at University College, London, where he had won an essay-writing award but was denied the prize money because he was not of 'pure' British stock, he founded the London Survey Players in 1933 with 'students of many nationalities' to enlighten his peers 'as to the character of the world they were living in, fraught with fascism and war'.[42] He wrote and produced sharply critical plays 'in a form bare of all but essentials', including a free adaptation of H.G. Wells' *The Shape of Things to Come* that featured masks by Duncan Grant and ballet choreographed by Hedley Briggs (danced by him and Diana Gould, an important protégé of Marie Rambert's, to music by Walter Leigh, a student of Hindemith's). In 1934 Menon joined the committee of Left Theatre, an umbrella group for left-wing theatre professionals, and acted in the group's production of *Sailors of Cattaro*. With other Left Theatre members, he formed a professional company,

Experimental Theatre, which gave two private performances at the Fortune Theatre of his play *Genesis II*, an ambitious and sprawling reworking of the first books of the Bible that deals with the oppression of one race by another and journeys from Eden and the British Museum Reading Room to a swastika-clad German police station and an Indian tea plantation. The group found a home in North London and pulled down its interior walls in order to build a 'space stage', which appeared not to be fixed to the ground, with two platforms at different levels and a cantilever support underneath entirely covered in black so that the audience could not see it. The group, which incorporated dance and music in its drama, responded to current events in Living Newspapers as well as presenting its play programme. The initial, twenty-week, season included an evening of Polynesian songs and dances, Gorky's *The Mother*, a classical Chinese play, *Apu Ollantay* (an Aztec drama of revolt against the Inca), classics from Tibet and Java, and Kalidasa's *Hero and Nymph*. According to one of its directors, the small auditorium was not financially viable and the venture soon collapsed. It is not clear how much of the programme was achieved, although one item, *The Mysterious Universe*, Menon's adaptation of the astronomer James Jeans's book, was produced at the Arts Theatre in 1935. Menon campaigned for India's independence at meetings around the country organised by the India League before going to live in India, where he wrote at least one play for radio, and then Italy.[43]

Another experimental artist who momentarily turned to the theatre in Britain was Samuel Fyzee Rahamin, whose play, *Daughter of Ind*, had three performances at the Arts Theatre in 1937. The story of a young Indian 'untouchable' woman whose love for a white English tutor brings down political and religious wrath, it began and ended with votive tableaux and acknowledged none of the conventional rules, demanding the audience 'discard their notions of what a play ought to be and exchange development of action for an unvarying situation only gradually revealed'.[44] The cast, it seems, was mixed white and non-white, as it was for Fyzee Rahamin's play *Invented Gods* (Embassy, 1938), which presents a philosophy of mystical acceptance through the life of its lead Indian character, played by an ex-RADA student from India, Vera Dantra.[45] Also in the cast was Mayura, whose solo performance of the Indian Temple Dance had been a highlight at the Mask Theatre Club the year before.[46]

During the war, the left-wing amateur Unity Theatre included in its 1943 repertoire *India Speaks* (a.k.a. *Map of India*)—a Living Newspaper in poem-form dealing with the famine in Eastern India—written by Mulk Raj Anand, who became one of India's leading literary figures. He recalled there being a cast of some three dozen, including several Indians. At one performance to raise money for Bengali relief, an astonishing £2,500 was donated following a speech by Krishna Menon, a local Labour councillor, secretary of the India League and future Foreign Secretary of India.

Accompanied by Menon, Unity took the play to London's East End for a special showing to Indian seamen, and to Birmingham, Leeds and Cardiff as part of the India League's campaign on the famine and the need for Indian independence. Anand went on to write a similar Living Newspaper, *Famine*, for the Army Bureau of Current Affairs Play Unit, which was heavily influenced by people associated with Unity.[47] In less ideological but no less practical vein, following in the tradition of South Asian charitable performance, *Sakuntala* was adapted as a ballet in 1946 to raise money to buy mobile health vans for India, with the celebrated Javanese dancer Retna Mohini in the lead.

Post-war period

In the decades after the war until 1975, there was little to change the major contours delineated in the pre-war theatrical map. Indian independence and partition—and in the 1970s the 'Asian' expulsions from Uganda as well as the creation of Bangladesh—formed the backdrop to the pattern and nature of the expansion or establishment of significant new immigrant communities. Self-organisation was strong, and out of that grew 'home' language drama, which offered community consolidation and comfort, yet could also exacerbate seclusion. Naseem Khan has written about the role of drama in these communities, pointing out that weakness of tradition meant theatre was slower to develop than music and dance, and that major cultural issues relating to religion, gender perceptions and language also played a significant part.[48]

In professional theatre, distinctive South Asian topics remained absent. Although appearances by South Asian performers, or those with South Asian roots, can be found in a number of West End productions, such as *This Way to the Tomb* (Garrick, 1946) and *Murder in the Cathedral* (Lyric, 1947), in which ethnicity is not an issue, or in plays that do touch on ethnic topics, such as *Teahouse of the August Moon* (Her Majesty's, 1954), based on a novel about the Americans in Japan at the end of the war, these appearances were marginal. This limitation reflects both a narrowness of vision by writers and a bias against artists of colour by producers. South Asian actors, if used, often portrayed characters from different parts of the continent regardless of any actual connection, as audiences still were overwhelmingly white and still, it was assumed, had little notion of the distinctions but did like to see what they regarded as acceptably 'real'.

On the fringes, Govindas Vishnoodas Desani, a Kenyan-born actor and writer who lived in Britain briefly in the late 1920s and from 1939 to 1952, had his poetic play about a prophet, *Hali*, published in 1950, with forewords by E.M. Forster and T.S. Eliot. It was staged that year at the Watergate Theatre Club at Charing Cross, but was little noticed. D.P. Chaudhuri, who managed the Irving Theatre, acted as an agent/promoter for 'coloured artists', and also in the 1950s owned the Princes Theatre in Edinburgh, which staged revue during the annual summer Festival. The Irving operated in the 1950s and early 1960s as a club theatre behind the National Portrait Gallery off Leicester Square, above what was then the City Morgue. It seems to have presented late night revue as well as more traditional fare. Apart from two Tagore plays in 1952, directed by Tarun Roy and presented by the East and West Drama Society, which appears to take its name from Das Gupta's organisation, and *Red Oleanders* in 1953, the only other show at the Irving under Chaudhuri that seems to have a South Asian connection is *Magic from the East* (a magician, fire-eater and other variety acts), a Christmas-time offering in 1953 that mined the conventional variety appeal of an illusory Orient.

It was still a time of individual initiative. Actors such as Zia Mohyeddin, Saeed Jaffrey and Alaknanda Samarth studied at RADA in the 1950s and 1960s but were isolated figures, as Rani and Devi had been before the war, despite the distinguished careers they went on to enjoy and the contributions they made to establishing a South Asian profile in British theatre. Collective activity was local and constrained by conservative attitudes within the diaspora and British racism without. The Indian government prohibited Partap Sharma's *A Touch of Brightness*, in which a young Hindu is tricked into becoming a whore and has to choose between the brothel and life with the man she loves, from being performed at the first Commonwealth Arts Festival in London in 1965. It was given a production without décor at the Royal Court two years later with a cast of Indian performers but did not lead to any further projects.

A breakthrough (however partial) in terms of 'mainstream' commercial theatre came in 1960, when E.M. Forster's *A Passage to India* was transferred from the Oxford Playhouse to the West End, with Zia Mohyeddin, Rashid Karapiet and South Asian extras in the cast. The novel was adapted for the stage with Forster's approval by Santha Rama Rau, an Indian-born writer who was educated in England while her diplomat father was based there. Her adaptation was seen on BBC TV in 1965 and used by David Lean for his 1984 film of the novel, in which Alec Guinness notoriously played Godbole in 'brownface'. Rau told a journalist that she had undertaken the project in response to a director who had asked her why there were no plays being written that interpreted India.[49] She chose not to write a play of her own or to adapt an Indian play but turned instead to an English novelist and an English view of India, a response that would be turned on its head in the 1970s with the forced arrival in Britain of South Asian exiles from Africa, who, with their exposure to theatre, responded in drama as well as in politics to the racism they encountered in order to create their own theatre of self-expression and self-representation.

Changing the map

This survey has tried to sketch the broad historical background against which such a change occurred. Connections that travel back over centuries of representation by non-Asians of the Asian Other are mixed with connections over mere decades to previous South Asian attempts to adjust the preconceptions of the 'hosts'. The connections may sometimes seem tenuous, but they are significant because theatre has been crucial to the creation of the British subject and its relationship to the Other. To take one example, a continuum can be traced from eighteenth-century shows such as *Aladdin, or the Wonderful Lamp* (Covent Garden, 1788) through *Sinbad the Sailor* (Covent Garden, 1838) and other nineteenth-century popular theatre to the wider popular culture of the twentieth and twenty-first centuries, whether in pantomimes, TV shows such as *It Ain't 'Alf Hot Mum* or the *Carry On* film series. (It should, therefore, come as no surprise that young British soldiers fighting in Iraq are reported as calling local men 'Ali Baba'.)[50]

Given the complexities of this historical process, it is not always easy or wise to draw definitive conclusions. Yet while the nuances of the indigenous drama should not be overlooked nor should the overall trajectory that diminished one set of peoples at the expense of another; mutual exchanges over centuries and advances in knowledge did not necessarily engender greater respect. The understandably fitful nature of the early and disparate South Asian theatrical response to imperial subjection and misconception stands in telling contrast to the persistence of the stereotypes contained in the 'host' drama. The issues of sex (and its progeny), religion, morality and status recur, even as the first eastern tropes, dominated by the tyrant and the harem, birthed more specifically South Asian figures of mystery and threat and objects of linguistic fun. The South Asian presence was marginalised whether on stage or in society, and that marginalisation came at a great cost. The trigger for the founding of Tara Arts in the mid-1970s, it should be remembered, was the racist murder of a young Sikh, and the outcome of that response, which spread beyond Tara and is detailed elsewhere in this book, went beyond mere encounter of cultures. Along with other postcolonial sensibilities active at the time, it changed the contours of the British theatre map for ever.

3

Bridging Divides

The Emergence of Bilingual Theatre in Tower Hamlets in the 1980s

Susan Croft

The London Borough of Tower Hamlets is famous for both its long-standing history of immigration as the classic 'Point of Arrival' and its tradition of left-wing political activism. Huguenots, Jews and Bangladeshi immigrants from Sylhet gathered in areas such as Spitalfields, which bear the traces of each new culture. The political activism is witnessed in the Match Girls strike, Sylvia Pankhurst's East London Federation of Suffragettes, workers' struggles in the docks and sweatshops, the battle of Cable Street against Mosley's fascists and beyond. These two histories were constantly overlapping and fuelling each other. In the 1970s and 1980s key struggles centred on the growth in joblessness, cuts in social provision and growing racial tension. The rise of the British National Party, lent support by Enoch Powell's infamous 1968 'Rivers of Blood' speech, the 1970s recession and, later, Margaret Thatcher's equally infamous 1977 rhetoric warning of Britain being swamped by an alien culture fed the increase in racial attacks.

Tower Hamlets also has a tradition of non-English language performance. It began with the Yiddish theatre, which became active and thrived from the 1890s onwards, taking over existing established venues such as the Pavilion Theatre[1] in Whitechapel Road and developing its own venues such as the Grand Palais, which survived until 1970. Similarly, the more recent growth of the Sylheti community in Whitechapel is reflected in the emergence of new cultural venues within the district and the re-emergence of old ones with a new focus. The success of these venues was built on the presence of an Asian community in the borough which goes back to the nineteenth century, when Lascar sailors arrived from Sylhet. Some stayed in cheap lodging-houses awaiting a working passage home, others found work, married and settled in the borough. The new migrant populations that arrived in the 1960s from what was, until 1971, East Pakistan, then Bangladesh, were initially slow to develop a cultural life. Naseem Khan's 1976 report *The Arts Britain Ignores* linked this to the male-dominated nature of the immigration, in which women made up only 15 per cent of the community and cultural activities were less likely 'to cater to family consumption'. At the same time, 'it is most often from among the women that dance and folk song teachers are found'.[2]

By the 1970s this had begun to change, and Khan instances the presence of the Bengali Artists Association in East London 'in existence as a number of individuals under differing names for very many years' (p. 18) and the work of the Bethnal Green Adult Education Institute. By 1976 the latter was hosting drama classes every evening but Sunday, led by Amar Bose. Its weekly showings attracted regular audiences of 200 people, many of them illiterate and therefore especially reliant on this entertainment. The production co-ordinator Shah Rehman describes an earlier tradition of Bengali drama in the area and his involvement in the group 'The Orientals', including staging a production of *Siraj-ud-Daullah* at the Barbican Theatre in 1963.[3] In 1973 the *Times Educational Supplement* reported the Adult Education Institute's groups' activities in drama in English, Urdu and Bengali, and in music and dance.[4] In its more recent incarnation the drama group had (in Khan's 1976 account) recently staged *Tippoo Sultan* at the Curtain Theatre, an Inner London Education Authority facility in Shoreditch.[5] Press articles in the borough archives give brief accounts of Bengali performances throughout the early 1970s at venues including Queen Mary College in Mile End Road, and by the Asian Artists Association at Tower Hamlets Girls School in Stepney. The press articles also point to the establishment of the Islamic Cultural Programme in Stepney (1974), marked by celebrations including poetry reading and singing in Urdu, Arabic and English.[6]

More Bangladeshi families settled in the area and, with the increase in numbers of children in local schools, the inner London Educational Authority (ILEA) was forced into a growing recognition of the need for increased language and, later, cultural provision. Norman Goodman, then a teacher at Daneford School, describes the establishment in the early 1970s of a 'Non-English Speaking Unit' in a context of racist attacks: 'It was a year or two before it was appreciated what a negative message this [title] was sending through the school!'[7] He recalls the development of the school's slowly emergent sensitivity to the impact of such well-meaning but problematic solutions to the 'language problem' and the need for active anti-racist strategies and policies. In parallel with this, Goodman describes an increasingly public celebration of Bengali culture. This was expressed both within the school, with recognition of festivals like Eid, the development of bhangra, provision of Bengali percussion instruments in the music department, and visits by storytellers and musicians, and outside, where 'Local melas became a feature of the summer and the Brick Lane Bengali Festival had become a major event, from small beginnings.' There was campaigning within the Bengali community and an increased recognition by arts projects of the need to include and address the experience of the Bangladeshi population. By 1986 this had led to an increasing number of spaces being listed in *Tower Hamlets Arts Directory* as programming Asian arts that included performance: Dame Colet House in Stepney Green, the Davenant Centre, the Brady Centre, the Montefiore Centre[8] in Hanbury Street and the recently opened space for women, the Jagonari Centre in Whitechapel.

Leftist political activism had also encouraged a long-standing theatrical tradition locally going back to at least the 1930s, in groups like the Rebel Players (to the north in Hackney) or the Yiddish-speaking Proltet. Numerous artists and theatre people had settled in the borough from the 1970s, attracted by cheap, often run-down accommodation (some rented, some squatted), and alongside it by the availability of run-down industrial and public spaces where work could be developed. The Half Moon Theatre grew out of the alternative arts community that was thriving in Tower Hamlets by the 1980s. The original Half Moon Theatre at 27 Alie St, E1, was set up in 1972 in an abandoned former synagogue and two adjoining houses. In a dangerous state of disrepair, it was nonetheless a flourishing centre of artistic experiment and a hugely atmospheric space. Maurice Colbourne, Guy Sprung and Mike Irving led a group of committed company members staging innovative productions which ranged from international plays from Eastern Europe to new home-grown work by local writers such as Steve Gooch and Billy Colville. The theatre's determination to stage a culturally and politically radical repertoire in a neglected part of London was allied to the efforts of other artists and grassroots initiatives in the borough with the aim of creating social transformation and access to resources for the culturally disenfranchised. This was achieved through housing co-ops, food distribution co-ops, community print shops that disseminated radical literature, and local newssheets and community festivals involving local people in celebratory activities and socialist consciousness-raising.

Alongside its main programme of plays in the theatre, the Half Moon involved itself in community activities. It set up the Half Moon Young Peoples' Theatre (HMYPT) with support from the Gulbenkian Foundation, and programmed the performance elements of the local E1 Festival (Stepney community festival, founded 1970), which operated as a platform to display local talent and campaigned in 1973 for a 'Docklands for local people'.[9] However, while elsewhere in Tower Hamlets artistic programmes of the Bengali language drama groups, together with music and dance initiatives, were developing in adult-education institutes, schools and other spaces, these two major strands of artistic development in the borough, the Asian and the 'alternative', remained largely separate. The E1 Festival centred on Bigland Grass in Stepney, which in the early 1970s was yet to become a major area of Bangladeshi settlement. There is no reference in leaflets and press materials to any events that represented cultural traditions other than those of the traditional white East End, despite Spitalfields forming a substantial part of that postcode. However, building on its E1 Festival involvement, in 1978 the Half Moon was instrumental in the establishment of TEEF! (The East End Festival) as an independent voluntary organisation. By this point there was an increasing realisation of the need to bring together the white East End and immigrant communities.

This new borough-wide festival was a deliberate initiative to try to foreground a range of communities and art-forms across an increasingly diverse borough where, as well as the Sylheti communities, there were Somalis, African-Caribbean, Hindu, Chinese and many other communities. The 1979 TEEF! programme included both The Wherehouse company[10] in a show called "@*&/?!" and the Wherehouse Bengali Drama Group in a dance drama, in addition to an evening of Bengali music. In 1977 and 1978 the shows programmed at Tower Hamlets venues generally suggest an effort to address the community's culturally diverse experiences, including Mutable Theatre's *Mother Country* at the Montefiore Centre,[11] Common Stock's *Bridget and Other Tales from Whitechapel* (1978), based on 'stories told by the children of Aldgate East' with an illustration showing a black man in a dinner-suit, and, at the Half Moon itself in 1977, Pirate Jenny in David Edgar's *Our Own People*, based on a strike at a Northern mill and the consequent government Court of Enquiry into discrimination against Asian workers.[12]

The Half Moon's 1981 Gorilla Festival of alternative theatre at both the old Alie Street venue and the New Half Moon, a former chapel in Mile End Rd, Stepney Green,[13] included Tara Arts in *Diwaali* (at Alie St). A 1981 document, 'The Bangladeshi Community', identified TEEF!'s increasing development as an umbrella organisation across the East End and attempted to address the 'vital' need that 'the input and involvement of the Bangladeshi community is reflected'[14] in TEEF!'s development. The document goes on to look at some problems encountered: 'We knew of two groups only, difficult to contact; and we didn't know whether to aim for Bengali events, aimed at the Bengali community, which we were not really qualified to organise, or fitting Bengali artists into a culturally mixed programme.' This candid assessment reiterates the sense of division between these worlds of performance practice, the Bengali and the (largely) white British alternative theatre scene. Even other Asian theatre companies such as Tara Arts, while sharing certain experiences and traditions with the Bengalis, came from other language and religious communities and were funded and professional, experimenting artistically and linguistically with new forms and aiming to reach a variety of audiences. Yet much local Bengali work must still have conformed to Naseem Khan's 1976 frank evaluation of a 'comfortable hermetically-sealed quality' of Bangladeshi/Bengali cultural activities, where 'Very few outsiders permeate, nor are they very seriously considered as a potential audience.' She recommended that 'Dance classes, which tend to embellish a young girl with another socially acceptable female talent, could do with the challenge of visits by professional groups.'[15] The divide between the local Bengali culture and the primarily white alternative scene remained.

However, in its large and costly new theatre, built behind the chapel, the now hierarchically-led main-house Half Moon concentrated on a policy of large-scale popular work including satirical musicals (in an attempt to bring in white working-class audiences) and leftist plays, including the first major British revival of David Edgar's *Destiny* (1985). The Half Moon Young People's Theatre, though saddled with a difficult space on the new site—a highly unsuitable breeze-block cube, a design on which they and their users were not consulted—began to develop a different policy, centred on responsiveness to the voices of company members and engagement at grassroots level with the urgency of bringing together the diverse communities of the borough. Issues around the empowerment and recruitment of performers and audiences and the representation of Asian characters were being grappled with in a continuing process, building on the best of the alternative theatre's traditions of collective working and self-appraisal. Dhirendra has described the HMYPT as a context where critical appraisal of the company's work was actively encouraged:

> *Raj* was the first play we did. And then I pointed out a lot of the problems I had, personally as a Brown person in the show, because it's a great piece to talk to White kids about. But all the imagery in the play was—and again you're going to eight to nine, eight to ten year olds—was very negative as far as the Indian guy who's grown up is taught by a White kid to do up his shoelaces. So they were all subservient images. ... And so then we decided that we're going to commission new plays. And out of that was born a play called *Video Wicked*.[16]

Asians were also actively involved in the company's developing employment policy:

> at that time basically we said that ... we set up a precedent that actors had to be employed, and the company had to reflect multiracial ... in its entirety. Like from administrators all the way to set-designers, writers ...[17]

In *Destiny* HMYPT company members Helen Awan's and Dhirendra's assigned roles reproduced the marginalisation of Asian experience in the play's foregrounding of the white characters and the rise of the ultra-Right. But the working processes of the YPT encouraged their critical engagement and creative input in determining the subject of new, commissioned work and the content of each final piece.

The HMYPT was originally set up in 1975, following the success of a pilot scheme of workshops in youth clubs in 1974. It operated from a series of temporary bases locally before moving to the site of the new theatre. Initially the performance company were largely white, with some Black company members. However, in the 1980s the company made a conscious effort to recruit Asian performers. There was a resident company of three or four actors and by the mid-1980s a director,[18] administrator, education worker and a bilingual education outreach worker, one of a gradual expansion of Asian workers within the core team. When the Half Moon itself was forced by its debts to close the HMYPT survived, constituting itself as a separate entity and eventually moving in 1994 into its current home, the converted former Limehouse Town Hall.

The HMYPT developed shows and workshops that went into youth clubs and schools. Accordingly, it was confronted on a daily basis with the issue of audiences for whom English was a second language.[19] When, in 1986, the Royal Court YPT hosted the ILEA conference 'A Meeting of Mother Tongues'[20] three members of the HMYPT attended. The conference was a highly influential event which led to the report *A Meeting of Mother Tongues: Bilingualism, Theatre and Schools*. Norman Goodman remembers its significance: 'It was a day filled with sort of amazing experiences and of meeting people in the discussions that were happening unofficially, you know, in lunch breaks and that kind of thing.'[21] There were presentations from, among others, Kwesi Owesu, director of African Dawn, George Eugenides of Theatro Technis, and BAT (British Asian Theatre). Jyoti Patel, from Leicester, performed a one-woman adaptation of the play *Awaaj* that she had written with the support of Youth Drama worker Jezz Simons. This was the first of a series of their bilingual collaborations in Gujarati and English, including *Prem* (Asian Co-operative Theatre), *Kirti, Sona and Ba* and *Subah O Shaam*, that were hugely successful at theatres in the East Midlands.[22] Also making a presentation were drama staff and students from Mulberry School for Girls, another Tower Hamlets pioneer, with which the HMYPT had built close links through its outreach worker Balbinder Biring. The conference both celebrated and established blueprints for the use of non-standard English and bilingual work in promoting inclusion, tackling racism and invigorating the art-form.

The published report gave accounts of seven projects working across languages, including Greek and Jamaican patois as well as Asian languages, and summarised debates around language, theatre and education. Recommendations included the revaluation of oral cultures, of other non-Western theatre traditions and of the role of bilingual and multilingual speakers of English in evolving new cultural and linguistic forms such as the 'Gringlish' (Greek Cypriot–English) of Theatro Technis, all of which could enrich the range of theatrical practice. The report identified the need for an injection of new forms of writing into theatre and the need for mainstream theatre-script committees to find ways of 'challenging their own assumptions about what constitutes good theatre'.[23] Circulated throughout the sector, it was influential in developing future practice in companies such as Theatre Centre and organisations such as New Playwrights Trust.[24] Through the agency of Elyse Dodgson, then Director of the Royal Court YPT, the report fed into the Royal Court's long-term practice through the development of the Court's programme of international workshops, exchanges, translations and commissions.[25]

The HMYPT's response, and the working process and projects to which it led, were eventually articulated in a paper by Director Deborah Bestwick, detailing the development of the devised bilingual show *Dear Suraiya ... Love Rehana*. Bestwick details the importance of bilingual work for educational, cultural and access reasons:

> Use of a child's home language carry crucial cultural implications which affect a child's sense of worth, value and therefore self-confidence and ability to learn. Working bilingually would also challenge our own relationship to English and the cultural assumptions it carries with it.[26]

In *Dear Suraiya ... Love Rehana* those actors who were not Sylheti-speaking undertook to learn the language and began an extended process of language-tuition, a commitment made possible by the HMYPT policy of extensive contracts for company members. The piece (aimed at 10–11 year olds) dramatised the relationship between two cousins, young girls growing up, one an aspiring teacher on a tea plantation in Sylhet, the other in East London. The narrative was built around the factual story of a union worker who represented the tea-pickers in Bangladesh. He arrived in the UK to attend the AGM of the Scottish company, which owned the tea plantations and to protest about the quality of drinking water available to the tea-pickers: 'War on Want came and bought one share in the company in order to be able to attend the AGM and he brought this bottle of water and invited the chair to drink it and she refused to do that.'[27] The production involved cross-casting that challenged a whole range of cultural assumptions: 'Andy (a white male actor) would have to represent an Asian woman with complete integrity, just as non-Bengali speakers would have to learn to speak lines in Sylheti convincingly.'[28] The process forced the actors to pay new attention to the nuances of language and physicality. The structure of the play as an exchange between the two women, and the fluidity of roles, created a context in which neither experience was privileged and foregrounded at the expense of the other.

In addition to the overt content of the play and the structure of the piece, the position of the performers in relation to the language spoken became in itself part of the meaning of the play. It dramatised a variety of relationships towards the words spoken, from those bilingual speakers equally fluent in both languages to those first-language-English speakers whose sometimes faltering command of Sylheti reflected in reverse the currently or recently-lived experience of first-language-Sylheti speakers in the audience. Watching it as a first-language-English audience member[29] was to experience and be compelled to reflect on the power relationships imposed by language proficiency and the ability to participate, reversing the usual position of English dominance. There were delays in comments being translated into English or inadequacies in translation when it became obvious that a Sylheti joke had not been, perhaps could not be, adequately translated into English. In a radical reversal of power roles, the deliberate experience of frustration and sensation of exclusion from full understanding became in themselves part of the encounter with the play.

The after-show discussions were translated, partly formally by members of the HMYPT team, partly informally by bilingual speakers in the audience. In these, first-language-Sylheti audience-members expressed both their pleasure at the willingness of the first-language-English performers to learn Sylheti, and a sense of enjoyment at a piece the structure of which celebrated the position and skill of bilingual speakers, with their resultant sense of empowerment. A professional theatre company had afforded non-native speakers of English a space in which they could legitimately speak. Both bilingual speakers and those learning English expressed a sense of enthusiasm for the authorisation to participate in a professional, extracurricular activity. For bilingual speakers it was important to experience a piece that reflected the complexity of their lived reality. They often acted as interpreters to older generations, and the play included the absurdities, misunderstandings and forced tactfulness in translation and the skill with which they learnt to operate and negotiate between languages. This sense of empowerment was reflected in a discussion to which many audience members contributed, switching rapidly between English and Sylheti and becoming animated and confident.

The piece was reworked several times over the next few years, reflecting an increasing sophistication in the working process and the English-speaking company members' command of Sylheti. This became the foundation of a new working method for the HMYPT.[30] This was explored further in *Korgosh o Kautwa (Hare and Tortoise)*, also 1989, which was aimed at 5–7 year olds, with a more consistent mix of Sylheti and English throughout. The animal world in which it was set did not 'exert a strong cultural pull towards the use of any particular language'. But it did make new physical demands on the performers, who were working with a Delhi-trained, Bengali co-director and in the performance style Yakshagana, described as 'a musical, physically declamatory, theatrical version of the classic Kathakali dance'.[31]

In 1990 *Aarekta Juta* (*The Second Shoe*) addressed issues of the purpose of education in a show for 10–11 year olds, who played the 'role' of a first-year secondary school class on the first day of term. For the first time the company worked from a bilingual devising process and involved the audience as participants, with the performers facilitating discussion between them in both languages. Wordplay between languages began to create the hybrid linguistic spaces, akin to what Jatinder Verma has described as 'Binglish' or the 'Spanglish' Guillermo Gomez-Pena explores in his performance and writings.[32] It represents alternative languages, a variation of what Salman Rushdie has said, in lauding 'mongrelisation' against the 'absolutism of the Pure': 'Melange, hotchpotch, a bit of this and a bit of that is how newness enters the world.'[33] It was a method that was successful in encouraging young people's participation in the work of the YPT, bridging gaps between language communities in Tower Hamlets and between the theatrical traditions of Asian performance and the leftist alternative theatre in the borough, pioneering new participatory directions.

4

Experiments in Theatre from the Margins

Text, Performance and New Writers

Rukhsana Ahmad

Text and performance: the conjoined twins

Let me begin with a minor truism: the perfect spectator neither wishes nor needs to deconstruct a piece of theatre into its constituent elements, but simply surrenders to the wholeness of the experience. S/he yields to the seduction of the text as performance in an uncritical spirit, straining forward to hear every note, absorbing gesture and movement, mood and music, light and colour subliminally. Indeed, the greatest productions resist deconstruction. Their seamless blend of textual and non-textual elements submerges the audience in the moment, erasing all sense of artifice, leaving them exhilarated and uplifted by the illusion. Conversely, new writers, bound to the text by definition, must unpack these elements to understand how all the constituents of performance orchestrate and meld with each other to generate theatre. Until they learn *not* to rely merely on words to drive the narrative, indeed acquire a degree of nonchalance towards them and exploit instead the physical/visual aspects of theatre, their plays sound wordy and undramatic.

Predictably, actor-playwrights or writers with thespian antecedents know the power of theatre's non-verbal elements. They understand the performance space and more importantly, the audience. Although this is not enough to produce an amazing play, it certainly raises their performance over writers new to theatre, especially over those committed to poetry or literature, who tend to rely on dialogue and mistrust or fail to exploit theatrical elements because of their lack of familiarity with the medium. Correspondingly, such new writers resist editorial interventions from collaborators that seem inimical to the text. Until they master the craft of theatre, budding playwrights would do well not to ignore the ubiquitous directorial rant: '*Cut out your darlings!*' The nation's love for Shakespeare notwithstanding, audiences are notoriously impatient with the 'poetic' or the 'literary'. Alas, that murderous, cautionary refrain encapsulating fear and mistrust of the playwright's darlings, or of that which sounds grandiose or epic in scale and ambition, is rooted in bitter experience.

My own roots are in literature, so I hugely empathise with playwrights who are in love with words: let me confess, I *am* too. But I learnt intuitively, early on, never to resist justifiable cuts. I believe any self-respecting dramatist's resistance must focus on what *is* 'a justifiable cut'? My guiding principle is: *meaning is sacrosanct; words, intrinsically, are not.* They may be negotiable, but only if their substitutes do not strike at the heart of the text to undermine its essence. Theatre is a tough discipline: you must learn to murder your darlings or they probably will return to haunt you.

Editors of literary fiction tend not to lock horns with writers with such ferocity. Not only are novelists prolix; in comparison, they never consider a ceiling on the number of characters to tell a particular story. Enough reason that for defection, distraction. It is the arena where the writer gets the most space, the most autonomy, the greatest freedom and perhaps the greatest satisfaction. A finished story or a novel is a viable artistic entity that does not need the paraphernalia and constraints of a production to find an audience. Words are its only currency—they do it all. Once published, it obligingly shifts shape and recreates itself for every reader. Anyhow, I suspect it is easier as a genre than any other—simply because storytelling comes to all of us quite instinctually. It is the form that came most naturally to me as a child and, admittedly, it still beckons: the challenge, the quest, the sheer pleasure and glory of a finished story.

I have now lost all fear of embarking on a new play: indeed, I love the challenge as much as I enjoy writing fiction. Initially, of course, the knowledge that it is a more demanding craft, where structure is supreme, daunted me. Recognising how vital directorial support and rehearsed readings are during the writing process we chose to offer these to new writers at Kali to enable them to eliminate repetition and overwriting.

Play writing is no less intuitive, of course, but it certainly demands an evolved story, which has already matured in the dark recesses of one's imagination, which submits to shape and structure easily instead of falling apart when exposed to air and sunlight and reflection. Whatever I learnt in the theatre about structure and dialogue has undoubtedly bled into my fiction, but I believe that I brought to my plays an inordinate commitment to story, characters, theme and tone.

Text matters

That commitment accounts partially for the fact that, for me, text has primacy and priority over all other aspects of the production. I see it as the starting point of 'a good play' as, I suspect, do most mainstream audiences. This degree of commitment to the text may be unacceptable to most students of semiotics and adherents of non-verbal theatre, but I hasten to clarify that my preference does not imply an aversion. On the contrary, non-verbal theatre has intrigued, entertained, fascinated and educated me, but I do experience it somewhat distantly, like a tourist who relishes a stint at a dream destination without ever wanting to move there forever.

The truth is that what enthrals and moves me deeply, and—if the play is memorable—haunts me is text-based theatre. I suspect this might be true of most spectators. The text *per se* may vanish from recall, but the most theatrical moments and images it sets forth on stage resonate long after the show is over and the actors' voices are silent. We carry the magic of those with us as we leave the theatre, we wake up to it the next morning and we can recall it for analysis and discussion. After all, text is what allows the creator to expose layers of meaning and the complexities hidden within the most conflicted and explosive relationships to any depth. It is what makes it possible for a playwright to define nuances and play them. It is the vehicle for thoughts and ideas: it not only delineates the world of the play but also contextualises the narrative and creates the space for exploring philosophical and political dualities.

Perhaps more than my commitment to play writing as a profession, this passionate defence of the text relates to a process of cultural conditioning, which I must proffer here as my excuse. The truth is that, until I began to write for the theatre, I viewed dramatic writing purely as literary text, sanctified by time and use. I discovered most of the plays that I love not as performances but as books that were part of my syllabus as a student of English literature. I still remember lines that I memorised decades ago.

To her great credit, our Professor of Drama at Karachi University managed to imbue us with a passion for the plays she taught even though there were few opportunities to see them mounted or even hear them if you discount the scratchy long-playing records of productions available then through the British Council Library. Nevertheless, we learnt to appreciate and love them one by one. They came alive as we read them and imagined them on stage, reverentially reaching out for notes and study guides, analysing them in class aided by literary criticism that eulogised the texts but never referred to productions. It seemed logical and obvious then to believe that the playwright was not just a cog in the wheels of a production but the presiding deity of this art form.

To further underline and strengthen this orientation towards text, my earliest experiences of live performance were quite rudimentary: school drama, folk theatre, occasionally popular comedy on stage (Urdu/Punjabi and even English) and amateur dramatics at various cultural institutes in Lahore and Karachi. Except the few Royal Shakespeare Company productions that toured courtesy of the British Council or the American

Cultural Centre, I had seen very few serious plays on stage before I came to live in London. Sadly, even that limited privilege is no longer available to students in Pakistan in today's climate of political extremism, dissension and violence. Television helped to fill the gap with black-and-white, rather poorly filmed early productions of the RSC, mostly of history plays.

Access to plays in a range of styles and at various scales of production was one of the great bonuses of my move to London. I have vivid memories of those early experiences: Janet Suzman playing Hedda Gabler, the thrilling sight of horses, their nostrils flaring, on stage in Peter Shaffer's *Equus*, the exhilaration and emotional power of August Wilson's *Ma Rainey's Black Bottom*, and countless productions of my greatest favourites: *Othello*, *King Lear* and *The Tempest*.

I discovered the fringe and loved it. When the arts editor at *Asian Post*, Reginald Massey, sent me to review plays, he opened a new chapter for me: here was an incarnation of British theatre in which I could finally see a space to inscribe myself. Sudha Buchar and Shaheen Khan were brilliant in Tara Arts' *This Story's Not for Telling* (1985, based on Manto's stories about partition). I found Tara's *The Little Clay Cart* (1984 and 1986) captivating too, but, for me, *This Story* was a significant production and the latter a bow to exotica driven by a search for definable differences in matters of style rather than thought-provoking ideas and content. I also reviewed a young new actress, Firoza Syal (now Meera Syal), who performed at a women's conference. These lively young actors seemed poised to step into the limelight and, indeed, some of them did.

My reviews and articles caught the attention of Ravi Randhawa, who had obtained funding to set up the Asian Women Writers' Workshop. She invited me to join the group. To step into that room full of kindred spirits was instant joy; I immediately knew I belonged with them.

Finding a voice

None of our contemporaries in the UK was dealing with the themes and subjects that drew us. We were all engaged in a quest for self-expression and, of course, for an audience. We became that for each other: an engaged and critical but, nevertheless, enthusiastic audience that promised a readership. Ravi's intention was to provide criticism in a spirit of support and co-operation rather than rivalry and competition, but so real was our appetite for the work that a sense of professional rivalry and hidden hierarchies soon emerged. Yet, the commonalties that united us then seemed more powerful than any possible fissures and divides in the collective psyche. No one foresaw the cracks that followed in the wake of that horrific date 9/11. (It was strange to hear Meera, who was once part of this group, berating Muslims on television and emphatically embracing an Indian identity to avoid any damage by association.)

These were the late 1980s. Rahila Gupta was a journalist with *Outwrite*, I freelanced for *Spare Rib*, and, slowly, the exchange of ideas, the debates and the readings within the workshop, as much as some events in my own life, politicised me further. I might never have written a play set in a refuge if Rahila's involvement in Southall Black Sisters had not raised my awareness and made it easier for me to research the play. The march for Balwant Kaur, for which she mobilised all of us, and her own elegiac tribute to Kaur prompted me to reflect on refuges and what they meant for women. I ran weekly creative writing workshops in a refuge to research my play. The story and the characters are fictional but newspaper accounts of a 'lockout' of some Asian refuge workers by the residents had sparked off the idea. Kaur's death lent it tragic force.

The writing emerging from the workshop was publishable and, authorised by the group to find a publisher, I contacted the Women's Press. Ros de Lanerolle, the late editor, immediately invited us. I co-ordinated the submission, but in true radical style we edited collectively, choosing to be inclusive and egalitarian within the agreed parameters of progressive politics; there was no space for reactionary agendas. Long before *Right of Way*, our first collection, was published, Jatinder Verma had commissioned me to write a short play for Tara Arts.

Text into performance: tensions and dilemmas

As drama suddenly transformed itself from pure text into performance before my eyes, I heard my own words with a degree of alarm, occasionally, even dismay. In the mouths of actors who queried if their character would indeed say this or that, every word sought justification in earnest. Suddenly text and performance were at variance, battling with each other for survival. It is difficult for a new playwright to determine whether the problem lies in the text rather than in the delivery. Eventually you learn to prune your excesses and stay within the range of performability on offer.

Over the years, through many assignments, I realised (in fitful flashes and insights) that this tension between text and performance is at the heart of the production process. It begins with a decision (whether stated openly or implied during the writer's first commissioning meeting with the director or producer) about the number of actors the company might budget for in a planned production of a commissioned play. That the text cannot completely elude or escape the impact of the producer/director and the realities of the production process was yet another (almost painful) recognition that came experientially.

Given that writing for the theatre is a craft, every playwright needs the experience of commissions and productions to grow and develop but you only ever learn to the limits of your learning opportunities. Yes, you learn from watching and reading plays and from lectures and workshops, but what you learn from writing a play yourself, seeing it through to production and then through a run, is invaluable. A sigh, a yawn, someone nodding off in the dark are salutary lessons that no amount of haranguing by a director, producer or dramaturge can match.

Each production is a journey and when the terrain is new, you rely on the wisdom and experience of your fellow travellers. Certainly, in the early stages *they* define the frontiers of success and failure for you. If they are novices too you muddle through together, but chances are you learn less than you might from a more experienced professional. As my career progressed, this knowledge deepened and my expectations dimmed before the limiting realities of fringe productions. Their impact on commissioned plays, the restraint they impose on the imagination when you begin writing, can be monumental, even though seasoned directors expect you to evade that.

Recognising this, I later sought experienced professionals (often mainstream) to help run my writing workshops for Kali Theatre Company in the 1990s. Likewise, to her credit, Rita Wolf prepared herself to direct *Song for a Sanctuary* by carefully consulting several directors and choosing to work closely with Sue Parrish from The Sphinx, formerly The Women's Theatre Group.

In search of models

Slowly, my work was weaning me away from the straitjacket of classical form, which had been my ideal as a student of drama in Karachi. Even my stint at Reading University, where my study of Yeats' *Collected Plays* corroborated the dangers of courting poetry and neglecting the golden rules, had only strengthened my natural conservatism about form.

My first commission from Tara Arts, *Sepoy's Salt, Captain's Malt* (performed 1985) was a resolute departure from conventional wisdom. I recognise now that I was engaged in pure agitprop theatre, with a young company that was political, combative, angry and still in search of its own theatrical vocabulary. To embark on that process was an act of faith, a leap in the dark. I put aside everything I knew about theatre as text from my student days and jumped in headlong, believing: 'When in Rome ...'.

The writing process allowed a week of research, three weeks of improvisations with three actors and a (first-time) director, Arti Prashar, followed by a fortnight to go away and write a 45-minute play for touring in schools. As a new writer with a reasonably clear visual map of my own expectations from this piece, I got my first insight into the chasm between text and performance when my text was handed over to the actors. Its relationship with their improvisations was remote, less literal than they anticipated. As they stumbled through their cold reading, searching for the meanings we had all sought to construct collectively out of our responses to the research in that freezing church hall over three weeks of improvisations, they waited for a verdict from our director and her boss, the producer. Luckily, she approved and so did he and I was given the weekend to address my notes.

As I watched the piece evolve slowly, liking some turns I saw on the floor and hating others, I discovered the potential power of the vehicle: an intelligent actor committed to the project becomes the playwright's ally. To my great relief design, lighting, costumes and sound slowly filled in the colours to deliver some of the coherence and depth that I thought had been in the script, but which were absent from the first cold read-through. The gap between what was for me the 'pinnacle' of theatrical writing, a proper 'grown-up' play like *King Lear*, and my own first script (based on our combined research and the actors' improvisations), which was stylised, polemical and charged with a degree of self-satire, seemed alarming and unbridgeable. Although I had enjoyed the challenge of a new creative process, I felt curiously distant from the text and the final production. It earned the writing credit I needed to become a full member of the Writers' Guild, but it was a collective rather than an individual effort. I realise now that I had no compass, or even a single lead, at that point in time, to find my way to the kind of plays I wanted to write in the years to come.

My second production for Tara was also a youth theatre piece, a free adaptation of a story 'New Constitution' by Saadat Manto. I stayed as loyal to Manto as possible. Jatinder Verma's direction demonstrated to me what image, action, gesture, movement, music, rhythm could add, how light and darkness could enhance the meaning, how props signified more than their real import; but the zany style of the production felt inappropriate to that text.

Many years later, Helena Bell (nee Uren) decided to pair my adaptation of my favourite Manto short story 'Black Shalwar' with Anu Kumar's first play *The Ecstasy* (too short to sustain an evening), as they were both poignant stories of love and loss. Kali marketed the show in 1999 with a somewhat romantic title: 'Love comes in at the window ...', although neither play was a conventional love story. The final, revised text written under Helena's direction with that agenda was, of course, substantially different from my adaptation for Tara, the company that had originally commissioned the piece. Her production, shot through with style and humour, sharply defined by a clear sense of Sultana's plight as a woman, was undoubtedly very different from what Tara's treatment, with its proposed element of song and dance, might have been.

Thrown in at the deep end as a practitioner, long before I had discovered the many different theatrical styles, schools and experiments current then, still discovering contemporary movements, I found myself on the cusp of a very sharp learning curve. It was a tremendously exciting journey, by no means over, but one that made me aware of the huge disadvantage most Asian women writers faced in this field.

Tara Arts offered me two further commissions, which I managed alongside assignments in the regions of similar ilk tied to Asian identity and experience in an age dedicated to multiculturalism. Desperate to earn from my writing, I accepted all commissions gratefully, producing the kind of 'community' plays expected of me, but I was longing to address subjects closer to my heart.

Learning to pitch

Writing is ultimately about self-expression. I knew and relished considerable autonomy and choice in the production of my own fiction and translations: inevitably, I longed for that in the theatre too. The opportunity presented itself with an invitation to meet Monstrous Regiment and pitch to them. I sold the idea for *Song for a Sanctuary*, my first full-length play. But Monstrous Regiment, who were about to move offices and were avowedly in financial straits, decided to abandon the play after receiving the first draft. This was distressing; I had no idea where to go with it next. Rita Wolf, having heard about the play, contacted me. With an iron will, she set out to produce and direct it. After a year pitted with rehearsed readings and rewrites we got the text into shape for a full professional production and Rita applied for funding to set up Kali theatre company.[1]

It was a tough lesson. All my earlier commissions had taught me very little about constructing a story for a full-length stage play or about the medium itself. Monstrous Regiment could not invest company time and resources into the play but one member of the collective offered to send it to a BBC Drama producer likely to want the play.

New writers and radio drama

That act of kindness opened another door for me, salvaging my faith in my abilities as a playwright. Although Kali's stage production preceded the radio version, the project became my calling card for radio work. Radio drama helped me quickly establish a small but regular income from writing, which was crucial: it paid for childcare, justified my absence from home and lent credibility to my perception of myself as a card-carrying, professional member of the tribe.

Women, blacks, Asians, disabled people, lesbians and gays were all knocking on the doors of the establishment in the eighties. I was amongst a group of thirty black and Asian practitioners invited to BBC Radio Drama for a day-long workshop. Senior executives welcomed us at the behest of a feisty black producer Frances-Anne Solomon, who denounced them openly for the institutional racism that had kept diversity off the airwaves until then. It was a break-through moment that gave us access to working producers (e.g. Anne Edyvean, Turan Ali, Pam Fraser-Solomon) interested in receiving ideas and pitches from minority writers and led swiftly to many black and Asian productions.

Radio, of course, closer to books than it is to the stage, is much more a writer's medium than film or theatre—it thrives on language and cherishes words. Like fiction, it addresses the audience's imagination directly, without an intermediary, offering greater intimacy with the characters. Not that there is room for laxity or verbosity here: on the contrary, each word must be the measured and perfect choice for the occasion. The dialogue has to be as convincing and credible as possible—any inappropriate word or line is far more clearly audible on radio than on a busy stage where a good actor can often cover lapses. The inflexibility of the time slot for each show exercises a fiendish rigidity in quantitative terms, enforcing discipline and economy.

Although written in prose, most radio plays demand the economy, precision and richness of poetry without the sentimentality and grunge. The best kinds of radio drama and documentary steadily spin out strong, clear images, evoking scenes that weave their narrative swiftly and vividly. The best producers are usually excellent dramaturges who help the writer achieve clarity; create narrative tension; identify missing transitions; envision the soundscape suggested by the shape of the piece; anticipate the set pieces; help the writer build the climax; and, finally, make it all work by identifying the perfect cast! As in theatre and film, ultimate success rests on effective collaboration.

Back then, BBC Radio seemed easier to sell ideas to than most theatre venues, which were guarded by coteries that remain to this day, harder for outsiders to penetrate. Radio drama was and remains a great training ground for our stages. Even today, the BBC's Writers' Room grooms new writers who might find it easier to attain a radio production than a theatre production.

Women in theatre, then and now

Soon afterwards I joined the Writers' Guild, playwright and novelist Bill Ash (husband of Dr Ranjana Ash[2]) encouraged me to join the Guild's Theatre Committee. There were very few black or Asian members in those days and his solicitous guidance was invaluable.

The Women's Committee at the Writers' Guild claimed that 'fewer than .5% of contemporary London's mainstream productions were scripted by women'. Barring Caryl Churchill and Timberlake Wertenbaker, few female playwrights were visible then. An *ad hoc* group of writers delegated from The Guild's Theatre and Women's Committees came together briefly to discuss, analyse and redress the situation and find ways of improving access for women. Both Monstrous Regiment and the Women's Theatre Group had already faded away as producers despite the crying need for their work. With no real resources at our disposal, we could do little except draw attention to the problem at Guild meetings.

Nowadays a quick tally of West End productions will probably elicit a better ratio for women than 0.5 per cent of all productions. Certainly the long-running successes of Yasmina Reza's *Art* and Marie Jones' *Stones in His Pocket* helped to prove the point that women's writing could gross millions and survive in the West End, but overall the figure for productions featuring plays written by women still remains low.

Charlotte Higgins ends her feature 'The Case of the Missing Women Playwrights' in the *Guardian* on a somewhat tentative note, but the blogs she attracted reiterate her concern at the disparity she highlighted:

> There are of course all kinds of historical reasons for this disparity. But it's pretty stark, and it doesn't seem to be ironing itself out fast. Depressing. Women novelists are everywhere; writing by women is on the whole booming. But women dramatists simply don't get the same kind of exposure.[3]

Tantalisingly, Higgins does not explore the reasons, but I suspect the glaring absence of women directors, identified by the Guild's *ad hoc* committee as one of the factors, continues to hurt women playwrights. This was one of the problems Kali Theatre Company recognised.

Over the years of rehearsed readings, I invited several women to direct the scripts our writers produced instead of relying on a single resident director. We soon realised that very new directors did not have all the skills to support new writers, but I do believe this single change, an increase in the number of women directors in the past decade or so, has impacted and will continue to impact favourably on the number of productions featuring women's writing.

Choosing a cause

My participation in the Guild's work, as well as my link with what was then an important forum for Asian women writers, made me realise that there was a serious dearth of Asian women playwrights. The awareness that theatre is a collaborative craft that needs structural support and perhaps infiltration into the powerhouses of production made me see that women, especially Asian women, would find it even harder to find work in this arena without a clearly defined access route. This absence was what Rita Wolf and I decided to address after we had delivered *Song for a Sanctuary*, Kali Theatre Company's first production in 1991. We worked out an ambitious plan to create stepping stones for new writers from our constituency.

We would offer skills workshops and script surgeries to generate scripts then present them as rehearsed readings before producing venues and companies to make productions happen for new writers. Realising we needed writers at an intermediate level rather than first-timers, we advertised our workshops in suitable sections of the press. Some writers applied, were interviewed and accepted for the very first set of workshops, but my main target for recruitment was the now mature and bustling Asian Women Writers' Collective. Ninety per cent of our first batch came from that group.

I invited inspiring workshop leaders: storyteller/writer Vayu Naidu, playwright Winsome Pinnock, experienced directors such as Debbie Bestwick (Oval House) and Vicki Featherstone (Paines' Plough) and, later on, successful playwrights such as Lin Coghlan to kick off the mornings. For the afternoons I devised writing exercises; participants wrote, shared their work and commented on each other's texts. Over the summer break they wrote and returned to attend script surgeries that led to some impressive first drafts in the very first round.

Presented at Tara Arts Studio with Tara's support, the readings included work by most, but not all attendees. The event was successful, attended by some artistic directors, literary managers, agents and a large number of actors. The writing was fresh and very 'new', but the plays were still incomplete. So although there was general recognition that these fledgling texts needed more time to evolve and mature, everyone agreed the work was promising and rich.

I did my best with dramaturgical input for those writers who sought it, but found it difficult to be robust with cuts or explicit with critical notes because of my overriding empathy for writers and a lurking fear of losing them. The finest writing came from the most fragile writing egos: easily hurt, easily defeated, and reluctant to revisit a text that was not immediately successful. *Daag Daag Ujaala* was possibly one of the most promising scripts submitted to the company in the second round; its scale was ambitious, the subject matter fascinating, but, inexplicably, after the rehearsed reading the writer vanished and never returned to finish it. All sudden unexplained departures felt like failures despite my recognition that for women it is often impossible to prioritise their own creativity.

My lack of dramaturgical experience meant I was better at creative input than at editorial direction. Instinctively, I sensed this was wrong and that we needed a professional dramaturge to cajole more work out of the writers by directing their excavations into their own imagination. Of the two script surgeries I organised over the summer, the writers had loved the one with Sita Brahmachari, but she worked for Talawa and we had no money to tempt her with a post. Rita had settled in New York and, with the additional burden of motherhood, soon found herself unable to work in London for the long stints required to direct. We set about finding a female director for Joyoti Grech's *Natural World*, the first piece completed and submitted to the company from our very first group of writers. Anne Edyvean agreed to direct the show for Kali, while the production role was delegated to Tara Arts for a small fee.

I invited Penny Gold to our second set of readings, 'More Dramatic Encounters' (1997), and persuaded her to join the circle of development enthusiasts I was trying to assemble within the company. Tony Craze, whose support had been invaluable from day one, offered to lead the board; Penny agreed too, because she believed in Kali's mission.

The parting of ways

The publication of my short story 'The Gate-Keeper's Wife' in 1990 found me a top book agent Anne McDermid, at Curtis Brown, without the travails most writers undergo to find one. This gave me tremendous confidence as a writer and I turned my face away from the theatre, but perhaps not resolutely enough. When Helena Bell came to meet me seeking permission to adapt the same short story into a dance-drama, we immediately clicked. Her request soon changed to a full writing commission from her Brighton-based company, Alarmist Theatre. A dancer was to play the role of a cheetah. For me, this was slightly alarming but it proved to be dramatically powerful and intense. The assignment changed my relationship with dramatic writing forever. It was a true collaboration: all the production elements Helena had envisaged instigated the structure and tone of the play without violating the spirit and core of the original short story.

Helena's passion for physical theatre taught me to recognise what worked best in the theatre. Her choices are always braver than mine but I trust her intuitive judgement and her experience. Slowly I learnt how much could be realised imaginatively by an audience within the stringent limitations of space and resources so inescapably present on the fringe. *Letting Go*, my last play commissioned by her, set out to paint an impossible scene of mountain-climbing in the Alps. She heard the story when I pitched it to her, without baulking at it for an instant, and made the scene perfectly credible on the tiny Oval House stage. The director's faith in the script and her ease with theatricality are deeply crucial to the success of actors' renditions of scenes that rely purely on the imagined.

Like Rita, she too was determined enough to pursue a production objective. But where Rita had been a first-time director, who never challenged me and had sought out Sue Parrish to mentor her, Helena had ten years of directing experience, an evolved style and clear preferences. We clashed over one detail (I think it was integrated casting, a principle which she normally upheld but '*not for this play!*'). We argued ourselves into an impasse. I conceded, realising I was being mistrustful, but, having taken the measure of each other's steely resolve, we managed never to clash again over several years of working closely on numerous projects.

Of stories and storytellers

I was working on *An Urnful of Ashes* for radio when I saw Vayu Naidu perform at the Barbican Centre. She sparked off the recognition that a storyteller would make it infinitely easier for me to frame and link my historical drama to the contemporary story of a young girl who elopes to Bombay to become a Bollywood heroine. Vayu played a significant role in the radio drama which later developed into a substantially different stage play.

When I pitched the story to Bill Alexander, the Artistic Director at Birmingham Rep, he loved the idea of a framed story and its grandiose location in a Mogul court. While commissioning the play he emphasised I should 'think big' and allow myself up to fourteen actors, as the play was intended for their main stage. The themes I was exploring had an epic feel to them and radio had already indulged my licence for a cast of thousands. It was easy to take his briefing to the letter.

Two years on, when it came to a decision about the production, budgets had become a huge issue in theatres round the country and he worried about the play's capacity to pull audiences. His letter declaring his decision not to produce it was deeply apologetic: he was not confident the play would achieve 55 per cent of capacity, the minimum his board expected. The play he chose to produce instead had a tiny cast but, equally, I suspect, my play set in Mumbai with a strong thread of Mogul history running through it felt remote and not especially pertinent!

A year or so later, when Kali's Board chose to produce it as *River on Fire* (2000), our limit was six actors and the play had to be considerably rewritten to allow for doubling. This transition was eased through a workshop process led by Helena and dramaturgical advice from colleagues, especially Tony Craze and Penny Gold. Their faith in the play was immense and their guidance through the complicated edit and restructuring remarkably useful. The forced economy helped me condense and clarify some of the themes, but the play's scale and ambition were clipped drastically to fit the smaller-scale production. The role of the Storyteller was almost excised. Instead, Seema, the dead mother (delivered by Shelley King) whose funeral sparks off the family feud, linked the two stories and became the chorus within the piece. The fiction I constructed around Akbar's life was read by some audience members as history. Equally, there was confusion between the fictional Seema (a feminist script-writer) and a real-life Urdu writer Ismat Chughtai whose funeral had sparked off a controversy that we chose to reference in the programme. For the record, Akbar's son's funeral story is totally fictional and Chughtai's story was a 'found' story that aligned with the material almost perfectly.

I returned to my use of the Storyteller with a commission from the Vayu Naidu Company, *Mistaken ... Annie Besant in India* (2007). It was a contractual obligation. While the decision of the company to make the production a 'history play' caused me considerable anxiety about accuracy and curtailed some of the freedoms I would have enjoyed had I resisted that label, it had the advantage of supplying a focus. Besant's long vigorous life, myriad interests and complex relationships were impossible to dramatise. In my original pitch, Gandhi had been a minor figure. The Company expanded the role and status of Gandhi as a character in *Mistaken ...*, admittedly at Annie's cost: her role in the Freedom Movement was minor and limited compared to his. But adding the political–historical context layered the adoption story with a powerful metaphorical significance.

I had created the role of Sidra for Vayu Naidu. My initial plan was to integrate the Storyteller fully into the drama as a character; but my director, Chris Banfield, persuaded me to split the role to preserve the integrity of the storytelling. I respect his exceptional sensitivity and imagination as a director, and I completely understood the logic of placing Vayu at a slight tangent on stage. It helped to maintain the unity of her role without giving her the impossible burden of a mixed bag of acting and storytelling. It also handed me a very simple device for signalling time lapses, changes in mood and tone, and occasionally for presenting complicated facts. It helped to separate the fiction (Sidra and her personal story) from historical facts. Predictably, our audience included descendants of the real characters. This division of the roles did cause one complication, however: it impeded the flow of the unfolding drama and snuck in some repetition.

If the play had not toured India, I might never have discovered its importance as a historical piece. Its stirring reception in Allahabad proved that the Company's dramaturgical influence and input had steered me in exactly the right direction. The story of Annie as a heroic, larger-than-life woman who evolved from the trade-union leader of her youth into a misguided do-gooder in India was the only one that made sense for a company with strong roots in India, Indian history and in a living storytelling tradition, as indeed it did for a writer attuned to politics.

Telling true stories

Of all the experiments on the fringe in which I have participated, one of the most special experiences for me was my work with the survivors of domestic violence in 2000 and 2002. The two projects facilitated by Southall Black Sisters, courtesy of Rahila Gupta, were different in scale and scope but the emotional vibe that held each together was equally powerful and stirring. In both instances survivors worked with stories they wanted to tell.

In the first show, *Meri Kahani*, they were paired with playwrights who wrote their stories. In the second, *Meri Kahani, Meri Duniya*, they wrote dramatic sketches themselves, in Punjabi and Hindi, some in English, prompted by workshops with actors and directors. This time, we had the time and resources to make it possible for them to achieve the tougher goal of writing. Helena directed the first show; the second show was directed by several directors with me providing the overarching concept. Neither group was homogeneous in terms of race, class or language. Most of the women had never been to the theatre in England. We organised a visit to Kali's production of Bettina Gracia's play *Singh Tangos*, which they loved.

Truth to life was a hallmark of the women's writing. That gave it force and validity but their work also sparkled with vigour and a lack of artifice that made it poignant and appealing even when the text seemed simple. There was liveliness here and humour. Some qualities in both the shows made them more entertaining and more engaging, perhaps, than the series of readings based on the work submitted to Kali by their 'normal' stream of more educated and able writers from a higher social class, who often 'seem' better equipped to write plays.

This made me wonder once again about the tension between text and performance and the secret of the perfect harmony between the two that renders the union successful enough to fill the auditorium with the magic of theatre. Had these pieces of writing generated better performances than our ordinary readings? Were we as audience members making concessions for a special category of writers? Were we viewing the sketches as documentary, so perhaps the bitter reality of the writers' lives lent them extra weight in the way fact-based drama lends special poignancy to moments?

For me, the answer to these questions is a resounding 'No!' I suspect what gave them greater power as pieces of writing was their freedom from the false notes that arise from facile literary impulses and ambitions, from faux or second-hand emotions and from an overload of ideas, from all contrivance and self-conscious design, from all imitation and borrowing. Here was text, pure and simple straight from the heart, matched perfectly with performance that observed those principles without fuss, fell into line without angst and strove for clarity and directness, giving the performances immediacy and the charisma of pure personality.

At their best, stylisation and elaborated artifice will always entrance an audience, but clearly there is an alternative route to the audience's imagination: through the power of truth and authenticity. It works very simply: by not trying too hard. What Kali had achieved in those workshops was a safe space for the survivors to play, dream and be themselves. Whether those dreams were pleasant or nightmarish mattered less: both kinds of dreams had a cathartic value for the subjects. Their stories, the happy ones and the saddest, had a certain potency because of their visceral connection with real life and their unstudied spontaneity.

Just as the text never quite captures the full promise of the first glancing vision of the writer, a performance seldom attains all the promise and possibilities of a text. Often, the obstacles are a fear of failure and of being judged. Surely, that elemental power of the imagination we saw in these two groups can work for all of us. All we need do as writers is find the truth of our own imagination and stand by it. Nothing works better than a commitment to the stories that matter to us, the ones *we really* want to tell. All we need are partnerships that achieve the perfect synchronicity between text and performance that might agreeably complement those stories and realise their full potential.

5

Dramatising Refuge(e)s

Rukhsana Ahmad's *Song for a Sanctuary* and Tanika Gupta's *Sanctuary*

Christiane Schlote

'They are in railroad depots. They are in old grain stores and recycled factories. Some are brand new, others are in adjuncts of prisons. One is on a ship anchored in the Dutch Port of Rotterdam. From Ireland to Bulgaria, from Finland to Spain, detention camps for foreigners have mushroomed across the European Union.'[1] In an ideal world, these unhomely places would not necessarily be the first images to come to mind when thinking of the term 'sanctuary', usually defined as 'a place of worship and a state of mind' and 'the most sacred part of a Christian church, the site where the altar is housed',[2] but also as 'the custom of allowing Christian churches to offer protection to criminals and other fugitives in danger of life or limb within their walls ... from the time of Constantine's Edict of Toleration, A.D. 303'.[3] Yet, these are the places which provide at least temporary shelter for refugees, asylum seekers and illegal immigrants across Europe, and it is the ambiguity of sanctuary spaces which will be the main focus of this essay.

In the last chapter, 'Living Diaspora Now', of her book *Contemporary Black and Asian Women Playwrights in Britain* (2003), the first book-length study devoted exclusively to Black and British Asian theatre, Gabriele Griffin includes a short discussion of the figure of the refugee and asylum seeker in Tanika Gupta's *Sanctuary* and Amrit Wilson's *Survivors*. But while, in the following, I will also concentrate on the dramatisation of refugees and 'refugeeness' in British Asian theatre, I will slightly shift the focus and explore and problematise the textual inscriptions of different forms of refuges in Rukhsana Ahmad's *Song for a Sanctuary* (1993) and Gupta's *Sanctuary* (2002).[4] Both plays share an engagement with refugee and migrant discourses, while already carrying the ambiguity of refuges in their titles.[5] I will begin by briefly sketching the terminological and conceptual issues inherent in terms and concepts such as 'refugee' and 'refuge' without dwelling on the history of international refugee law or the emergence of the 'refugee figure' in detail, as, as Liisa Malkki explains: 'There is no "proto-refugee" of which the modern refugee is a direct descendant.'[6] Suffice it to say that, although people have always sought sanctuary throughout history, the refugee 'as a specific social category and legal problem of global dimensions' emerged only during World War II largely as a result of the establishment of refugee camps and administrative procedures as key elements of standardised means of power:

> The basic blueprint of the military camp and many of its characteristic techniques were appropriated by those new spatial and disciplinary practices that were emerging in the 1940s refugee camps in Europe. There is bitter irony in the fact that many of the hundreds of work and concentration camps in Germany were transformed into 'Assembly Centres' for refugees when the war ended.[7]

Moreover, as Giorgio Agamben explains in his well-known essay 'What Is a Camp?': '*The camp is the space that opens up when the state of exception starts to become the rule.* In it, the state of exception, which was essentially a temporal suspension of the state of law, acquires a permanent spatial arrangement ... outside the normal state of law.'[8] Secondly, I shall be proceeding from the notion that concepts of refugees as 'ahistorical, universal humanitarian' subjects[9] can be perpetuated and intensified exactly in and through those moments when it is being represented and discussed. I will consequently address the question of the extent to which the aforementioned plays may, on the one hand, lead to forms of acceptance and the reaffirmation of notions of refugeeness, or, on the other, function as literary modes of questioning these notions. Within this second part, there will be a particular focus on the following two aspects: a) the refugee as social actor and b) illusionary spaces such as 'home' and 'refuge'. Without attempting to provide a closure where there can be none, in the third and last part of this essay I will propose some perspectives in regard to the plays' potential to challenge essentialist representations and discourses of refugeeness. In his study of selected refugee narratives in Norway Stephen Dobson defines 'refugeeness' as a process where 'refugees in exile are the source of hybrid exile cultures, founded existentially, through ontologically valued choices, which give rise to different ways of Being'. Dobson also observes that 'refugeeness', just as importantly, 'entails changing conceptions of self' and 'boundary experiences'.[10]

Escape, exile and migration are part of some of mankind's oldest experiences and are, in fact, considered as 'the "normal" state of affairs' in the field of Migration Studies. An awareness of the historical dimension of refugeeness can thus help to reconceptualise 'images of displacement as an anomaly in the life of an otherwise ... stable ... society'.[11] But while so-called 'forced migration' has strongly contributed to social transformations throughout the ages, the processes that have taken place within the context of globalisation during the past two decades have brought about unprecedented changes and have affected people worldwide in all fields of life.[12] According to estimates by the UN Refugee Agency, at 'the end of 2008, the number of people of concern to UNHCR stood at 34.4 million' (including 10.5 million refugees).[13] On the one hand, the global scale of these movements has made it increasingly difficult to maintain conventional dichotomies such as '"modern and traditional" ... "the South and the North"' and to analyse local affairs without taking into account the global framework.[14] On the other hand, globalisation has forced people to reconstruct and produce new concepts of 'home', 'community' and 'locality', which, in turn, have contributed to a growing significance of cultural processes in analyses of the effects of globalised social transformations.[15] These phenomena are also mirrored in the plays I have selected, and I will argue that *Song for a Sanctuary* and *Sanctuary* are dramatic interventions in current debates on refugees, gendered migration and the negative and positive socio-cultural and psychological effects these transformations can bring about in the daily lives of displaced people. They also provide a stage, as it were, for critically rethinking the challenges and limits of notions of agency in regard to refugees, migrants and other social actors.[16]

My reading of the plays draws on the work of anthropologists such as Liisa Malkki, who has examined constructions of refugees and displacement as 'an anthropological domain of knowledge',[17] and on analytic frameworks of transnational theories, such as Avtar Brah's concept of 'diaspora space'. This Brah defined as a site of 'intersectionality of diaspora, border, and dis/location' which is marked not only by the border crossings 'across the dominant/dominated dichotomy' but by the 'traffic within cultural formations of the subordinated groups ... not *always* mediated through the dominant culture(s)'.[18] My use of the term 'transnationalism' is based on Sallie Westwood and Annie Phizacklea's definition, in which transnationalism commonly denotes the process 'by which immigrants forge and sustain multi-stranded social relations that link together their societies of origin and settlement' and which allows them 'to lead political, economic and social "dual lives" through the creation of "dense" cross-border networks'.[19] The basic legal definition of refugee status, as cited in the 1951 Geneva Convention Relating to the Status of Refugees, reads as follows:

[T]he term "refugee" shall apply to any person who ... owing to well-founded fear of being persecuted for reasons of race, religion, nationality, membership of a particular social group or political opinion, is outside the country of his nationality and is unable or, owing to such fear, is unwilling to avail himself of the protection of that country; or who, not having a nationality and being outside the country of his former habitual residence as a result of such events, is unable or, owing to such fear, is unwilling to return to it.[20]

The fairly new interdisciplinary field of so-called Refugee Studies, marked by the establishment of the Refugee Studies Programme at the University of Oxford in 1982 and the launch of the *Journal of Refugee Studies* in 1988, has contributed significantly to developing a theoretical framework, together with what Aristide Zolberg calls 'the international refugee regime', including UN organisations, NGOs and relief agencies.[21] At the same time, there has also been an increasing essentialisation of the so-called 'refugee experience', which can primarily be identified in view of the following developments, which are also crucial in regard to the literary representation of refugees: a) the construction of one single, essential 'refugee experience', what Malkki describes as '[a]lmost like an essentialised anthropological "tribe"'[22] with its own identity and psychological condition; b) the belief that any kind of displacement automatically results in the loss of a person's identity, tradition or culture; and c) the assumption that 'going home'— apart from the fact that it has ambiguous connotations of nativism—is the overall panacea. As Malkki rightly observes, 'mass displacements occur precisely when one's own, accustomed society has become "strange and frightening" because of war, massacres, political terror, or other forms of violence and uncertainty'.[23] In the following analyses of the two plays I will argue that it is exactly these assumptions which are being subjected to a dramatic critique.

In *Song for a Sanctuary*, the inaugural production of Kali Theatre Company, written by the Pakistani playwright, writer and Kali co-founder Rukhsana Ahmad and first performed on 8 May 1990 by the Kali Theatre Company at the Worcester Arts Workshop in Worcester, any notions of exclusionary identity politics based on cultural or national origins are problematised. As Ahmad explains, the play is based on the real story of a Punjabi woman (Balwant Kaur) who was killed in an Asian shelter in 1985:

> My play *Song for a Sanctuary* was very much about being in London and exposure to a London event. I was at that time involved in the Asian Women Writers Collective kind of to give myself an anchor in my writing. There were amongst them women who were much more political than I was and I think somebody was involved in the refuge movement. My play is not based entirely on the true incident but it got sparked off by the murder of a woman who was living in a refuge by her own husband. And that happened in London, actually very close to where I used to live. ... and I went to meet a few people who were running a refuge, and they told me about a huge quarrel between residents and workers and it was an Asian refuge.

And I think those two things troubled me greatly. ... So it became a play not directly about domestic violence but about differences within the refuge and the play was produced later on by the Kali Theatre Company. I suppose I'm always preoccupied by that subject of divisions between people.[24]

In *Song for a Sanctuary* Ahmad shows that even the common experience of domestic violence does not necessarily lead to the construction of a strategic community of women, but that so-called 'communities', whether based on national, cultural, religious or gender affiliations, need to be seen as constructed and context-specific. Ahmad centres the plot around the relationship between a mother (Rajinder Basi), a middle-class Pakistani, who speaks Punjabi, and her daughter (Savita), and the subjugation of both to Pradeep, Rajinder's violent husband and Savita's abusive father. Yet she also emphasises the conflicts evolving from the different national, cultural and socio-economic positions of the residents and workers in the women's refuge. As Griffin observes, these clashes are presented 'through juxtaposing two sets of characters in the refuge ... functioning as both mirrors and opposites to each other':[25] Rajinder and Sonia, a white British working-class woman who has also sought refuge from her abusive partner Gary, and the refuge workers Kamla, who is from South London but of Indian Caribbean descent, and the older Eileen, who has been working at the refuge for eleven years and who tells Rajinder that 'I came to this place for refuge myself'.[26]

Ahmad portrays Rajinder not only as a victim but also as a woman trapped within her own prejudices and contradictions, which make it impossible for her to feel any kind of solidarity with her fellow refuge residents and Sonia in particular. Interestingly, the play opens with the first encounter of Rajinder and Sonia in the gendered space of the refuge kitchen, where Rajinder is cleaning its shelves: 'Hai, hai, ainna gund! You'd never guess how filthy it is inside, disgraceful'.[27] The portrayal of Rajinder in the very first scene immediately sets her apart linguistically and with regard to her national, ethnic, social and religious background, and thus apparently makes her an outsider even within the group of abused women. It is also important to note that Rajinder immediately takes over the refuge space by trying to improve its 'dirty' image, which, in turn, corresponds to the common and metaphorical image of a refuge, described by Rajinder as follows: 'It's hygiene I'm worried about. Can you imagine all the millions of germs in here?'[28]

Despite her middle-class background ('I've always lived in a nice house'[29]), however, Rajinder still shares the experience of domestic violence with Sonia and Eileen, and, according to Griffin, all three characters can be read as representing the typical patterns of domestic violence: 'cycles of abuse, repeated attempts to break free, and often inadequate support from the authorities'.[30] But just as there is no alliance between Rajinder and Sonia as sufferers of domestic violence, there is also no inherent bond between Rajinder and Kamla, based on their presumed similar cultural heritage. Not only does Kamla not speak Punjabi, but she is also unable to read Rajinder's refugeeness and her cultural beliefs because of her lower-class status and mixed parentage as well as her embodiment as a social worker, who, unlike Eileen, has not experienced domestic violence herself.[31] In the following scene Kamla tries to convince Rajinder to press charges against her husband's abuse of Savita and, importantly, it is Sonia who actually informs Kamla and Eileen that Savita told her that she was abused by her father:

> KAMLA: Social Services get involved. She has to have a medical
>   and then all the parties talk and decide what to do
>   next.
> RAJINDER: I can't agree to that. ... Where I come from we deal
>   with things within the family.
>   . . .
> KAMLA: There's a principle involved here and I do think men
>   like him should be prosecuted.
> RAJINDER: Ah! So that's it! I wondered about your motives.
>   . . .
> KAMLA: So you're not going to co-operate? ... You're still
>   avoiding facing it.
> RAJINDER: I'd like to avoid a scandal. She's got to marry one
>   day. But then you don't know what it is to live in a
>   community. I don't know where women like you come
>   from. Call yourself an Asian, do you?
> KAMLA: I am one.
> RAJINDER: I wouldn't go that far! Black you may be, Asian you
>   certainly are not.
> KAMLA: You can't deny me my identity. I won't let you. You
>   people with your saris and your bloody lingo and all
>   your certainties about the universe, you don't have a
>   monopoly on being Asian. You can't box it and contain
>   it and exclude others. I'll define myself as I bloody well
>   want to.[32]

As this exchange shows, *Song for a Sanctuary* is marked by overlapping discourses, all culturally and structurally sanctioned, through which Ahmad disrupts familiar and often problematic representations of domestic violence. On the one hand, there is the physical violence perpetrated by Pradeep. On the other, there is Rajinder's refusal to enter into a discourse with Kamla or most other women in the refuge, because, as Rajinder puts it: 'I'm not one of your illiterate working class women to be managed by you.'[33] Apart from their different postcolonial and diasporic histories, Rajinder and Kamla are also separated by a generational gap which allows Rajinder to communicate, at least partly, with Eileen, but not with Kamla, whom Griffin sees as belonging to 'a particular moment in the refuge movement',[34] which is also shown in her often rather textbook-like rhetoric. Yet, as in the opening scene, Rajinder holds her ground, albeit it seems for the wrong reasons, and refuses to be reduced to the status of victim, as defined by Kamla and the British authorities.[35]

This perspective ties in with recent trends in Migration Studies, where increasing attention has been paid to the notion of agency in regard to both refugees and policy makers, in contrast to traditional approaches in which migrants and refugees have mainly been pictured as passive victims.[36] In this respect, agency has been defined as 'a certain knowledge-ability, whereby experiences and desires are reflexively interpreted and internalised ... and the capability to command relevant skills ... and engage in particular organising practices'.[37] Philomena Essed et al. argue that a focus on agency allows researchers to address the rhetoric of current refugee and migration discourses as much as to emphasise the fact that identities and social relationships can change during and after violent conflicts and displacements. Studies have shown, for example, that gender identities have been redefined in refugee camps and can even, at times, reinforce women's socio-economic empowerment. Likewise, Dobson states that 'it is a mistake to regard the refugee as merely the product of and constrained by overlapping discourses in law ... on the nation, race, class, gender ... While they are obviously influenced by such discourses, what is interesting is how they are chosen, denied and reworked into hybrid refugee cultures.'[38]

Thus, a reconceptualised notion of displacement and refugeeness would not only focus on the loss of culture and identity but also on its transformative potential. What Essed et al. describe as the 'more sophisticated awareness of their social situation' of refugees, and their potential to 'grow assertive in negotiating social space',[39] can be observed in regard to Rajinder's behaviour in the refuge. It may also be observed in the development of a similar female character called Petra Karagy in Timberlake Wertenbaker's refugee play *Credible Witness* (2001), who, as a refugee from Macedonia, searches for her son in England and is intimidated by neither British immigration officers nor detention centre workers. Moreover, as Malkki explains, the '"making strange" of the asylum country often corresponds to the assumption that the homeland ... is not only the normal but the ideal habitat for any person ... the place where one fits in, lives in peace, and has an unproblematic culture and identity'.[40] Viewing the dominant spaces of refuge and Rajinder's home in *Song for a Sanctuary* along these lines sheds light on Rajinder's seemingly contradictory behaviour. On the one hand, she has had the courage to transgress boundaries by seeking refuge in the first place, yet on the other she refuses publicly to acknowledge the breakdown of her family and to initiate further legal action against her husband.[41]

As such her behaviour also shows her continuing belief in the communal prescriptions of honour and shame, which are being promoted by the more conservative segments of South Asian diasporic communities. At a telling and disturbing point in Scene Six of Act One Rajinder asks her sister Amrit: 'Must you have blood always? Would you rather I died, so you wouldn't have to explain to your friends? ... Would you rather I set myself alight in my back garden?', whereupon Amrit answers: 'Honour is always preferable to disgrace, but the choice of course is yours.'[42] According to Shamita Das Dasgupta, diasporic Indian community leaders have been eager to suppress intra-communal dissent and to create a monolithic notion of 'traditional South Asian culture' symbolised by the figure of the 'pure and chaste South Asian woman': 'South Asian women are given the task of perpetuating anachronistic customs and traditions. ... The practice of making women emblematic of a nation's cultural survival is in the tradition of locating family *izzat* [honour] in its female members.'[43] Inevitably, as Anannya Bhattacharjee observes, 'anything that threatens to dilute this model of Indian womanhood constitutes a betrayal of all that it stands for: nation, religion, God, the Spirit of India'.[44]

On a broader scale, May Joseph also sees these expectations as part of a dilemma concerning notions of cultural and legal citizenship faced by Rajinder (and other South Asian women), who are caught between aspects of 'common law' and 'customary practice', in this case 'between British concepts of individual rights and her culturally specific realm of experience, where notions of duty and honor supersede ... Western concepts of individual rights'.[45] Ahmad uses the spatial metaphors of the claustrophobic and overcrowded refuge and Rajinder's former home, haunted with the memory of Pradeep's physical abuse, to illustrate this dilemma and to deconstruct essentialised notions of refugees and South Asian womanhood. Her problematisation of the concept of 'home' also shows that, particularly in the case of the women in the refuge, it is clearly not 'the place where one fits in, lives in peace, and has an unproblematic culture and identity'.[46]

Ahmad also refuses to give into what Sue Kossew has called 'the appropriation and spectatorship of violence'[47] by foregrounding Rajinder and Savita's life in the refuge, and by providing only snippets of information through their often contradictory narratives. However, in the last scene of the play Ahmad further complicates modes of representation and spatiality by having Pradeep stab his wife in her room at the refuge onstage, an ending which, as Griffin notes, is already foreshadowed in the play's 'elegiac title'.[48] The play is partly based on a true incident, and although Ahmad does not see *Song for a Sanctuary* as 'a documentary or a biographical play',[49] this final scene may be read as a strategy to refuse to fictionalise domestic violence and to prevent easy consumption and accommodation of the dramatic text.[50] In this respect, like Amrit Wilson's play *Survivors* (which is also based on a real event of two Pakistani brothers fleeing to London in the undercarriage of a plane), in terms of its aesthetic and dramaturgical strategies *Song for a Sanctuary* could be seen as part of 'the socialist-realist tradition of theatre-making'.[51]

I would argue, however, that Ahmad, as she did in her first novel, *The Hope Chest* (1996), transcends what Jatinder Verma has called 'the dead hand of realism'[52] and also resorts to what may be termed Márquezian supernaturalisms. Like other Black and South Asian British playwrights, Ahmad makes use, for example, of 'ghostly presences', by demonstrating Pradeep's threatening power as a hovering and silent presence who intermittently appears throughout the play.[53] At the same time, however, Pradeep's demonisation can also be seen as problematic, in that it reproduces stereotypes of South Asians caught in 'barbaric' cultural practices and traditions.[54] Both—ghostly presences and the danger of reproducing stereotypes—also mark Tanika Gupta's play *Sanctuary*.

Gupta's *Sanctuary*, which was produced during the 2002 *Transformation* series of The National Theatre in London,[55] is, like Ahmad's *Song for a Sanctuary*, a disturbing exploration of human behaviour in times of distress. But while Ahmad chose to address issues of violence, gender relations and class differences by dramatising a real-life event, Gupta's *Sanctuary* has mainly been classified as a post-modern morality play. Gupta stages the encounter of a diverse group of characters, some of them refugees and migrants, in the metaphorical setting of a beautiful garden of an English church graveyard. In this seemingly idyllic place, which, like the title of Ahmad's play, already foreshadows the tragic future events, we get to meet Kabir Sheikh, an Indian Muslim gardener marked by the trauma of having seen the killing of his wife in Kashmir, the Afro-Caribbean journalist and war photographer Sebastian Cruz and Michael Ruzindana, a pastor from Rwanda with an equally troubled past.

In a manner similar to Ahmad's use of Pradeep's 'ghost', Gupta also reveals the characters' partly traumatic pasts through the use of 'ghostly presences' as well as a series of flashbacks, as when Kabir relives the moment when his wife was raped and murdered: '*KABIR hides behind a small shrub. He is clutching an imaginary child in his arms. The gunshots and shouting stop. ... KABIR watches with horror. ... Nusrat's voice calls out KABIR'S name, but he remains where he is.*'[56] Commenting on her use of a ghost figure in her play *The Waiting Room* (2000), Gupta explains her intertextual references:

> Drawing on Hindu cosmology and Buddhism and making bits up along the way, I invented a journey. ... One of my big influences was Charles Dickens's *A Christmas Carol* (1843). I loved the character of Scrooge being forced to look at his life, refusing to recognise himself

or his mistakes, fighting all the way but inevitably bowing to the ultimate truth.[57]

Apart from the male protagonists, there is Jenny Catchpole, the woman vicar, who fights against the conversion of the church into, ironically, 'a health club ... a new fitness studio',[58] her perceptive and controversial grandmother Margaret Catchpole, and the fifteen-year-old bicultural pupil Ayesha Williams, who completes this transnational *ersatz*-family. As the drama critic Michael Billington put it: 'Not since *Hamlet* have I seen a graveyard so bustlingly populated.'[59] With her international character set-up Gupta questions the exclusive nature of nation states as much as conventional concepts of political and religious refugees.[60] As in Ahmad's play, in *Sanctuary* the assumption that an individual would return home immediately if conditions changed is not at all taken for granted, and the distinction between forms of voluntary and involuntary displacement is problematised.

Again like Ahmad, Gupta draws on spatial metaphors to examine the fundamental moral and ethical decisions and questions with which her characters are confronted. As already indicated by the character list, *Sanctuary* can, at times, be overbearing in regard to its thematic overload and its often overt symbolism. While the garden functions foremost as a supposedly safe refuge and a place where the characters look for peace and quiet and the occasional friendly chat, it can also be read as a metaphor for England as an island welcoming refugees, yet ultimately rejecting them.[61] In fact, Griffin argues that '*Sanctuary* creates a diasporic space in the graveyard and church grounds which act as the site for multi-cultural encounters ... suggesting that the displacements generated by political conflict create new and fragile micro-communities'.[62] Apart from this political implication, the setting also hints at the religious and mythological dimensions of the metaphorical garden as a primal and pristine Eden where nothing is lacking, and at its association with Paradise.[63] As to be expected, this pastoral image has been completely dismantled by the end of the play.[64] While the church itself is being transformed from a sacred to a secular space, the characters can be seen as exemplary sites of violence on a global scale, whether in the form of the Kashmir conflict, the Rwandan genocide, the Black Atlantic or the British Empire as a whole.[65] Interestingly, the latter is embodied by Margaret, who lived in different places as the wife of a military doctor and who remains staunchly colonialist: 'Whole place is teeming with foreigners and now there's that peculiar Negro hanging around here.'[66] At the same time, however, ironically she also accuses Jenny of a similar backwardness: 'You've wasted your life marrying yourself to a dying institution.'[67]

Kabir and Michael literally see the garden as their 'home' (Kabir: 'This is my home, my resting place. ... [to Michael] You are coming here every day—this is being as much your home as mine.').[68] But the sanctuary of

Gupta's title is as misleading and, moreover, as fatal a space as the sanctuary in another important intertext of the play, which (like the murder of Balwant Kaur) is based on a real event. In the course of the play, it turns out that, according to Sebastian, Michael was heavily involved in the massacres during the civil war and the genocide in Rwanda in 1994: 'This wolf in sheep's clothing ... ordered over five thousand killings. ... His name isn't Michael. It's Charles Bagilishema. ... Herded them into the church ... handed out machetes ... Kibungo ... the Church.'[69]

Reportedly, in April 1994 there was indeed a massacre at a Seventh-day Adventist church in the Rwandan town Mugonero, where about 3,000 Tsutsis had fled to seek refuge in the church and with its Hutu pastor, Elizaphan Ntakirutimana. Yet the refugees were brutally slaughtered in exactly that space that gave the word 'sanctuary' its most important meaning in the first place. Before that, a number of Tutsi Seventh-day Adventist pastors had actually sent a letter to Ntakirutimana informing him of an upcoming attack and asking for his help. The French journalist Philip Gourevitch used a part of this letter for the title of his impressive documentary account, mainly based on interviews, *We Wish to Inform You That Tomorrow We Will Be Killed with Our Families: Stories from Rwanda* (2002). Gupta refers directly to this massacre in Scene Four of Act Two, when Sebastian and Kabir find a letter which Michael had hidden in a cigar box and buried in the graveyard:

> KABIR: Our dear leader, Pastor Charles Bagilishema. How
>   are you! We hope you will be able to come to our
>   assistance. We wish to inform you that we have heard
>   that tomorrow we will be killed with our families. We
>   therefore ask you to speak up for us especially to the
>   mayor.[70]

Eventually, Michael is killed by Kabir in the garden, turning the refuge, as the character of Pradeep does in *Song for a Sanctuary*, into a site of extreme violence in the manner of a Jacobean revenge tragedy:

> KABIR *brings the machete down ... on MICHAEL'S arm.*
> *MICHAEL'S arm is hacked off. Blood gushes out across the floor.*
> *... KABIR picks MICHAEL up by the scruff of the neck and drags*
> *him backwards towards the shed. ... we hear the roar and crackle*
> *of a huge fire. ... KABIR picks up MICHAEL'S charred body and*
> *... smashes the skull with the machete and then collapses weeping.*[71]

While it may seem that Gupta provides a too-neat closure in having the villain killed off in this most brutal manner, it should be noted that she problematises the ethics of judgement throughout the play. Again, at this point, parallels can be drawn between the characters in *Sanctuary* and those in *Song for a Sanctuary*, who are all divided by seemingly unbridgeable gaps regarding their traumatic experiences and cultural backgrounds. Thus, despite their friendship, Kabir reprimands Jenny at the beginning of Act Two, thereby dismantling Margaret's colonialist mindset as much as contemporary neo-colonial attitudes:

> KABIR: You don't know. You and I are living in very different worlds. ... You have never been suffering. How can you be giving comfort to people when you have never been in any bad situation? You are living in a cocoon where everyone is being "nice" and giving charity to all those poor little starving babies in the "third" world.
>
> JENNY: Stop it. ... How dare you?
>
> KABIR: You are collecting money in your church to ease your own little conscience when it is your Church that caused the fuck ups in those countries in the first place![72]

But, as in Ahmad's portrayal of Rajinder's husband, what may be seen as problematic regarding the depiction of Michael is the combination of his refugee status with his apparently monstrous and evil character. Refugees have repeatedly been identified as 'the other within the other' and the ultimate alien.[73] As Jacqueline Mosselson explains in her study of young Bosnian refugees: 'To be in flight presupposes the possibility of having done wrong, of being an outlaw. "Fugitive" implies "from justice"' and so 'refugees are turncoats or traitors of sorts ... definitely not someone you can trust.'[74] Hannah Arendt has called this process 'the pathologising and even criminalising of refugees'.[75] The figure of Michael is represented in a way that not only allows but may actually promote such a negative reading of his refugeeness. The play's suspense is based on the gradual revelation of his horrendous actions. Moreover, even when his garden-friends find out about his past, he refuses to repent: 'We had to be seen to show no mercy. The Tutsi women were part of the problem ... They had to be dealt with, punished, humiliated. ... And in war, gang rape is more effective than any military weapon.'[76]

In a similar vein, the medium through which, *deus ex machina*-like, the so-called truth comes out can also be seen as problematic. Sebastian produces a photo from his war photographer days to prove Michael's responsibility ('I was there—in Rwanda. I took photos of the carnage').[77] On the one hand, the use of photos in migrant and diasporic literatures functions as a popular strategy to provide at least an illusion of continuity and belonging, since images are used to establish a link between the identity of the author or protagonist and a specific place.[78] But this link proves to be fatal in Michael's case. Thus, on the other hand, Gupta also shows how the characters, in their search for the 'truth', neglect one of the most important characteristics of the medium of photography: namely, that photographs are never neutral representations, but cultural constructs themselves that can omit details and be strongly manipulated. This is also mirrored in the structure of the play, which alternates between day-time scenes and night-time scenes, often showing the three male protagonists at dusk or night time and the more innocent character of Ayesha on bright sunny days. Gupta's use of a photographer figure could further be read as an attempt to displace conventional media representations of refugees and what Malkki calls 'clinical humanitarianism' (i.e. U.N. officials reporting from a dusty African landscape, surrounded by innumerous black people): 'the possibility of persons stepping forward from the milling crowds, asking for the microphone, and addressing the glassy eye of the camera: "Now, if I may, Sir/Madam, there are numerous things that you have not considered, many details about our history and political circumstances that might assist you in helping us."'[79]

On the whole, both Ahmad and Gupta problematise the notion of sanctuary spaces and provide, albeit sometimes ambiguously, spaces to challenge conventional ways of representing and contextualising refugee and migrant discourses. In that respect, their plays can be seen as part of a growing number of recent artistic explorations of displacement and migration, including plays such as Kay Adshead's *The Bogus Woman* (2001), Ping Chong's earlier performance piece *Undesirable Elements* (1992), Stephen Frear's film *Dirty Pretty Things* (2002), Wertenbaker's *Credible Witness* (2001) and Michael Winterbottom's documentary film *In This World* (2002).[80] All, in very different ways, dramatise the anguish, the pain and the loss as much as the discovery of new possibilities caused by the experiences of migration, exile and flight. From a geographer's perspective, Doreen Massey once explained that 'the home may be as much a place of conflict as of repose',[81] and in the view of these two plays the same assessment may be applied to so-called sanctuary spaces. Thus, when, at the end of Gupta's *Sanctuary*, Jenny takes her mother and Kabir with her to her new parish, the drab perspective that 'there's no garden, just a car park around the back of the church hall' may perhaps even prove to be a respite from the deceptive nature of their former Eden. As Malkki rightly concludes: 'But if "home" is where one feels most safe and at ease, instead of some essentialised point on the map, then it is far from clear that returning where one fled from is the same thing as "going home"'.[82]

6

Directing Storytelling Performance and Storytelling Theatre

Chris Banfield

Introduction: the nature of this enquiry

In this discussion I have tried to reflect on my work as director for Vayu Naidu[1] and the company named after her, established with Arts Council support in 2000.[2] Vayu completed a PhD at the University of Leeds in the Indic Oral Tradition, and amassed more than a decade's experience as a highly acclaimed and skilled solo storyteller in the UK and abroad. By 1999, she was seeking to develop her craft alongside a musician in a new telling of the great Hindu epic *Rāmāyana* for the Leicester Haymarket Theatre, a story that had been in her repertoire from earliest days. Following my collaboration with Vayu on *Nine Nights: Stories from the Rāmāyana*, I have been fortunate enough to have the opportunity of working with Vayu Naidu Company on a number of further occasions. My discussion here will also be based on two further productions: a devised piece entitled *South* (2003) and *Mistaken ... Annie Besant in India* (2007), a commissioned play written for the company by Rukhsana Ahmad. So the three selected productions I shall discuss span approximately an eight-year period.[3]

The nature of my enquiry here concerns the role that a theatre director might play in storytelling performance and storytelling theatre. Why have a director for a storytelling performance, given the frequently and perhaps expectedly improvised nature of telling a story? What working methods might be adopted? What constraints and what advantages might present themselves? Another set of questions concerns the relationship between storytelling and other performance modes such as music, dance and drama. What is the nature of the interplay between these modes in combination?

I would like to consider these questions firstly in relation to Vayu Naidu as solo storyteller working with a musician. I will make *Nine Nights* the main point of reference here. Secondly, I will discuss the case of a third performance element, dance, being introduced, and use *South* as an example of such work. Finally I will consider some of the consequences of positioning storytelling at the centre of a dramatic text realised in a theatrical production, basing this discussion on *Mistaken*. To make clear the conceptual distinction, these last two I regard as 'storytelling theatre', the first 'storytelling performance'. The discussion that follows is based on the premise, therefore, that 'storytelling' is essentially an individual-led process that need not be based in a theatre, while 'storytelling theatre' involves a broader collaboration of individuals working with a director to produce work intended for performance in a theatre. I should perhaps add that the questions I will consider here have emerged out of the work rather than prefigured it. None of these projects began life explicitly as a research exercise. The approach was nevertheless goal-oriented in each case: to produce an engaging and effective performance or theatrical event for an audience.

Although my own journey into this field has followed a practical route, the relationship between storytelling and theatre (and by implication between storytellers and actors) has been examined from an academic perspective in recent years, perhaps most prominently by Michael Wilson. In offering a conclusion to a chapter on this very topic, the author seeks even-handedness as he attempts to summarise contemporary practice, and goes on to speculate about the likely 'convergence' of the actor and the storyteller in the future:

> There are many ways to skin a cat and storytelling remains, as it has done for centuries, a primary concern of the theatre. It is interesting that recent trends in storytelling in Britain suggest that as the storytelling movement begins to gather in confidence and storytellers begin to push the boundaries of their art, then we are likely to see more storytellers creating longer shows based on a single narrative, such as have been seen recently. In shows like this the differences between storytelling and theatre become more blurred and less distinct, as storytellers readily adopt the techniques and means of performance and production of the actor, whilst theatre companies continue to produce shows that adopt the techniques and repertoire of the storyteller. If these trends continue, then theatre and storytelling will once again converge, become indistinguishable from each other, and the terms 'actor' and 'storyteller' will be interchangeable.[4]

Without at this point stopping to unpack several generalities here ('gather in confidence', 'push the boundaries', 'shows like this', 'once again'), I feel that Wilson's writing glosses over and, indeed, in many ways signally fails to take account of some fundamental differences between storytelling and theatre, and between narrative and dramatic voices in the theatre. Such differences emerged for me, at least, quite forcefully over the course of working as director on the three productions I will now turn to.

Nine Nights: Stories from the Rāmāyana

I first worked professionally with Vayu Naidu at Leicester Haymarket Theatre in 1999. As Artistic Associate with responsibility for Natak, the Asian theatre initiative then in place at the theatre, she had invited me to help develop her remarkable telling of the great Hindu epic *Rāmāyana* to incorporate a musical dimension. This involved trying to integrate Vayu's captivating solo storytelling with music created by Colin Seddon, a versatile musician whose expertise across an extensive range of percussive and melodic instruments provided a rich palette on which to draw. This painterly metaphor proved a useful one to me at the time, insofar as the colour and texture of an expansive narrative could find aural complement, underscoring or counterpoint through, say, the rhythmic drone of Colin's *berimbou*, the rapid flutter of his hands over the *djemba*, or the lyrical scattering of harmonics struck high up the fret board on the *bouzouki*, to name but three instances. Colin also made use of an electronic recording loop at various points in the story. Skilled use of a foot-pedal control allowed sounds to be built through layers of live recording and playback during specific sequences, such as the demon Shoorpanakka's disguised appearance to Lakshmana and Rama while in their forest exile, her brother Ravana's aerial abduction of Sita over the seas to Lanka, and the final battle between Rama's monkey army and the ten-headed emperor Rakshasa's legions as the forces of good and evil clash in one last epic struggle.

Yet as soon as a musical dimension is introduced to a story told orally questions immediately arise regarding its role and function. What should be the relationship between story and music, and between the storyteller and the musician? In the bardic tradition, the storyteller *was* the instrumentalist; a self-accompanist on the lyre or other instrument. In the case of the separation of story and music production, decisions regarding what, whether and when to play have to be negotiated between storyteller and musician. As a creative team, it was our collective view that both needed to be acknowledged as equal partners in the endeavour.

Storytelling and music can, and often do, work most successfully within an improvisational context. Some of the reasons for this are entirely practical; rehearsal time and space is expensive so there are financial advantages to keeping things loose enough to evolve freely in performance following limited rehearsal. Over the years Vayu has worked as part of a performance duo alongside many outstanding single instrument musicians such as Sarvar Sabri (*tabla*), Soumik Datta (*sarod*) and Ansuman Biswas, who plays the haunting, contemporary instrument of Swiss origin called the *hang*, in the telling and retelling of the Rāmāyana, as well as in other narratives. Such duets have only very rarely been scored in any way, still less directed by an outside eye, emerging instead through concentrated listening on the part of both artists as part of the creative process 'in the moment'. Preparation for the performance will usually begin by Vayu telling a particular story to the musician, who listens without playing in order to literally and metaphorically tune in to the narrative. They will then begin to rehearse the story together, stopping and repeating episodes and phrases during the process of adding musical shape to the piece, each adapting to the other's contribution. It will never be the same twice, either in rehearsal or performance.

I have come to appreciate there may be good reason to avoid outside interference (in the shape of a director) during such extempore story creation, precisely in order not to fix that which is by nature spontaneous. There can be few theatre directors who do not tend in some measure towards fixity in their work (Joan Littlewood being a notable exception).[5] While it can be helpful in general terms to have a listener's feedback to a developing oral narrative, for many storytellers storytelling is too fluid a form to benefit much from directorial interventions of the 'set it this way' variety. So under what circumstances might a director be helpful in storytelling and music performance? I think this question is answerable in relation to the degree to which the storyteller and musician can self-manage their joint performance.

Whether the instrument is percussive, tuned percussive or melodic, I would argue that storytelling alongside a solo instrumentalist offers a more manageable improvisational framework for the performers than one in which the performance context includes a multi-instrumentalist or indeed several musicians. Once a single instrument is established in the audience's mind as a feature of the storytelling performance, its sound will vary about an established mean. The instrument may be foregrounded in narrative gaps, or recede to occupy an almost subliminal space 'behind' the story. It can contradict or complement the rhythms of the narrative; it can build or resolve moments of tension. Atmosphere can be created through tonal variation, but within certain fixed parameters determined by the characteristics of that particular instrument.

When more than one instrumental choice is available, the question of the selection of the appropriate sound for a story event or episode needs to be decided. While this may be just as straightforwardly dealt with as the negotiation between storyteller and single instrumentalist during their improvised performance, it seems to me that it can be advantageous with a multi-instrumentalist to have an outside eye and ear helping in this selection and shaping process. This is partly, I think, because what might be termed the 'improvisational error stakes' are higher in performance.

Errors, lapses or miscues between storyteller and musician seem to me more easily accommodated and less audible (and visible) to an audience where a solo instrument is in play than where choices are having to be made between instruments by the musician(s). For example, striking a gong rather than plucking a melody on a thumb-piano offers a tonal contrast qualitatively more marked in effect than, say, playing an evening *raga* on a *sarod* where a morning *raga* had been intended. Picking up the wrong instrument at a point in the story, or picking up the right instrument only to find that the storyteller has departed from the anticipated narrative, can appear awkward and clumsy. It's not that improvisation is impossible between a storyteller and multi-instrumentalist, but it is a riskier business and less easily managed by the artists involved where things are happening on the hoof. The concomitant is that more preparation and rehearsal time is required; both parties need to know exactly, rather than approximately, what's coming up next in the story performance. If a director can make any contribution to the process, it is in helping to facilitate the smooth orchestration of the variety of sounds available from the palette to work with rather than against the story. In this context, the director is not quite a composer, but able to suggest and advise on instrument selection and kind of effect desired; not quite a conductor, but able to attend to the ebb and flow of narrative and sound in an attempt to create an aesthetically effective whole.

The paradox, as I have already mentioned, is that the more the storytelling performance is rehearsed, fixed and planned in advance the more likely it is to lose spontaneity and become 'produced', its artifice and construction emphasised through theatricalising this freest of forms. Storytellers are practised adaptors to their performance circumstances; perhaps more than any other performers they are used to taking into account and responding to the nature and needs of their audience. Theatre directors generally want to work to create specific and replicable effects for audiences, rehearsing things to get them a certain way. This tension between the quest for directorial organisation and the scope for performer spontaneity seems to me ever present with regard to directing storytelling performance.

It was illuminating running a workshop with Vayu and Ansuman Biswas during their run of performances at the Edinburgh InvAsian Festival in 2008, in which Ansuman outlined to participants what he saw as the key elements of the contribution to storytelling made by music and a musician. These were hierarchically ordered, he felt: from the purely 'illustrative' (an arrow is fired and hits its target, perhaps), to 'turning a page' and 'marking chapter endings', to the creation (highest order) of a particular 'fragrance' during different episodes of the story. Ansuman thought that a further vital contribution of the musician was as 'active listener'—one might even say 'model' listener—for the watching audience.

It is intriguing to find a musician invoking metaphors of page turning and chapter ending so clearly rooted in a literary tradition; perhaps these aspects might be contested by other musicians, not to say storytellers.

Nevertheless, Ansuman's distinction between the illustrated moment and episodic 'fragrancing' is a key one for music in its relationship to storytelling performance, and a vital one when thinking from a directorial point of view. This notion of 'fragrance' can clearly be seen to chime harmoniously with the Indian performance concept of *rasa* or 'flavour'.[6]

Unsurprisingly, perhaps, Ansuman was least enamoured of the illustrative musical event, though acknowledged it was sometimes required. The 'When I nod my head, you hit it' approach leads to a reactive response from the musician that is not a particularly satisfying one to execute. From a directing point of view, I think there is (or should be) an ever-present consciousness of the danger of *redundancy* in the simultaneous operation of narrative and music. Do we really need to hear the clock chime midnight if it is described in words by the storyteller? Do we really need to hear the storyteller describing the clock chiming midnight if we are listening to the sound on the musician's triangle? Redundancy is the director's bane when working with storytelling performance; an ever-present behemoth raising its head at every turn.

If the sphere of performance elements is enlarged still further beyond the nucleus of the simple oral story, then things can become yet more problematic. Storytelling with music *and* dance or movement, for example? Do we really need to *see* the hands of the clock reach midnight, as well as hear the midnight chimes, as well as learn from the story that the clock is chiming midnight? What about stage design? Lighting? Sound effects? Should these be included in storytelling performance? Or do such theatrical trimmings and trappings rapidly defuse the power and simplicity of pure narrative which operates so effectively on the audience's imagination?

The real problem with redundancy seems to me the attendant risk of banality through overstatement. This is, of course, significantly audience-dependent. Young children delight in the same thing being presented again and again in identical or very similar ways. No problem for them in getting the midnight description from the storyteller and hearing the musical chimes striking the hour. At a recent Vayu Naidu Company workshop on ensemble storytelling, held at Drama Centre in London, I was also reminded by a visually impaired participant that what I might regard as redundancy could equally be seen as *accessibility*; a fair point when, say, physical movement requires audio description to be meaningful to a person with a visual impairment. Some audience members may require the keeping open of more than one channel of communication. But is 'storytelling theatre', the theatricalised extension of storytelling performance, actually a paradox; neither fish nor fowl or, to continue the culinary metaphor, a pudding in danger of constantly being over-egged?

South (2003)

This question was to come to the fore during our preparation of Vayu Naidu Company's production of *South* in 2003. Vayu wished to develop a devised piece that would combine storytelling not just with music but with *bharatanatyam*[7] as well as contemporary dance, to tour to small/ mid-scale theatre venues. This wasn't just to be storytelling performance, but storytelling *theatre*. The devised production which emerged, involving jazz musician Orphy Robinson, *bharatanatyam* dancers Shane Shambhu and Magdalen Gorringe, and Lia Prentaki, a contemporary dancer, became in essence a practical exploration of some of the questions I have touched on above. The artistic process was often driven by questions of redundancy that had their origins in the work on *Nine Nights* at Leicester four years earlier. But the real difference now was the inclusion of movement. In *Nine Nights*, Colin Seddon's physical transitions to and from myriad instruments as the story progressed meant that, for the watching audience, the musician almost seemed to make as much of a kinaesthetic impact as an aural one. But this was an accidental choreography as far as I was concerned as director; now all movement had to be considered and, always, justified.

In *Nine Nights*, the gestural dimension of the storyteller's movement was something that, if I choreographed at all, I preferred to direct with the lightest of touches, attempting to move along the trajectory of whatever, often beautiful, physical shapes Vayu was creating in relation to the words she was speaking. I learned that breaking this link between improvised word and natural gesture and demanding of the storyteller that she reproduce a fixed pattern of movements had a deleterious effect on both the fluency of her speech and spontaneity of her physicality. If a physical image arose spontaneously that I thought really effective then I might request that she keep it in mind for the next time she tried that section of the story. But I found that, if overdone, this could induce a physical self-consciousness on her part and a rather stilted gestural representation as a consequence. A case in point was the moment in the final battle between Rama and Ravana where the hero takes aim, pulls back his bow and releases a deadly arrow that slays the demon king. I felt Vayu's gesture for this needed expanding and enlarging to allow it to be synchronised with the musician's striking of a brass bowl that I wanted turned into a ringing sound to mark the arrow's flight. Yet while she tried hard to match the shapes I (perhaps speculatively) demonstrated, the choreographic fixity seemed antithetical to the spontaneity of expression that is storytelling's hallmark. I was trying to turn a storyteller into a dancer–actor.

The dominance of the visual sense for audiences is a major constraint (but also opportunity) when directing storytelling theatre. The eye will always be drawn to movement first: light travels faster than sound, perhaps? Vayu has long been adept at conjuring graceful gestural images during her storytelling performance, momentarily complementing description in her stories using her hands, sometimes with *mudrā*-like[8] precision. With the presence of the dancers, it was possible to amplify these physical impulses. Now the distinction between the illustrative and 'flavouring' that had come to the fore with music and story offered more complex permutations as we set about trying to integrate movement into the work. I felt this was potentially liberating from Vayu's perspective also, since while floor patterns relating to the storyteller's movement within the ensemble would need to be attended to, the gestural component of her work could be left up to her without too much directorial interference; my principal choreographic attention would turn to the dancers.

The south Indian Classical dance tradition of *bharatanatyam* mapped neatly onto this terrain because its practice is separated into the forms of *abhinaya*, or storytelling dance, and *nritta*, or movement that is abstract in nature and which might be regarded as the technical language of expression necessary to acquire in order to practice *abhinaya*.

Not having *bharatanatyam* dance training, I was very much reliant on the dancers to generate choreographic ideas which could then be integrated with musical and narrative elements. Vayu was clear about the culturally diverse stories that she wished to include in the piece: the Greek myth of Arion and the dolphin, an Indian folk story about the goddess Kanya Kumari, and a dark Norse myth about Odin. But what was the best way to get the artists to work together in their development? How could redundancy be avoided in the performance? How could these three disparate stories be tied together in a unified way through a production that did more than illustrate three oral narratives with music and dance?

Unsurprisingly, improvisation offered a key way into developing a working relationship between the artists. I purposefully relegated narrative in the early stages to focus on ways in which music and dance could originate rather than follow a story. Orphy would improvise on the marimba and the dancers would follow. The dancers would initiate a movement and Orphy would follow, on a drum, perhaps. Finally Vayu would be asked to weave a narrative through these unfolding choreographic and musical ideas. We'd stop and reflect on the interplay and begin again, perhaps focusing on a shorter section of what had been just produced in order to refine some of the ideas that had emerged.

Our working methodology developed over two periods of rehearsal separated by several months and involving one personnel change; the Dutch *bharatanatyam* dancer Kalpana Raghuraman had participated in research and development of the Arion story prior to Shane Shambhu's arrival. Shane's male energy brought new possibilities for the second of the stories we developed, Kanya Kumari. Here, I wanted to combine the explicit storytelling style of *bharatanatyam*'s *abhinaya* in a self-consciously illustrative manner with Vayu's narrative in order to produce a much

2. Vayu Naidu Company's *South* (2003), Arion's Story. (Photograph: Moira Blackwell)

lighter, comic effect. It would be more accurate to say that *abhinaya* was really the starting point; the dancers proved themselves adept at handling mimetic material in a contemporary style which integrated elements of *bharatanatyam*. This process was really about signalling awareness of the problem of redundancy in storytelling theatre to an audience, and exploiting its comic potential.

It is worth pointing out how imbalanced directorial attention was on the artists during the process of making *South*. It might take hours to find a workable, non-reductive physical counterpart in movement for what the storyteller could achieve in seconds with a couple of well-turned phrases. The focus on the visual was so much greater than on the other elements. For example, the making of the brief shipwreck sequence in the Arion story took days to get right, involving the dancers creating the shape of the bow of the ship travelling through the waves, with Vayu holding its mast and sail and moving with the dancers as they rose and fell. This sequence led into a storm conjured by Orphy's percussion during which the ship-image was thrown asunder, which was in turn followed by the reconstruction of the image as the ship was seen to continue its journey.

3. Vayu Naidu Company's *South* (2003), A quest for direction.
(Photograph: Moira Blackwell)

For Vayu and Orphy there were often interminable delays while the
movement was attended to, which was frustrating for them both. This was a
major factor behind our collective decision that it would be best for Vayu to
work only with music for the Norse myth. In doing so, I followed a similar
pattern with Orphy that I had taken with Colin and Vayu on *Rāmāyana*.

What ultimately bound these stories together and became the central
theme underpinning this devised piece was the celebration of creativity,
imagination and infinite possibility in story-making. We chose to develop
a framing narrative about an every-Man figure 'seeking direction'. This
narrative intersected with the three main stories we had developed at their
start and end points, with each main story linked to one of the cardinal
points toward which Man would travel in his quest for direction: West
(Arion), East (Kanya Kumari), North (Norse myth). The established, implicit
performance relationship between storyteller and the other performers
(essentially 'I say, and, watch ... they follow') was subverted in a final
sequence, in which the storyteller began a quick-fire starting and stopping
of enacted stories. This began with 'There was a man ...', ultimately
prompting a rebellion of the dancers, and challenging their subservient role
as illustrator-demonstrators of the storyteller's imagination. The literality of
the representations through this sequence provided a much-needed lightness,
and I was grateful to Assistant Director Adam Meggido for his assistance
in creating some of these images. Resolution to the frustration was achieved

4. Vayu Naidu Company's
South (2003), Vayu Naidu.
(Photograph: Moira
Blackwell)

following Man's phone call to God—a telephone box image created by the dancers—in which the direction he is given is the only one remaining: *South*. A *bharatanatyam* duet concluded the piece.

The thematic centrality of the compass and seeking direction offered an entirely appropriate metaphor for the project. If we (I?) struggled to find bearings and some kind of resolution at the end, the voice of God from the telephone box provided just the kind of *deus ex machina* conclusion to which the ancient Greek poets had resorted; we were in distinguished company. Though I have not yet mentioned them, the circular shape of the compass and angular dividers became integrated into Marsha Roddy's magically atmospheric and geometrically suggestive set-designs for *South*: a set we were able to light in many different ways to change the mood. Vayu's costume also, a long burnished orange cloak with three-quarter length sleeves, decorated with sweeping rainbow arcs of darkening silvery-blue bands, evoked the great magus John Dee's conjuring within a magic circle; not Faustian, diabolical forces this time, but spirits of the storyteller's imagination.

I came to appreciate that key determinants of individual responses to *South* were not merely the rigidity or flexibility of views held about the nature of storytelling as an art form, and the degree to which these expectations were met or dashed in the mind of the spectator during the performance. Responses also related to more fundamental issues about what happens to storytelling, from an audience's perspective, when it is theatricalised. For example, why, I was asked, did I choose to dim the house lights when the storyteller entered and go on to make extensive use of lighting cues throughout the performance? What is interesting about this question is the particular discourse of storytelling in which it is embedded. In this discourse the storyteller must be seen to make eye contact with, and speak directly to, a visible audience of listeners, occupying the same physical space without artificial separation through lighting. Stage lighting and, by implication, other theatrical devices that impede this immediacy of contact between audience and storyteller and hold the spectator at arm's length fail to serve the art of the storyteller. The 'presence' of the storyteller, a characteristic fundamentally connected to the spontaneity that the storytelling art form promotes, is compromised by theatricalisation. Fixed lighting cues are merely symptomatic of the more general problem of storytelling being constrained by having to follow the theatre's rehearsed route; indeed, from this viewpoint 'storytelling theatre' might be regarded as an oxymoron. The final implication of this position is that storytelling is best left a solo art.

Purist objections to the kind of hybridity *South*'s storytelling theatre represented could be equally matched from the music and dance camps. Music as *mere* accompaniment to storytelling? Movement as *mere* servant of narrative? Surely outdated notions? And what of the theatre, particularly dramatic theatre? What relationship has storytelling to drama and how might the storyteller be accommodated within the drama?

Rather than attempt to provide comprehensive answers to such questions (which, it will be noted, have been subject to theatrical experiment and exploration for the last 2,500 years), I shall instead turn to one final example of a Vayu Naidu Company production to discuss some of the issues that arose in my own practice.

Mistaken ... Annie Besant in India by Rukhsana Ahmad (2007)

Being invited to take on the dramaturgical development and direction of a play set in colonial India, whose protagonist is an occidental octogenarian female theosophist with a political zeal for the Indian Independence movement and a fantasist's conviction that her adopted Brahmin son is the new messiah, was clearly a rather different undertaking from my previous projects directing storytelling performance and theatre for Vayu Naidu Company. In many ways it was a project I approached feeling more confident than I had previously, since it seemed far more consistent with my own drama- and theatre-directing background and experience. As a director, what could be more straightforward than having a playscript in my hands and setting about realising it?

The idea for a stage play about the later life of Annie Besant had come from writer Rukhsana Ahmad, who was subsequently commissioned by Vayu Naidu Company in 2005 to develop an idea she had been exploring as a screenplay. I had anticipated what I envisaged would be the major challenges. Rukhsana's play would demand as much meticulous research in its direction as the playwright had given to its writing. The political scope and cultural significance of remote historical events would need to be communicated with absolute clarity and conviction to a contemporary British audience (it was not envisaged at that stage that the play would be presented to an exclusively Indian audience, as came to pass).[9] There would be the 'King Lear problem' of casting an actor in the very sizeable title role who was capable of playing an elderly character, yet would possess sufficient energy to survive a sustained theatre tour (we were fortunate to find one in Rosalind Stockwell). Critically, the interplay of narrative and drama would need to be carefully and sensitively worked out given the centrality of the role that had been envisaged for a storyteller in this commission.

The production of the play, in fact a co-production with Guildford's Yvonne Arnaud Theatre,[10] went on an Arts Council England-supported national tour in early summer 2007. Thanks to the Vayu Naidu Company's securing of private sponsorship to pay for flights, the production also travelled to India in late November, where it was performed in Allahabad, Delhi and Chennai.

If Annie is known at all these days in England, it is usually for her early trade-union activism in relation to the matchgirls strike in London of 1888. Annie Besant married young and was, scandalously for the times, separated from her Anglican clergyman husband following her refusal to take the sacrament during one of his communion services. He succeeded in obtaining custody of the couple's two children following a court ruling in his favour. Annie Besant was a proto-feminist and sometime Fabian Society member who, as well as seeking to improve young women's factory working conditions, also campaigned for women's access to birth control information. However, her meeting with Madame Helena Blavatsky became pivotal in propelling her diametrically away from the atheistic, socialist circles she moved in towards the spiritualism of the Theosophical Society (TS) which Blavatsky had co-founded; this was a move that would ultimately take her to India and a leading role in the advancement of this pseudo-religion's esoteric doctrine.

While Besant's early life was certainly of interest to Ahmad, it would be accurate to say that the playwright was more intrigued by the metaphor of misguided adoption that she saw emerging from Annie's later period in India. Besant had taken under her wing two young boys, the sons of a clerk at the TS headquarters in Madras, later formally adopting them and sending them to England for their education. The relationships between Annie, the two boys, Krishnamurthi and Nityananda, and their father, who was to take legal action to regain custody, had colonial resonances, and paradoxes, too; Annie had, after all, by this time become President of the Indian National Congress party and a staunch advocate of Indian Home Rule.

Reviewing an early scene-breakdown of the play from January 2006 offers insights into the shaping of the drama that would eventually unfold. Already by that stage the five main characters had been determined: Annie herself; Narayaniah, a clerk at the Theosophical Society headquarters in Madras whose sons Annie adopted; Krishnamurthi, the elder son and later philosopher; M.K. Gandhi, whose political influence in the Congress Party waxed as Annie's waned following her equivocation over the Amritsar massacre of 1919; and Sidra, Rukhsana's entirely fictional creation of Annie's housekeeper (all the others being real historical figures), who would hold a key narrative function. Rukhsana envisaged that this would be the part that Vayu would play.

Storytelling and acting are significantly different kinds of performance. I sometimes give an exercise to students in which they explore moving between what I call dramatic and narrative voices. In pairs they must tell a story for an audience, alternating who leads from time to time: A must use the first person ('I'm standing alone at the edge of the sea ...'), B the third person ('She begins to walk along the shoreline ...'). A is always in her own space and never makes eye-contact with the watching audience, investing her account with an affective quality that must come from complete emotional involvement with what she is doing. B *always* makes eye-contact with his audience, but remains utterly unemotional and physically detached in his commentary, which A must follow silently in action during B's passages of narration. It is, of course, an archetypically Brechtian exercise. What is interesting is that it proves surprisingly challenging for some excellent actors to divest themselves of affective expression during the narrative 'She' account; and many excellent storytellers struggle to engage completely at an emotional level with the embodied dramatic 'I'. An extension of the exercise is to have a single performer attempt to switch between these two styles of performance, which is an even trickier task.

So what's the point? Some actors are adept at making the switch between dramatic and narrative voices. But the best storytellers (and I am not alone in counting Vayu Naidu among them) must, of necessity in my view, keep one foot on the narrative voice side of the dramatic–narrative divide. This is firstly because of the requirement for rapid shifts between the use of descriptive language and reported speech when they 'play' a character; and secondly because any committed leap into the dramatic voice risks loss of contact with an audience—a fundamental of storytelling, as has previously been observed. From a storytelling perspective and handled in the right way, calm, underplayed detachment in the use of the narrative voice (definable characteristics of Vayu Naidu's approach to storytelling, I

5. Vayu Naidu Company's
*Mistaken ... Annie
Besant in India* by
Rukhsana Ahmad (2007):
Vayu Naidu, Storyteller
(Act 1, Sc. 1).
(Photograph: Robert Day)

think) can invite a listener to listen more actively. Conversely, a storyteller's extended over-emotionalism in the use of the dramatic voice makes the listener more passive, a recipient of the performance yet ironically pushed away from it, rather than a joint constructor of narrative in imagination.

I have taken this slight digression in order to explain and justify my decision to ask Rukhsana to rewrite what she had conceived as the single role of Sidra, Annie's housekeeper, and split the role into two parts: a younger Sidra represented in the dramatic voice (who would be played by Ruby Sahota), and an older Sidra, the storyteller (played by Vayu Naidu) looking back on events in the narrative voice.

The link between the two was made apparent in the writing. Signalling the *physical* connection for the audience between the performers playing the younger (dramatic present) and older (narrative past) Sidras was relatively straightforward. It was obviously helped through casting and the plausibility of Ruby being a younger Vayu, as it were. I chose to reveal their connection on a number of occasions in the play, mainly through physical means, such as at the beginning, when Sidra was about to present herself for employment in Besant's household; during the aftermath of the Amritsar massacre, when Sidra visits Jallianwalla Bagh with Annie; and at the end of the play, as she knelt at the dying Annie's bedside. In the first two instances connections were achieved choreographically. The two performers walked towards one another maintaining eye-contact before circling and moving away into their own space and time. At Jallianwalla Bagh, Vayu physically echoed the slow and respectful salaam paid to the murdered by the young Sidra when leaving the compound. In the death-bed scene, Rukhsana wrote dialogue between the two that bound both Sidras together in a past-present moment of remembrance of Annie's death and cremation, a simultaneity of affect and detached observation which seemed to me to complete the circle. Here, again, it was possible to justify eye-contact between the performers. Other than at these points, during the essentially linear chronology of the play's action, I chose for there to be no direct acknowledgement by the dramatic Sidra of her storytelling counterpart. This made the storyteller somewhat isolated from the other performers. 'It's so lonely never making eye-contact with the others!' Vayu would half-jokingly complain.

Having an additional performer to take the cast size to six rather than five was one consequence following the decision to split Sidra's role. But there were much more important consequences. I may have done Vayu a disservice in not envisaging that she would be comfortable in moving with total commitment and assurance between narrative and dramatic voices, as would have been demanded in casting her into a single Sidra role. Yet, in spite of being largely freed from performing dialogue, she nevertheless still had extended passages of monologue in the play to learn by rote. I think she would agree she did not always find this an easy process, unfamiliar as she was with word-for-word learning in previous storytelling practice. While in theory both the playwright and I as director were happy to allow Vayu free rein to adjust her lines through paraphrasing, to convey essence rather than exactitude, in practice the requirement for accuracy in a play about real historical figures and events did not always permit a looser treatment of the script. For example, the full impact of the storyteller's account of the Amritsar massacre (Act 2, Sc. 2) depended on Rukhsana's detail in the writing. Who was the commanding British officer responsible for the atrocity, O'Dwyer or Dyer? How many exits were there at Jallianwalla Bagh? How many bullets were fired into the crowd? How many were wounded? How many were dead? It is also difficult to accommodate paraphrase where other stage events are contingent upon a storyteller's cue. Here, the final echoing ring of Sarvar Sabri's pre-recorded, slow and steady *tabla* rhythm needed to coincide with the final word of the storyteller's Amritsar narrative, 'dead'. Even a few words gained or lost in the telling might compromise this effect. The interaction of storyteller with the other performers, as well as with the technical crew, raised such issues. When should an entrance be made? When should a lighting cue go?

Another issue as far as this production was concerned was that my decision to divide the Sidra role exacerbated the dangers of redundancy I have already discussed in relation to *Nine Nights* and *South*. A single performer cannot both 'do' and 'comment on the doing' simultaneously; two performers can end up inadvertently achieving this with ease, especially where my own dramaturgical eye failed to identify places in the writing that were not always quite taut enough to make separation between them 'clean'.

One of the advantages from a playwriting point of view of having a storyteller is the expositional convenience it provides. But it can often be hard to get the balance right between commentary that sets up events we then see played out in the drama, and commentary that describes events we then see re-presented in dramatic rather than narrative form. Sometimes narrative commentary after an event presented dramatically proves equally redundant. Seeing the production afresh some half-dozen performances into the tour, many instances jumped out at me. Rukhsana agreed to make a number of changes to the text to address issues that I should have had the discernment to pick up earlier. Amongst others, out went storyteller lines such as 'Krishna ji went into a dark, stunned silence where no one could reach him ...' just prior to Narinder Samra *acting* Krishnamurti's reaction to his brother Nitya's unexpected death, in a scene with Sidra and his adoptive mother, Annie (Act 2, Sc. 6). Dispatched was 'She waited, and waited ... slowly losing her strength and hope. I did my best to cheer her up and sustain her ...' immediately prior to *watching* a bedridden Annie being coaxed by Sidra to drink some soup (Act 2, Sc. 10). Gone was 'Such a chasm of hatred and mistrust had opened up between father and son', following a fiery scene of failed reconciliation and traded accusations between Krishna and Narayaniah, *played* with bitter anguish by Ranjit Krishnamma (Act 2, Sc. 3).

Character in drama needs to emerge from action not narrative, an Aristotelian tenet that still holds good. The choral voice in drama, if we consider the history of its use in theatre practice, has for the most part been character-*less*. Of course, individual characteristics may be contrived for Sophocles' Counsellors of Thebes telling us about the city's plague, or Shakespeare's Chorus painting the scene on the eve of the Battle of Agincourt, but none is intended more than schematically in the writing. Successful (I mean dramatically effective) character-narrator figures such as Arthur Miller's Alfieri (*A View from the Bridge*) tend to be very few and far between in drama. And even in this example the lawyer's sketchy personal circumstances are merely relevant in so far as they intersect with his client Eddie Carbone's case. Where playwrights have adopted storytellers in their drama it has been in order to exploit the art form of storytelling's strengths. The narrative voice in drama can set a scene, turn the clock's hand, establish

6. Vayu Naidu Company's *Mistaken ... Annie Besant in India* by Rukhsana Ahmad (2007): Ranjit Krishnamma as Narayaniah (Act 2, Sc. 3). (Photograph: Robert Day)

7. *Mistaken ... Annie Besant in India*: Narinder Samra as Krishna and Ruby Sahota as Sidra (Act 2, Sc. 6). (Photograph: Robert Day)

mood, introduce characters and help orient us towards what is at stake with extraordinary economy. But these narratives are written with an implicit understanding that an audience's dominant, empathic engagement in the drama will be withheld until after the arrival of the protagonists, when the dramatic voices will take over. Playwrights understand that audiences are, in truth, much less interested in storytellers than in the stories they have to tell. This is why, it seems to me, playwrights do not much care to have us focus on the psychological characteristics of their storytellers, if they use them. Yet it was precisely the psychological development of Sidra that was of significance to Rukhsana Ahmad's *Mistaken*. In particular, Sidra's journey was bound up with her concealed Muslim identity, withheld from her mistress for fear of Annie's negative judgement of her. With the benefit of hindsight, I think I failed to take into account that splitting the character resulted in an imperfectly conjoined psychological link for the audience; an unbridgeable gap between the storytelling Sidra and the Sidra realised through dramatic action.

Conclusion

In this discussion I have attempted to focus on some of the challenges of directing storytelling performance and storytelling theatre based on my own experience of working on three productions for Vayu Naidu and her Company. But what was the Company's collective vision for this work? Was it defined from the outset, or did it emerge through the process of production?

In my experience, 'vision' forms in the crucible of practical creation rather than being decided upon in advance. For my own part, I don't believe that I was professionally engaged by Vayu Naidu Company as a director to implement a particular vision held by the company about what 'storytelling theatre' meant. Rather, I was fortunate enough to be given the opportunity to help explore and negotiate a multiplicity of meanings through a range of practice, practice that I have attempted to explain and perhaps justify here. Often it is only through the act of writing that one discovers what it is one has to say; how much more persuasively does this truism hold for the collaborative act of theatre-making.

Sadly, for me, it is a journey that looks unlikely to continue. Vayu Naidu Company's 54 per cent cut in Arts Council England revenue funding announced at the end of 2007 (193 other funding cut recipients were originally listed, a minority of whom appealed successfully against their cuts) has had a profound impact on its ability to initiate theatre projects such as *South* or *Mistaken ... Annie Besant in India*. This cut followed, and was ostensibly linked to, ACE's negative appraisal of (the aptly named?) *Mistaken*, the first truly mid-scale theatre production that the resources of the company had allowed. Although it was not made clear by the funders in advance, it appears the Company had one chance to 'get it right' at mid-scale level; we were adjudged to have failed. I think the ACE reviewers were correct in raising the issue of dramaturgical difficulties in the play's development; this was cited as one of the main reasons behind their decision.[11] Yet they were unable to articulate those difficulties with much insight, or engage in dialogue that might have allowed them to understand that those involved with the production had long been actively reflecting on and, indeed, learning from the choices made in the company's developing work. Given this uncertain future, I have been particularly grateful to record something of the VNC's experimentation over recent years in this essay.

I am aware that much of what I have written, and certainly what now follows in conclusion, is readable as either attempted post-hoc rationalisation of my own directorial failure to make 'storytelling theatre' work, or as articulation of the justifiably problematic nature of this particular form. I leave it to the reader to decide which.

I began my discussion by taking issue with Michael Wilson's view that the actor and the storyteller are destined for convergence. In examining the production work I have directed, I have tried to explain what I think are the fundamental differences between dramatic and narrative voices in the theatre and provide evidence as to why, in my view, such a hypothesised convergence misunderstands the unique essences of acting and storytelling.

Attempts to direct storytelling are likely to constrain the imaginative and physical freedoms of the storyteller, if direction means seeking to exercise control over the storyteller's spontaneity in creating words from instant to instant or reproducing patterns of gestural movement through choreographic fixity. But would an actor 'play the part of' a storyteller any better? It must be acknowledged that actors, who are arguably more pliant in responding to directorial intervention, do not always make good storytellers; a learned-by-rote story is qualitatively inferior to one that is crafted in the making and made up with *an* audience rather than *the* audience in mind.

I have further suggested that a key concern for a director of storytelling performance and storytelling theatre is addressing the difficult issue of redundancy. I have attempted to consider the interplay of storytelling with other performance modes such as music, dance and drama in this context. I'm aware that much of what I am trying to reveal is buried in practice linked to specific productions of which the reader is likely to have no knowledge. However, I hope that general conclusions may still legitimately be drawn from particular observations.

The examples I have selected here illustrate the storyteller's progressive loss of autonomy as storytelling is firstly theatricalised and secondly accommodated within a dramatic framework, albeit a 'purpose-built' one. In theatre, playwrights and directors strive for replicable, cue-dependent effects. Yet it is apparent that the fundamental constraint of having to learn a script verbatim compromises the storyteller's ability to extemporise; this is something that many rightly regard as storytelling's *sine qua non*.

With continued support, Vayu Naidu Company may yet survive its straitened financial circumstances, capitalising instead on storytelling's formal advantages and making a virtue of being leaner, lighter and more mobile as it focuses its work beyond the conventional theatre, to reach new audiences for storytelling and once again thrive in yet-to-be-explored physical and imaginative spaces.

7

Engaging the Audience

A Comparative Analysis of Developmental Strategies in Birmingham and Leicester since the 1990s

Claire Cochrane

This essay focuses on the audience development record of two theatres, Birmingham Rep and Leicester Haymarket, both established in cities which have seen the growth of Asian communities significantly influence the whole landscape of cultural relations. Given the multiplicity of geographical, linguistic and religious heritage represented in the British Asian population, however, identifying exactly what constitutes an 'Asian' audience is particularly challenging. The policy-makers in regional producing theatres may be tasked with providing artistic product which is relevant and accessible to all members of their local communities irrespective of heritage and skin colour. For them, the challenge is not just about meeting or, more often, *creating* distinctive cultural expectations for potential audiences; it is also about a much more precarious artistic, economic and social balancing act.

During the period from the 1990s to the present both Birmingham Rep[1] and Leicester Haymarket[2] suffered major financial crises and both had to be put into 'recovery' by the Arts Council. The Rep, with an accumulated deficit for the financial year 2001/2 of £926,562 did not close, although the artistic director Bill Alexander had resigned a year earlier.[3] Leicester Haymarket, with debts in 2003 of nearly £500,000, did go dark for over a year. The board of trustees, including the chairman, was replaced. One of the nastier aspects of the recriminations generated by the closure was the belief expressed in some quarters that the problems had been exacerbated by the attempt to engage more fully with Asian audiences.[4] As the only regional producing theatre in the UK to have a joint dual-heritage artistic directorate in the white Irish Paul Kerryson and the British Indian Kully Thiarai, the Haymarket's strongly stated policy of total integration was very exposed.

As every chief executive of a building-based theatre is only too aware, programming to enable more challenging or more 'minority-interest' product is frighteningly difficult. If lavishly resourced, feel-good shows such as musicals and pantomimes, deliberately planned to make sufficient profit to cushion any loss on riskier work, fail to meet financial targets, the whole edifice can come crashing down. In their 2003 annual report the directors of the Leicester Theatre Trust acknowledged a generalised shortfall in box office receipts, but singled out the loss of vital revenue caused by the cancellation of four performances of the musical *Hot Stuff* as a result of industrial action.[5] Also in a familiar pattern associated with the priorities of local politics, Leicestershire County Council had withdrawn a £100,000 annual grant.

The Ramayana and *Bali—The Sacrifice*: aspiration and disaster

Both Birmingham and Leicester theatres had invested a great deal of money in two high-profile, main-stage productions targeted at Asian interest. In 2000 in Birmingham, Indhu Rubasingham directed a new version of *The Ramayana*, which featured a large multi-cultural cast, a script by Peter Oswald, designs by Ultz, original tabla music played onstage by Kuljit Bhamra, and choreography by the Indian dancer Piali Ray. The production was promoted as a kind of festive pantomime for Diwali that borrowed from the traditions of Kathakali. Efforts to market the show included an initiative which brought together a twenty-strong panel of advisors drawn from Birmingham communities to stimulate strategies for South Asian audience development. These strategies included commissioning Asian artists to lead community performances on Ramayana themes. In the event, however, this witty, multi-cultural, hybrid approach to an ancient Sanskrit text sold 6,537 tickets, and in an auditorium which seats 824 that represents 33 per cent of capacity.[6] There were those, outside the magic circle of enthusiastic, mainly mono-chrome white theatre critics, who had doubts about what might have been perceived as yet another example of colonial cultural appropriation. Pervaiz Khan, not a Hindu but a Birmingham-based Muslim theatre- and film-maker, went on record in protesting about 'hotchpotch originality' which lost 'sight of the underlying truths of the epic, which are to do with revelation and epiphany'.[7]

The parallels with Leicester Haymarket's 2002 production of *Bali—The Sacrifice*, directed by Nona Shepperd, are striking. Based on a tenth-century Jain epic about the triumph of faith and non-violence and written by Girish Karnad, the main stage production starred the well-known Indian actor and Bollywood star Naseeruddin Shah. Just like the Rep, the Haymarket made extensive efforts to involve the community. The theatre's foyers were filled with artworks made by children and local artists. In the Studio there was *Safe Passage*, an interactive multi-media performance based on the Iranian childhood of the trainee director Nazli Tabatabai. 'Blueprints for Peace', a series of symposia, including a performance by the Haymarket's Asian young people's Peacock group which took place within different religious community settings and debated issues round non-violence. Faith Sculptures were created by four local artists working in four denominational primary schools and the results each celebrated a different faith. Other marketing strategies included a charity gala event and a £1 matinee.[8]

The detailed evaluation commissioned by Arts Council England showed that, in terms of box office revenue, *Bali* was a disaster.[9] Attendance for the run reached just 26 per cent of capacity in an auditorium which seated about 750. The attempt to capture audience data, although unscientific and incomplete, did appear to show that the production had attracted some new audience, including a small but solid core of Asian attenders. The critical response, however, was ambivalent. Lyn Gardner, writing in the *Guardian* (10 June 2002), was clearly very supportive, praising Nona Shepperd's 'canny, beautifully acted production'. But she also admitted that the play was neither great nor even particularly good. For her the experience was greater than its parts. Rhoda Koenig's review in the *Independent* (12 June 2002) was brutally dismissive of an adaptation of a tenth-century epic written originally to win converts: 'I think the Jains would have about as much success if they threw a brick through someone's window with their message wrapped around it.' Her final paragraph delivered a knock-out blow which would have dashed any hopes that *Bali* as an audience development exercise in itself had been a success:

> There are three deep mysteries about *Bali—The Sacrifice*. Why did anyone foist this thing on the public? Why did Naseeruddin Shah decide to squander his considerable distinction on the role of the mahout? And how did the Indians of Leicester, who I assumed would roll up in droves to see him, know to stay at home?[10]

Theatre and city

One very basic question which could be asked is why it is worth persevering to make what Hardial Rai has dubbed a 'white space' relevant to the cultural lives of Asian communities.[11] I asked this question of Dipak Joshi, who as BBC Roots Co-ordinator in Leicester was seconded to work with the theatre to develop stronger links with the Asian community just a few weeks before the opening night of *Bali*. His reply was also very basic. *All* the citizens of Leicester had the right to enjoy the resources which they, through their taxes, actually pay for. As a public service provider, the subsidised theatre in the heart of the city has to share its goods.[12]

There is a very important issue here which relates to the whole landscape of British theatre and the way it is dominated by London. Although

Birmingham and Leicester, along with Manchester, are competing in current statistics to become the first non-white majority city by 2011, the population of London, with its many diverse communities, is much bigger. All the major British Asian theatre companies—Tara, Tamasha, Kali, Yellow Earth are the most obvious examples—are based in the capital and there is no company of comparable status in the regional cities. London is where ambitious artists gravitate in search of professional fame and fortune, and where they appear to encounter the most receptive audiences. When Birmingham Rep's *Ramayana* transferred to the Olivier auditorium of the National Theatre 13,000 seats were sold, which is 95 per cent of capacity.[13]

The consequence of this imbalance is that there is rarely more than one building-based subsidised *producing* theatre in each major city. One theatre is *the* dominant provider of original work. It alone has the resources and the infrastructure to create dynamic and exciting scenography, for example, and sustain at least relatively large acting companies for each show directed in line with a coherent artistic policy. Birmingham Rep's *Ramayana* and the Leicester Haymarket's *Bali* may have been conceptually and artistically problematic, but they were produced on home ground, for local audiences, and that in itself offers valuable opportunities for a wide range of skills and interests. These buildings also play host to the touring London companies and it is usually through the theatres' receiving programmes that local communities can access their work. For the past decade, again because of centralised funding strategies, the more hidden activity of education and community outreach departments has grown considerably. Just my brief description of the *Bali* project gives some idea of the scale of the activity involved and the possibilities it offered. It was also part of 'Arts Connect', a major collaborative audience development initiative in partnership with two other Leicester venues, Phoenix Arts and De Montfort Hall, which also programme artistic product of potential interest to Asian audiences.[14]

What none of this does, however, is support the assumption that these generously resourced opportunities for creative, intercultural engagement are going to be automatically accepted by the 'target' communities. The history of separateness and alienation is too long and deep. The civic authorities have had to fight hard to obliterate the damage done by a past record of troubled race relations. In Leicester in 1972 after the city council placed an advertisement in the *Ugandan Argus* warning potential migrants to stay away, the city was branded as the most 'unwelcoming' in the country. Thereafter, as a major centre for National Front activity, it was considered the most racist city in Britain.[15] In the report produced after the Handsworth rebellion in 1985, Birmingham was accused of being the 'racist capital of Britain'.[16] As the disturbances between the African- and Asian-heritage communities in the Lozells district of Birmingham in 2005 prove, there are still many problems. Social and economic complexity and inequality are features of all urban environments. For the idealised and subsidised regional theatres, there has always been a disjunction between the artistic ethos *within* the enclosed walls of the theatre and the very complicated and far from idealised reality outside.[17]

The architectural aesthetic which literally shaped the Birmingham Rep and Leicester Haymarket as purpose-built producing theatres derived from a conscious desire to create physical synergies with the surrounding environment, albeit from different ideological perspectives. The 'new' Rep building and the Haymarket opened within two years of each other in 1971 and 1973 respectively. But the origins of the Rep's design as a bold, modernist architectural statement lay much further back in a 1950s' dream of a spacious civic centre. In the event, the theatre suffered an alienating and windy isolation for the best part of twenty years, before the opening of the £180 million International Convention Centre and the creation of Centenary Square integrated it into a visually and socially much more dynamic space. Even so, from the outset, the broad sweep of glass windows which created the Rep's façade and the way the entrance doors and foyers formed a continuous unit with the street were designed to welcome and attract.[18]

The concept behind the original Haymarket theatre emerged from a very different theory of social interaction. Constructed out of reinforced concrete with red-brick cladding, the building was deliberately designed to be almost indistinguishable from the surrounding commercial properties. It was part of the shopping centre, signalling clearly that theatre-going was ordinary, accessible—no more daunting than, but by implication as necessary as, a weekly trip to buy provisions.[19] In contrast to the Rep's heroically proportioned end-on stage and fan-shaped undifferentiated 900-seater auditorium,[20] the two-tiered Haymarket auditorium and proscenium opening, which incorporated a fixed thrust stage was deemed both more intimate and artistically manageable. But as the steady stream of researchers commissioned by the Arts Council in the 1980s and 1990s to produce reports on Black and Asian audience engagement in the arts discovered, no amount of physical space manipulation in the interests of social engineering was going to make white arts venues feel culturally relevant or accessible.[21]

The demographic context

It would be an obviously crude and inaccurate generalisation to suggest that the Asian-heritage citizens of Leicester and Birmingham do not shop in or walk through these city centre complexes. Yet the history of migrant community development has of necessity created an inwardness and gathering together in psychological and, indeed, physical separateness which has made it difficult for the white spaces of theatre to reach out and draw in. Indeed, the economic context within which every local neighbourhood functions, irrespective of race and ethnicity, is crucial to an understanding of levels of receptivity to externally provided arts activity. Social class is a very important factor; so too is generational difference. Within every first- or second-generation migrant community that looks back and clings exclusively to old ways, traditions and values, there are young, third- or even fourth-generation 'new' British who look sideways to their wider peer groups and forward to a wholly different future.

The circumstances which gave rise to the main waves of migration into Birmingham and Leicester have resulted in admittedly very broad but also quite distinctive differences between the Asian communities. In particular, the contrasting socio-economic profiles derive from two key original points of embarkation. In Birmingham, of the 20 per cent of the total population which is classified as Asian (just under a million), by far the largest group (52 per cent) came from Pakistan and the majority of these are Muslim. Most came from the Mirpur district of Azad Kashmir and were displaced because of the building of the Mangla Dam. Thus first-generation migrants arriving in the 1960s came to a heavily industrialised city from very rural areas, and from livelihoods based on smallholdings, animal husbandry and textiles. Initially men came on their own, before achieving enough security to bring wives and families. Fifty years on it is this sector which is growing very rapidly. The Birmingham-based sociologist Tahir Abbas attributes this to a high birth rate and to 'specific within-group marriage practices'. In addition, as he identified in 2005, there are higher than average unemployment rates and poor health statistics.[22] This is not a group for which theatre-going is likely to be a major priority. In 1998, a three-month Mirpuri community project in the Washwood Heath and Saltley areas of the city initiated by Birmingham Youth Services culminated in a packed-out, one-off afternoon performance at Birmingham Rep. The project with primary and secondary schools, called *Kahanian*, was designed to capture oral story-telling techniques through theatre. At the time it was reported that some of the audience members had never been to the city centre, let alone to the centrally located host theatre.[23]

Demographically Leicester is significantly different. As a whole the city is smaller. In 2001 the total population was estimated to be 279,921, of whom 36 per cent were from an ethnic minority background and 30 per cent were classified as Asian. The overwhelming majority of these were of Indian descent, comprising 25.7 per cent of Leicester's total population. A survey conducted in 1983 showed that half of those had migrated from East Africa.[24] Given the political circumstances which provoked the exodus of East African Asians from countries such as Kenya and Uganda, patterns of migration were also different. Whole families came, rather than just male individuals whose wives joined them later. To be sure, many East African families had lost everything. But in terms of what they brought in intellectual and entrepreneurial expertise—much of it developed within urban environments—and which incorporated the influence of their own layered colonial and migratory past, they tended to straddle cultures more readily and were more open to educational opportunity. This was certainly the view of Vayu Naidu, who came to England from India in 1988 and was appointed to lead the Asian Theatre Initiative at Leicester Haymarket as a producer in 1999. Asked about her experience of working in both Birmingham and Leicester, she stressed that there was a stronger leisure culture amongst the Asian community in Leicester, and more disposable income to support it. In addition, for her, the more powerful status of women within Hindu or Sikh families was a major determining factor in levels of interest and engagement.[25]

While this is just one individual opinion, evidence based on interviews collected for consultancy-led research reports in the 1990s and 2000s tended to confirm the perception that it was the women within families who took the lead on arts attendance.[26] In her comparison of the two cities Vayu Naidu related it to the gender orientation of the dominant dance traditions. The 'very male, high testosterone' enjoyment of the Punjabi agricultural folk-dance bhangra within Birmingham's Muslim communities, where women had less involvement, was contrasted with the Garba, the traditional dance from Gujarat integral to the Mother Goddess festival of Navratri.[27] Historically, of course, dance has been an important factor in infiltrating Asian art forms into Western theatres. Arguably, however, the principal beneficiaries were interested white audiences, rather than Asians, who prefer family leisure pursuits within the family environment. Indeed, the cost of going to the theatre in large family groups was also perceived to be a problem.[28]

Relatively speaking, Leicester communities were more homogeneous. The intervening migration, therefore, had led to cultural traditions associated with the 'home' country which were very firmly established. The celebration of Diwali and Navratri, for example, is known to be the largest and most spectacular outside India. As Joanna Herbert's research into Leicester communities has shown, migrant associations 'proliferated in the 1970s and 1980s', with the formation of clubs for sports such as hockey and cricket, female exercise classes, dance and music clubs and, of course, the social networks based in Hindu places of worship often converted from disused Christian churches. By 1992 there were in total some 186 ethnic minority associations in Leicester. The city's first purpose-built mosque was completed in 1987. As Herbert points out, '[c]onsequently the meaning of the landscape was dramatically altered so that it acted not as an index to the dominant white culture, but an alternative cultural and religious identity'.[29] Ironically, Belgrave Road, where the most visible concentration of Asian shops, restaurants and other businesses is to be found, and the location of the famous 'Golden Mile', led directly into Belgrave Gate in the city centre and thence to the Haymarket Theatre itself.

Expectations that local Asian audiences would gratefully respond to any culturally specific theatre product on offer from an unfamiliar source, no matter how well-intentioned, proved unrealistic. As Suman Buchar recalled, even companies such as Tara and Tamasha had great difficulty in attracting local Asian audiences to their toured-in productions at the Haymarket. She complained of a 'narrowness' of outlook.[30] Vayu Naidu contradicted this perception on the grounds that a community strong in its own sense of cultural identity would object to 'imposed ... top-down approaches from metropolitan-based companies'.[31] For her '[s]ensitivity to the systolic and diastolic function of trust between a theatre and its audience/s is the greatest learning curve. I learned that art as creating theatre must strike at truth, in its making and through a sociological awareness.'[32]

Sociological awareness and selling the product: Tamasha and Birmingham

Creating trust through sociological awareness and from a position of perceived cultural legitimacy has arguably been the most important factor in successful audience engagement. Suman Buchar's account of her work marketing Tamasha productions to Asian communities in Birmingham is evidence of the need for determined interaction. For the best part of eight years, Birmingham Rep became a second home for Tamasha, beginning in 1994 with a Studio production of *A Shaft of Sunlight* by Abhijat Joshi and ending in 2001 with a main stage revival of their popular *Fourteen Songs, Two Weddings and a Funeral*, which had received its first performance in the Door (as the Studio is now known) at Christmas 1998. Two of Tamasha's productions, *A Yearning*, a version of Lorca's *Yerma* (co-produced with Leicester Haymarket), and *Balti Kings*, were set in Birmingham.[33]

What Buchar describes is a labour-intensive process undertaken at a time in Tamasha's history when there was no proper marketing budget; telephone calls had to be made by landline, and email and even fax were rarely used.[34] Lists of community groups provided by the town hall or local race relations office were the main source of information, and appointments had to be made before visits to promote a production could be attempted. One successful contact was a route to more. If temples had community centres attached, user groups were accessible and in general there was greater openness and flexibility. The subject matter of plays would be described, photographs of the actors would be shown and flyers distributed. Out of this personal effort an audience base was built. This strategy contributed to the success of *East Is East*, which premièred in the Studio in 1996, and to a gathering momentum of interest, so that tickets for the première of *Balti Kings* in 1999 sold out quickly.[35]

Growing the audience in Leicester

Leicester Haymarket's status as one of the venues specifically selected and funded by Arts Council England for the Asian arm of their Black Regional Initiative in Theatre (BRIT), launched in 1994, meant that strategies to attract the Asian community had to be integrated into the company's overall mission. Under the auspices of BRIT, Vayu Naidu and, before her, the actor, writer and director Sita Ramamurthy were appointed as successive Artistic Associates working with Paul Kerryson, who became sole Artistic Director of the Haymarket in 1994. Kerryson, himself something of an outsider as a non-university-educated, self-confessed 'strange boy from Ireland',[36] built up the theatre's specialist reputation as a producer of high-quality music theatre and invested in such audience-pulling strategies as the casting of the comedian Eddie Izzard as Marlowe's Edward II in 1995. As early as 1992, when he and Julia Bardsley were appointed as co-artistic directors, local playwrights Jez Simons and Jyoti Patel were commissioned to write *Safar*, a trilingual fusion Hindi, Gujarati and English play based on fantastical animal stories and the Lord Shiva, which was staged in the Studio in 1993 and toured into the community. The relationship with Simons and Patel continued that year with *Kali Mata*, another commissioned play about superstition, rebellion and fear of the unknown in British Asian society.

The Simons–Patel writing partnership enabled the theatre to make one of the first moves into the production of original home-language drama and raised the possibility that the acknowledgment of Leicester's linguistic diversity might break through community barriers and bridge intergenerational cultural divisions. Both Patel and Simons—the latter a former highly influential drama teacher at the local Soar Valley College (whose protégées included Parminder Nagra)[37]—also brought links to the community youth theatre Hathi Productions. In the Studio in 1996 their Gujarati–English musical *Nimai: The Spirit of Vrindavan* was again an east–west fusion of dance and drama. By this time Sita Ramamurthy was also directing her own work in the Studio and other Indian-themed and authored drama was programmed. The Studio was beginning to host companies such as Tamasha (*A Yearning* was a co-production with Birmingham Rep), Kali Theatre and the East Asian company Yellow Earth. In September 1996 David K.S. Tse, the founder of Yellow Earth, was brought in to direct *The Pandavas in Leicester*, billed as devised by the Asian community with ages ranging from nine to forty. By the 1997–8 season there were Asian faces in the brochure, 'Bollywood Nights' hosting evenings of local talent, and the emergence of the Haymarket's own Asian Peacock Youth Theatre.[38]

While this microcosm of Asian-heritage practice in a 140-seater Studio theatre was helpful in growing confidence for the artists and the community participants, the wider impact was very modest. In addition, the programmer/producer had to navigate a much more acute awareness of generational difference in cultural allegiance. Even where first-generation migrants from East Africa might never have been to India, there was and remains a longing to connect to the imagined homeland. As Vayu Naidu found when she arrived at the Haymarket in 1999, 'they continued to converse with anecdotal references to the epics *Ramayana* and *Mahabharata*. They had lived in Leicester for 35 odd years with the Theatre just down the road they felt a kind of emotional apartheid as the programming did not reflect their interests.'[39] At the same time, a very buoyant programme of new Asian comedy had been developed to appeal to the younger, media-savvy generation, with more irreverent jokes and Singh-songs (sic) calculated to 'make you wet your chuddies'.

Walking the tightrope of conflicting sensitivities meant refusing to programme some of the more overtly retaliatory racist elements in the Punjabi comedy circuit. It also meant facing down the outrage whipped up in the Gujarati community at the prospect of *Krishna's Lila: Playboy of the Asian World*, a bold Indo-Irish pairing with J.M. Synge's *Playboy of the Western World* designed to mark the first Haymarket-produced Asian play on the main stage. Naidu herself has written a detailed account of her artistic rationale for Krishna and Radha and the subsequent negotiations, supported by Kathleen Hamilton, the theatre's Executive Director, with the communities and their City councillor spokesman. With hindsight, the threatening reminder that 'bricks have been thrown at buildings' looks like a prophecy for the *Behzti* riot in Birmingham five years later. At a time, however, before the heightened post-9/11 nerves, and with compromises which, crucially, did not extend to permitting the agitators into the rehearsal room, the retitled *Krishna's Lila: A Play of the Asian World* went ahead, bolstered by Naidu's acute sensitivity to the nuances of Hindu classical texts and spiritual priorities.[40] The personal relationship built up with senior members of the local Elderly Activity group had already paid dividends. There was a positive response to *Nine Nights*, which reflected the *Navaratri* festival by weaving together stories from the *Ramayana* using folk and classical performance styles.[41]

While promoting short consciously intracultural and intergenerational Asian seasons of classical and contemporary theatre, music and dance under the umbrella title of *Natak* gave them a distinctively coherent brand name, the overall strategy still appeared peripheral to the theatre's main artistic policy. The writer and director Timeri N. Murari, whom Naidu commissioned to direct his own stage adaptation of his film *The Square Circle*, later wrote an account from a 'homeland' perspective of a somewhat bumpy experience. Arriving from India in September 1999, a month before rehearsals were to begin, to encounter a dark tiny studio theatre and no agreed budget, he 'panicked at the thought of compressing my play and India into such a claustrophobic and eccentric space'. Naidu wrote that she thought the play 'would work well for integrating audiences with its unique theme of cross-dressing in an Indian ethos enabling its characters to understand the psyche of vulnerability and liberation across genders'. Murari was blunter about the way his scenes of gang rape and transvestism were written to shatter romantic Bollywood-generated illusions about India. 'This is the India where women are casually molested and most men are male chauvinists.'[42]

In the event Parminder Nagra proved perfect casting as Sita, the illiterate village girl kidnapped for prostitution on her wedding eve and then raped after her escape. Indian film actor Rahul Bose as the itinerant, transvestite actor Lakshmi/Lakshman, who befriends her and gives her protective and empowering male clothing, was praised by Lizz Brain in the *Leicester Mercury* for 'a wry, beautifully arch performance'. As an artist with an international reputation, Murari noted the sparse if 'important' first night audience and lamented the damp squib of a press night, when metropolitan critics were conspicuous by their absence. By the end of the run there were, largely through word-of-mouth publicity, full houses, but again Murari commented that 'eighty-five per cent of my audience was English [sic]. The Leicester Asians weren't about to embrace theatre.'

In 'Staging a Play in England', written for the newspaper *The Hindu* (which part-sponsored the production), he described the drunken white youth out on Friday nights in Leicester city centre 'competing to be drunk and bedded first ... jeans, shirts hanging out, and ugly shoes'. His production of *The Square Circle* was firmly set in contemporary India with sound and light effects of revving motor bikes and car headlights. But in the aftermath of what, with British Asian actors, had finally been an artistically satisfying experience, he commented that 'a play about Friday night drunks would be more socially relevant'.[43]

New Asian playwrights and community critique

Murari was quite definite in his views on first-generation migrants, namely that 'expat Indians are very conservative'.[44] In the light of this, the need of young British Asian artists to address socially relevant issues in their own communities raises other and demonstrably more urgent questions about audience engagement. Birmingham Rep's capacity to commit to the development of new playwriting, largely through well-established funding mechanisms and producing partnerships, has encouraged new British Asian dramatists to explore and indeed interrogate aspects of their lived experience of multicultural contemporary society. Perhaps most characteristic of the new British Asian plays which have been presented in The Door is that their dramaturgical roots are in what is usually described as 'gritty' social realism, albeit usually laced with a surreal black humour—the *East Is East* model of playwriting. There are small-scale domestic settings—the households of small shop-keepers and other first-generation migrants who have struggled to gain an economic foothold in British society. Themes include unrealistic dreams and aspirations, and intergenerational conflict or confusion.

Following the formal launch of The Door as a new writing dedicated space, in 2000 the Rep produced its first Asian-heritage play. *My Dad's Corner Shop* was a relatively gentle depiction of different generational priorities, which travelled round Birmingham and the wider Midlands as the Sir Barry Jackson Community Tour. Wolverhampton-born Ray Grewal, who wrote *My Dad's Corner Shop*, was a beneficiary of the Rep's Writers Attachment Scheme and won the 2001 Meyer-Whitworth Award for the play. In performance the easily transportable set evoked the shelves and clutter of tins and boxes of a recognisable corner shop where two young brothers, Rajesh and Kumar, are left to look after the business while their father is in India attending their dying grandmother. At a time when Door audiences in general were beginning to stabilise after a very wobbly start, Grewal's play sold over a thousand seats before touring to schools and community venues.

With the Tamasha relationship nearing an end, and with it the automatic support of their local loyalists,[45] audiences for a community representation of the ubiquitous Asian-run shop would have been as heterogeneous and unpredictable as the communities themselves. Even so, the cultural dichotomy explored in this modestly surreal story of two boys with very different life aspirations would have been familiar to many of the young people who saw it. When it comes to the development of tougher-minded, more consciously polemical plays, the social and intellectual disjunction between the lives of the representative *dramatis personae* and the witnessing audiences raises very thorny questions.

This is obvious in the bleak Birmingham setting of Amber Lone's *Deadeye*, which, as a co-production with Kali Theatre Company, was given its première performances at the Rep, followed by a run at the Soho Theatre in 2006. The stage directions for the opening scene are typical: 'Back room of the Chaudhrys' terraced house on an inner-city street, West Midlands. Peeling, painted wallpaper and general disrepair'. Tariq, the drug-dependent son of the family, enters 'carrying a white plastic bag, quite full'.[46] Amber Lone was brought up in Birmingham and her first Rep commission, *Paradise* (2003), explored what drove young Asian men to Islamic extremism, while *Deadeye* emphasises the Kashmiri origins of a family which might well feature as one of Tahir Abbas's case studies.

Gurpreet Kaur Bhatti's first play, *Behsharam (Shameless)*, was also developed through the Rep's Writers' Attachment Scheme. Co-produced and presented again with the Soho Theatre and first staged in 2001, it depicts the lives of three generations of a completely dysfunctional Birmingham family, ranging from a foul-mouthed, shop-lifting Punjabi granny and an unemployed would-be poet father to the drug-dependent isolated eldest sister, all hiding a dreadful secret about the fate of divorced and long-vanished Mummy One. Despite the strand of wild comedy—granny arriving with bags stuffed full of stolen Boots' toiletries, and little sister Sati inseparable from a life-size cardboard cut-out of footballer Ian Wright—the physical and emotional landscape is bleak, shifting from confrontations in 'a seedy pub/club in a hopeless Birmingham suburb' to a dank and rubbish-strewn bedsit and 'the dole office', all radiating out from the core of family collective deceit in 'Uncle Comrade's Shop'.[47]

Although the initiatives which nurtured *Behsharam* came from Birmingham, the business partnership with the Soho Theatre and the resultant performance trajectory gave the play a metropolitan imprimatur. Written by a London-born British Sikh playwright, and given its first important weeks of performance at the Soho Theatre, it was well-placed to draw audiences from both the London Asian community and arts professional networks and the new writing cognoscenti. The play received more attention from national newspaper critics, and after breaking box office records in Soho it did well in Birmingham.

Like Lone, who has worked in South London refuge and resettlement projects, Bhatti's career also includes refuge and youth and community work. The psychological and physical damage and abuse, especially of women, which results from economic and cultural dislocation is exacerbated by defensive exclusionary community strategies and further complicated by the multiple ethnicities to be found in British urban contexts. *Behsharam* is set in an imagined Birmingham environment, but the life crises and issues explored are real enough. The problem is that the dramatised objects of sociological scrutiny, given their economic circumstances, will not and arguably cannot share the gaze of the audience. The vast majority of the violent protesters who forced the closure of Bhatti's second Rep-developed play, *Behzti (Dishonour)*, and subsequently threatened the playwright and her family, had not only not seen the play but had never set foot in the theatre at any time. The glass panels of the Rep's façade were an invitation to easy destruction, not windows into a welcoming world of theatrical illusion.

When *Behzti* was scheduled, inadvisably, for performances in The Door over Christmas 2004,[48] it was against a background of multiple city-wide attempts to maintain the fragile balance of intercultural and interfaith relations in Birmingham. Unlike *Behsharam*, there was to be no preceding London showing; the producing partner was Sampad, the Birmingham-based South Asian arts agency led by Piali Ray, who was building up audience-promotional networks.[49] Despite this potential buffer, and nervous about the consequences of offence, the Rep management took the decision to expose the vulnerable and pressured process of new play evolution and rehearsal to senior, and thus more powerful, members of the very community under scrutiny. Indeed, in the context of the Birmingham bishopric of Uganda-born John Sentamu, the presence of an Anglican interfaith advisor in support of Sikh elders at the very troubled open dress-rehearsal is indicative of the extent to which civic politics had been allowed to intervene in the process of professional theatre-making.

It is clear from recollections by actors of the reading at the end of the first week of rehearsals, which were observed by two male elders and a few, more enthusiastic, younger women, that the response from the Sikh community would inevitably divide on both gender and generational lines. That there were the usual differences to be found in any institutional religion between orthodox social rigidities and more liberal openness to critical enquiry became apparent in attempts to visit two local gurdwaras: one rejected the visitors from the theatre while the other offered encouragement.[50] The gurdwara very simply indicated in *Behzti* is given no specifically identifiable location. Indeed, Anthony Frost has read it as 'a dramatic, and metonymic representation of Sikhism corrupted and in need of cleansing'.[51] But in the witnessed dress-rehearsal Bhatti's characters/actors trod on dangerous ground. The white-sheeted scenographic delineation of the gurdwara floor, where for the few permitted performances front-row audiences could literally place their feet, became the locus for a violent, enacted disjunction between visual signifiers.

Like the female suffering disclosed in *Behsharam*, the depiction of sexual abuse legitimised by traditionally accepted gender hierarchies in the second play is interwoven with scabrous comedy and eccentric characterisation. The fairy-tale qualities of the ending, in which the evil monster is slain by an avenging, zimmer-frame-clutching mother with an unreliable bladder while her dowdy Cinderella daughter (Min) wins her black carer Prince Charming, are grounded in the instantly recognisable, quotidian realities of difficult lives maintained in the interstices between cultures. But the blood on the back of Min's shalwar kameez, and the shock of the two comic shoe-lifting women workers beating the raped girl for imagined sacrilege, were made doubly disturbing by the implication that women knowingly collude in corruption.

That the play was written to provoke is beyond doubt, albeit, as Bhatti publically stated, from a position of commitment to the fundamental values of Sikhism.[52] *Behzti* sought to expose the isolation and vulnerability of those excluded by hypocritical and ultimately abusive power structures. If extremism of language and image and emotional frankness are characteristic of the dramaturgical principles of in-yer-face theatre, then *Behzti*, like *Behsharam*, can be classified as belonging to that genre. The tension for the young Asian woman dramatist is that this is a genre which owes its critical currency to the small but privileged audiences who have sat in the equally small, experimental spaces of ambitious theatres, and whose sensibilities are honed enough to withstand battering. The economic imperatives which make studio theatres marginal spaces for minority audiences give way to the advantages of a degree of creative seclusion to enable the informed dialogic possibilities offered by live performance.

Coherent strategies and wholehearted engagement

Paradoxically, the *Behzti* debacle has now potentially elevated the status of British Asian dramatic writing, aligning it with the best-respected traditions of campaigning Western theatre. After silencing, Bhatti's text now speaks volumes. In the immediate aftermath of the *Bezhti* incident a rising trajectory of 'mixed' audiences attended both The Door and the Rep's main house, if anything encouraged by the controversy. In March 2005 the final performance of Yasmin Whittaker Khan's *Bells*, which graphically explores the sexual trafficking of Pakistani girls, was witnessed by a packed all-age, multi-heritage Door audience. In the main house Roy Williams' *Little Sweet Thing*, which was presented as part of the Eclipse Theatre initiative, also saw unusually large audiences.[53]

However, there was a much more humdrum dimension of industrial inefficiency to the *Behzti* production process from which lessons could be learned in other contexts: inappropriate scheduling and marketing which promoted the play as an edgy, but genial, Christmas treat; three hugely pressured weeks of rehearsal for a work that needed more development; and difficult, business-driven negotiations with the Soho Theatre, which lost the play the safer haven of a London venue.[54] In Leicester, the evaluation report on *Bali* picked up on comparable factors which undermined the enterprise. Artistic and, by extension, marketing strategies have to be seen to be whole-hearted in their engagement. The report referred to a loss of strategic momentum when Vayu Naidu left and a new chief executive, Mandy Stewart, was appointed. The provision of transport for Asian community groups brought just two groups of elders to the Haymarket for the first time, and in general there was confusion across the three collaborating venues (Phoenix, Haymarket and De Montfort Hall) about the scheme. Naidu's profile-raising strategy to distribute five issues of the newsletter 'Samachar' proved no more effective than the use of well-produced season brochures and, as always, word-of-mouth proved the most effective publicity tool.[55] Most importantly, there had to be recognition of the generational implications of the fluid and hybridised nature of cultural identity, which can confound preconceptions about popular preferences.

Between them the three venues provided a very diverse range of Asian-oriented arts events, but perception about accessibility, ambience and relevance varied considerably. Phoenix Arts, formerly the Phoenix Theatre, offers both live performance and a varied range of Asian films, but was seldom visited by those interviewed for the report. The response to the Gujarati drama programmed at De Montfort Hall, amongst the high-profile and very eclectic music events for which the venue is best known, vividly demonstrated the impact of growing community heterogeneity. Prices were high, and the imposing building, which had served Leicester audiences since 1913, appeared to project a middle-class White liberal ethos. But the less Western-acculturated women, for whom Asian arts events did not inhabit a separate sphere but were 'part of our way of living', valued the plays as all-generation and family-friendly. For respondents with a broader knowledge of the arts available in Leicester as a whole, the Gujarati plays were of poor quality, unchallenging and with 'banal' subject matter. The language itself was problematic: 'pure' rather than 'street' Gujarati was difficult to understand, and nonsensical when translated into English phonetic script for the season brochures.[56]

The whole issue of facilitating access through language is very complex. The language of home and then is not necessarily the same as here and now. An elderly woman resident in England since the 1970s, but still not comfortable in English, is not the same as a recent immigrant from the Indian sub-continent. Engaging with the audience through box-office assistants who, ideally, can speak Asian languages or, more pragmatically, simply pronounce a word such as 'Bali' correctly, as Dipak Joshi was brought in to ensure, demonstrates sensitivity to multicultural need.[57] By the time the Haymarket reopened in September 2004 the marketing department had moved to publishing brochures which, alongside complete listings of what was on offer, printed multilingual promotions of selected productions. But more searching dialogue with audience members also showed that even Bollywood home-language films could create difficulty for young British Asians. English is their 'home' language, and the integrationist strategies of interculturalism best serve their interests.

Any discussion of the 'Shared Space' projects initiated by the partnership of Kerryson and Kully Thiarai, who arrived in 2001, has to take cognisance of the fact that on one level the strategy failed. The theatre went dark for a year in 2003 and then reopened in September 2004, only to close for good in January 2007. The second closure, however, was planned to enable work to begin on the Curve Theatre, the stunning twenty-first-century 'sleekly ovular glass' vision of the Uruguayan architect Rafael Viñoly, which places an unambiguously theatrical space at the heart of the regenerated St George's conservation area. The opening by the Queen was celebrated before Christmas 2008, and all the key stakeholders (trustees, city councillors and funding officers) have had to put a brave face on the final cost of nearly £61 million. A major new building project, which also demands the closure of the former theatre, places huge strains on managerial structures and human and financial resources. One consequence of this was that Kully Thiarai left the company shortly after the Haymarket closed, leaving Kerryson as sole artistic director.[58]

The importance of the Kerryson–Thiarai partnership, which also incorporated the role of Maya Biswas as artistic co-ordinator, far exceeded the act of putting work by and for the Asian and Black community at the centre of artistic policy rather than at the margins.[59] At the time of the publication of *The Eclipse Report*, which examined institutional racism in the theatre,[60] the appointment made a strong statement about higher-level managerial structures within the industry as a whole. Thiarai was not a token British Asian presence, but had equal status directing across the full spectrum of dramatic genre. Her first production was of Arthur Miller's *Death of a Salesman*, which featured the Black British actor Joseph Marcell playing Willy Loman as the head of a mixed-race New York household.[61] Indeed, one of the key criticisms to emerge from the New Audiences research report was that the Haymarket's view of their target audience was too narrow: 'Does it mean because I am Asian I can only watch an Asian play?'[62] Local Asian audiences were also just as likely as their white counterparts to frustrate the avant-garde ambitions of theatre professionals with their preference for feel-good western musicals such as *Fame* or *Grease*.

Amanda Whittington's specially commissioned *Bollywood Jane*, which Thiarai staged in May 2003, ironically just as the Haymarket's trustees decided to close the theatre, aimed to learn the lessons of *Bali*. Described as 'a unique mix of English theatre and Asian cinema ... bursting with life and sizzling with Bollywood song, dance and masala', it is the story of a naive sixteen-year-old local white girl finding escape and romantic dreams in the unlikely setting of a failing Bollywood cinema on the Belgrave Road. Dipak Joshi, with his role in Roots Phase 2 extended until 2004, proved vital as a 'human bridge' between theatre personnel and communities alienated by the short-lived relationships of the past. He negotiated additional promotional features on BBC Radio Leicester and brokered new links and advertising capacity on MATV and Sabras radio. He organised launch events developed with four different community groups, including one from the kind of predominantly white, working-class, outer estate where Jane herself might have lived.

Moving between the different Haymarket teams, Joshi provided Bollywood reference materials and wrote and rewrote the words of Bollywood songs, writing out lyrics phonetically so that actors could lip-sync effectively. He advised box-office staff on sensitive language issues and recorded an audience mobile-phone instruction in Hindi. When it looked like a *Krishna's Lila*-style protest was about to develop out of an incident in the play when Jane drops a Ganesh figurine, Joshi assisted Thiarai and the Communications Director Ruth Doyle in their attempts to placate the offended. The press night was covered by the BBC Asian network and the show was reviewed on Asiangigs.com by Ashvin-Kumar Joshi, who noted the packed-out house. In terms of what audience demographic data could be captured, the result was gratifying. Over 60 per cent of the audience surveyed were from black and minority ethnic (BME) communities and of those 55 per cent were Asian. The 'Asians' who opted to classify themselves were Indian, British Asian and, in relatively small numbers, Pakistani.[63]

Nothing at this time could swiftly ameliorate the deep-seated structural problems the theatre was experiencing. But it was clear that it was necessary to embed the kind of facilitating role that Dipak Joshi represented within the fabric of the organisation for long-term benefits to be achieved. As the writers of the report pointed out, such strategies could also be applied to other disenfranchised or marginalised groups. In 2004, in the city which had once actively tried to discourage immigration, a major public-/private-sector cultural strategy saw the Haymarket team join with other important educational and religious stakeholders in collaborative community projects.[64] Paul Kerryson worked on *Divine* with Smita Vadnerkar, the founder of Nupar Arts, the leading East Midlands company, which trains young people and adults in a range of classical and popular Asian dance forms. As a practising Roman Catholic, Kerryson brought his own faith to a project which used story telling, dance, song and drama to celebrate different religious faiths, and which culminated in performances presented in the disused medieval All Saints Church.

Thiarai later commented on what had been a very fraught, but nonetheless extraordinary, experience which had not needed her facilitation as the official 'Asian' in the directorate. 'As a consequence of that, Paul's relationship to some of those communities is stronger than mine, and his relationship to his faith and the faith of others is stronger than mine.'[65] Her background in social work with young people in the 1980s took her to a project with fourteen 'hard to reach' young people from five different areas of the city to create the site-specific *Captured Live* for three performances over the August Bank holiday weekend. Again, bringing together young people who might never usually meet to encounter the discipline and achievement of live performance was a way of encouraging cross-community participation and engagement in the capacity of theatre to nurture self-esteem.[66]

A changing demographic and new audiences

In 2000 the *Parekh Report* was at pains to show the extent to which cultural identities were in transition in multi-ethnic Britain, and that there were 'few stable patterns from which future projections can be made'. All the migrant peoples described were 'busy negotiating place and space within a rapidly changing larger whole'.[67] Nearly a decade on the results of that commercial and educational business may be seen in significant changes in the socio-economic status of growing numbers of British citizens of colour. Arguably it is that which is the most substantive contributory factor to the changing demographic of mainstream theatre audiences.

In Birmingham by the 2007–8 season it looked as though there had been a turning point in overall audience diversity. Roy Williams' *Angel House* (another Eclipse production) exceeded its financial target. Data produced from the all-important Christmas production of *Peter Pan* suggested that the 11 per cent of the audience that came from BME communities were looking for family-friendly content rather than cultural specificity. It seems likely, however, that the success of the National Theatre's touring production of *Rafta Rafta* ..., Ayub Khan-Din's adaptation of Bill Naughton's *All in Good Time*, benefited from word-of-mouth publicity which drew 'walk-up' Asian patrons to the box office. This theatrically prestigious but warm-hearted attempt to point to the commonalities rather than the differences experienced in family marriage crises also provided an ideal mutual networking opportunity with members of the Asian Business Institute, who were treated to 'a meal/see the show/and have a backstage tour' promotional package.[68]

While the ghost of *Behzti* still hovers, and the Rep has had to think carefully about community liaison practice, there have been no tokenistic attempts to build bridges with the Sikh community or, indeed, apologies for giving the writer a voice. The relationship with Kali Theatre and with it the company's commitment to powerful women's writing have been sustained on a contractual basis. In May 2008 Kali's production of Satinder Kaur Chohan's *Zameen*, which tackles the disastrous human consequences of globalisation on rural Punjab, did exceptionally well in The Door. Marketed with her customary tenacity by Suman Buchar, the success of another Sikh woman's play, albeit set on much safer ground, encountered no obstacles.[69]

Using theatre to engage with communities where deprivation and social exclusion have been exacerbated by heightened tensions around religious and cultural allegiance challenges everyone concerned. The Rep's network of youth theatres includes all Asian groups in Small Heath School, and Park View Specialist Business and Enterprise College in the Alum Rock area of the city, where 90 per cent of the pupils are Muslim and some forty languages are spoken. There has been help to pump-prime the emerging activity of Ulfah Arts, which prioritises Muslim women's access to, and participation in, the arts.[70]

As I write, *These Four Streets*, a play about the 2005 disturbances in Lozells which had been commissioned from six women playwrights, Naylah Ahmed, Sonali Bhattacharyya, Jennifer Farmer, Lorna French, Amber Lone and Cheryl Akila Payne, has completed a community tour following sell-out performances in The Door. Each writer's individual heritage permitted her access to local people whose lives were affected by what happened, and their experiences formed the basis of the text. No audience was, or could be, purely 'Asian' or, for that matter, 'Black'. The play aimed to reflect the reality of lives which daily grapple with the challenges of cultural alignment, but in a spirit of hope. In Leicester a production of *As You Like It* directed by Tim Supple with a multi-heritage cast has just completed its run. The marriages at the end of the play were celebrated in ceremonies which reflected the city's different communities and the heterogeneity which will inevitably characterise the audiences of the future.

8

Patriarchy and Its Discontents

The 'Kitchen-Sink Drama'
of Tamasha Theatre Company

Victoria Sams

In recent interviews and articles, Kristine Landon-Smith, joint artistic director of Tamasha with Sudha Bhuchar, has expressed dissatisfaction with the ways the company's theatre work is categorised, whether it is as 'British Asian' or 'community' drama. She does not wish to deny that the company takes an interest in the access of British Asian theatre practitioners and audiences to theatre, but objects to the preconceptions, and possibly the condescension, that can accompany such designations. She explains:

> Of course we do work from an Asian sensibility, but that's about who we are and what we want to say. With the burgeoning interest in all things Asian, the label sticks. Its effect is to sideline the company's work as not necessarily legitimate and not part of mainstream British theatre. It's exhausting; we've been around for a long time.[1]

She continues to discuss the ways that 'community' is a loaded term:

> We have found that the mere mention of the word has undervalued our work. Why? A mainstream company doing the same thing is praised for its diversity. When we explore subject matter from our own community, it can be viewed as unsophisticated.

Landon-Smith's objections to labels stems from an understandable resistance to a simplistic reception of Tamasha's work, as well as to reductive understandings of British Asian identities, which are irreducible to any fixed notion of a community. Any theatre artist who seeks to be understood in context but not necessarily in a frame would share such objections. The connotations of such labels pose a challenge to theatre artists and cultural critics alike. Yet they can also create useful connections between isolated plays or productions and a broader theatrical landscape, or between plays and cultural legacies. Such use can be tactical, whether embraced for the productive associations the labels may form across other categories, or challenged for their reductive associations, even if in a positive theatrical mythology. As seen in the reactions of diverse playwrights and historians to the 'dominant' narratives of postwar British theatre history, it can be as disturbing to be placed within a mainstream or a movement as it is to be excluded from it. Yet Tamasha's strengths seem to lie in its infiltration of multiple theatrical institutions, whether through collaboration with larger building-based theatres or through its absorption and revision of genres, from Bollywood film to documentary theatre to kitchen-sink drama.

Tamasha's realism and its approaches to script and production

Tamasha's approach has been largely (but not exclusively) realist, and in their dramatisations of these 'underexplored realms' of Indian and British Asian experience they have illuminated the intra-familial and cross-cultural tensions that shape contemporary life for many in both Asia and the UK. In its first production, an adaptation of Mulk Raj Anand's *Untouchable* (1989), the company combined a focus on contemporary Indian society with a humanist approach to character and story development. After *Untouchable* toured the UK with alternating English and Hindi performances, Landon-Smith and Bhuchar collaborated on a dramatic adaptation of another social realist Indian novel, one that depicts the post-Partition lives of a group of Sindh migrants. Meira Chand's *House of the Sun* (1991) takes place entirely within one apartment building in Bombay, in which multiple classes and generations of its Sindh occupants interact. *House of the Sun* introduced the use of a domestic setting to depict various forms of social claustrophobia and tensions within individuals, families and communities, which have characterised many of Tamasha's later productions. Yet, in their next production, *Women of the Dust* (1993), their focus was the more public domain of the workplace, in this case a construction site in Delhi. This production also marked Tamasha's movement from text-based theatre to a fusion of documentary and realist drama. In these respects, one can read *Women of the Dust* as a precursor to Tamasha's later research-based *Balti Kings* (1999), which is set in a working restaurant kitchen. Where *House of the Sun* focuses on the domestic lives of its female characters, both *Women of the Dust* and (to a less exclusive extent) *Balti Kings* place women's experiences, labour conditions and perspectives at the heart of their plots. *Women of the Dust* drew on research and interviews that Bhuchar, Landon-Smith and their cast conducted in India. For this project, they collaborated with UK-based writer Ruth Carter, demonstrating an early commitment to developing new writing for the theatre that has significantly expanded in recent years.

Where more explicitly feminist theatre companies such as Shared Experience or Kali sought to promote female writers, Tamasha developed new writing by both male and female playwrights.[2] Following *Untouchable* and *House of the Sun*, Bhuchar and Landon-Smith worked with playwright Abhijat Joshi on his new play *A Shaft of Sunlight* (1994), beginning a relationship with Birmingham Repertory Theatre that would continue with their next production. *A Yearning* (1995) marked Tamasha's first UK-set play and their second collaboration with Ruth Carter. This adaptation of Federico Garcia Lorca's *Yerma* to a Birmingham Punjabi community developed a bond with both the Birmingham Rep and the broader community in the city that would significantly deepen with *Balti Kings*.

Tamasha's productions have shifted between text-based (where source material is a novel or new play) and research-based (where the script derives from oral interviews and other forms of research). Both Bhuchar and Landon-Smith place a high value on what they call the 'authenticity' of all of their productions. This they attribute primarily to their methods of production research, whether interviewing female construction workers in Delhi for *Women of the Dust* or involving workers and customers in the Birmingham balti restaurants in the conception and production of *Balti Kings* (including materials for the programme, which contains a history of Indian cuisine in the UK). One way the research has fed directly into the performances is through a script development technique called 'hotseating', in which the actor is called upon to embody rather than describe their interviewees. More than a means of understanding their subjects as characters, these practices have served to connect the company to the communities in which they work. This research is not only content-driven but has also become an element of their marketing strategy. Interactions with the communities range from leafleting to interviewing to encouraging local businesses to invest in production, all of which has contributed to the company's aim of drawing more first-time theatregoers and building more culturally diverse audiences.[3]

Both Bhuchar and Landon-Smith have distinguished their approach from the more stylised or epic dramaturgy of other companies, most notably Tara, and from the physical theatre of such companies as Complicité. In a 1998 interview with Anjum Katyal, Landon-Smith describes their approach as more text-based and 'Western-based' with respect to characterisation and acting styles. While Tara's work self-consciously engages in a postcolonial approach with the adaptation of European and Indian classical myths and texts, Tamasha does not explicitly concern itself with cultural canons or legacies. Nevertheless, many of its productions directly revise and revive dramatic foci widely considered central to modern British drama: domestic realism and workplace drama.

Tamasha's realism and the British 'New Wave' of the 1950s

Tamasha's emphasis on social realism and on new writing aligns the company closely with the building-based Royal Court Theatre, which has a long history of nurturing new playwrights, and particularly new realist playwriting in the above genres. Playwright Ayub Khan-Din's *East Is East* marked Tamasha's first co-production with the Royal Court Theatre, and went on to gain Tamasha national acclaim through its tour and subsequent film adaptation, which became one of the UK's greatest film successes. The research and preparation for *Balti Kings* (not a collaboration with the Royal Court) resembles an earlier collaboration between the Royal Court and Joint Stock on Hanif Kureishi's *Borderline* (1981), which drew on research and interviews conducted with residents of Southall in the aftermath of violent clashes with National Front protestors. *Balti Kings*, Tamasha's second Birmingham-based play, written by Naushaba Shaheen Khan and Sudha Bhuchar, presents a range of migrant characters within the seemingly insular kitchen of a fictional Ladypool Road balti house called Shakeel's. The characters' references to Pebble Mill (site of the BBC studios in Birmingham), the Bosnian war (as experienced by the refugee brother and sister who work in Shakeel's) and other local landmarks situate the play in its particular time and place, while regional idioms flavour the characters' speech (bad culinary puns are irresistible with this play, as repeatedly evidenced in its reviews).

These two productions share particularly strong intertextual connections to several post-World War II plays linked to the Royal Court and commonly associated with the 'New Wave' of British realist drama. The term new wave conveyed the sense that significant shifts in British postwar culture were taking place, even though it actually constituted neither a movement nor an organised collective. John Osborne's debut *Look Back in Anger* (1956), Shelagh Delaney's *A Taste of Honey* (1958), Brendan Behan's *The Quare Fellow* (1957) and *The Hostage* (1958), and Arnold Wesker's *The Kitchen* (1959) are often credited with establishing the reputations of the Royal Court and the Theatre Workshop (at the Theatre Royal Stratford East) as promoters of young playwrights and as vital sources of new British drama in the late 1950s and 1960s.

Tamasha's *East Is East* and *Balti Kings* not only enact the kinds of familial tensions and personal struggles prevalent in modern realist drama, but situate these struggles in specific geographic and social environments in ways that strongly echo these precursors. Deeply embedded in their respective settings of Salford (as is *A Taste of Honey*) and Birmingham, these plays further resemble their predecessors in their depictions of intercultural as well as intracultural tensions. While critics of *East Is East* note its Salford or Lancastrian setting, very little is made of either its regional realism or its other connections to these earlier plays.[4] The reception of *Balti Kings*, on the other hand, does link it to its Birmingham setting and to Wesker's *The Kitchen*, which dramatises the lives of immigrant and native restaurant workers in 1950s Britain. One critic finds echoes of the earlier play's depiction of the social landscape of a 1950s restaurant kitchen in *Balti Kings*' presentation of the social hierarchies of immigrant lives in the restaurant trade of the 1990s: 'Here is the caste system of Asian Britain (with a Bosnian refugee underclass) in action.'[5]

Both these plays produced by Tamasha share many qualities ascribed to 'kitchen-sink drama', a label freighted with both pejorative and neutral connotations. Art critic David Sylvester coined the term 'Kitchen-sink Realism' in a 1954 article about the paintings of the Beaux Arts Quartet (John Bratby, Derrick Greaves, Edward Middleditch and Jack Smith).[6] Sylvester states that their paintings chronicle the 'ordinary lives of ordinary people' by depicting every element of domestic life, including the kitchen sink. The term crossed over quickly to theatre, first referring to the work of contemporary playwrights John Osborne and Arnold Wesker, whose 1956 *Look Back in Anger* and the aforementioned 1957 *The Kitchen* famously focus their dramatic action around an ironing board and a restaurant kitchen, respectively.

Like another term linked closely to the New Wave dramatists, 'Angry Young Man', or the more recent term 'in-yer-face' drama, 'kitchen-sink drama' is a label that invites resistance (as any label might) for its constraints. Recently, Arnold Wesker wrote a *Guardian* column in which he protested the use of the term kitchen-sink drama to describe his plays.[7] Is this resistance simply because any categorical description of a play (in-yer-face, state-of-the-nation, country-house, etc.) would come across as reductive? Or is it that the terms kitchen-sink drama and kitchen-sink realism, perhaps more strongly than realism alone, connote a literalism and didacticism—a kind of slow journalism? Popular usage of the term is frequently disparaging, often suggesting that the work to which it is applied is limited in artistic value or depth. The condescension with which some critics treat such drama tends to belittle its depiction of the sites and the labour that sustain a home or workplace, and its emphasis on the material conditions and physical environments that shape the lives of its characters. The emphasis of some New Wave plays on declamatory male protagonists and their predicaments has inspired sardonic critique as well as more sustained analyses of their gender politics and their purportedly revolutionary qualities.[8] Yet playwrights of this genre, such as Wesker and Delaney, often focus their plays' action around the plights and the desires of their female protagonists. Troubling labels and catchy terms such as 'Angry Young Man' and 'kitchen-sink drama' serve limited use as analytic categories; but they can provoke dialogue about and more nuanced readings of these plays and their reception.

Authenticity has tended to be the paradigm by which kitchen-sink drama is evaluated in its critical reception. As one aspect of this, its accessibility and intimacy has at times been the pretext for the treatment of playwright and subject as virtually indistinguishable: John Osborne notoriously came to be aligned with his protagonist, Jimmy Porter, as an 'Angry Young Man'. A similar pattern emerges in the reception of *East Is East*, although Khan-Din admits to modelling his central character, George Khan, after his own father, aligning himself most closely with the youngest child, Sajit.[9] Such emphasis on the linkage between real-life subject and fictional creation (even, or perhaps especially, when invoked in the defence of the authenticity of a character's behaviour or stereotypical qualities) risks overlooking the artistry, the distillation, and altered perspectives often at work in these plays.

Unexplored realms: depictions of the family and labour in *East Is East* and *Balti Kings*

What is often obscured in the autobiographical or sociological criticism of 'kitchen-sink drama' is the sharp delineation of their characters. So, for Tamasha's *Balti Kings*, many critics felt that Khan and Bhuchar's depiction of the familial and interpersonal tensions among the characters was trivialised by the chaos in the kitchen and the disparate plot strands.[10] This is less true of the critical reception of *East Is East*, which overwhelmingly praised Khan-Din for his multidimensional portrayal of a close-knit family and a complicated marriage.[11] In fact, Khan and Bhuchar and Khan-Din show tremendous sensitivity in their dramatisations of these characters' personalities, idiosyncrasies, temperamental differences and senses of humour. Each play develops a multi-strand plot through intricate choreography of an ensemble of characters. Their characters become multi-dimensional in performance through the ways that they work and share space as much as through their dialogue. Practising the social extension attributed to modern realist drama, and paralleling Tamasha's stated aim of examining the 'underexplored realms' of Indian society, both *East Is East* and *Balti Kings* focus their dramatic gaze on the underexplored realms of British Asian society.

The plays present multiple perspectives on and experiences of immigrants and their families, as well as the relationships between their home and working lives. In both plays, the businesses (a fish and chip shop in *East is East*, a restaurant in *Balti Kings*) are owned by the patriarchs of these families. Where the fish and chip shop is managed and staffed by the Khan family and one close friend of Ella's, the restaurant in *Balti Kings* is managed by the family but staffed by immigrant employees of varying backgrounds, ages and relationships to the family. These employees regard the restaurant owner, Yahsin Anwar, alternately as paternal authority figure and potential exploiter. He frequently invokes his benevolence and his shared history with his employees as a means of retaining their loyalty, which inspires mixed feelings in them. The characters that remain on stage at the close underscore the play's illumination of the overlooked labour (sometimes invisible even to its owners) that sustains the restaurant.

Both of the families in these plays are depicted as interdependent, almost symbiotic organisms, even as their intermittently present patriarchs dictate their fates. Although they are often displaced or in danger of becoming superfluous, the fathers in these plays function as controlling figures within the lives of the other characters, whether it is those who depend on them as their employees or as their family members. Both George Khan and Yahsin Anwar inspire varying degrees of resentment and rebellion in their families, neighbours and employees. They indirectly drive or provoke much of the action on stage, even if they do not dominate all the scenes they are in, and figure only peripherally or not at all in many scenes. More often than not, we see the repercussions of their decisions or actions (or their anticipated decisions or actions), or we witness characters' responses to them. That they often, wilfully or not, cause these characters great pain prompts the audience to view them with less sympathy, possibly even with hostility.

Patriarchal authority in *East Is East* is embodied by the two fathers who appear in the play (George Khan and his proposed in-law, Mr Shah), and largely resisted by the children and by their mother, Ella, as well as her friend Annie. Where George's authority is challenged by his native-born family and neighbours, Yahsin's is questioned by his workers, who are even more vulnerable to social marginalisation than he is. His sons internalise their employers' privilege differently: Shakeel, the elder, is paternalistic towards the object of his affection, the young Bosnian cleaner, Mariam, and deferential in making demands of the older workers. Shahab, the younger son, is predatory and exploitative in his business and his sexual pursuits. Yet we also catch glimpses of the tenderness and compassion that each of these men can show, and we are shown moments when their intentions are misconstrued or they are judged unfairly by other characters. Such glimpses occur more frequently with Yahsin, whose recent heart trouble and role as sole parent to his sons Shakeel and Shahab both render his authority over them less reliant upon their fear and more a function of their concern and loyalty. Nevertheless, the pressures placed upon these men by themselves and others are made visible through more than dialogue and gesture. Correspondingly, both plays emphasise the burdens placed upon women whose life choices are dictated by poverty, patriarchal values (whether imposed on them by relatives or internalised) and cultural displacement.

The playwrights for *East Is East* and *Balti Kings* employed techniques of documentary theatre, and these practices result in plays that cling much more closely to the conventions of realism than *A Taste of Honey* (which employs a jazz band acknowledged in character asides) or other oft-cited cornerstones of British realist drama. In numerous interviews and in the preface to his adapted screenplay, Khan-Din describes how his early drafts of the play were both oral history and personal therapy.[12] Where he drew on his mother's and his own personal recollections of their familial life in Salford, *Balti Kings* co-writers Bhuchar and Khan worked from observation and interview. Their production research took them into the kitchens of numerous balti restaurants, and they and their actors interviewed balti house workers at all levels, from dishwasher to head chef, as well as customers and owners of the restaurants.[13]

Khan and Bhuchar transformed their research into an abundantly populated but nevertheless character-driven realist play, in which the onstage kitchen connects not only to the restaurant dining room, to Ladypool Road and Birmingham, but beyond all this to Europe and Asia through the relationships between these characters. For instance, the conflict between Yahsin's sons Shakeel and Shahab simultaneously involves a clash of business approaches and temperaments, differing responses to their own class privilege and competing desires to prove to their father that his faith in them is well founded. The tensions between the workers—head chef Billa and his young nephew Nadim, Khalida (widow of a longtime friend of Yahsin), the middle-aged Yacoub, the Bosnian refugees Mariam and Isaac (Mariam's brother)—and their employers, Yahsin and his sons, reveals faultlines that run across and within family, gender and culture.

The choreography of each scene exposes these faultlines as vividly as the dialogue. For instance, Yacoub and Khalida's respective entrances at the play's opening reveal how their responsibilities and physical burdens (starting work before daylight in the unheated restaurant, stooping under the lowered shutters) are borne according to their different temperaments. Yacoub curses his absent co-worker Nadim, but gets to work uncomplainingly. Khalida enters and immediately provides the audience with a litany of grievances against the owners, tracing her misfortunes to the exploitation of her late husband by Yahsin and to the 'gori' wife of her beloved son. Khalida decries her own oppression (by the Anwars and by her own family) while passing judgements upon others that suggest an uncritical imposition of the very patriarchal values she resents.

The role of the set, space and place in both plays

As with the earlier realist plays, décor and space illuminate the tensions and different worlds being reconciled (or not) within the plays.[14] The split set in *East Is East* contains George and Ella Khan's house and chip shop, where they and their seven children live and work. Two rooms and a kitchen with an outside shed comprise the house. From the laundry piled on the Lazy Susan (itself a relic of the 1970s) on the kitchen table to the overall spatial design, it is clear that the family lives in very tight quarters, but it is equally clear that they (not all of them) have made an effort to make the rooms presentable. The kitchens in these plays are simultaneously public and familial places, both dwelling spaces and places of business. The set design of both plays emphasises the tensions and the bonds produced through closely sharing space in the everyday sense, whether in a family home, a neighbourhood or a workplace. In *Balti Kings*, characters argue with and console each other as they chop produce, navigate hot burners and dodge opened oven doors, with a choreography that links the spatial order of the kitchen to the hierarchies of class, family, generation and culture that operate on all of the characters. In the Khan household, the nuances in the relationships among the children and their parents are conveyed as much through their physical interaction within and between the rooms of the house and the chip shop as through their dialogue. The Khans' living spaces parody the mainstay of early realism, the bourgeois living room, which is highlighted by daughter Meena's caustic response to the 'posh' accent her mother adopts when inviting Mr Shah into the 'parlour'.[15]

The plays' use of space (and the characters' movement within those spaces) to convey both emotional and social relationships is matched by their use of language. The characters' use of language further defines their relationship to place. Lancashire, and more specifically Salford, carries deep resonances for all the characters, including George, who is the only Khan who does not speak with the local accent, even as he has adopted some of the expressions. To George, Salford is the geographical stepchild of Bradford, which in turn is a poor translation of the original hometown in Pakistan. Khan-Din's introduction to his screenplay suggests this additional source of insight into the nostalgia and displacement felt by his father and other migrants. Furthermore, he explains that the onset of his mother's Alzheimer's disease coincided with the proposed demolition of the neighbourhood (in Salford) in which he grew up, which motivated him to try to recover and preserve an eroding familial and local history through his play.[16] *Balti Kings* was born of a similarly articulated desire to make a theatrical record of a place and a community in Birmingham with which Tamasha shares a history and a relationship.[17]

Both plays stage the characters' struggles for belonging and their claims to communal affiliation in the face of impossible conditions for the fulfilment of those claims. The settings in these productions frequently emerge as spaces in which characters negotiate differently held values or expectations within themselves, their families and their communities. Through these practices, they illuminate the repercussions of cultural displacement and the processes of 'making oneself at home' in a challenging, even hostile, environment. They highlight the perceptions of cultural differences between a Britain still associated with a white Anglo-Saxon heritage and its immigrant or minority inhabitants still marked as racially or ethnically Other. In *Balti Kings*, set over twenty years later than *East Is East*, such a monocultural Britain seems to exist in the form of Shakeel's potential customers and their appetites, but otherwise bears an irrelevance to their life in the UK that inspires a tenuous optimism.

This perspective marks a reversal of the ways that immigrants and minority characters featured as contrapuntal 'others' to native British subjects in such plays as *A Taste of Honey* and *Look Back in Anger*, where such characters featured either peripherally or entirely offstage, and even in *The Kitchen*, where these characters were central to the play's action. Wesker's mainly European immigrants seem to be negotiating temperamental rather than cultural differences (although such differences often express themselves as cultural prejudices in the play), whereas in *East Is East* and *Balti Kings* characters' cultural and religious practices are the sources of intense debate and conflict about their life choices. *East Is East* seems to hold out various prospects for its younger generation: the possibility of positive cultural fusion and genuine belonging to both family and community, the vision upheld by George of conformity to the dictates of his desire for acceptance (also conditional) into the Bradford Muslim community as the only route to belonging, or the complete rejection of all that George demands and values. *Balti Kings* seems to posit multiple if tenuous forms of cultural and personal reconciliation, from Yahsin's acknowledgment of the success of both Shakeel and Shahab's business strategies, to the return of Billa to the kitchen, to Khalida's grudging acceptance of her son's wife. The intimacy of the characters' interactions with each other and with the spaces they inhabit in these plays can serve to illuminate the characters' interior lives and build a rapport between the works and their audiences.

A critical focus: home and away, and the absent family, in *East Is East*

Where *Balti Kings* meshes melodrama with comedy in its dramatisation of the working and familial lives of many characters in ways that occasionally misfire, *East Is East* more gracefully fuses its tragic and comic (and at times farcical) elements in depicting the simultaneous pull of Pakistan, Salford and Bradford within one family. The confusion, conflict and violence that permeate the Khans' domestic life emerge in sharp relief to the verbal and visual comedy that runs through the play, just as the tensions and long-held grudges between family members and employees simmer and flare up around (and occasionally because of) the kitchen choreography in *Balti Kings*. Unlike Yahsin, who rules with an emotional rather than an iron grip, George Khan maintains a physically violent and authoritarian hold on his family. Upon leaving Pakistan in the 1930s, George also left a first wife and children, with whom he remains in contact, sending goods and money to them from England. His sense of obligation, perhaps based on feelings of guilt, produces a strong sense of affiliation to that family and to his home state of Azad Kashmir.

In the preface to his screenplay (adapted from the play), Khan-Din's explanation of his own father's behaviour suggests the autobiographical inspiration for George's characterisation:

> I think part of his problem was that he always felt slightly embarrassed by us in the company of his family, who had settled over here ... In many ways, he must have felt extremely isolated and would have liked to have lived in a Pakistani community like Bradford.[18]

Khan-Din does not shy away from depicting George's tyrannical, brutal behaviour and its often devastating consequences, but he also allows George's longings and his sense of isolation to surface in some quietly moving moments in the play, rendering him a more sympathetic figure. History's invasions into the Khans' home take the more obvious form of the television news features on the independence war in the former East Pakistan. As these broadcasts punctuate the days and nights in the Khan household, George agonises and fumes over the potential fates of his first wife and family in Azad Kashmir. The Bangladeshis' struggle for independence from an increasingly militarised Pakistan parallels the children's conflicts with their authoritarian father. His fears about the impact of border disputes on the security of his Pakistan-based family are matched by fears of the encroaching influences of non-Pakistani social and cultural values on his children. Similarly, his mingled feelings of guilt and relief—guilt for not returning to this family and relief at not living with the struggles and demands of everyday life in Pakistan—hold his feelings for both families in a kind of tension with each other.

This absent family shadows the family that we see on stage. George paints them as both a perfect and a typical Pakistani family: respectful of the patriarch, harmonious, untainted by the 'outside' influences he finds so fearsome in England. His views appear to be a source of both comic and real tension for his current wife Ella and most of his English-born children. They are sceptical, even scornful, of George's praise for the country and family from which he has been apart for forty years, arguing that such distance lends enchantment, and he and Ella enjoy an ongoing comic banter about his quirks in spite of his temper. The Khans' house is also haunted by the absence of their eldest son, Nazir, disowned by George for resisting the marriage George arranged for him. The family is ordered to treat him as dead, though, as Ella tartly observes, 'No, he's not, he's living in Eccles. He might be dead to you but he's still my son.'[19]

Moments such as these reveal the strengths of Khan-Din's development of those who might otherwise be considered minor characters. Ella, Meenah and Ella's best friend Annie all display keen senses of humour, independent minds and strong inclinations to assertiveness (curbed only by George). The sole sister among seven siblings, Meenah is well able to hold her own, even with her elder brothers. Annie, like Ella a native of Salford, possesses both a tremendous compassion for all members of the Khan family and a gift for deflating the pretensions of others. Where Ella's responses to George's behaviour are alternately funny and painful but nearly always self-aware, Annie's challenges to George's authority emerge comically and seemingly accidentally. For instance, when Annie pops in to the Khan house to find them entertaining Mr Shah, she interrupts their discussion of childrearing to praise the Khan children for being 'good Samaritans', provoking a potential crisis with the disapproving Mr Shah. She echoes Mr Shah's affirmation of his wife's firm hand with their children by offering her own insight into discipline: 'Oh aye, yeah, mind you, our Peter knows how far he can go, before I knock him to kingdom come—and that's just me husband Mr. Shah!'[20]

George's aspirations of impressing and ultimately belonging to the Bradford Pakistani community produce some of the funniest moments in the play, even as they demand painful sacrifices from Ella and their seven children. The tensions between George and his children reveal his own conflict within himself over his visions of England and Pakistan. Interestingly, George's authority erodes in one of the few scenes set outside their home. After an embarrassing debacle at the mosque, Ella and George take their youngest son, twelve-year-old Sajit, to be circumcised at the local hospital. When the doctor approaches them after the operation, Ella takes control of the situation, shushing George deprecatingly and urging him to go and call them a taxi while she talks to the doctor. Her strictness with Sajit and George derives from a parallel desire for social acceptance: 'I'm not having my kids being accused of bad manners. People are a lot quicker to point the finger if they see they're a bit foreign.'[21] Her behaviour is more assertive than in their home. These scenes suggest that George has had a succession of disempowering experiences—as a target of both English racism and Pakistani racism and elitism—resulting from his marriage to Ella and choice of Salford as home as well as from his decision to raise his children as Muslims. In this respect, they suggest the complicated sources or triggers of his insecurity and rage.

As his exclusionary and racist treatment in England is internalised, George's reaction is to embrace more conservative Pakistani and Muslim values than he might have done had he remained in Pakistan or found England a less hostile environment. Thus the household has become George's domain through a combination of threatened and actual violence and the tactical concessions of his wife Ella and their children. Constantly living under the cloud of 'what Dad did to Mam last time', which emerges implicitly as his near-fatal beating of her after Nazir fled the house, the children must negotiate their lives outside of the house around their parents' strict demands of their time and behaviour. Ella mediates between a kind of conspiratorial complicity with her children, for instance by allowing Salim to secretly study art instead of engineering and warning Abdul and Tariq that their father is planning their engagements, and a submission to the often tyrannical will of George, as with her concession to twelve-year-old Sajit's circumcision and to Nazir's banishment from their home after his rebellion. The flow of action through the space of the set illustrates the numerous codes and nuances by which Ella and the children can gauge George's moods and circumvent his authority. George's impending entry into the house frequently precipitates a flurry of covert activity, as the children hide the evidence of their sausage eating, or Salim's art portfolio, or anything else forbidden by their father. As George struggles to gain social acceptance for his family within the Pakistani community in Bradford he becomes an outsider in his own house.

When Mr Shah, the would-be father-in-law to Abdul and Tariq Khan, makes his first formal visit to the house the tenuousness of George's control emerges both through their chronic eruptions of rebelliousness and, more implicitly, in the impossibility of sustaining his purist vision. George's desire for acceptance within the Pakistani community in Bradford leads him to embrace a paradoxical fusion of materialist social ambition and devout commitment to Islamic religious practices and beliefs. Mr Shah appears as the standard-bearer of the 'traditions' defined as Pakistani by the social elites of its expatriate community in Bradford, and his enthusiasm for his role as the paragon of Bradford Asian respectability is matched (and possibly enhanced) by his complacent pride in his wall-to-wall carpeting and double glazing. George's position of authority within his home, held more by fear than respect, shifts quickly to one of social inferiority and obsequious deference in the face of the self-satisfied Mr Shah.

Concluding comments: the critical value of 'kitchen-sink drama'

The idea of kitchen-sink drama as aesthetically or dramatically limited has fed on presumptions about what constitutes challenging or significant or timeless theatre. Plays that feature domestic settings and labour seem to be read in contrast to 'state-of-the-nation' plays that focus on public life or leaders, a distinction that often aligns with gendered expectations of domestic labour as 'women's work' that is less politically and dramatically significant. Feminist critiques of realism often emphasise its privileging of core patriarchal structures and values in its dramatic focus and its resolution.[22] Both the plays produced by Tamasha and featured here retain a consistent focus on the patriarchal structures and values imposed by their central characters, as is typical of their New Wave precursors. This focus is frequently but not always a critical gaze, however, one that invites the audience to identify more strongly with those characters who live and work within the confines of these structures, while at the same time potentially exposing the contradictions embedded in their very foundations. Yet these examples of kitchen-sink drama also demonstrate the genre's capacity to do more than engage in literal social diagnosis or didacticism. The plays offer more nuanced depictions of the characters' predicaments than many critics, even those who praise the plays, credit them with doing.

Both plays invite an identification with the female protagonists' (mainly Ella and Mariam, but also Meena and Khalida) struggles to assert themselves, but do not do so at the expense of audience understanding of the male characters. Such depth of characterisation can serve an important function. In George's case, it allows audiences insight into the intimate and everyday experiences of a figure often stereotyped or caricatured, even as he embodies some of those very stereotypes. His struggle against the scorn of his family and community inspires empathy. However, his constant invocations of religious authority, cultural pride and familial honour to force his will upon his wife and children inexorably reveal his flaws.

While both plays set up a somewhat predictable conflict between western individualism and a stereotypical non-western paternalism, the purportedly universal desirability of the former and the latter's invocation as religious or cultural tradition are both hotly contested by other characters, suggesting a more realistic intracultural and intragenerational diversity. In *Balti Kings* all of the characters are Muslim, each with his or her interpretation of what that might mean. In *East Is East* George's interpretation (or imposition) of proper Muslim behaviour is set against his own contradictory practices, the secular and Catholic views of his neighbour Annie and of Ella, and the idealised Muslim practices of his family in Pakistan and the Bradford community. *Balti Kings* depicts a multiplicity of Muslim beliefs and practices, from the charitable impulses of Yahsin, to the paternalistic chivalry of Shakeel, to the older workers' visions of divine will and their own destinies. It is a subtle and complex picture, and one that does not invite simplistic judgements.

To return finally to the New Wave era, Wesker's introduction to *The Kitchen* makes an implicit appeal for a more generous reading of kitchen-sink drama as engaging core issues and institutions of far-reaching significance. Defending the dramatic potential of the kitchen, Wesker declaims: 'The world might have been a stage for Shakespeare, but to me it is a kitchen, where people come and go and cannot stay long enough to understand each other, and friendships, loves, and enmities are forgotten as quickly as they are made.'[23] It is an appeal that, as this essay hopefully has shown, may readily be applied to our critical reading of Tamasha's 'kitchen-sink drama'.[24]

9

The Marketing of Commercial and Subsidised Theatre to British Asian Audiences

Tamasha's *Fourteen Songs, Two Weddings and a Funeral* (1998 and 2001) and *Bombay Dreams* (2002)

Suman Bhuchar

In this essay, I will examine the marketing methods of two shows, *Fourteen Songs, Two Weddings And a Funeral* (1998 and 2001), produced by Tamasha Theatre Company, and *Bombay Dreams* (2002), presented by Andrew Lloyd Webber, in order to explore similarities and differences in the following three areas: marketing strategies for commercial and subsidised theatre; the development of new audiences for theatre; and the imperatives that drive the marketing within these sectors. As someone with a proven track record of marketing to niche audiences, I was involved in the successful marketing of both shows. This was at a time when it was considered by everyone involved in theatre—from funders and venues to companies—to be challenging to reach out to specifically Asian audiences.[1] One should bear in mind the complexity of the challenge of targeting Asian audiences; the Asian communities do not constitute a single, homogeneous group and the marketing of each production must be specifically tailored to each individual targeted community or age-group.

Bombay Dreams constitutes the first inter-cultural musical presented in the West End in contemporary times.[2] Its marketing was unique in commercial theatre, marrying as it did established techniques with community outreach and Asian marketing, values more at home in subsidised theatre. This article will analyse the chosen marketing strategies used by the production company, the Really Useful Group (RUG), and the marketing company, Dewynters. In addition, two special 'Asian' marketing consultants were hired to ensure that the show had the widest possible audience reach but at the same time did not alienate the audiences drawn to Andrew Lloyd Webber musicals. By contrast, the marketing for Tamasha's *Four Songs, Two Weddings and a Funeral*, an Asian-led production which transferred from small- to mid-scale, was carried out by the company, and in line with its existing marketing strategies.

Tamasha Theatre Company: building an audience development policy

In 1989 my sister Sudha and Kristine Landon-Smith founded the Tamasha Theatre Company to mount a play based on a classic novel by Mulk Raj Anand, *Untouchable*, in English and Hindi on alternate nights. They found the venue, the Riverside Studios in London under the directorship of Jonathan Lamede, who took a chance and offered them a box-office split.[3] There was an untested but prevailing perception that the Asian community did not go to the theatre (in the western sense). So the company felt that by performing the production in Hindi and English they were maximising their opportunities to reach out to a range of Asian audiences, especially those who might not understand the English-language performance. The priorities were to render the performance with authenticity and in rigorous detail, and to undertake what is now called 'audience development': identifying and targeting those people from whose cultural antecedents the story was drawn. The directors felt this community would enjoy the show, but it would also put paid to the stereotype that Asian people did not go to the theatre.

This is where my involvement in marketing British Asian theatre began. I offered to try my hand at both press and marketing, and Kristine and Sudha as directors of Tamasha agreed. I had no formal training in this area, except enthusiasm and a passion for theatre.[4] It was all very heady. I 'cold-called' different press contacts—the nationals, features, previews, Asian media, and critics—and, surprisingly, they responded. At that time there was no formal model for a strategy to attract an Asian audience. Instead, the idea was to directly approach the different Asian communities in their own spaces, such as community centres, shops, streets, youth clubs and voluntary groups. I made it a personal policy never to go into a religious institution which focused only on prayer, but would go to places that had a community centre attached and/or would send them postal communications.

The method was simple. First we set up the tour, then researched the Asian demographic at each location. To do this I first looked for names of groups through local services, such as the community relations or arts departments of local boroughs. Then, having obtained a sense of the Asian demographic surrounding each tour, I used this direct approach alongside usual marketing methods for theatre such as mailings and distribution of posters and flyers. First I called people on the list of groups, then wrote letters, and then finally put a box of flyers in my car and drove up and down the M1 to meet people. Indeed, over the years I have clocked up thousands of miles doing this, and even today, when there are more sophisticated channels for marketing and the Asian media have developed considerably, there is no more successful method than that known as 'word of mouth'. In those early years I would give people a flyer of the show, talk to them, engage them in the content, show them pictures of key cast members, tell them a little of their biography and introduce the theatre company. There was little awareness amongst these people about the contemporary culture being produced by the second-generation Asians, so those were important tasks.[5]

I carried flyers everywhere and never lost an opportunity to hand one to someone. I stood outside big hotels where formal dinners hosted by Asians were held, Asian club events, cinemas screening Indian films and classical music concerts at venues such as the Queen Elizabeth Hall, London. I was always asked one key question: 'Are you acting in it?' My reply was always negative, and people were always disappointed to hear this, since they wanted to rub shoulders with 'celebrity'. Nevertheless, they were welcoming and interested in hearing about the arts. Another audience I assiduously targeted was the 'Indophiles', Westerners who were interested in Indian literature, music, film, dance and theatre. I felt that here were people who already engaged with Indian culture, so the new British Asian culture that was being forged by companies such as Tamasha was only a short step away from familiar territory. What made it possible to employ such an untested approach in Tamasha's early years was the support of the company's directors. They were producing plays with popular appeal and a social message, and wanted to attract Asian audiences who would appreciate the humour and pathos within the productions.

The production of *Untouchable* was performed in English and Hindi in the round, with a whole village being created in Studio Two at the Riverside. Here were British Asian actors who had to speak in two languages on alternate nights; however, it was so visual and direct that one reviewer from *City Limits*, who had mistakenly ended up coming on the Hindi night, nevertheless enjoyed herself. The success of the London run of *Untouchable* at Riverside Studios from 4 to 30 December 1989 was replicated on its national tour.[6] That success, and the company's ability to attract a diverse audience, led to an invitation from Philip Hedley at the Theatre Royal Stratford East (TRSE) to create a production there that would appeal to the local Asian community.[7] This was Tamasha's second production, *House of the Sun*, an adaptation of the novel by Meira Chand, which tells the story of the residents of Sadhbela, a Bombay apartment block peopled by Sindhi refugees, who fled from Sind to India at the time of Partition. The TRSE season brochure described it as a 'Bombay *Coronation Street*' (the title of a long-running ITV soap), and the show featured fourteen actors playing over forty characters, with the block of flats—and even a working lift—recreated on stage by designer Sue Mayes.

. The Sindhi community featured in the story was sparse in the London Borough of Newham, where the theatre was situated. However, Kristine and Sudha spent several months researching the socio-ethnic intricacies of the Sindhis resident in London and Bombay; this authentic aspect of the company's process was reflected in the use of the direct-mail letter as part of its marketing strategy.[8] Alongside this, another part of the TRSE marketing strategy for *House of the Sun* was to hire me to identify the reasons why the local Asian community did not use the theatre, and to develop a marketing plan for the forthcoming show. It was here that a 'formal strategy' took shape, and one which would form the basis of Tamasha's evolving marketing strategy. The play ran from 12 April to 11 May 1991, and from January until the press night (16 April) I was in Newham as an arts ambassador, foot-soldier, audience-development and marketing person, wandering around Newham and neighbouring Waltham Forest, and to some degree Redbridge and Barking. I met people in the voluntary and youth sector, community colleges and in local authorities, as well as local Asian councillors, and attended small community events, as a way of fostering a relationship. I put this experience in a small report for the venue, pompously entitling it 'There Is No Simple Solution'.[9]

Looking at that report eighteen years later, it is really a practical guide packed with information about the local Asian community. It focuses on the question of how to target the local Asian community, and presents future programming suggestions as well as a marketing plan for the show. The methodology is all relevant, even today, although some content would need updating. It carries information on the demographics of the borough, methodology, perceptions about the theatre and a suggested plan of action on programming. This incorporates targeting the local Asian community for future shows through grass-roots contacts, selling tickets through video outlets and using shared mail-outs, and outreach work via the theatre's education department.

Tamasha's fourth production, *A Shaft of Sunlight* (1994), marked the beginning of a relationship with the Birmingham Rep, which was followed by five shows in the Studio theatre there: *A Yearning* (1995), *East Is East* (1996), *A Tainted Dawn* (1997), *Fourteen Songs, Two Weddings and a Funeral* (1998) and *Balti Kings* (1999). This was a new venue for the company, and the relationship had been brokered by Sudha Bhuchar, who wrote to Anthony Clark, then Associate Director at the Rep. Although the venue was not known for its 'Asian work', the Studio (now known as The Door) was committed to developing new writing, and *A Shaft of Sunlight* by Abhijat Joshi was a new stage play. It had originally been written for the BBC World Service, and Tamasha had asked Joshi to adapt it for the stage. It is a serious, gritty piece set in Ahmedabad and dealing with the tensions that exist within a mixed marriage between a Hindu and a Muslim against the backdrop of the explosive communal politics of India during the 1990s. It is not exactly a light-hearted show, and I was left to sell it to a new Asian audience, who knew the location of the venue, situated as it was next to the main library in the busy, city-centre Centenary Square and on Broad street, but rarely visited it.

In Birmingham, I continued with a similar approach, aimed at identifying and pulling in Asian audiences for this show and ensuing productions, which entailed marrying conventional marketing methods with a grass-roots style. In summary, despite Tamasha's success at the Rep and after making significant progress in attracting a regular Asian audience to the venue, my suggestions that the Rep continue to foster a sense of 'ownership' for this audience and target them for other non-Asian shows at the Rep, were not pursued. This point is eloquently made by Hardish Virk, another independent marketing consultant, who worked on other Asian productions at the Rep in later years.

> Historically a lot of these people were aware of the Birmingham Rep only through passing through the Centenary Square. They may have walked in to see some Tamasha productions beforehand, but there was no sense of ownership of the space or the venue or where it was located.[10]

Fourteen Songs, Two Weddings and a Funeral

These early productions give an indication of the initial marketing 'method' that I developed with Tamasha, which then evolved more formally into an integral aspect of a marketing strategy. A closer examination of the campaign for *Fourteen Songs* will illustrate the fundamental principles that underpin the formal marketing strategy pioneered by Tamasha.

In March 1998, members of Tamasha Theatre Company went to Bombay to undertake research for their next show, a British musical based on a Bollywood film, *Hum Aapke Haim Koun ...! (Who Am I to You?)* (1994). They had sponsorship from Emirates Airlines to go to India, so the two co-directors, Sudha Bhuchar and Kristine Landon-Smith, together with the set-designer Sue Mayes and myself, spent the week travelling to film sets, meeting people at Rajshri Productions, the company who had made *Hum Aapke Hain Koun ...!* and watching three different versions of the film, all approximately four hours long.[11]

Feeling much inspired and daunted, the directors found in this film, with its sweet nature and homespun values, a story that lent itself to the stage. The show they crafted ultimately became *Fourteen Songs, Two Weddings and a Funeral*, which was really Sudha Bhuchar's description of the plot of the original film (and stage musical), and the title stuck. This proved very useful in marketing as it encapsulated the story in a nutshell to audiences who knew nothing about its provenance, and brought a smile to the faces of people who knew the film *Hum Aapke Hain Koun ...!*. The plot was very simple and clearly illustrated in the publicity blurb:

> Pooja falls in love with Rajesh. Prem, Rajesh's brother, falls in love with Nisha, Pooja's sister. But when Pooja dies suddenly in tragic circumstances, Nisha finds herself betrothed to the wrong brother. Will Nisha's secret love for Prem be discovered before it's too late? Featuring all the classic ingredients—romance, comedy, melodrama, song and dance—*Fourteen Songs, Two Weddings and a Funeral* is an enchanting love story lavishly told in true Bollywood style.

Most of the action takes place in a large family home, designed around a central staircase, a useful feature for the later tragedy. The play delves into Hindu cultural mores and family values, where duty and sacrifice are prized, along with some goofy comedy. The creative challenge lay in taking the best of British musical traditions and that of Bollywood and blending them seemingly effortlessly together. Firstly, the music of the original film was adapted to render it effective for a stage performance.[12] Secondly, all the songs were translated into English by Sean McCarthy and then recorded by the cast, so that on stage they were lip-synching to their own pre-recorded voices, perfectly mimicking the idea of playback in Hindi films. As director Landon-Smith explains in the original programme note:

> The film also had key song-and-dance routines. They were all in the right place for a stage musical and we were therefore careful to include all those classic numbers such as Prem & Nisha dancing by the poolside (a blueprint of Fred Astaire & Ginger Rogers numbers) and the climactic number right at the heart of the piece, *Jute De do Paise Lelo* [Take the Shoes and Give Me the Money].[13] This reminds me about so many musical numbers about young love where the boy's side meets the girl's side en masse (*West Side Story* or *Grease* to name just two). Fast choreography and the dove-tailing of one scene to another helps give the illusion of a stage peopled with actors.[14]

By 1998, although Tamasha had a track record of producing high-quality, populist work that appealed to its core audience of Asians, the musical form was a new departure. The company therefore maintained its rigorous approach to ensuring the production was marketed to its core audience comprised of families and professional Asians, in addition to introducing the conventions of Bollywood films to Western audiences.

Initially the production was to play a small-scale tour of three venues where Tamasha had a history. These were the Lyric Studio, Hammersmith, London (11 November–5 December 1998), Bristol Old Vic (New Vic Studio) (8–12 December 1998) and Birmingham Rep (The Door) (15 December–9 January 1999). However, the marketing strategy still had to be thorough and closely targeted to this core audience, since it was not possible to assume that they would attend. The marketing concept involved incorporating the traditional techniques used to promote Bollywood films in all the visual imagery for the show. So, firstly, an artist was commissioned to draw big faces of the two lovers, Prem and Nisha, against a blue backdrop filled with stars and fireworks. This was an idea reminiscent of the billboard images of Bollywood films, the original method used to promote films in India. The font for the lettering was a romantic one, again mimicking front- and end-credit styles in films, and the publicity information (as mentioned above) was also 'filmic' in concept, highlighting the 'feel good' and 'family friendly' nature of the production.

An Education Pack containing information on the history of popular Indian cinema, as well as suggesting explorations on key themes of the play, along with those from Hindi movies, was created for schools. The cover of the programme booklet featured the main protagonists in their Bollywood archetypes. Actor Pravesh Kumar, who played Prem, is shown with a bat; Paterfamilias Shiv Grewal appears contemplative; and Shobu Kapoor, a well-known face from *Eastenders*, is shown with a hair dryer, highlighting her vanity. A young actor, Raza Jaffrey, who trained at the Bristol Old Vic Theatre School, played Rajesh.[15] Inside, the programme carried a note by the director, Landon-Smith, explaining her reasons for adapting a Bollywood film for stage and giving some background information on Indian cinema and the original film before moving to the cast and crew details. The programme itself always comes later in the actual marketing schedule, as it is sold during the run of the production; however, the background information is prepared in advance, circulated to venue staff and press and used for any promotion on the show.

In the summer of 1998 the company produced a small postcard which was distributed at numerous Asian events, including melas and youth festivals. The circulation of the core publicity leaflets and posters then began eight to ten weeks before the opening. Forty thousand flyers were printed for London and Birmingham and ten thousand for Bristol, reflecting the amount required for the length of the runs at each venue. Five hundred posters for London and Birmingham, with a hundred for Bristol, were also produced. In line with Tamasha's existing commitment to reaching out to the Asian community through various direct marketing methods, the company provided me with a budget of £4,500 to both employ an assistant to help me contact groups and subsidise tickets for community groups.

In a process of this kind, firstly you try to identify groups of Asians living in a particular city; secondly, you write to them explaining the show and identifying the cast members they may recognise from other television or stage shows; and, thirdly, you follow this up with a call or a personal visit. This procedure is very onerous and time-consuming, and there are no guarantees that any ticket sales will ensue as a result. As this show was deemed suitable for all the family, the age, gender and class of individuals were not considered relevant. Pricing can be another issue, as it may be a barrier, but this show was priced reasonably, with tickets ranging from £5 to £9 at all venues, and the company was able to offer subsidies towards travel and the cost of the tickets to concessionary groups.

In the files I kept on the marketing for the show, there is an evaluation for the community groups targeted in the London area, across the boroughs of Barnet, Brent, Ealing, Haringey, Newham, Hillingdon and Hounslow. The groups vary in range and size: examples include Asian Action Group, a youth group from Haringey, a Lions club in Stanmore who bought the whole show (102 people; capacity 110) and an Asian Women's Project in Newham. Most groups, I discovered, want you to come and perform the show at their own venues, which is sadly not possible for a produced theatre piece, and although very polite they tend to be non-committal about purchasing tickets, so they have to be visited or called several times. I sent letters and booking forms for the groups to complete and return to me. This meant that I then had to liaise with the venue to confirm the booking was on the system, pay the theatre and ensure that the group received their tickets in advance of the performance. This was a time-consuming and bureaucratic process, but there was no other way of achieving a direct sale.

At the end of three months' work the total number of people who came to see the performance at the Lyric Studio through this type of work was 312, of whom 70 were senior citizens from Newham, who were also given a coach subsidy by Tamasha to get them there. This process was replicated in Bristol and Birmingham, alongside normal theatre-marketing activity. In 1998 this involved distribution of flyers and posters through traditional theatre-marketing agencies picking the best type of 'runs': different geographical areas of the city, demarcated according to specific 'taste', where a potential audience might congregate and pick up a flyer or spot a poster. Specific direct mail was sent out to previous attenders of Tamasha shows, reminding them that this was the company that had brought them *East Is East*.[16] I also shared mailings with other promoters marketing classical Asian music or fusion concerts to reach the 'Indophile' and Bollywood audiences for this show. This meant that they inserted the *Fourteen Songs* flyer in mail-outs for their show, and vice versa. I was also able to afford one advert in a glossy Asian youth magazine, a rarity for a small-scale show.

It is worth recalling that although the Internet did exist in 1998 it had not been tried and tested for marketing purposes in theatre. In 1998,

Tamasha, like other companies, had a website, but the general perception was that 'effective' marketing was confined to the traditional approach of using the postal service, telephone, fax or ambassadorial work. However, when Tamasha remounted *Fourteen Songs* in 2002 the use of the web had become ubiquitous and the company used it in parallel to traditional marketing. In 1998, the hard work paid off and the show was almost sold out at all three venues. In a brief audience survey undertaken during that period a few key things emerged. Firstly, 42 per cent, a very large number of the audience, were new to the venues, and overall 34 per cent of the audience said they first heard about the show from a friend or relative. Of the Asians, 64 per cent said they would return to see the play if it was produced again. At that point there was no talk of a revival, but this result was encouraging.

Fourteen Songs ...: from small- to mid-scale

The show went on to win The Theatrical Management Association/Barclays Theatre Award for Best Musical, as well as the BBC Asia Achievement in the Arts Awards in 1999. Accordingly, the company decided to remount the production, and applied for extra resources to do so with more actors and bigger production values for a middle-scale tour. Although the remounts of *East Is East* had amply demonstrated the Company's ability to reach wider audiences, this production represented an even greater challenge for Tamasha to see if its work could attract similar audiences, ranging from 500 to 800 people for any given performance.[17] With the support of an award from Barclays Stage Partners with the Arts Council of England,[18] the show toured to middle-scale performing venues from 14 February until 21 April 2001. It opened in the main house of the Lyric Hammersmith on Valentine's Day. Sir Andrew Lloyd Webber and composer A.R. Rahman came to see the show; it would have given them a good insight into their forthcoming venture. It ran in London until 3 March and travelled to Nottingham Playhouse (6–10 March), Lawrence Batley Huddersfield (13–17 March), The Lowry Manchester (20–24 March), Bristol Old Vic (27–31 March), Yvonne Arnaud Guildford (3–7 April) and Birmingham Rep (10–21 April).

With such a range of venues, the marketing was scaled up and the image for the flyer now consisted of photographs of the cast incorporating some press quotes: 'The chirpiest musical of the year ... Charming and utterly entertaining. Grab a ticket if you can', said the *Evening Standard* (2 December 1998),[19] while the *Sunday Times* intoned: 'All heart and humour, irresistibly charming and shamelessly enjoyable ... A treat' (15 November 1998).[20] Somehow this production struck a chord with Asian and middle-scale theatre audiences, and was able to garner major press coverage. Mainstream newspaper preview and review coverage was targeted: examples include the *Evening Standard*'s 'Hot Tickets Magazine' and 'Going Out' page and local papers in West London such as the *Hounslow Chronicle*. Specialist critics unable to review the show during its earlier incarnation were also targeted.

Other important aspects for marketing were ancillary activities organised around the show. This was usual practice for the company for any productions, but this time the programme of events was on a more ambitious scale, going beyond the normal education work around content of plot and stage-craft, and encapsulating the broader theme of popular Indian cinema. The events included a couple of talks on Bollywood posters at the Lyric and Lowry by Brighton-based artist, Christopher Stevens, who had photographed how these posters were created in India; Bollywood dance workshops by choreographer Anand Kumar at the same venues; and an exhibition of my personal collection of Bollywood posters at the Lawrence Batley. The company was committed to 'inclusivity', and as such organised a 'signed' performance of the show for hearing-impaired audiences by Zane Hema in London, mainly attended by the Deaf Asian Women's Association from Newham, and another at the Birmingham Rep. A Bollywood club night hosted by D.J. Ritu also took place at the Lyric in London. All these events were expensive to undertake, but they were considered important to communicate the message of the inter-relatedness of the provenance of the musical to other aspects of Asian culture and music, and to celebrate the vibrancy of Bollywood.

Behind the scenes a flurry of marketing activity continued alongside advertising on Asian radio, press and mainstream papers. This was our opportunity to explore Internet marketing using email and website alongside conventional techniques. It was a tentative first step, limited to sending out simple HTML information emails about the show and maintaining a regular presence on the company website with images and press quotes. We used email as a fast means of communication with other venues and services alongside the fax; but, at that point, it was only designers and printers who had fast Internet access, and others were limited to 'dial-up' access options. It is worth mentioning that at that time most of our theatre venues did not even have Internet ticketing systems in place. My over-riding concern was how I could maximise the show's presence in the burgeoning Asian media with its niche satellite channels, specialist radio stations and several newspapers and magazines devoted to Bollywood.

The production had been filmed for archival purposes during its 1998 run in London, and a few short segments of the 'Shoe-stealing Song' were transmitted by the BBC when it televised its award event; the song is a visually striking sequence, with its purples and greens, as well as being the English rendition of a popular Bollywood number. TV magazine shows, both Asian and British, wanted to cover the show; specialist Asian radio programmes on the BBC covered the show on tour. For the press night in London, I invited dignitaries such as the Indian High Commissioner, peers, presenters from Asian television and Bollywood distributors, together with actors and press. Our marketing budget allowed us to purchase select advertising on specialist Asian stations such as Sunrise in London, XL in Birmingham and Asian Sound Radio, Manchester. I took an advert in the monthly in-house magazine of the *Cineworld*[21] cinema chains, which could be picked up free by consumers at their sites. The issue for February–March 2001 distributed in Bexleyheath, Wolverhampton and Wakefield featured a full-page A5-size advert for the show in London, Birmingham and Huddersfield respectively. This was a simple way to get the word out to a Bollywood audience and cover a large geographical spread where I was unable to concentrate the marketing. I brokered a relationship between Milapfest, a Liverpool-based specialist Asian promotion and programming outfit and the Lowry, Salford, in order to target a wider geographical spread of audience in the North, one which has subsequently endured. Finally, in London, a great deal of effort was made to ensure flyers were circulated in those postcode areas where the Asian population lived. All these activities may appear a little random; but the strategy was about reaching out to a non-homegeneous Asian audience of varying age ranges, tastes and social backgrounds, competing as we were with other entertainment choices on offer for this group.

The show went on to perform a hat-trick when it was remounted for the third time, but only in London, at the main stage of the Lyric, Hammersmith (19 September–3 November 2001). This time the marketing focus was totally 'Bollywood'. The flyer image was modelled on a West End style, with lots of beautiful photographs interspersed with press quotes. Several co-promotion and sponsorship relationships were established in areas of Bollywood culture, from taking out adverts in *Movie* Magazine, a monthly Bollywood fanzine, to undertaking a media partnership with B4U Movies and B4U Music. These were two related and specialist satellite channels devoted to Bollywood, which ran a thirty-second advert of the show in return for their logo being featured on the publicity. I also promoted the production on an Asian entertainment website portal, Clickwalla. The plan was now to reach out to audiences along the Western corridor up to Oxford and Reading. The company offered Bollywood workshops to schools in this area as well (led by Anand Kumar, who had worked with the company previously), and there was a small exhibition of Bollywood-inspired work by an artist in the Lyric foyer areas. As had been earlier identified through the marketing survey in 1998, the show had great word-of-mouth and repeat value, with many audience members returning to see the show several times.[22] My direct association and involvement with Tamasha continued professionally until 2001, and my subsequent relationship with them has been on a freelance consultancy basis.

The West End: *Bombay Dreams*

Fourteen Songs went on to enjoy a high press and audience profile, something which could not have escaped the West End, and in a way 'test drove' on a smaller scale all the methods used successfully for *Bombay Dreams*. I was hired to work on the production because of a proven track record in generating new audiences, plainly underpinned by my work at Tamasha. The canvas for a West End musical is larger, and the methods were replicated on a bigger scale. It was a risky strategy, as it had not been tried in this terrain, and could have backfired.

It is hard to identify any major differences between the visioning of the marketing of *Fourteen Songs, Two Weddings and a Funeral* and that of *Bombay Dreams*. The former, beginning in 1998 and continuing until 2001—a year before *Bombay Dreams* opened—provided a good blueprint for the latter production. It was visibly popular and grew slowly from an 'ethnic curiosity' to a 'feel-good musical'. As the *Daily Telegraph* said: 'By the end of this beguiling show, I guarantee that you'll have tears in your eyes and a goofy grin on your face' (20 February 2001).[23]

Bombay Dreams is a musical set in Bombay, a story about a poor boy rising from the slums to become a big star in Bollywood and falling in love with a rich girl. The plot is a generic rags-to-riches romance in the mould of much West End musical fare, but its setting, musical language and hybrid British–Asian artistic team might be unfamiliar to a West End audience.

Once Lloyd Webber had announced his intention to produce a musical from Bollywood, he set about putting together that team. The core team consisted of established professionals with whom he had previously and successfully worked, and British Asian and Indian professionals. The actor/writer Meera Syal (of *Goodness Gracious Me* fame, as it was expressed in the publicity) wrote the book,[24] the song lyrics were by Lloyd Webber's long-time collaborator Don Black (*Tell Me on a Sunday*, 1977; *Aspects of Love*, 1989; and *Sunset Boulevard*, 1993), and the choreography was by Anthony Van Laast (*Joseph and the Amazing Technicolour Dreamcoat*, 1968; *Jesus Christ Superstar*, 1970) along with the established Bollywood choreographer Farah Khan (who had worked on hit films including *Monsoon Wedding* (2001), *Kabhi Khushi Kabhie Gham* (2001) and *Dilwale Dulhaniya Le Jayenge* (1995)).

The forty-strong cast was a mixture of dancers and British Asian actors with an experience of working in professional theatre. The two leads were Preeya Kalidas, a graduate from Silvia Young Theatre School (whose celebrated alumni include Emma Bunton and Denise Van Outen), and Raza Jaffrey, who had played Sky in the hit musical *Mama Mia* (March 2001–March 2002) and Rajesh in *Fourteen Songs, Two Weddings and a Funeral* (1998)). Both leading actors were able to sing and dance, essential requirements for a West End musical. Other British Asian performers included Raj Ghatak, Shelley King, Raad Rawi and Ramon Tikaram. Dalip Tahil, an experienced character actor from Bombay, with a background in English-language theatre and more than a hundred Bollywood films under his belt, was cast as the musical's movie mogul, Madan Kumar Kumar. The composer, Kuljit Bhamra, performed live percussion during the show. The production was directed by the now late Steven Pimlott, who directed *Joseph* in 1991 at the London Palladium, with Indhu Rubasingham as the associate director. The show itself was quite 'daring' for a West End commercial producer to undertake, as it was entering uncharted waters. But what drew Lloyd Webber to this idea was his interest in the music of Bollywood composer A.R. Rahman.[25] This then led to a collaboration between artists from Britain and India on several creative fronts, from music production to choreography, casting and directing.

Once this team was assembled, Lloyd Webber set about promoting the composer, A.R. Rahman, a household name in the Asian world, but not so to the western musical public. An initial postcard was printed: on the front was the imagery in bold colours of a couple surrounded by a border of marigolds, and on the back was Lloyd Webber's heartfelt message about the composer.

> I have always been fascinated by Bollywood ... As I listened to more and more soundtracks one name kept coming up—A.R. Rahman. Rahman is a phenomenon in his native India ... He is India's greatest ambassador in the world of music and, I believe, one of the most exciting young composers of our time and a melodic genius.[26]

Rahman has said that is was the director, Shekhar Kapur, who brought him and Lloyd Webber together, as Shekhar Kapur was a key player in the gestation of this project. The composer revealed he got a call one day from the director, saying:

> 'Rahman, would you like to speak to Andrew Lloyd Webber?' I said: 'What?' And the next thing he has given his phone to Andrew who said: 'Oh I love your music and I want to do something with you.' I went and met him and the whole concept of *Bombay Dreams* was formed and the rest is history.[27]

The postcard continues to describe *Bombay Dreams* as 'a uniquely **new** musical in London's West End. I am delighted to be producing *Bombay Dreams* and look forward to sharing its magic, spectacle and romance with you', and was signed with a flourish.[28]

These main points were constantly reiterated in all the ensuing print, although some wording in the text did differ. The key information highlighted was as follows: melodic genius; Bollywood: glamour, epic, spectacle, heart-aching romance; and a new musical voice for the West End produced by Andrew Lloyd Webber.[29]

The London production of *Bombay Dreams* cost £4.5 million to mount.[30] Lloyd Webber was directly involved with the marketing and the show was promoted as the 'big new musical of the year' to core musical theatregoers. His name helped enormously in maintaining confidence, but it was still an unknown venture.

Overall, the production and marketing was a good package that melded the worlds of the Bombay film industry and Western musicals. It had something for everybody—comedy, romance, tragedy, visual spectacle, poppy tunes—and was family friendly and an enjoyable evening out. As reviewers later noted:

> It's as subtle as panto, but then so is Bollywood, which this show joyfully echoes. Great fun, great costumes, and a refreshing change from every other West End show. (*Daily Express*, 20 June 2002)[31]

> A loving lavish celebration of Bollywood ... and it brings a new sound, new choreography, a whole new style and vibrancy with it ... I love it. (*Mail on Sunday*, 23 June 2002)[32]

> Bombay Dreams is really a throwback to Busby Berkley. Life and art, poverty and illusion, romance and kitsch and realism all intersecting. (*Financial Times*, 21 June)[33]

> Raza Jaffrey and Preeya Kalidas as the romantic leads also have charm and sex appeal, but the acting honours are stolen by such familiar British-Asian performers as Raad Rawi as the white-coated Mafia boss and Shelley King as an astringent gossip columnist. (*Guardian*, 20 June, 2002)[34]

Lloyd Webber had actually closed *Starlight Express*, a musical that had been running for nearly eighteen years at the Apollo Victoria, one of the largest venues in the capital with a capacity of 2,208, in order to open *Bombay Dreams*.[35] It can be argued that his marketing team also had the foresight to realise that they would have to mix and match a range of marketing approaches in order to get the word out to the widest possible audience and generate ticket sales. They identified and hired two Asian consultants to work with them on the campaign six months before the production was scheduled to open. They were Hardish Virk and myself; between us we had a varied range of marketing experience in developing new audiences. We met with the RUG and Dewynters core marketing, promotions and press team, and after several planning meetings and conversations the tasks were divided up according to our areas of expertise, knowledge, and location, in order to bring best results to the production. We shared aspects of the marketing. I was based in London and Virk was in Coventry; I focused on strategic planning, networking, press, promotions, celebrity profile, while Virk ran training, audience development, and flyering in areas outside London.

Marketing is all about getting consumers to know about your product, exciting them, making the experience easy and comfortable and ultimately getting them to spend money to buy tickets. There are, however, key differences in marketing shows from the subsidised theatre sector and those from the commercial sector. In the former the imperative is not necessarily a financial one, whereas for the latter people need to buy tickets in order for the product to be sustainable in a competitive marketplace. So the key concepts in targeting British Asian audiences were identified as follows: **Ownership**—Asian audiences must feel the show has specific relevance to them, because of the storyline, music, look, cast, costumes and experience, which might mirror their enjoyment of popular entertainment; **Bollywood**— *Bombay Dreams* must be positioned as 'authentically Bollywood' in terms of the creative personnel, and follow all the conventions familiar in this cinema tradition; **Access**—RUG were aware of the need to rise to the challenge of welcoming large numbers of theatregoers with no previous experience of the West End: key issues included pricing and performance times. The normal price for tickets for a West-End show ranged from £14 to £40, but the top group-sales price would be £25 for ten or more, before the show officially opened; **Education**—the need for theatregoers, staff at the theatre and ticket agents to go through a process of education about dealing with the buying- and booking-patterns of an unfamiliar customer base, alongside gaining knowledge about Bollywood and the cast and the creative team.

It can be argued that all these ways of considering marketing might have been new for a West End musical but were common practice in the subsidised sector. This view is certainly shared by Virk: 'Again, if it's a commercial project or a community project or a subsidised theatre production, the principle's exactly the same.'[36]

Direct West End marketing took the form of direct mail, telesales, email and on-line bookings, and often seemed to be one place removed from the consumers. Audience development could be interpreted as initiatives targeting large group bookings, such as inviting hotel concierges to previews so they could talk to tourists about shows to see, and focusing on group bookers and ticket agents. In the West End, tickets are sold by ticket agents on a commission basis and theatres are rented just for specific productions; some have their own box office, but there are always several outlets for ticket sales.

Flyers and postcards are placed in different outlets, while posters are a different size (commonly folio) from those used in the subsidised sector. Bigger budgets mean bigger campaigns, with a regular presence of the

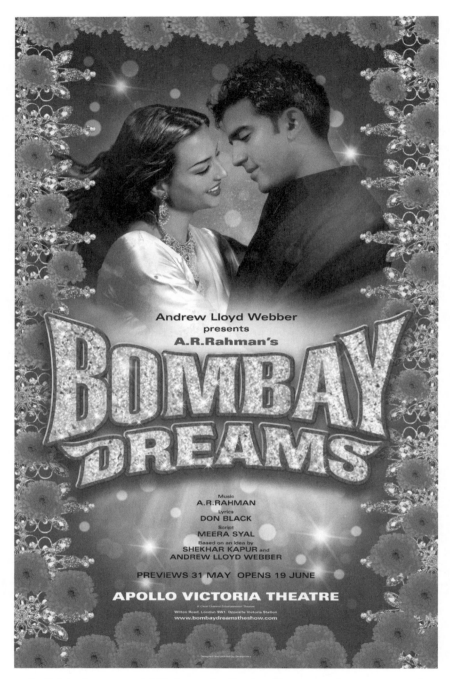

8. Original poster and folio image for Bombay Dreams used to promote and market the show before the preview and the official opening on 19 June 2002. (Courtesy of Really Useful Group)

brand on bus-stops, side-panels of buses, escalator-panels in tubes and big posters in train stations. It is also imperative to sell tickets before the show opens, as start-up costs are very high and it is important to get a sense of revenues generated.

The start-up marketing budget for a musical can vary from £350,000 to £1 million up to the opening, and then a regular weekly spend has to be maintained during the run.

Advertising and competitions in papers and radio feature on a regular basis and everything is tried to see what works. This may involve the daily papers, specialist magazines such as those of big department stores, train magazines, and co-promotion partnerships with restaurants and drink—in this case, Cobra Beer and a curry range in Sainsbury's supermarkets. Classified listings in papers have to be paid for and maintained throughout the run. The tourist trade is targeted, and once the show opens merchandising at the venue includes the cast album, T-shirts and mugs. In addition, there is a souvenir programme, normally an A4 or larger glossy booklet of production photos. This sells for a higher price than the normal programme, which provides only cast and creative team biographies as well as a short history of the theatre with some adverts.[37] The marketing for *Bombay Dreams* sought to mix these approaches for its core and specialist audience.

By contrast, a normal marketing campaign in the subsidised theatre sector would have the following pattern. The theatre venue is the main box office for the purchase of tickets; direct mail letters go to the theatre's regular audience, along with the audience of the company producing the show. The outlets for flyers, postcards and posters through direct distribution fall into a certain circuit.[38] Advertising is something that can rarely be afforded, and is the icing on the cake. Listings information is sent to an agency and may or may not be picked up by papers and magazines such as *Time Out* or the *Guardian Guide*—it usually depends on space, knowledge of the company and the location of the venue. Such productions rarely have any merchandising, except for the cast programme, which occasionally includes the show script.

RUG and Dewynters team used the traditional marketing methods that they would normally do for any of their West End shows and sought ways of engaging with the South Asian community in order to achieve the four goals listed as above, aided by the expertise and knowledge of the two consultants. I would certainly argue that the campaign achieved outcomes in the areas that were identified as key for Asian audiences: **Ownership**—the plot was totally Bollywood with the crucial *masala* (spice mix), from the character of the *hijra*[39] Sweety to the underworld and slums, and music with some familiar film numbers, such as *Shakalaka Baby*[40] and *Chaiya Chaiya*.[41] Some of the Asian cast were familiar to Asian audiences from their own work in theatre and television. Lloyd Webber spoke and wrote about A.R. Rahman with genuine admiration at every opportunity; **Bollywood**—the authenticity

9. Outside section of folded A4 flyer printed to promote the show after the official opening and press night on 19 June 2002, featuring copy and press quotes. (Courtesy of Really Useful Group)

of the Bollywood look was there in the visual imagery of all the publicity produced, from the flyers to posters on underground trains, which featured all the archetypal characters (the hero, the heroine, the villain). It was there in the creative team, and also in the production, from the dance numbers, songs, and even a wet sari sequence! It should be pointed out that the original image of the couple was the only one which ran until after the show officially opened on 19 June 2002,[42] after which new imagery was created which featured quotes from reviews and production shots, making it even more Bollywood than it had previously been; **Access**—ticket agents were briefed; pre-recorded phone messages in different Indian languages were created (later not used); escalator-posters were put in tube stations in areas of high Asian concentration; special Sunday shows were created—an expensive venture for the West End, owing to staff costs, but the ideal evening for Asian audiences to dress up and go out; the pricing structure for group bookings was an 'escalator' style (the earlier you book, the cheaper it is), but without compromising the brand; and a welcoming front of house environment was created at the venue; and **Education**—training was offered to ticket agents and theatre staff regarding Asian customers, booking patterns and knowledge of the product. The company even tried to recruit Asian ushers, but this proved unsuccessful because of a lack of

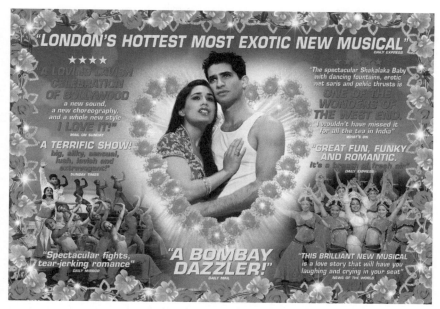

10. Inside section of the A4 flyer, featuring production images and press quotes, with central image of stars Preeya and Kalidas and Raza Jaffrey. (Courtesy of Really Useful Group)

candidates. Direct mail letters were written to key South Asian people including community leaders, high-profile politicians and peers, celebrities, glitterati and literati, who were invited to a launch held twelve weeks prior to opening at The Cinnamon Club. Guests included people from the Indian High Commission and Tourist Board, British Film Institute and Bollywood film companies and individuals such as Mr J. Sachar of *Asian Who's Who*, Nisha Paul from Caparo group and journalists Yasmin Alibhai-Brown and Zee News reporter Ashish Joshi (now at Sky).

Sponsorship and tie-in opportunities with ethnic brands and retailers were pursued with vigour, since everyone wanted a slice of this celebrated brand. Andrew Lloyd Webber was also lucky in that he was assisted by external events. The year 2002 seemed to be the zeitgeist for Bollywood in the UK: another Rahman-composed film, *Lagaan*, was short-listed for the Oscar in the Best Foreign Language film category; Selfridges, a big department store in Oxford Street, was running a month-long Bollywood Season;[43] the Victoria and Albert Museum (London) had a poster exhibition on Bollywood posters; and the British Film Institute (London) ran a film season entitled ImagineAsia.[44]

Another key adjunct of marketing was the press campaign, which was run like a military operation. In the South Asian context its function was to build and continue to promote *Bombay Dreams* through engaging the community, getting press coverage and continually having a presence at events (e.g. *Eastern Eye* Business awards; EMMA Awards) attended by Andrew and Madeleine Lloyd Webber, Shekhar Kapur, Rahman and key cast members. A video was made of the English version of *Shakalaka Baby* from the show, which was played in record shops. Many preview events were arranged, which were focused on including the Asian constituency. Several media nights were held before the official opening (19 June 2002), and invitations were sent to several key Asian businesses and press and community organisations who would enjoy the show and spread good 'word of mouth'; a special matinee for young children took place, which included children of Asian celebrities; a special Charity preview for the Millennium Memorial Gates Trust was hosted by businesswoman and fundraiser Surina Narula and attended by the Asian rich.[45] The press night on 19 June 2002 was attended by many Bollywood celebrities, including star Shah Rukh Khan and director Ashutosh Gowariker.[46] People could not get enough of this and the brand continued to exude magic well after the show officially opened.

For the purposes of the study of marketing strategies that target Asian audiences, questions remain: how successful was *Bombay Dreams*, and how might this success be measured? I would argue that the show was successful on many levels. Although the reviews were mixed, the production ran for just over two years until 16 June 2004. It also opened in New York and ran for 284 performances from 29 April 2004 to 1 January 2005. The marketing was successful in that it brought in a new and specifically Asian audience to the West End, as well as a repeat audience; anecdotal evidence suggests that many people saw it as many as four times. Although this article has talked in detail about the specialist approaches for Asian audiences, the show also attracted the core West End musical audience as well as American tourists.

Conclusion

In conclusion, in this essay I have analysed the marketing methods employed to target new audiences for two productions in the subsidised and commercial sectors. I have identified that both *Fourteen Songs* and *Bombay Dreams* employed what would have been considered daring or visionary marketing methods, veering as they did from the normal blueprint for such productions. Both productions proved that there is a marketing strategy that can work when it is properly planned and carried out. However, it is easier to promote a populist product, such as a stage show that has its antecedents in popular Bombay cinema, than a 'niche' show. Nonetheless, that is not impossible, as my own later work with the Royal Shakespeare Company's production of *Midnight's Children* at the Barbican, London, from 18 January to 23 February 2003, demonstrated.

Bombay Dreams established that there was a marketing strategy that could work to attract Asian audiences, and this was noticed by the West End theatre sector, as Richard Pulford, Chief Executive of SOLT/TMA commented:

> They had spent some time trying to work out, obviously with some success, how to reach a market that they hadn't previously, specifically addressed. And if you mean did it succeed in attracting a new audience to the West End theatre for the first time, I should think the answer to that is certainly 'Yes'.[47]

However, the West End failed to capitalise on this endeavour. In the latest West End Theatre Audience Report published in September 2004, only 2 per cent of the population who attended West End shows cited themselves as 'Asian' or 'Asian British', whilst 92 per cent of the population described themselves as 'White'.[48]

This could be considered to be typical, because most commercial producers would only be concerned with targeting an audience that they consider to be the core audience for their production, and not waste time or resources undertaking 'audience development' for which they get no subsidy. Conversely, 'The Tamasha Marketing Method', if I can term it so, was noticed and has been replicated by other individual theatre companies, as well as venues in the subsidised sector, as it encouraged them to target a new audience and paved the way for many mainstream initiatives in this field.[49]

10

Mixing with the Mainstream

Transgressing the Identity of Place

Jerri Daboo

There has been an increasing number of Asian-led productions over the past ten years which have taken place within what are considered to be 'mainstream' theatre venues, thus raising questions about what happens when theatre usually considered to be at the 'margins' is filtered into the 'centre', and how this centre is both challenged and revealed in the process. As Tim Cresswell explains, marginal 'elements and events in society are interesting in themselves, but they are more interesting when we examine the role they play in defining the "normal", the classical, the dominant. The centre could not exist without the margin.'[1] The meeting, or mixing, of margin and centre, of British Asian[2] and mainstream theatre, will be examined in this essay through notions of place/space in relation to identity and cultural production. For this research I have studied a range of productions, including the Birmingham Rep and National Theatre's co-production of *The Ramayana* (2000–2001); Andrew Lloyd Webber's production of *Bombay Dreams* at the Victoria Apollo (2002); the National Theatre's 2007 season featuring *Rafta, Rafta …* and *The Man of Mode*; *The Ramayana* adapted and directed by David Farr at the Lyric Hammersmith (2007); and Tim Supple's production of *A Midsummer Night's Dream* (2006–2008). However, for this essay, the main examination is of the relationship of these productions to the venue, the place/space in which they are performed, as well as the audience that comes to see them. This leads to questions of how this relationship defines, transgresses and/ or reinforces the identity of the place, the play and those who journey to the place to see the play. In relation to this, I will also be discussing the audience development work of Hardish Virk within both the venues and with local communities.

In order to approach this subject, I draw on theories from cultural geography which highlight the inherent inter-relationship between space/

location, identity and culture. I suggest that the notion of 'mainstream' itself in this context may be considered within these terms. 'Mainstream' theatre is usually connected to spaces—that is, to specific venues or places, such as those within the West End or Broadway—which are labelled as mainstream venues. Therefore, mainstream theatre productions can be considered to be what happens within these particular spaces (on their 'main' stages, at least). So mainstream theatre is both the physical space, and what happens within that space. Christopher Innes states that mainstream productions 'are usually considered to represent the highest level of commercial theatre in the English speaking world',[3] referring specifically to those within the West End. However, the National Theatre and the Victoria Apollo are also seen as effectively part of this mainstream, even though they are not physically within the boundaries of the geographical West End. The West End thus becomes an imagined and ideological as well as a territorial space, which contains within it the idea of the epitome of 'mainstream' theatre. Venues in the regions, such as the Birmingham Rep, are also usually labelled as 'mainstream' even if they simultaneously have a marginalised identity in relation to the centre-space of *the* mainstream of London and the West End. This idea of place, both imagined and physically real, contains within it the ideology and practice of what is considered to be 'normal' or 'acceptable behaviour' within that space according to the reinforcement of its identity. As Kay Anderson states, '[c]ultural norms are located in the practices of their institutionalisation'.[4] These 'norms' are not necessarily fixed, but can be challenged and/or redefined through the negotiation and practice of power relations from within and without.

I suggest that in this way 'mainstream' theatre, and what happens when 'British Asian' theatre is mixed with it, may be considered through three aspects: space/location, identity and aesthetics. Space/location refers to a specific site or place, either an actual theatre building or an imagined geographical site such as the West End. The sense of identity operates on multiple levels. There is the identity of the building as a mainstream theatre house. Those who work within it also have a sense of personal identity relating to this. Playwrights and actors can identify themselves as being 'mainstream' because they have worked in those venues. Likewise, a play or production can also be labelled as 'mainstream' owing to the location of its performance. There is also the identity of the audience that comes to see a 'mainstream' production in those spaces. In terms of aesthetics, if what is performed in these spaces is considered to be the epitome of mainstream theatre because these are mainstream spaces, then this will define what the form and aesthetics of mainstream theatre are. The effects will then be felt in demands for those aesthetics and forms to be considered as the 'norm', and to be perpetuated as such. In this way, the mainstream operates as a structure of power for those involved in making theatre. It offers the possibility of high visibility and accessibility to performances and to those playwrights, actors, directors and designers involved in them, as well as a greater level of security in terms of finance and potential future work. It also provides a higher likelihood of being given a review within a national newspaper, therefore, again, gaining greater visibility. However, the security of the building and institution is often financially dependent on public subsidy and box-office success, and the demands of both these can dictate what is produced on the stages in order to fill the houses. What is seen on mainstream stages has to be considered 'worthy' of investment, so the institutional directors hold considerable power over how this is defined in relation to centre and margin.

As stated previously, the sense of place and identity is not fixed in an ahistorical time, but is rather in shift, or in process. This is also reflected by the identities of those within these specific places: they are in process and change, in relationship to the space and time that they are living within. This is not only a personal but also a community identity, with shifts and changes created through migration from both within and outside the nation. In discussing the relationship between space, time and identity, geographer Claire Dwyer explains that: 'I theorise identities as contextual and relational positionings ... which are articulated across different spaces and at particular moments.'[5] For Radcliffe, 'these geographies of identity provide positionalities. In theoretical terms, such a relationship between community, place and identity implies that previous discussions of national identity have not sufficiently taken on board the multiple geographies in and through which subjects articulate their communities and places.'[6] When looking at Asian theatre within the mainstream, these ideas of geography become very important in terms of understanding how and by whom a space is defined, and how this relates to a sense of personal and communal identity. Mainstream theatre spaces are potentially seen as 'white places', where the dominant ideology of what is perceived to be the 'highest level of commercial theatre', to repeat Innes, is at the centre, and the voices from the margins are not heard, unless invited into the space/place of the mainstream. When this happens, it can create what Cresswell describes as a 'transgression'[7] of the space, an interruption to the established norm, a 'heretical geography' which 'causes a questioning of what was previously considered "natural", "assumed", and "taken for granted".'[8]

The mixing with the mainstream questions the nature not only of the centre but also of the margin, and definitions and identities of what 'British Asian' theatre is. Black theatre practitioner Felix Cross states in relation to Black theatre: 'In my twenty years of being in theatre ... I don't know what Black theatre means. ... Is it when Black actors get on stage? Is it when a Black writer writes a play? Is it when a company's owned by Black people? Is it when it's only a certain subject matter? Is it when it comes from a certain sensibility? Is there a style? Is there a different kind of language? Is there a different play structure? I don't know. I know Black music, I can understand that one, probably even do Black dance. You can tell me about that, but I'm not sure that I can understand this one.'[9] These same questions can be applied to the notion of British Asian theatre, particularly when it is performed in 'mainstream' spaces. For playwright Tanika Gupta, who has questioned her own identity of being labelled as a British Asian writer, 'I don't know what [British Asian theatre] really … means. I mean *Rafta, Rafta* … was on at the National Theatre, directed by Nicholas Hytner—is that British Asian theatre? If you have a story that is Asian, does that make it Asian or does that make it theatre?'[10] This is even more complicated by the fact that *Rafta, Rafta* … is Ayub Khan-Din's adaptation of a play by an English man about an English family. Does Khan-Din's transferring this to an Asian family make this into a British Asian play, particularly when that play is performed within the mainstream institution of the National Theatre, directed by its Artistic Director? Does the nature of mixing with the mainstream contribute to, or diminish, a sense of how questions concerning British Asian identity are played out on stage?

Mainstream theatre spaces can be considered to be what cultural geographer Kay Anderson defines as 'cultural domains'. These domains are responsible for creating and maintaining the hegemonic (or mainstream) narrative and ideology which is defined through its choice of productions. She states, 'Central to these concerns is the role that institutions (as structured forms of agency) potentially play in processes of cultural construction. … Just as people frame their actions in terms of shared definitions of situations, so do organisations and institutions operate as cultural domains.'[11] To examine ways in which mainstream theatres mix their ideology with the British Asian voices at the margin, I will focus on the audience development work undertaken by Hardish Virk to transform both the physicality of the spaces and the demographic of those who visit them, reflecting the interrelationship between the space, its identity and the aesthetics of the building and what is performed within it.

Virk has worked on audience development for a large number of productions, including those considered to be within the realms of British Asian theatre and performed in mainstream theatre spaces. His first production in this respect was the Birmingham Rep/National Theatre co-production of *The Ramayana*, which received a contribution from the Arts Council's New Audiences Programme, an initiative which ran from 1998 to 2003, investing £20 million into encouraging new audiences and social inclusion.[12] This version of the well-known Hindu epic was written by Peter Oswald and directed by Indu Rubasingham, who wanted to create a multi-cultural production that would appeal to a culturally diverse audience. Despite the cultural diversity of the population of Birmingham, the Rep theatre was perceived to be what Hardial Rai calls a 'white space'.[13] Virk stated that, historically, the range of Asian communities within

Birmingham had been aware of the existence of the Rep only when walking past it, and that they 'had no sense of ownership of the space, or the venue, or where it was located'.[14] The building itself, as the home of mainstream theatre, was in a 'negative',[15] or invisible, space to the community. It was an object that they walked past and not part of their sense of personal or communal identity in terms of the building, what happened within the building and the types of theatre that it produced. The challenge for Virk was to change these communities' perception of the theatre building and its productions by forging links and a sense of trust between the theatre and the communities. He also needed to alter the actual physical space of the inside of the theatre building itself, creating a shift in the practice of the cultural domain, to allow the Asian audience to have what he calls an 'ownership of the production'[16] as well as the space of the theatre.

Over an eight-month period, Virk worked closely with members of the local community and set up an Ambassador scheme of twenty-six local people who represented 'different sections of the Asian community'[17] so that it was not sold as a faith production, since Rubasingham wanted the play to reach beyond the Hindu community. The role of the Ambassadors was to advise on the publicity material and assist in its distribution; to promote the production to their family and local community; and to work in different departments of the institution of the Rep itself, including marketing, education, programming and front-of-house. Virk conducted training sessions with front-of-house and box-office staff to ensure that they were able to deal with a South Asian audience who might be unfamiliar with the booking process. The box office, often being the first entrance or gateway into a mainstream theatre-house, has great importance in the perception of that space by those attempting to cross the physical and ideological boundaries into it. Femi Elufowoju Jnr, Artistic Director of Tiata Fahodzi, demonstrated in the Eclipse Report that the behaviour and assumptions of box-office staff about the cultural 'norms' of the institution of the theatre space can reinforce the feeling of alienation for non-white audiences. He mentions the instance of his father, who

> turned up in his traditional robes at the Royal National Theatre to purchase day seats for *My Fair Lady*, and he was told by a front-of-house person that the cleaner's vacancy had just been filled two hours earlier. ... [I]t is not unaccustomed these days [for a non-white person] to turn up at the theatre, where maybe say a Brechtian or Alan Ayckbourn play is being performed, and what you get at the box office is a gob-smacked or better still incredulous gaze from the often non-Black or Asian box-office attendant, as if you've turned up at the wrong theatre. Unfortunately this example arguably sums up the general myopic consensus, which probably affects every single stratum within the theatre infrastructure.[18]

To repeat Kay Anderson, '[c]ultural norms are located in the practices of their institutionalisation',[19] and it is these practised 'norms' which Virk was seeking to transgress. In addition to working with the staff and infrastructure, he also transformed the space of the building itself to assist in the sense of ownership, for, as Cochrane points out, the 'challenge for so-called "white spaces" is to make non-white audiences feel comfortable'.[20] Virk felt that the foyer was 'too clinical',[21] and so dimmed the lights, had Indian music playing throughout the run, and also included a new bar menu with South Asian food and beer to complement the 'normal' menu. This created a transgression, or 'heretical geography', to use Cresswell's term, of the cultural domain of the Rep, transforming the space from a negative or invisible building into one of local identity and belonging for the Asian communities, at least for the duration of that production. All of Virk's development work allowed space for new ways of approaching and understanding the impact and interpretation that a performance and the promotion surrounding it can have for a different audience. As an example, the poster for the production contained a cartoon image of Rama firing his bow, which is a connection to the picture-book stories of the *Ramayana* found in India, which have also migrated to the UK along with the community. This identification of an image from 'home' had a strong effect: Virk spoke of a shop-owner who started crying when he saw it. In this sense, 'home' is also both a real and imagined space for a migrant community. For Salman Rushdie, 'our physical alienation from India almost inevitably means that we will not be capable of reclaiming precisely the thing that was lost; we will, in short, create fictions, not actual cities or villages, but invisible ones, imaginary homelands, Indias of the mind.'[22] Appadurai also states that 'the homeland is partly invented, existing only in the imagination of the deterritorialised groups'.[23] The story of the *Ramayana* itself, presented on the mainstream stage, became a metaphor for the act of migration for those who have experienced it. Dominic Rai, Artistic Director of Man Mela, speaks of his response to seeing the story in a new way: 'The bridge-making scene transformed by milk crates—representing the bridge to Lanka—I found myself thinking how pertinent this story is—pregnant with the mythology of *Pardes* (away from home), *Desh nikala* (banishment from the homeland), and *Hijrit* (migration)'.[24] Both the space and the story told in the performance were transformed and transgressed by stepping outside the 'norm' and allowing for new readings and meanings to be created. The metaphor of migration was present not only within the story but also in a community taking steps into a theatrical space which did not appear available to them before. In this way, the homeland of the hegemonic mainstream became inclusive of those that the mainstream usually excludes, both in terms of the audiences and of the types of productions that it puts on, which are clearly related. Anderson states:

The discourses that [these mainstream] organisations articulate to interpret themselves to each other and the world at large can clearly uphold unequal relations between people and places. Powerful institutions (including nations) can work to ensure that what are partial, culturally-bound interpretations of reality are accepted as 'natural' and 'correct' by the public at large.[25]

This idea of the interpretation of reality seen through a geographical territory and the forms and aesthetics of cultural productions is particularly apparent in the real and imagined space of London's West End, which, as stated, includes theatres such as the Victoria Apollo and the National Theatre. After its run at the Birmingham Rep, *The Ramayana* transferred to the Olivier stage at the National, with Virk doing direct marketing and outreach work similar to that which he had undertaken in Birmingham. This included working with communities within the proximity of the South Bank which have a high proportion of Asians, including Tower Hamlets, Southwark and Camberwell, and then branching out to Wembley and Southall. Certainly these communities would not consider the National to be in their 'local' space or have a sense of ownership of it. This is made clear by the name: it is not local, or even London, but the 'National' theatre, and, even beyond that, the 'Royal National Theatre', and so becomes the self-labelled representation and upholder of the nation-state and British tradition and history. In this way the place/location of the building and what takes place within it become the identification with and definition of what theatre is at a national level, both to those within and outside the nation.

Virk highlights the difficulty of sustaining and monitoring audience development in mainstream spaces, seen particularly in the case of the National Theatre. After the production of *The Ramayana* there was no sustained monitoring of the evolution of new audiences. He had been paid by the Arts Council to do the initial work, but there was no meaningful continuity of this approach. It was only in 2007 that he was called back to the National to promote their production of Khan-Din's *Rafta, Rafta ....* In the meantime, there had been other productions with an Asian focus on mainstream stages which had been aimed at attracting the 'brown pound', most notably *Bombay Dreams*, which Virk also worked on promoting, in part because of the success of *The Ramayana* in playing to almost full houses at the National. Despite the clear economic incitement to develop a new audience, Andrew Lloyd Webber was also impressed by the effects that Virk's training of his staff to welcome Asian audiences had on his Really Useful Group, and was 'amazed at the real shift in thinking brought into his organisation'[26] as a result. In the 'Indian summer' of 2002, the Bollywood theme and aesthetics of the production drew an unexpectedly large proportion of Asians into a mainstream West End theatre and, although it was not a critical success, the production raised interest in the economic potential of this new audience.[27] According to Virk, Lloyd Webber and Cameron Mackintosh were called into the Mayor of London's office to discuss how to sustain this audience. They did not appear to know the answer to this question, and since this was not an Arts Council project Virk was not expected to do an evaluation report for the production.

Rafta, Rafta ... was part of the 2007 season at the National which also included a production of Man of Mode, George Etherege's 1676 comedy with an Asian and white British cast, and some of the Asian members from both casts played in other performances throughout the season. Both these productions were directed by Nicholas Hytner, the Artistic Director of the National. Khan-Din adapted Rafta, Rafta ... from Bill Naughton's 1963 play All in Good Time, about a newly married couple who are forced to live with the husband's father. Khan-Din transferred this to an Asian couple in present-day Bolton. Khan-Din became well-known for his play East Is East, first produced by Tamasha in 1995, which was later made into a successful film. It is worth questioning whether the choice of Khan-Din, out of all contemporary British Asian playwrights, to place on the Lyttleton stage may be due to his name being familiar amongst non-Asian, 'mainstream' audiences who may have seen or heard of East is East. But whereas that play had a freshness and originality, Rafta, Rafta ... is a somewhat tired, formulaic play that explores the issues of a northern Asian family in a dated and superficial manner. As stated by Tanika Gupta earlier, it is questionable whether this play, an adaptation from issues faced by a white English family in the early 1960s, is capable of addressing questions of contemporary British Asian identity and culture in a meaningful way, even while drawing that community into a mainstream theatre space. Virk, in his promotion of the production to that community, stated that the main attraction for Asians was not Khan-Din, or even Meera Syal, who was acting in the play, but to whom Virk does not feel that British Asians generally relate; the attraction was rather that the main character of the father, Eeshwar Dutt, was played by the famous Indian actor, Harish Patel. Although Patel is an experienced and accomplished stage actor, it is his appearance in many Bollywood films that makes him a significant and recognisable figure for many British Asians. The Bollywood theme is reflected in the National's programme for the production, which included an essay by Rachel Dwyer entitled 'Bollywood Cinema and the UK', in which it is stated that 'British Asian directors such as Gurinder Chadha ... have made films that have been successful with mainstream audiences in the UK and abroad.'[28] This creates a clear correlation between Bollywood and the mainstream, and this being so explicitly indicated in the programme demonstrates that the mixing of British Asian theatre with the mainstream means Bollywood, as this is the economically driven force by which a 'mainstream' audience will be created for an 'Asian' production.

The production itself offered a somewhat safe and conventional approach

11. Scene from *Rafta, Rafta* ... at the National Theatre.
From left to right: Harish Patel (Eeshwar Dutt), Meera Syal (Lopa Dutt),
Rudi Dharmalingam (Jai Dutt), Simon Nagra (Jivaj Bhatt), Shaheen Khan
(Lata Patel), Kriss Dosanjh (Laxman Patel), Natalie Grady (Molly Bhatt),
Arsher Ali (Etash Tailor).
(Photograph: Catherine Ashmore)

to a play which, in Naughton's original version, tackles difficult subjects in
a far darker way than Hytner chose to do with Khan-Din's adaptation. The
set, designed by Tim Hatley, was a two-storey construction showing rooms
in the Dutts' house. Combined with the proscenium arch of the Lyttleton,
it results in a fairly flat, two-dimensional effect, perhaps intended to appear
familiar to those who are more used to watching television and film rather
than theatre. This took away from the potential power of theatre as a
medium to work with metaphor and physical image and presence, offering
instead a 'flat screen', straight telling of the story. There were many pointers
in the setting toward the types of furnishings and decorations that could be
perceived as being 'typical' of a British Asian family, such as Indian cloths
and furniture, a shrine with surrounding lights and Bollywood posters in
the bedroom. However, these elements felt 'tacked on' to the set in order
to create a stereotypical image of what an Asian house may look like, and
often they were not used in a meaningful way. The naturalistic look of the
set was not always matched by the style of acting and the portrayal of the
characters. This was seen particularly in the contrast between the acting of
Harish Patel and that of the rest of the cast. It is no criticism of Patel, who

is a fine actor, that his approach to speaking the text and his physicalisation were quite different in style to those of the other actors. His character, who was portrayed as a stereotypical Indian father, emphasised Patel's own Bollywood background, with Eeshwar Dutt's singing and dancing, particularly of Bhangra.

The issue in casting an actor from India in a British production was noted in Tara Art's version of *Cyrano*, performed in the National Theatre in 1995, which placed the well-known Indian actor Naseeruddin Shah in the main role. Difficulties arose with Shah's unfamiliarity with the devising process that was fundamental to the production and with a style of acting that contrasted strongly with that of the rest of the cast. Anuradha Kapur, Director of the National School of Drama in Delhi, points to some of the differences in acting styles in India compared to the UK. She feels that, partly as a result of the influence of traditional performance forms (students at the School will spend two months in a region of India learning such a form), there tends to be more of an emphasis on the training of and expression through the body, rather than the voice. Additionally, there is a particular focus on melodrama when performing realism, which produces a style of acting, particularly through the body, that is unfamiliar in the west. The influence of Bollywood on acting results in what Kapur describes as an 'exhaustion' in acting vocabulary: if Bollywood becomes the dominant aesthetic in acting, 'a whole range of the psychological gets glossed in a certain way'.[29] Bringing over an actor from India who is well-known to Asian audiences will draw more people to the production, but this difference in acting styles can lead to confusion in the overall aesthetics of the play. *Rafta, Rafta ...* certainly did not offer a challenge to portrayals of British Asian characters that tend to be seen in the mainstream of theatre and the mass media. Yet it is this production that became representative of what the hegemonic institution chooses to portray as British Asian theatre, because it occurs in the high visibility of the mainstream.

I suggested earlier that the very label 'Royal National Theatre' makes a statement that what happens within the cultural domain of the building is the epitome and definition of British theatre, to both those within the nation and outside it. This was highlighted by renowned Indian playwright Girish Karnad in comments he made at the conference 'British Asian Theatre: From Past to Present' at the University of Exeter, 10–13 April 2008. He stated that in India all he had heard about recently in terms of Asians on the British stage was adaptations such as *Rafta, Rafta ...* and *Man of Mode*, and also adaptations from Hindi films, rather than original work. In relation to *Rafta, Rafta ...*, he asked: 'A second-rate English play being adapted by the National Theatre. What's it supposed to do?'[30] In this, he was pointing out that the themes present in the play are not actually addressing issues of contemporary British Asian life, but rather defining what these issues are through mainstream eyes. This point of view was confirmed in comments made by the theatre critic Michael Billington, who stated of the play that 'the real pleasure lies in seeing Khan-Din use a northern folk comedy to explore the recognisable fissures in Asian family life',[31] again defining and reinforcing, as a white man, that the play presents the essence of the current issues in the Asian community. Karnad suggests that perhaps situations such as a dominating father are now being framed as being predominantly an 'Asian' issue because they are not seen as acceptable within white British society; so they are not a comment on Asian but rather on white British life. He also criticised the emphasis on Bollywood as an aesthetic for Asian theatre, particularly for the resultant perception that this is the sum total that Asian theatre can be about within the mainstream. As he says: 'It defines the nation.'[32]

This is the inherent problem with the cultural domain of the mainstream being the voice, setting the 'norm' which 'defines the nation', and thereby silencing the voices from the margins, even whilst 'mixing' with them and drawing in the margins to the centre as an audience. Karnad asked the participants at the conference if it is true that adaptations of white British plays are the only form of contemporary British Asian theatre. He received a rousing 'no' from those present, including theatre practitioners who have worked for decades producing work in companies and communities that directly and meaningfully address the issues of British Asians. However, these are not the theatre works and voices that are necessarily being heard beyond their localities, and certainly not by Karnad in India. Kristine Landon-Smith, director of Tamasha, gives the following picture when discussing the effectiveness of the publicity for *Rafta, Rafta ...* in attracting Asian audiences into the mainstream:

> How quickly the theatre marketeers have realised the value of the 'brown pound'! But the industry built around marketing to ethnic minority audiences is booming because companies like Tamasha, Nitro, Talawa and Kali—all run by multicultural practitioners 365 days of the year—provide a product in the national arena for marginalised groups of people. This is what gets them into theatres in the first place. It's important to remember that these companies, through their artistic output, have given the suggestion to the mainstream venues that the brown pound is out there to be tapped for theatre revenue.[33]

Landon-Smith is suggesting that there is an influence from the margins to the mainstream centre; but what is seen in the National Theatre when this occurs is a diluting, or filtering, of the marginal voice to accommodate a dominant vision.

The question of sustainability, of a true transformation or transgression of a mainstream space as a cultural domain, must also involve the power structures within it. Maddy Costa has questioned Nicholas Hytner's genuine commitment to diversity in the mainstream fabric of the National:

> And then there is Hytner's own manifesto, as delivered at the beginning of last year: the National should be 'forward-looking ... a theatre that will discover new things to say, and new ways of saying them'. It should be home to 'a diverse audience ... that will support adventure, innovation'. Most of all, it should 'give as many people as possible a good time'. ... [However] Philip Hedley, artistic director at Theatre Royal Stratford East, asks why black directors are still missing from the National; Mike Bradwell queries the small number of women writers and directors in its roster. Certainly, of the 16 associates Hytner last year invited to be part of his creative thinktank, only five are women and only one (the actor Adrian Lester) is black. ... 'I wouldn't want us to be culturally homogeneous, but I don't want to be ticking boxes either,' Hytner responds.[34]

As a representative of the national mainstream, the real narrative is revealed through what is unspoken. Why are there no Asian associates? It is also worth noting that the proportion of Asian actors in the 2007 season at the National season has dropped considerably during 2008: there is a feeling that the 'Indian theme has been done'. There is also a question of directors. Of the six mainstream productions I listed at the beginning, five were directed by white men. Deirdre Osborne points out a similar situation in contemporary black British theatre, in relation to black plays in the mainstream during 2003–4:

> of the eleven plays staged during this time, nine were directed by white directors, primarily male. While the staging of plays by Black British dramatists in mainstream London theatres might reveal an increasingly contested sense of the 'mainstream' and revisions of what has been perceived as the traditional theatre market, traditional theatrical hegemonies remain evident. White men continue to remain at the helm.[35]

These issues of theatrical hegemonies and the mainstream are obviously not limited to race, but can also be applied to class, gender and sexual orientation.

It is important to note that there have been attempts to make stepping from the margins into the mainstream centre by Asian-led productions and companies more meaningful, although what these tend to highlight are the problems with sustainability. During the time of Richard Eyre's directorship of the National Theatre Tara Arts was invited to work in collaboration with the National, and produced several works, including

Tartuffe (1990), *The Little Clay Cart* (1991), and *Cyrano* (1995). Although these productions, apart from *Cyrano*, were successful, this collaboration has not been sustained in the years since, and the glimpses of visibility that they afforded the company are now part of a brief history rather than a continuous transformation and establishment within the mainstream space. As Verma says, 'When it comes to Asian or Black Arts, there is no History, only "moments of significance". So we lurch from moment to moment of visibility, separated by a void of invisibility.'[36] The sporadic nature of these initiatives may be due to changes in funding policies; specific individuals and institutions may develop a particular focus for a programme season by season; or there may be changes in culture and fashion, as was seen in *Bombay Dreams*, leading to the financial incentive for finding a new audience.

There have also been 'moments' of support for the development of new Asian playwrights, though again this has not been sustained, and nor has it led to a significant visibility of Asian writers on mainstream stages producing high-class work. The Birmingham Rep has had 'moments' of staging new productions by Asians, such as the collaboration with Tamasha which began in 1994 and included *A Shaft of Sunlight* (1994), *A Yearning* (1995), *East Is East* (1996), *Fourteen Songs, Two Weddings and a Funeral* (1998), which transferred to the main stage after a successful run in London, and *Balti Kings* (1999). Cochrane points out that a range of South and East Asian plays was put on as part of the Door season at the Birmingham Rep in 2004–5, but it is worth questioning why they were produced in the studio space, rather than in the greater visibility of the main stage. Cochrane notes that, during the same season, plays by two Black playwrights, Roy Hart and Kwame Kwei-Armah, were staged in the main house,[37] whereas the Asian plays, with the exception noted below, were confined to the Door. Both Hart and Kwei-Armah have received great support and cultivation from the National Theatre in developing their writing, facilities which have not been extended to an Asian playwright to the same degree.

A further issue is raised by the reception of the one Asian play which was shown in the main house of the Birmingham Rep in 2004: Gurpeet Kaur Bhatti's *Behzti*. The response of some members of the Sikh communities to the play highlighted an ongoing concern connected to the placing of Asian-led plays within the mainstream. The concern is that some sections of Asian audiences and communities have been critical of portrayals of Asian characters on stage when they do not conform to certain conventions and representations which are seen to be acceptable within those communities. Actress Shelley King noted that in her first high-profile role as an Asian nurse in the BBC television series *Angels*, which began screening in 1975, there was an outcry from many Asian communities about her portrayal of an Asian character who encountered such issues as alcoholism and four abortions, stating that she was showing Asians 'in a bad light'.[38]

There were undoubtedly some notable film and television productions during the 1980s which overturned the usual stereotypes of Asian characters, such as Hanif Kureishi's *My Beautiful Laundrette* (1986) and Farrukh Dhondy's *King of the Ghetto* (1986). But King maintains that mainstream theatre has now reverted to the safety of non-controversial subject matter and familiar characterisations of Asians in order to attract an Asian audience with plays that will avoid a negative response from any members of the Asian communities and fill the auditorium. Thus the voices of some of the audiences and communities could be seen to create their own hegemonies of how Asians are portrayed on stage and the themes and nature of the plays which are seen. Particularly after *Behzti*, a mainstream theatre institution may be even less willing to stage a production that might challenge the stereotypes for fear of a controversy which would drive away that audience. So shows such as *Rafta, Rafta* ... stay on the side of safety and entertainment, rather than attempting to push the boundaries of both writing and production. The popularity of Bollywood, mentioned earlier as being the dominant aesthetic used to represent British Asians, may also lead to certain genres and themes of plays being seen as more popular, and thus able to attract greater funding and audience numbers. This can result in an overabundance of forms such as musicals, or plays with songs, as well as themes involving the family, arranged marriage or a problematic love affair resolved with a happy ending. Tamasha has done much to promote new writing by Asians, yet some of their productions, such as *Fourteen Songs, Two Weddings and a Funeral* (1998/2001), reflect this more popular appeal in genre and theme. Their own website acknowledges the bringing together of the ingredients to create a production that draws on these popular elements, which can both attract funding and ensure greater audience numbers rather than necessarily push out the boundaries. The play is described as '(f)eaturing all the classic ingredients—romance, comedy, melodrama, song and dance—*Fourteen Songs, Two Weddings and A Funeral* is an enchanting love story lavishly told in true Bollywood style'.[39] As Anuradha Kapur states about the tendency towards the dominance of Bollywood in British Asian theatre, '[i]f it has a Bollywood twist, it's fine. If it's doesn't have a Bollywood twist, it's not Indian.'[40]

However, there is still a potential for the transgression, for the 'heretical geography' of an increasing Asian audience, created in part through the successful work of developers such as Virk, to have an effect in the cultural domain of the white mainstream. To repeat Cresswell, 'transgression is important because it breaks from "normality" and causes a questioning of what was previously considered "natural", "assumed", and "taken for granted".'[41] A break from the 'norm' of 'acceptable behaviour' within the mainstream space can be seen in several of the productions discussed. There is transgressing both in terms of the physical spaces, adapted to make a new audience 'feel welcome' (whilst the audience were arriving at the Olivier theatre for the performance of *The Ramayana* one of the actors on-stage called out to them to 'make yourselves feel at home'), and in the shift in behaviour of these new audiences, disrupting the expectations of the hegemonic space. During performances of *Bombay Dreams* some of the younger Asian audiences arrived late because they were used to going to the cinema rather than the theatre, and so expected there to be advertisements before the show.[42] A tradition became established that the musicians, led by renowned percussionist Kuljit Bhamra, would continue to play after the performance whilst the Asian audience members would get up and dance in the aisles and at the front. When this began to happen, the ushers in the theatre did not know how to deal with this transgression of the usual behaviour of a mainstream theatre audience, but the new behaviour transformed itself into an accepted 'norm' for the space of the production. Virk stated that Ayub Khan-Din was angry that people were making a lot of noise through performances of *Rafta, Rafta ...*, pointing out that he 'doesn't know the Asian audiences'.[43]

The transgression of the dominant space can create new meanings, but this occurs in reaction to the established structures of that space. For Cresswell, '[t]ransgression's efficacy lies in the power of the established boundaries and spaces that it so heretically subverts. It is also limited by this established geography; it is always in reaction to topographies of power.'[44] On leaving a production of David Farr's *The Ramayana* at the Lyric Hammersmith in 2007, I overheard two comments which illustrate this. A young white English girl was saying to her friend: 'It made me cry. It reminded me of being in India. How everything is sacred. With the lamps at the end, it made me cry.' A group of young Asian girls, on the other hand, were saying to each other that they thought it was 'crap', and that they would never go back to 'this theatre', the Lyric, again, owing to their bad experience. The views of the English girl indicate that Farr's version was essentially based on his idealised view of Indian culture, and did not reach to the heart of the story within a Hindu context. In the programme, Farr states: 'Ever since I went to India I have had a strong attachment to the story. ... It reminded me of Shakespeare in the way it combined adventure and action with the most beautiful and profound meditation on loss, love, wealth, materialism and spiritualism.'[45] So it is Indian, but not *that* Indian, and lost much of its potency in being filtered through Farr's attempt at rewriting the epic. This was seen in the reaction of the Asian girls, which also demonstrates the potential problem with so closely aligning a production to a theatrical building. For them, it was not just the play that was 'crap': the theatre space itself was identified with that production, and this meant that they would not be entering it again, even for a different production.

The process of mixing with the mainstream, of the journey from the margins to the centre, is fraught with potential difficulties, subversions and paradoxes, as much as is any form of migration and integration. Questions of how to sustain a new audience beyond a single production; of shifting power structures within organisations; of highlighting the work of 'non-mainstream' Asian companies producing exciting new work; and of finding meaningful ways of addressing issues concerning British Asians are all still major concerns for those working both at the margins and in the central cultural domains, and those who move between the two. Reflecting on the history of appropriations and reinforcing of stereotypes that have occurred in many of the productions designed to attract new audiences within the mainstream, each making use of particular funding opportunities and cultural fashions, it is worth asking if there is any meaningful future for these types of productions in mainstream institutions. Jatinder Verma believes that a solution would be for a company such as Tara to have their own permanent theatre space:

> [T]here are no dedicated theatre buildings pushing forth the ethics and aesthetics of multiculturalism. In all areas of the infrastructure of theatre—writers, performers, designers, administrators, publicists, critics—the representation of Asian, Black and other 'minority' practitioners remains either small or inconsistent, despite the enormous investments of the past three decades.[46]

I question, however, whether this would be an appropriate long-term solution. Might it instead again create an-'other', a space which becomes representative of the 'minority', thus leading to mainstream institutions deciding to abandon any attempt to bring such performances into their own cultural domain, as they are happening elsewhere? This may result in a further separation, rather than a way of transgressing the dominant to develop high-quality theatre which engages meaningfully with the issues of Asian communities. For a transgression to become a transformation that creates a genuine shift in the 'norm' there needs to be a willingness for the space, both physical and ideological, to be changed by those within it. In such a process, rather more than lip-service would have to be paid to the need for mainstream theatre to become the space/location for engaged representation, and for debate on the realities of contemporary British life, with all its cultural complexities.

11

Between Page and Stage

Meera Syal in British Asian Culture

Giovanna Buonanno

'The Rose—the bleedin rose! Ten lines and a stupid frilly costume. But I know I'm the best actress in the class. Why haven't I got a bigger role?' The director (alias the woodwork teacher) took her aside and said kindly, 'Now then Feroza, we can't have an Alice with a brown face, can we?' and I knew my battle had begun.[1]

I soon realised how many untold stories lay silent on the lips of Asian women in this country (Britain). Silenced by both their inability to verbalise their frustrations in a society which regards them as second-class citizens and a theatre and media in which the Asian presence is minimal and often merely nominal. I wished to give voice to this silence in the best way I knew. Through my acting.[2]

As an acclaimed writer and media personality, celebrated as 'the feisty face of multicultural Britain',[3] Meera Syal has been at the forefront of British Asian culture in contemporary Britain and has successfully engaged with various art forms over a number of years. Her fame has been consolidated by her increasingly frequent presence on television following the huge, and in some ways not entirely predictable, success of the BBC 'ethnic' TV series *Goodness Gracious Me* (BBC2 1998–2001) and *The Kumars at no. 42* (BBC2 2002–2006). Both shows have been crucial in furthering Syal's media career, while mainstreaming and popularising British Asian culture.

As both a writer and a theatre and screen actress, Syal has explored the link between writing and acting in the attempt to visualise the experience of Asians in Britain. Her work has run counter to traditional views and easily fabricated cultural stereotypes, and has engaged with issues such as representation, visibility and the performance of identity as they emerge out of contact and interstitial cultural zones.[4]

In this article I intend to focus on significant moments of Syal's career and argue that her performance of a gendered and ethnic identity is a key element of her work. Her work across genres and media emerges as a response to an overall lack of images of Asians, as well as to a very limited range of roles available to British Asian women. Since the mid-1980s Syal has helped to enlarge the scope of representation of Asian women on stage and screen by offering a multiplicity of roles that could capture the plurality of their experiences, while also reflecting on the possibilities opened up to herself as an actress of Asian parentage in Britain. Similarly, the protean, transformative quality of acting has influenced her writing. Both acting and writing have been deeply instrumental to the process of self-fashioning a female identity on which she has embarked, one that intersects questions of ethnicity, cultural translation and typecasting.

Being part of an emerging British Asian theatre scene has, in and beyond the 1980s, shaped Syal's writing. As Kaur and Terracciano have pointed out, 'drama became an exceptional medium to convey the changing modalities of BrAsian identities well before the film industry would take an interest in this area of British urban life.'[5] The 1980s were an important decade in the process of imagining a culturally diverse Britain, as well as in the creation of what were then defined as black arts, despite the fact that they were still largely ignored in the wider mainstream artistic circuits.[6] This was the decade in which second-generation writers and artists such as Syal came of age: artists who, as Ponnuswami has argued, 'are uniquely positioned to be agents of intercultural communication and exchange'.[7] Their role as translators and mediators through images was crucial and has contributed to what Donnell has defined as 'the shift in terms of identification and representation, from being perceived as the black presence in Britain to the black dimension of Britain', that began to take shape in the 1980s.[8]

Syal's awareness of the singular positioning of the first generation of British Asians informs her interviews and non-fictional writings and is also enacted in her screenplays and novels by a number of characters who take on a distinct liaising role. An instance of this is Simi, the advanced feminist and coordinator of the Saheli Women's Centre in the film *Bhaji on the Beach* (1993), who is constantly called upon to mediate within the group of Birmingham Asian women she is taking on a day trip to Blackpool, while also in the course of the day proving her ability to facilitate the group's rapport with society at large. Another case in point is Tania, a London-based film director in the novel *Life Isn't All Ha Ha Hee Hee* (1999), who expresses her awareness of having 'translated' the south-east area of London she was brought up in—itself a transitional/translational space hinging on a 'corner which separated the Eastenders from the Eastern Enders'.[9] Tania paved the way through 'her mini-wars' for a younger and more assertive group of local British Asians performing their newly fashioned identities, 'loafing around in their mix and match fashions listening to their masala music with not a care in the world'.[10]

Syal paid a tribute to the spirit of the 1980s in an article published in 2003 and entitled 'Last Laugh' in which she looks back on her early days in London and describes this period as a very exciting as well as formative experience. After having graduated in English and Drama at Manchester University, she co-wrote and played in a one-woman show called *One of Us* (1983) that was staged at the Edinburgh Fringe festival. She subsequently worked as an actress at the Royal Court Theatre in London, and considered herself to be part of the 'rainbow' population that the newly elected GLC, led by Ken Livingstone, had decided to embrace. Syal points out that as a student in an 'all white drama department' before moving to London, she had never acted in parts that would reflect who she was or that could offer her the opportunity to come close to her experiences. She admits that in London she was impressed by the wealth of opportunities available to her: 'there I was, suitcase in hand, doing what I'd always dreamed of doing for a living but never imagining a funny looking Punjabi girl from the Midlands would ever achieve.'[11] However, this period of celebration of diversity also made her aware of the constraints of the 'female' burden of representation for minority artists, an issue that was being increasingly debated at the time and sparked her reflection on how narrow the scope of images of Asian womanhood on the stage was.[12] As she recalls, in 1980s London important organisations such as the Newham Asian Women's Project began activity which addressed in particular the issue of domestic violence and testified to the plurality of the lives of Asian women who were negotiating public and private roles while striving for visibility. This context influenced her decision as an actress not 'to be in plays by middle-class white writers about angst in Hampstead' and, in particular, her work with the Newham Project helped to build her awareness of the inequality of the representation of gender and its misrepresentation on the stage, all of which she would then transfer onto the page.[13] The standard roles she was offered as an Asian actress she defines as laughable, such as 'the meek subdued teenager escaping an arranged marriage, the subservient wife bewildered by her surroundings, the exotic princess pouting with Eastern promise'.[14] Such roles did not at all reflect the reality of Asian women in the 1980s, who were involved in community work and in organisations fighting racism, patriarchal oppression and tackling questions of gender and cultural identity.

At the time Syal was active in Asian Co-operative Theatre, one of the first London-based British Asian companies that included in its repertoire both modern classics such as Lorca's *Blood Wedding* and the work of budding British Asian playwrights such as Farrukh Dhondy. The company experimented with forms of integrated casting, and Syal interpreted both Asian and non-Asian roles.[15] Her involvement with Asian Cooperative Theatre and her work as an actress outside the British Asian circuit, most notably her appointment at the Royal Court, proved significant in focusing her attention on the crucial role that the practice of acting can play in imagining the experience of real Asian women and in undoing the impact of widespread racial stereotypes. Her own experience there also confirmed her concern over what she defines as the 'unimaginative' casting of Asian actresses that, even in 1990, rarely went beyond the usual typecasting. Despite tentative multi-racial and integrated casting initiatives in mainstream theatre, Syal maintained that this was 'one of the profession's besetting sins' and still a hindrance to 'an automatic acceptance of, say, an Afro-Caribbean or Asian Ophelia'.[16]

Syal gives us a further reflection on this theme in an essay suggestively entitled 'Finding My Voice', which I have quoted as an epigraph to this article. The essay begins as a humorous recollection of her days as a young schoolchild longing to walk the stage. She then moves on to reveal how from very early on she had seen acting as an instrument of rebellion and as part of a process of identity formation that aims to 'achieve presence', in Verma's words, allowing space for the projection of subjectivities that are normally socially excluded.[17] In Syal's view, training as an actress encouraged her to find the connections between her creative capacities and political awareness and allowed her to explore the dimension of playing in a space that is in between British and Asian cultures. In 'Finding My Voice' she particularly elaborates on the question of choosing exacting roles for women and assessing their representative value: the danger when interpreting Asian roles is that of being reduced to a 'didactic mouthpiece', and therefore in her view it seems paramount to be able to find a script that would combine both sides of her personality and ultimately express her feelings as an Asian woman.[18] As she recalls in this essay, as part of her quest to 'find her voice' she co-authored with Jacqui Shapiro the show *One of Us*, an exploration of female identity in an in-between cultural space, which stands out as an early attempt to write a play and perform in it as a British Asian woman.

In 'Finding My Voice' Syal responds and gives her contribution as an actress to the collection in which the article originally appeared, whose aim was to showcase and discuss black women's creativity, exploring the link between gender and ethnicity in the arts. Published with the title *Passion: Discourse of Blackwoman's Creativity*, and edited by Maud Sulter, the volume featured the work of many visual artists such as Chila Kumari Burman, Ingrid Pollard and Lubaina Himid, along with writers and performers committed to expanding the limits of female representation on the page and on the stage, such as Syal herself and writer Bernardine Evaristo, who at the time was involved in setting up the company Theatre of Black Women. The category of *Blackwoman* was then an important signifier conveying a need for both agency and representation, resounding with the spirit that informed the Asian Women Writers' Collective set up in 1984, which would later propel other Asian women's cultural endeavours such as the London-based Kali Theatre. This establishment of creative cultural spaces was the product of both the social tensions that surrounded them and their desire to make sense of the changing positions of Black and Asian women in Britain, visualising their experiences in many walks of life, not least in theatre and the media. As director Pratibha Parmar put it in 1991, reflecting particularly on the situation of diasporic Asians:

> As diasporic Asians, we hunger for images which in some way reflect our images and our desires and realities. Media representations are a critical component of our identities, particularly for those of us who are perceived to be on the margins of the mainstream, the malestream, and the whitestream. Our need for reflections of ourselves and our communities is pivotal to our survival. As cultural outsiders, representations of ourselves, both on the big screen and on the small screen, are important in shaping our sense of self.[19]

The hunger for new images and the need to reclaim an active role in challenging current representations of oneself finds its way into Syal's own work, and features strongly in her writing debut, the autobiographical novel *Anita and Me* (1996). In this novel Meena, the nine-year-old protagonist, is constantly longing for images that would adequately reflect her. Set in the early 1970s in Tollington, a fictional ex-mining village in the Midlands, the novel follows Meena as the only Asian girl in the village in her journey of self-discovery over a period of two years. As a child 'caught between two cultures', according to the easily fabricated formula defining second-generation young Asians growing up in Britain in 1960s and 1970s, Meena's experience of culture clash is often one which involves a clash of visual representations. Her hunger for British food—jam tarts and fish-fingers as opposed to her mother's Indian 'soul food'—is complemented by her hunger for images that can accommodate her constant juggling between the two extremes of 'real Indian girl' or 'real Tollington wench',[20] the latter symbolised by her local, sassy, blonde friend and unattainable model Anita.

Anita and Me has been thoroughly investigated as a coming-of-age novel and a quest for belonging, capturing the emerging, culturally contested world of 1970s Britain.[21] In its depiction of this world through Meena's eyes, the novel gives voice to her plight in not being able to find reflections of herself in the world that surrounds her. As a child with a talent for storytelling and a secret ambition to become a writer, Meena fantasises about appearing on *Opportunity Knocks*, a TV talent show and one of her favourite programmes, but she is concerned that she has 'not seen anyone who was not white on the show yet'.[22] The fear of exclusion certainly accounts for Meena's painful non-acceptance of her body and colour: 'I wanted to shed my body like a snake, slithering out of its skin, and emerge reborn, pink and unrecognisable', while by focusing on the lack of any real visual representation of the young protagonist the novel further investigates the question of the invisibility of blacks and Asians, and points to their all too negligible presence in the media.[23]

Meena is aware that Tollington as a small village in the Black Country is only a 'footnote in the book of the Sixties', but she is even more sensitive to the fact that her family and friends are 'the squashed flies in the spine', largely invisible from newspapers and televisions to the extent that:

> If a brown or black face ever did appear on TV, it stopped us all in our tracks. 'Daljit! Quick!' And we would crowd around and coo over the walk-on in some detective series, some long-suffering actor in a gaudy costume with a goodness-gracious-me accent (...) and welcome him into our home like a long-lost relative.[24]

Meena reflects on 'how starved we were of seeing ourselves somewhere other than in each other's lounges';[25] yet she seems aware that the 'occasional minor celebrities' seen on TV were merely unrealistic, stereotyped representations of Indians. In the novel Syal does not mention directly the stereotypes that were being peddled in the television series of the 1970s which, as has been argued elsewhere, contributed to the racialisation of blacks and Asians,[26] but nonetheless she voices Meena's desire to challenge the far too exaggerated and exotic versions of Indian identity. As an actress Syal has often been confronted with these reductive versions. She refused to appear in the 1980s film series *Viceroy* because of the 'indefensible' choice of having a 'famous actor blacking up as Nehru', and because she felt that it was imperative to 'turn down work that was insulting or limiting—the stereotyped roles of Indian mothers in shops or the ubiquitous girl running away from her parents'.[27]

By the mid-1980s Syal had already vindicated Meena's desire to appear on television by acting on both the big screen—in Frears-Kureishi's *Sammy and Rosie Get Laid*—and on television in the BBC2 production *The Real McCoy*, a comedy which drew on the experiences of black Britons, as well as by both acting in and writing for the 'ethnic' TV comedy *Tandoori Nights*. Despite their still largely relying on familiar stereotypes (e.g. the Indian restaurant setting), these TV comedies, as Sarita Malik has argued, represented a significant move towards 'an integrated mode of Black production, with black writers, actors and producers actively involved'.[28] Furthermore, thanks to their policy of casting black and Asian actors, these programmes were all significant in challenging the invisibility of non-whites and provided an effective counterpoint to the nostalgic Raj revival that was being offered on television with the popular TV series *Jewel in the Crown* and *Far Pavilions* where, as Rushdie argues, the trend was still to cast predominantly white actors. Reflecting on these popular recreations of colonial life, Rushdie ironically quips that only occasionally did they 'allow

Indians to be played by Indians (one is becoming grateful for the smallest of mercies)'.[29]

In her later writing of the 1990s, Syal expands the scope of representation of Asian women with scripts for the feature film *Bhaji on the Beach* (1993), the BBC drama *My Sister Wife* (1992) and the short feature film *A Nice Arrangement* (1990), produced by Film Four, in which Syal also acted, taking up for herself the rather challenging role of the unsettling, divorced Auntie Sita. In these scripts Syal places herself as a writer—and actress in the case of *A Nice Arrangement*—in multiple subject-positions, encompassing a plurality of female experiences cutting across generational, class and religious differences.

These texts clearly reflect her dissatisfaction with available roles for Asian actresses in the way that they both elaborate on the potential of staging identity and present contrasting images of Asian women. Judith Butler's reflection on gendered identity as 'performatively constituted by the very "expressions" that are said to be its results' resonates well with Syal's writing, which enacts the performability of female identity.[30] This appears to be a central feature of the film *Bhaji on the Beach*, directed by Gurinder Chadha, in which a cross-generational group of Asian women from Birmingham experience, each in her own way, some 'female fun time' on a day trip to Blackpool. By presenting a gallery of women differentiated by age and class and giving voice to their problems and desires, the film manages to convey the sense of the plurality of both gender and ethnic identity and challenges the widespread monolithic view of minorities in Britain. *A Nice Arrangement*, also directed by Chadha, looks at the complexity of keeping to cultural and religious traditions and captures the anxiety of a North-London Hindu bride on the day of her sumptuous wedding, which is the result of an arranged and loveless match.

In *My Sister Wife*, the first screenplay written by a British Asian woman to be produced by the BBC, Syal explores in the form of a melodrama the identity crisis of two Pakistani women in Britain bound in the very uneasy relationship of being sister wives. They are first portrayed as strikingly different, with Farah the second and younger wife standing for the second-generation Asian woman in Britain who is only moderately influenced by her parent culture, but nonetheless is attracted to the already married Asif who understands 'both sides of her' (Asian and British). Farah is mirrored by Maryam, the first wife who is first presented as a silent, submissive Asian woman. However, the initially clear-cut divide between the two women is increasingly blurred, and detailed stage directions testify to their visual and physical transformation.

The performability of identity in culturally contested terrains is further developed in her two novels, in which Syal presents characters who explore the fine line between acting and being. Meena in *Anita and Me* enacts various strategies in order to find herself, and exhibits protean qualities while indulging in her ability to create alternative stories in order to fill in gaps and fabricate history. As she quips: 'I'm really not a liar. I just learned very early on that those of us deprived of history sometimes need to turn to mythology to feel complete, to belong.'[31] The three thirty-something friends and protagonists of *Life Isn't All Ha Ha Hee Hee* all challenge predefined models of Asian womanhood and are seen to grapple with their multiple identities in both public and private life. However, as a career-minded TV director, Tania is the character who offers an especially perceptive analysis of the performability of the self and reflects on the link between gender and ethnic stereotypes. As a racialised ethnic subject, often denied individuality in the public perception, Tania plays up to the 'burden of representation':

When I get asked about racism, as I always do in any job interview when they're checking whether I'm the genuine article (oppressed Asian woman who has suffered), as opposed to the pretend coconut (white on the inside, brown on the outside, too well off and well spoken to be considered truly ethnic), I make up stories about skinheads and shit through letterboxes, because that's the kind of racism they want to hear about. It lets my nice interviewer off the hook, it confirms that the real baddies live far away from him in the SE postcode area, and he can tut at them from a safe distance.[32]

Tania fulfils racist expectations by resorting to her ability to perform identity and make up stories, offering a rather more sophisticated and urban version of the young and village-bound Meena of Syal's debut novel, who is equally keen to elaborate on her own family history.

The two novels marked a moment of increased fame for Syal while contributing to the expanding field of British Asian fiction. It is significant that at the end of the 1990s, in the era of 'cool' and supposedly culturally diverse 'Britannia', her work managed to cross over and become mainstream, reaching out to large TV audiences with the BBC2 TV show *Goodness Gracious Me*.[33] The show emerged out of the desire to challenge easily stereotyped views of Asians and claim for Asians a long-denied presence on TV. Reflecting on the success of the show, Syal seems acutely aware of the difficulty usually faced by Asians and Asian culture in Britain in the ambition to be understood beyond deep-seated stereotypes and received ideas and, even more so, for Asian life finally to become material for successful media recreation. As she argues: 'It's trendy to be Asian at the moment. It was always trendy to be black, but never Asian. We used to be all tank-tops, side partings, too many kids and maybe a bit of mysticism. This was our slot.'[34] The success of the programme was proof of the relatively recent ascent of Asian popular culture in Britain at the turn of the millennium, where Syal believes—a little triumphantly, perhaps—that 'brown [is] indeed the new black, in couture, in music, in design, on the high street.'[35] As Malik suggests, the show 'frequently laughs at "Old Britain" in a style that could only have materialised from this distinctly hybrid British-Asian comic register'.[36] It should be noted, however, that the success of the show has attracted criticism, based mainly on the assumption that it has managed somehow to offer commodified versions of the British Asian experience and South Asian culture in Britain, accommodating it too much to western audiences.[37]

Goodness Gracious Me was followed by the *The Kumars at no. 42*, which humorously situated Asian popular culture within the popular genre of the TV talk show and cast Syal in the comic role of Granny Kumar. Syal's success on TV was paralleled by that of the popular West End Bollywood-inspired musical *Bombay Dreams* (2002), produced by Andrew Lloyd Webber, for which she wrote the script. Though quite different works, both the BBC shows and *Bombay Dreams* draw on forms of entertainment that have proved successful with various cross-cultural and transnational audiences, the 'ethnic' comedy and the Bollywood genre, respectively, and seem to move in the direction of what Huggan has defined as the 'postcolonial exotic', namely the 'global commodification of cultural difference'.[38] Huggan analyses the work of writers such as Kureishi, Naipaul and Rushdie as 'celebrity minority' writers and introduces the concept of strategic exoticism. This can offer a critical perspective on Syal's more recent work, which seems equally 'designed as much to challenge as to profit from consumer needs, while exploring their own ironic relation to majoritarian notions of British national culture'.[39] According to Huggan's analysis, both the TV shows and *Bombay Dreams* have offered 'commodified perceptions of cultural marginality' involving a 'strategic redeployment of commercialised forms of the exotic'.[40]

This element of marketing marginality or strategic exoticism may be seen to be at work in Syal's return to the stage at the National Theatre in Khan-Din's play *Rafta, Rafta ...* (2007), the play that marked the much awaited return of playwright Ayub Khan-Din to the London stage with a portrayal of family life in the British Asian community of the North West of England. In her performance as Lopa Dutt, a middle-aged wife and mother, Syal certainly brings a halo of media celebrity and popularity to the production, reflected in the fact that she actively promoted the play in interviews and press conferences, where she stressed what she personally valued about performing in it. She has described the play as refreshing thanks to the absence of issues such as arranged marriages or terrorism, and has also remarked on its broad cross-cultural appeal. When interviewed on ITV she admitted being particularly pleased with the fact that she did not have to play the victim of an arranged marriage or the mother of a victim of an arranged marriage.[41] This way of describing and promoting her role seems to be still framed in Syal's idea of the 1980s and 1990s, when the range of roles for Asian actresses was admittedly limited to that of a 'Mrs Patel' in a corner shop with one line, or to a social worker with one line, and when actresses of colour hardly ever walked the boards of the National Theatre. As critics have remarked, in her version of what could be seen as a rather traditional matriarchal role in Khan-Din's play, Syal gives a 'strong, unshowy performance'[42] laced with 'grumpy good humour',[43] and posits herself in a genealogy of the British Asian actress by creating a role that both mirrors her acquired celebrity status and offers a nuanced creation to add to her gallery of British Asian female characters.

Syal's recent performance as Lopa Dutt at the National Theatre offers us an opportunity to look back on her career as both an actress and a writer and retrace her long-standing commitment to expanding the range of roles for British Asian actresses. This process started with her one-woman show *One of Us* in the early 1980s and reached a significant and productive stage when she worked as an actress at the Royal Court Theatre and joined Asian Cooperative Theatre in the 1980s. In this formative period Syal was also being progressively drawn to acting in film and television, in this way contributing to establishing an Asian female presence on screen. The significance of the 1980s for Syal as an actress is reflected in her essays and interviews, in which she puts herself forward as a kind of marginalised *ingénue* and elaborates on the relationship between acting and the exploration of ethnic and gender identity. Similarly, as a writer she has committed herself to spinning tales of self-affirmation, experimenting with a variety of genres, ranging from scripts for film, TV and the West End theatre to the novels of the 1990s. In her pursuit of multiple images of British Asian women in her writing, Syal has challenged deep-seated stereotypes surrounding Asians in Britain whilst raising a series of issues related to the lives of British women of Asian parentage, such as racism, abuse, female sexuality and inter-generational conflicts. Most notably, in her novels Syal has drawn on her engagement with theatre and her experience as a professional actress to write stories that explore the performative nature of identity and investigate the complex issue of the representation of Asians in British culture. Her fiction reflects the changing perceptions of South Asian women in the 1990s, and marks a significant stage in her negotiation between a marginal and a mainstream cultural position. Her move into the cultural mainstream following her successful TV shows, as well as her foray into the West End musical world with *Bombay Dreams*, has opened up a debate as to the marketing potential of British Asian culture, its ensuing commodification and Syal's role in this process of staging marginality. However, as Huggan has argued, 'staged marginality (...) may function in certain contexts to uncover and challenge dominant structures of power.'[44] Syal's work over the years has been shaped by her determination to challenge the theatre and the media 'in which the Asian presence is minimal and often merely nominal'.[45] By acting and writing against the grain she has pushed forward the limits of representation of British Asian female subjectivities, articulating a plural and increasingly visible Asian presence on the page and on the stage.

12

Imagine, *Indiaah* ...
on the British Stage

Exploring Tara's 'Binglish' and Tamasha's Brechtian Approaches

Chandrika Patel

Tara means 'stars', and Tamasha is a form of folk theatre from the Maharashtra region of India, with the word also meaning 'commotion, creating a stir'. So the 'Indian' identities of both theatre companies are etymologically suggested in their names, and are indeed evident in their productions and collaborations since their inception in 1977 and 1989 respectively.[1] Tamasha's work ranges from a literary adaptation of Mulk Raj Anand's *Untouchable* in 1989 to a 'Bollywood' musical, *Fourteen Songs, Two Weddings and a Funeral* (1998, 2000), based on the Indian film *Hum Aapke Hain Koun (Who Am I to You?)*. Tara Arts is firmly rooted in British history, in terms of being formed in response to the racist murder of a young Sikh man in Southall. But Tara has looked towards India to create its distinctive 'Binglish' approach, which is based on a combination of influences from the Sanskrit performance treatise the *Natyasastra*, Indian cinema and European theatre traditions. Tara's work includes the adaptation of Indian classics such as Sudraka's *Miti Ki Gadi (The Little Clay Cart*, 1986) and *The Ramayana* (1998), the 'Indian' adaptations of European classics such as *A Midsummer Night's Dream* (1997), and *The Merchant of Venice* (2005), and the research-based trilogy *Journey to the West* (2002), drawing on the South Asian diaspora experience.

Diaspora and audience

Bearing in mind Tara and Tamasha's Indian sub-continent associations, their 'mission' statements, according with their role in the representation of 'cultural diversity', invite reflection on the nature of their audiences.[2]

No passports: Positioned between East and West, Tara champions creative diversity through the production, promotion and development of world class, cross-cultural theatre.[3]

Implicit in Tara's 'No passports' mantra is the notion of a non-place identity, evident in the phrase 'positioned between East and West'. That points towards a 'diaspora' definition, suggesting a culturally dislocated position for their 'cross-cultural theatre'. But for whom is Tara's theatre made? According to the critic Gandhi,

> in its postcolonial incarnation, diasporic thought reviews the colonial encounter for its disruption of native/domestic space and is [...] generally concerned with the *idea* of cultural dislocation contained within this term, and as such may be used as a theoretical device for interrogation of ethnic identity and cultural nationalism.[4]

Gandhi's definition helps to clarify Tara's mission statement in terms of the 'location' of its work and the purpose behind it, and so may provide insights into the nature of its audience, who might accordingly be those who share concerns of 'ethnic identity and cultural nationalism'. Tara's premise of a 'cross-cultural' form is firmly derived from the company's development of a *Natyasastra*-inspired, 'Binglish' approach. But it may be considered to have had more contemporary influences upon it, notably Bollywood, which would point towards the Indian diaspora audience:

> under the direction of Jatinder Verma between 1983 and 1989 ... Tara focused on the study of Indian and other non-European theatre techniques, along with Sanskrit drama and anti-realist genres in theatre and cinema, for which Bombay movies provided a source of inspiration.[5]

The term diaspora is valuable, but its precise dimensions and implications are hard to track, as scholars have noted. For Ahmed, the term has

> centuries of pain and dispossession inscribed in it and questions arise regarding the possible applicability of those sentiments to the migrants who came to the UK directly from India, Pakistan, Bangladesh, who were perhaps more likely to have been motivated by economic ambitions as opposed to driven out by persecution.[6]

Ahmed is understandably cautious about its application: 'No generalisation can be offered for so large and complex a phenomenon [meaning immigration] involving so many individual biographies.'[7] Does Brah's conceptualisation of diaspora, imagined 'via a confluence of narratives as it is lived and re-lived, produced, reproduced and transformed through individual as well as collective memory as well as re-memory', provide a better 'location' for an Indian diaspora?[8] Brah uses the concept of diaspora as an 'interpretative frame to analyse economic, political and cultural modalities of historically specific forms of migrancy ... [and the] relationality of these migrancies across fields of social relations, subjectivity and identity'.[9] For Brah, terms such as British Asian-ness or Black Britishness are 'not mutually exclusive configurations', but crosscut with other British identities, thus decentring notions of Englishness, British-ness or Indian-ness.[10]

> My argument is that they are not 'minority' identities, nor are they at the periphery of something that sees itself as located at the centre, although they may be presented as such.[11]

Brah's contentions about the nature of 'British' and 'Asian' identities are not necessarily reflected in the socio-political framework of Britain, as is evident in the Arts Council funding policy, in which the Black Minority Ethnic section (currently called the 'Sector') is exclusively concerned with the funding of Black and Asian works and with the perceived role of representing 'cultural diversity'. Such a policy will inevitably receive responses from the artists concerned. In its mission statement, below, Tamasha's attempt to place 'British Asian talent ... [at] centre stage' recognises the continuing 'minority' status attributed to British South Asian artists and arts that Naseem Khan's report, *The Arts Britain Ignores*, first brought to wider notice in 1976. Tamasha's statement promises a theatrical intervention by placing British South Asian practitioners at 'centre stage':

> Our goal is to transform theatre to create a space where British Asian talent takes centre stage, through original writing and productions that provoke debate, ideas, passion and laughter.[12]

The language chosen here has moved significantly away from that which Tamasha advanced a decade ago in the flyer of their 'Bollywood' musical *Fourteen Songs, Two Weddings and a Funeral* (1998), expressing the company's aim 'to reflect through theatre the Asian experience, from British Asian life to authentic accounts of life in the Indian subcontinent'.[13] This suggests the changing nature of mission statements, marking a clear shift from the company's Indian sub-continent associations towards the British politics of 'cultural diversity'. If the concept of diaspora is to be understood in Desai's terms as 'a deterritorialised geopolitical community succeeding the nation in an age of increasing globalisation', then a distinct nature for the Indian diaspora audience may possibly confirm itself. This is an audience for whom the existence of Satellite TV channels and relatively cheap travel has made it possible to exist in what Desai describes as a 'third space', maintaining a separate cultural identity through an 'imaginary' and 'tourist' relationship with India.[14] British South Asian theatre practice is undoubtedly mindful of the Indian diaspora audience and their love of 'Bollywood' cinema, and has explored and exploited this relationship in productions through utilising its songs and conventions.

Despite some general bearings that may be taken with confidence from theoretical reflections on diaspora, the position of the British South Asian practitioners and their audience remains complex. This is reflected in the individual mission statements of Tara and Tamasha, and is thoroughly apparent in the strikingly different theatrical approaches of the two companies.

In the rest of this essay I shall be examining two productions that illustrate the different approaches taken by these companies, adopting a complex form of analysis that draws on three sources. The first of these is the Sanskrit aesthetic treatise, the *Natyasastra*; the second is the Brechtian theory of *Gestus*; and the third is semiotics, seen through the lens provided by Roland Barthes. As a brief orientation to the analyses of the productions, I shall first provide my own summaries of these three theoretical sources.

Natyasastra

The thirty-six chapters of Rangacharya's English translation of *Natyasastra* (1996) reveal a strong sense of religious engagement associated with the treatise, in which its discussion of compositional signs is situated. The narrative style of the *Natyasastra*, in which the Hindu god Brahma is said to have given a *Veda* (sacred text) of *natya* (drama) to Bharat Muni, who passed the knowledge to his hundred sons, implies a distinct *guru–shishya* (teacher–pupil) relationship. This dictates not only the mode of exposition in the treatise but also its mode of reception, with both rooted in a particular socio-cultural context. The treatise recognises three models of forms: *nrtta* (pure dance), *nritya* (pantomimic dance) and *natya* (drama).[15] The types of *natya* are elaborated in chapter twenty-two: 'a play in which speech is artificial and exaggerated, actions unusually emotional, gestures graceful ... and voice and costumes are not from common use is *Natyadharmi* (dramatic)'. In contrast, *Lokdharmi* (realistic) is 'a play in which men and women, in their own nature, without any change ... without any gestures, behave naturally'.[16] The treatise's complex network of sign-making places the human body as a primary signifier, with an emphasis on caste/status referents, appropriate conduct and illustrative conventions. This is evident in the component parts of the skill of *abhinaya* (acting)— *angika* (bodily signs), *vacika* (verbal), *aharya* (make-up and costumes) and *sattvika* (emotional)—which together constitute a system that 'carries the performance towards the spectator', serving as the vehicle of *natya*.[17] For example, in the chapters concerning *angika abhinaya*, illustration appears to be the main convention controlling movements of the head, nose, cheeks, lips and chin and the major limbs, showing emotions and illnesses in a stylised and often exaggerated manner. The twenty-four *mudras* (hand gestures), however, are governed by distinct principles that apart from being illustrative also contain social-status referents, although they may not carry such an interpretative value when utilised in *nrtta* (pure dance).[18] The *Natyasastra*'s unequivocal acceptance of the distinctions of the caste system can be seen in chapter eighteen on the *vacika* (verbal) *abhinaya*, with its prescribed Sanskrit (refined) and *Prakrta* (demotic) dialects and modes of address based on principles of caste and status.[19] Moreover, the notion of 'appropriate conduct' is implicit in the treatise's caste- and status-conscious signs, evident in terms such as 'superior', 'inferior' and 'middling' used in reference to characters. This emerges strongly in chapter twenty-three, on the *aharya abhinaya*, which is concerned with conveying caste, social status and the individual circumstance of the character though costume, colour and make-up, as well as in chapter twenty-four on the *samanya abhinaya*, which prescribes types of behaviour related to love.[20]

The governing concept of the *Natyasastra* is that of the *rasas*. Understanding it adequately remains a complex task, as it is not only the overall aim of *natya* but also the principle ruling the various *abhinayas*; as a result, it is also applied to the reception of the performance. There are eight *rasas* encapsulating eight different emotional states, and subordinate to the *rasas* are the *bhavas*, which carry the emotions through and across to the audience. The ultimate goal of the theatrical experience is related to the concepts of *rasas* and *bhavas* and their complex relationship with the *abhinayas*, and is concerned with evoking feeling as opposed to meaning, this being one of the distinct qualities of the treatise. The principles of the sign-making sections suggest that the treatise assumes that a particular set of emotions can be distributed in categories and can be demonstrated through *bhavas*, embodied by *abhinaya*, through which *rasas* can be evoked in the 'cultured' spectator. The treatise's sign-making ultimately relies on the aesthetic response that the spectator would recognise as a 'feeling', which in the terms of the theory is equivalent to what we might call the 'meaning' of the performance.[21]

Gestus

Brecht's theory of *Gestus* shares important similarities with the *Natyasastra* in the sense of portraying social relations through physicality and stage properties. Moreover, *Gestus* assumes that the *gestic* actor can control the physicality of behaviour and gestures in order to portray the 'social relations' that shape the character's actions. But, unlike the *Natyasastra*'s sign-making, which is concerned with an emotional response through recognition, Brechtian *Gestus* seeks a 'distancing' from the character's situation in which recognition does not automatically align the spectator with an 'emotional response'. Such an approach demanded a socio-politically aware actor who was not only the 'reader' of a character but who could control his actions to convey expressions of the social relationships prevailing between characters.

In terms of aesthetics, this meant that stage properties such as costumes, objects and placards were not exclusively confined to the stage world and often functioned independently. Brecht sought to challenge the conventional, interpretive habits of the audience and the actor through a 'distancing' that was required of both parties. From this duality, created by the actor's presence in demonstrating a character, emerges a '*gestic* split' that aimed to facilitate a social reading of the character. The audience was required to read two different signs in the same bodily space, one which originates in the stage world and one which originates outside the stage world.[22] When the *gestic*-split actor engages with other elements of the stage properties, such as placards and captions, a 'distancing' through the contradiction between the *gestic* split (telling and told) and the placards/captions (told) is created in which each informs and contextualises the other.[23] So the audience is required to construct a meaning through separate registers. Auslander speculated on the metaphysical limitations of the *gestic*-split actor in reference to Derrida's concept of *différance*, where 'the actor's self is not the grounding presence that precedes the performance, but an effect of the play of *différance* that constitutes theatrical discourse'.[24] Such deconstructive strategies employed in the Epic theatre define not only the rhetorical quality of a *gestic* discourse but also the characteristics of an 'appropriate spectator.'[25]

Semiotics

The roots of theatre semiotics can be traced in literary semiotics, and there are some difficulties in transferring an argument about sign-making in language to the variety of verbal and non-verbal signs involved in performance. However, semiotics draws attention to the significance of the role of the spectator in the creation of meaning. Peirce's trichotomy of *icon*, a sign similar to its object; *index*, a sign which points to or is connected to the object; and *symbol*, where there is connection agreed by convention rather than similarity between the sign and the object, provides a useful starting point for considering the analysis of the material aspects of theatre.[26] Barthes and Geertz's works were concerned with exploring the socio-cultural contexts within which the signs operate. Barthes's concept of *myth* combined the Saussurean concept of how material objects function as 'signs' with the Brechtian concept of the interrogation of their ideological weighting. It attempted to uncover the covert meanings of seemingly 'natural' products/images. Thus Barthes's concept of '*myth*' is based on the principle of 'intertextuality', what he describes as '*a type of speech*', where meaning is generated by texts drawing on existing cultural meanings—ultimately, that is, on other *texts*.[27] Geertz viewed a cultural event as a 'symbolic structure', as a 'means of saying something of something', the cultural meaning of which can be decoded by exploring its dramatic shape, its metaphoric content and its social context.[28]

These three bodies of theory will inform my analyses of Tara's *The Marriage of Figaro* (2006) and Tamasha's *A Fine Balance* (2007), which are based on my observations of the performances staged at the New Players Theatre and Hampstead Theatre, and seen on 27 October 2006 and 6 April 2007 respectively.

Tara Arts—*The Marriage of Figaro*

> Returning the famous opera [*The Marriage of Figaro*] to its theatrical roots and re-locating it to India is a means of making new a very familiar story ... I passionately believe stories have no passports; in these times of cross-cultural wars, it's even more urgent to simply see familiar stories in unfamiliar dress and colours.[29]

Ranjit Bolt's script-adaptation of *The Marriage of Figaro* is set in eighteenth-century Moghul India, and the director Jatinder Verma gives the original French play by Beaumarchais a distinct 'Indian makeover'. The Gujarati Figaro is a butler to the Nawab (Count), who dreams of marrying Rukhsana, the Nawab's maid. However, before the wedding Figaro learns of the Nawab's plans to exercise his ancient 'privilege' to 'receive' the bride on the servant's wedding night. With help from the spurned Begum (Nawab's wife), Figaro and Rukhsana plot together to punish the Nawab for his intended infidelity.

The presentation is dance-like, one in which the Indian-costumed actors move in a stylised manner using the Gujarati folk-theatre *Bhavai*'s steps and gait as their signature 'tune' to the sound of V. Chandran's drum beat. Verma first encountered the traditional *Natyasastra* conventions of theatre when Tara was producing the Sanskrit play *The Little Clay Cart*, by Sudraka, in 1984. In the construction of its dramaturgy he was drawn to the conventions of *Bhavai*, a Gujarati folk theatre, as 'it took liberties with its audience ... which was not alienating or offensive.'[30] This type of *Bhavai* was created by *Bhavayas* who practised 'down to earth street theatre verging on vulgarity and in crude taste'.[31] Its foundation is rooted in the caste-dilution of Brahmin actor/singer Asait Thakur of Unjha. Asait rescued a kidnapped Kanabi girl from a Muslim house by performing for the kidnapper, Sardar Jahan Roz. Asait claimed that the Kanabi girl was his daughter, so the kidnapper Roz asked him to dine with the girl, who was of the lower caste. As a result of this 'unholy' dinner between the Hindu

Brahmin Asait (Brahmin is considered the highest caste) and the lower-caste girl, Asait was excommunicated. It is said that he eventually married the Kanabi girl and chose to live by his art—the performance of *Bhavai*.[32]

In a succession of productions from the mid-1980s forwards, *Bhavai* became for Tara and Verma a part of their 'Binglish' approach. *Bhavai* is associated with the *Lokdharmi* practice as described in the *Natyasastra*, which, according to Mehta, would be acquired through hereditary skills and considered to be not as sacred and inviolable as *Natyadharmi* practice.[33] However, its exclusively *Lokdharmi* status is ambivalent; when it is performed by the higher-caste Brahmins and Princes during the *Navratri* festival, its social status is classified as *Margi*[34] (associated with the *Natyadharmi* practices). On the other hand, when it is performed by the *Bhavayas*, *Kolis* and *Kansaras*, who are considered to be of lower caste, then the form acquires *Desi* (folk) status, normally associated with *Lokdharmi* practice.[35] Thus the form and the class/caste of the people performing it are intrinsically linked in determining its identity. Vatsyayan describes *Bhavai* as the 'village theatre ... of the so-called outcastes, who entered and influenced caste society in many meaningful ways'.[36] Vatsyayan's definition carries the notions of caste-dilution and 'outcast' that are associated with *Bhavai*. It provides for Verma an ideal metaphor for using the form on the British stage, one that echoes the socio-political dimensions of 'Asian' identity and the 'Sector' position of his company in Britain. Moreover, Verma's choice of *Bhavai* may be interpreted as a way of maintaining a theatrical dialogue with 'Indian tradition' on the British stage. In this respect, it might be seen to reflect the South Asian diaspora's imaginary and tourist relationship with the Indian subcontinent,[37] described by Verma as 'not in terms of "them and us", but "us" being a part of "them" ... because part of your body, part of your blood, part of your memory is actually of that landscape'.[38] So it might be said that the 'representative' (of the South Asian community) identity of Tara Arts is implicit in the choice of *Bhavai*, chosen *not* on the basis of its regional Gujurati identity but on the basis of the form's social and caste identity. This suggests a symbolic usage, captured theoretically by Geertz as a 'symbolic structure ... a means of saying something of something', where cultural meaning is located in the form's dramatic shape, its metaphoric content and its Indian context.[39] In this sense, the *Bhavai*'s status—one rooted in caste-dilution—also reflects the 'outcast' socio-political identity of a BME (Black Minority Ethnic) theatre company such as Tara Arts.

The characteristics of Tara's production of *The Marriage of Figaro* are predominantly physical and material, embodied in the *Bhavai* movements and a materiality associated with the region of Gujarat, amplified by the use of other theatre forms and conventions such as masks, shadow-puppets and the *tawa'if* (courtesan) tradition associated with the Moghul period.[40] Yet there are also elements of the physicality of the performance that suggest an application of *Natyadharmi* style that would not normally be associated with *Bhavai*. These include the use of *angika abhinayas*, such as the *sringara mudra* that Rukhsana portrays at the start of the play, signifying a mirror; the reclining body postures (*sthanas*) conveyed by the Nawab; and other body positions assumed by the masked characters throughout the performance. The image of a Karnataka musician, V. Chandran, at stage right can also suggest more the presence of a *gandharva* (celestial) musician associated with the *Natyadharmi* convention than a 'popular' singer associated with *Bhavai*. Moreover, the heavy usage of Gujarat-associated textiles (linked to the regional identity of *Bhavai*) and the status-conscious costume styles strongly suggest an application of *aharya abhinaya*, but one associated with the *Natyadharmi* style in which the 'voice and costume are not from common use'.[41] In contrast, the vocal register of the production, combining the colloquial Brummi and Mancunian English accents spoken by the play's mostly Asian cast, roughly contradicts the *Natyadharmi* style, suggesting more an affiliation with the *Lokdharmi* style. The use of other Indian subcontinent-associated forms, such as shadow-puppets, the *tawa'if* (courtesan) tradition and *garbas* (Gujurati dance form) that are 'of the people' and not 'of the celestial world', also suggests an association with *Lokdharmi* style, while in addition contributing towards the creation of a distinct 'Hindu–Muslim' synergy that complements the eighteenth-century Indian context.[42] This mixture of styles may be considered an outcome of the 'Binglish' methodology that Verma had been developing, characterised by 'heaping together fragments of diverse cultures' in an attempt to 'culturally locate [the] British Asian subject' by theatrically 'placing cultural hybridity at the "centre" stage'.[43]

I would also argue that on the British stage the unfamiliar appearance of *Bhavai*, in terms of its distinctive gait and its 'demonstration-like' execution; the Indian-subcontinent-inspired costumed cast speaking in Brummi and Mancunian accents; the mimed demonstration of *raga* singing by the Begum; and the on-stage presence of V. Chandran and the heavy 'materiality' of the production all combine in attributing a Brechtian, 'quotable' quality to the form. They do so by simultaneously offering dissonance and recognition, and so reinforcing the 'branded' nature of Tara's 'Binglish' aesthetics. This is accomplished specifically by the suggestion of the elevation of the *Lokdharmi*-associated *Bhavai* to the more elevated *natya* status, which is facilitated by the usage of *abhinaya* conventions firmly associated with the *Natyadharmi* style.

It may seem that I am suggesting for this production a complementary collaboration between the conventions of the *Natyasastra* and Brecht's acting theory of *Gestus*. However, the 'individual-centred' premise of a human being as 'the sum of all social circumstance'[44] behind Brecht's Epic theatre is very different from the *Vedic* worldview suggested in the Sanskrit theatre, in which an individual was at the mercy of fate.[45] Moreover, whilst the *abhinaya* conventions were based on the principle of caste/status,

Sanskrit theatre was not necessarily concerned with the exposure of status considerations. It was far more associated with the celestial world, judging by the pre- and post-preliminary rituals that are found in the prescriptions for the *Natyadharmi* style. In addition, the notion of the *guru–shishya* relationship and the *Vedic* status of the treatise do not sit easily with the autonomy of a *gestic* actor, who was afforded the privilege of conveying a personal viewpoint that was ultimately to be 'decided outside the theatre.'[46] Bearing these differences in mind, the collaboration of *Gestus* and the *Natyasastra*-based conventions in the 'Binglish aesthetics' of *The Marriage of Figaro* offers signs that share technical similarities but contain distinct worldviews, inevitably contributing towards its complex and conflicting status as a performance.

Tamasha—*A Fine Balance*

Set in the 1975 State of Emergency in India, Tamasha's production of *A Fine Balance* (based on the Canadian–Indian Rohinton Mistry's novel) is focused around the Parsi widow Dina Dalal and her relationship with her two employees, Om and Ishvar, from the untouchable caste. Determined to avoid a second marriage, Dalal takes Maneck, a student boarder, and the two tailors Om and Ishvar into her tiny flat and runs a sewing business from home. As the Emergency's forbidding policies bring chaos to the city, the four strangers, whose lives have become inextricably linked, find themselves crossing divides of caste, class and religion to form the most unexpected of friendships.

The expansive set bearing a large billboard of Mrs Gandhi was inspired by photographs of India and was conceived in consultation with the production team and after the designer Sue Mayes's observation of the actors' workshops.[47] Mayes has designed almost every production for Tamasha for the last eighteen years, and values her close relationship with the two artistic directors Bhuchar and Landon-Smith. Her involvement begins right from the idea of production and continues throughout, even after the first and second runs as it was in the case of *A Fine Balance*.

The two-tier sprawling set, in muted beige and brown tones with a film-style billboard of Mrs Gandhi floating in a black space, is a silent character that initially greets the audience on their arrival into the Hampstead Theatre. The combination of the billboard of Mrs Gandhi, with its porous texture, the overloaded telegraph pole bearing numerous illegal wires, and the bamboo poles that hold the front part of the set but not the back create a setting of a rundown part of an Indian city, with notions of 'still under construction'. The other metaphorical image that Mayes has pursued from the novel is the patchwork quilt. Mayes saw the quilt as 'a metaphor of the pieces of the characters' lives joined together', and decided to incorporate this imagery in the construction and in the texture of the floor of the set: 'I am saying life is a patchwork ... People come together in completely unusual ways and then move apart.'[48]

The signs constituting the set may be categorised in Peircean terms. The large billboard of Mrs Gandhi created to signify the historical context of the 1975 Emergency may be considered *iconic* (inspired from a photograph), *indexical* (related to the other material objects as well as to the context of the play), and *symbolic* (the style of the poster is created by adopting a film-billboard convention). The overloaded telegraph pole and the three-panel rickety structure supported by bamboo poles may also be considered *iconic* (resembling the objects) and *symbolic* (pointing towards a particular context). They may also be considered to be *indexical*, pointing towards the patchwork quilt which is used metaphorically to represent the nature of social relations between the characters from different castes. However, if one considers the overall quality of the whole set, taking into account the number of objects and their spatial positions, then the set may be considered to be mostly *iconic*, consisting mainly of materiality that resembles the objects. This *iconic* register contributes towards its realistic quality.

Yet there is much in the performance of the play that invites a Brechtian approach to analysis, concerned less with portraying reality and more with pointing towards it, not least in the 'voices' of the production. The production did not attempt to authenticate the 'Indian' context of the play through the use of inflected Indian English in the dialogue, which might have sounded contrived or patronising. Nor was there any indication of the 'coached' Hindi spoken by British Asian/non-Asian actors that was employed in Stuart Wood's *Mahabharata* at the Sadlers Wells theatre.[49] Instead, true to the Brechtian ethos of the actor being privileged over character, Tamasha appears to have taken into account the presence of the mixed-race cast (Asian and Turkish) and their respective heritages. By accommodating their culturally inflected voices, Tamasha has allowed them to contribute towards the *gestic* quality of the production by creating 'transparent signifier[s] ... and a focus on "voice" itself as a site of contestation'.[50] In the opening scene, when Shankar the beggar shouts '*ek paisa aapo*', instead of '*ek paisa de do*' as in the published play-script, one senses that the play has been allowed to develop organically in the rehearsals, with the actor Divian Ladwa's Gujarati identity heard in his own words, which I recognised as a fellow Gujarati.[51] Contrastingly, when Dina Dalal passes by searching for something, Shakar, the beggar offers to help: 'I am like A to Z where you want to go?'[52] These diverse auditory signifiers in Gujarati and English may be considered *gestic* in nature, revealing both the Brechtian portrayal of the Indian beggar's social status as well as the voice of the actor (Divian Ladwa) speaking through him in his 'British' accent and references.

The evidence of the cast's voices can be heard in other scenes, such as that in the market, in which a woman (Rina Fatania) selling chapatti flour is shouting '*rotli no aato*' in an East African Gujarati accent. Moreover, when the Beggarmaster (Taylan Halici) visits Dalal to collect 'protection' money, he uses the Turkish greeting '*e gunlar*' ('goodbye/see you'), thus allowing presumably his Turkish identity to surface in the sound of a play that is set in India. Yet, in addition to the 'voices' of the cast, one can also as distinctly hear the translated voice of the *characters*, plainly apparent in the potency peddler's call, offering magical cures for sexual disorders: 'Apply once a day and your wife will be proud of you. Apply twice a day and she will have to share you with the whole block.'[53] The spontaneously delivered Indian film songs in the production serve as third-person narratives that may be understood as the externalisation of the unspoken emotions of the Indian street performers.[54] The deconstructive strategies apparent in these multiple voices highlight the complexity of reception involved in the realisation of a *gestic* approach between the 'telling and told', the '*gestic split*' whose interpretive registers demand mutually exclusive readings of the same subject.[55]

In addition to the mixed voices, the inclusion of puppets contributes to the Brechtian nature of the play in portraying the demonstrative quality of Brechtian *Gestus*, by showing both the manipulator and the manipulated on the stage. There are puppets for Leila the performing monkey, Tikka the dog and Chunni the performing girl (the Monkeyman's niece).

Yet the inclusion of the mixed-race cast's voices highlighted in the linguistic element of the text is not extended to the characterisation of the play, where original names from Mistry's novel have been strictly retained. Om, Ishvar and Shankar, the names of the central characters, carry deified connotations in the Indian context that perhaps suggest Mistry's intention to elevate them from their 'untouchable' status in a literary context. The names Om and Ishvar are associated with the Hindu religion, with the former being the powerful and sacred mantra *Om* and the latter *Ishvar* being another name used to address god. The name Shankar given to the beggar, who is literally elevated on his wooden *gadi* that carries his severed limbs, is another name for Lord Shiva. Shankar's Hindu funeral in the play is also ceremonious, resembling that of a VIP, which can imply his elevation at death. Even the widow Dalal (who is not shown to have direct relationship with him in the play) decides to attend his funeral, provoking outrage and anger from her older brother Nusswan: 'What will people say if they see my sister prancing in a procession of beggars?'[56]

The notions of elevation are more apparent in the pivotal scene in which Dalal invites her two employees Om and Ishvar to dine at her table laid out with her best china and cutlery. In the context of the play this suggests a massive leap in Dalal's attitude: in the earlier scenes she would not even allow her two employees to use the frosted water glasses in her home that were exclusively reserved for her and Maneck. This transformation scene displays the 'temporary' social elevation of the slum dwellers Om and

Ishvar, who are more accustomed to sitting on the floor and eating with their hands solely with their 'own' people. It is difficult to ascertain whether Dalal's transformative act is motivated by the tragic story about Ishvar's father's murder at the hands of the local *thakur* (landowner) that Maneck shared with her in the preceding scene, or whether she has her own selfish interests at heart in keeping the two tailors in her cramped rented flat so that she can deliver the garment orders in time. Within the context of Mayes's realism-inspired set, such utopian displays of 'acceptance' and even the suggestion of the beginning of a 'friendship' between the Parsi widow Dalal and her two employees of the untouchable caste would seem unrealistic, taking into consideration the social conventions and constraints associated with widows living alone in India. Tamasha's production contains tension between realism and a Brechtian exposure of class/caste relations, one that may register more in the contemporary than it 'realistically' portrays the social relations of the time.

This juxtaposition of a subaltern community (Om and Ishvar of untouchable caste) with individuals of the writer's own culture (like Dina Dalal, the Canadian–Indian writer Rohinton Mistry is a Parsi, a minority group of Zoroastrian faith that migrated to India from Iran in the thirteenth century to escape persecution) invites consideration of JanMohamed's theories on the presentation of racial difference in colonial literature. He argues that such works of literature

> not so much represent as present the native for the first time ... Since the native does not have access to these texts (because of linguistic barriers) and since the European audience has no direct contact with the native, imperialist fiction tends to be unconcerned with the truth value of its representation.[57]

Moreover, as the 'native' is often presented for the first time in such a text, subtle changes can occur in the relationship with the reader. Such a work of fiction

> is rarely concerned with overtly affirming the reader's experience of his own culture and therefore does not solicit his approval: it exists outside the dialogic class discourse of European Literature.[58]

In these formulations, JanMohamed carefully defines the audience of such texts, of which the writer can also be a part, and which Abeysekere determines as being 'subconsciously conditioned by a market that has grown around that audience, that readership'.[59]

It is interesting to note that in *A Fine Balance* the character of the Parsi widow, Dina Dalal, does not represent the archetypical 'Indian' widow, dressed in a widow's sari, as worn by Mrs Gandhi in the billboard, but rather a modern entrepreneurial [Asian] woman, dressed in skirt/top and sensible shoes, who is trying to carve out an independent living in her tiny rented flat. It might be argued that the character of Dalal is more a representative of a 'western' woman than an 'Indian' widow bound by society/family conventions. The theatrical portrayal of Dalal's personal and professional relationship with Om and Ishvar of the untouchable caste suggests a classic 'dominant model of power- and interest-relations', at the core of which lies 'the Manichean opposition between the putative superiority of the European and the supposed inferiority of the native'.[60] According to JanMohamed,

> power relations under-lying this model set in motion such strong currents that even a writer ... who may indeed be highly critical of imperialist exploitation is drawn into its vortex.[61]

The issue of social relations between castes is at the heart of Mistry's literary text set in India, but the novel may also be seen as a narrative about the writer himself and his explicit subject. It is also possible that, to an extent, the director Landon-Smith may have utilised Tamasha's adaptation to explore the caste-consciousness of British South Asians, which she had highlighted in *Strictly Dandia*.[62] These considerations add significantly to the mix of signs registered by the production.

Conclusion

In conclusion, I return to the question of audience. The analysis of *The Marriage of Figaro* revealed a complex network of signs to which the sign-making theories of the *Natyasastra* and Brechtian *Gestus* can be considered applicable. The idea of 'being English' and 'not-quite English'[63] suggested in Verma's 'Binglish' aesthetics attempts to create, in Rushdie's words, a 'different sort of noise in English'[64] theatrically. Lines such as 'Pardon my Hindi' spoken by the Gujarati Figaro can also bring what Bennett describes as a 'not-like-us' quality to the performances, where the attractions of the production for audiences may lie in its 'otherness ... [and] its seeming inability to be understood (and, as such, to be really consumed) by conventional receptive processes'.[65] Moreover, Tara's distinctive, *Natyasastra*-inspired 'Binglish' aesthetics invite a reconsideration of Barthes's question: 'Can we westerners really consume a fragment of civilisation totally isolated from its context?'[66]

In Barthes's use of the term 'westerners', the British South Asian audience may also be included, as many of them might have inherited an Indian heritage but not the lived experience of the Indian subcontinent, or necessarily any affinity with its culture. To quote from my earlier study of sign-making in British Asian theatre, 'I would suggest that this estrangement from the culture of the Indian subcontinent is as much part of the "Asian" narrative as is their "imagined" affinity with it.'[67] This is a view that resonated at the 'British Asian Theatre: from Past to Present' conference held at Exeter in April 2008, in which practitioners such as the playwright Parv Bancil declared their disassociation from India and their frustrations at an identification with it. Colin Counsell has argued that theatrical forms 'manufacture different audiences', who assume a particular 'interpretative posture' in interpreting a particular kind of performance in which the 'logic is written into the form itself'. If that is so, then the obscure nature of Tara's 'Binglish' aesthetics does not appear to seek connectivity either with the Asian or the non-Asian audience.[68] A branded approach such as 'Binglish' aesthetics, which is reminiscent of the work of European practitioners Brook and Barba, can turn the 'form into an icon rather than a force for communication'.[69] Furthermore, the particular 'effect' intended by the 'other-ness' of such an approach can eventually fade, resulting in a performance becoming more about the company/brand than about the performance itself.[70]

Against Mayes's realism-inspired *iconic* set, the portrayal of 'Indian' characterisation in *A Fine Balance* offered both unified and un-unified readings, drawing upon the *gestic*-split British Asian cast's interpretation as well as on the Canadian–Indian Mistry's text. My analysis of the performance revealed that selective aspects of Mistry's text were given a 'Brechtian treatment', evident in the materiality of the set and in the inclusion of the 'voices' of the mixed-cast actors. Contrastingly, I have suggested, in adopting some observations by JanMohamed, that the central theme of the friendship between the Parsi widow Dalal and her two employees of untouchable caste was portrayed from the writer's point of view. In that connection, the shifting interpretations of 'Indian' character-isation suggested in Landon-Smith's direction did not add conviction to this ideological theme—the portrayal of a friendship between the Parsi widow Dalal and her two employees of untouchable caste that attempted to transcend caste and status differences. Bearing in mind the notion of an 'imaginary' relationship with the Indian subcontinent associated with the Indian diaspora identity, such a contemporary adaptation for the British stage might have been more fruitfully utilised to reflect the current economic migratory trends in the UK that include the arrival of Indians as well as Eastern Europeans. So, for instance, Tamasha might have shown the 'British Asian' Dalal's two employees as newly arrived economic Indian migrants (which the two employees in the play are, in the sense that they had left their village to find work in the city), so providing a more current and global interpretation of Canadian–Indian Mistry's novel. In addition, bearing in mind Tamasha's ethos of placing British Asian talent at 'centre stage', the adaptation of India-based plays such as *A Fine Balance* can also highlight the complexity of representative politics. Here one needs to take into account the British-Asian community's history of political/artistic representation; their imaginary and tourist relationship with the Indian subcontinent; and their status within the Indian context, in which they are not necessarily recognised as 'Indian', 'British' or 'Asian' but often as PIO (Person of Indian Origin) and NRI (Non Resident Indian). In this sense, the representation of the 'Indian' identities on the British stage by an 'Asian' cast can be complex and open to multiple readings, depending on the context and the audience and the interpretations offered by the production itself.

In *A Fine Balance*, Tamasha returned to its Indian-diaspora profile reflected in the earlier productions of *Untouchable* (1989), *House of the Sun* (1991), *Women of the Dust* (1992) and *A Tainted Dawn* (1997). The 'Binglish' treatment of *The Marriage of Figaro* also reveals Tara's continued affiliation with exploration of Indian forms and material and their application to the European places that the company had explored in the mid-1980s to the early 1990s. The question of the audience for both companies remains hard to answer confidently, as these productions do not necessarily attract South Asian diaspora audiences. Indeed, the presence of diverse audiences might be regarded as a significant achievement of both the companies, one that implicitly contradicts the Arts Council's 'new audience' initiatives,[71] concerned as they have been with attracting a British Asian audience to British Asian productions. With the arrival of new migrants and the tragic events of the London bombings of 2005, associated as they were with British Asian youth, it remains to be debated further whether these two distinctively different approaches reflect either the changing 'new' India or the complex socio-political landscape of Britain. The two productions, in the complexity and contradictions of their aesthetics and sign-making, reveal the uncertainties that still lie within the theatrical confidence of two of Britain's leading Asian theatre companies.

13

British Asian Live Art

motiroti

Stephen Hodge

Live art is now recognised as one of the most vital and influential of creative areas in the UK: it is a research engine driven by artists who are working across forms, contexts, and spaces to open up new artistic models, new languages for the representation of ideas, and new strategies for intervening in the public realm.[1]

These words, written by the Directors of London's Live Art Development Agency in an attempt to define the broad cultural strategy that is live art, are easily applied to the last twenty years of work by Keith Khan and Ali Zaidi, who have operated together for a large part of the time under the name **moti**roti.

There are over fifty projects attributed to **moti**roti,[2] and this essay will focus on a few key episodes, examining the company's shifting relationship with performance (theatre and live art). These episodes will be selected, formative collaborations between Khan, Zaidi and others; the move from street to stage in *Moti Roti, Puttli Chunni* (1993); the contrasting contexts of two works of 1995 (*Maa* at the Royal Court Theatre and *Wigs of Wonderment* at the ICA); the legal incorporation of **moti**roti in 1996; the international intermedia work *Alladeen* (2003–5); and recent work by **moti**roti after Keith Khan left the company.

Pre-**moti**roti: formative collaborations

Time and age is a great benefactor when you look back at things. So, there's a very clear trajectory there. Very clear. And I think displacement happens to be that.[3]

Naseem Khan has described Keith Khan as 'a determined polymath',[4] outlining three major influences on the young artist in the 1980s: 'varied forms of contemporary western culture—gay culture, club culture, music, dance, video, film';[5] the cultural heritage (in particular the carnival) of Trinidad, where his Indian–Muslim relatives had moved to in the nineteenth century; and his fine art education, specialising in sculpture (at Wimbledon School of Art and Middlesex Polytechnic).

Born in Bombay, Ali Zaidi migrated to Pakistan at the age of four, and spent his youth travelling back and forth between the two. Issues of displacement and identification were hardwired into Zaidi, 'because in Pakistan we were always seen as the Indians, and in India we were always seen as the Pakistanis'. Zaidi displayed a talent for drawing and painting, but was not interested in shutting himself off in the studio, and was persuaded by his film-maker father that the job prospects of a fine artist were poor. Instead, he chose to pursue avenues in graphic design, photography, advertising and teaching.

Zaidi, who had received a British Council scholarship to study at Chelsea School of Art, met Khan at a play in the basement of the Soho Poly Theatre in 1988. Zaidi was interested in the way that the personal image was projected into public space, and Khan, who 'was an anomaly' in terms of the way he dressed and wore his hair, fascinated him.

Soon after they met in 1988, Khan employed Zaidi to paint a set with him, and it was not long before their working relationship slipped into collaboration, rather than employment. Whilst it took years to articulate and formalise both their working relationship and any shared set of aims and objectives, they quickly developed a working strategy that was 'not about one person taking the control, but it was actually allowing the others to come in and have their space to work within'.[6] This reflected Khan's body of experience in carnival design in Trinidad and Notting Hill, which had instilled a deep sense of the importance of social and artistic collaboration at the heart of his practice.

Two pre-**moti**roti works of 1990 demonstrated an early desire on the part of Khan and Zaidi to draw on their diverse training and experience, collaborate with artists from other disciplines (such as musician Gavin O'Shea), approach major commissioning bodies and take on large-scale projects. These were *Revisionist Queens*, a series of giant sculptural street interventions commissioned for the Houston International Festival, and *Aiya's Apples, Aisha's Eye*, a video work exploring British and Indian identity funded by the Arts Council of Great Britain's Black Arts Video Project.

For *Flying Costumes, Floating Tombs* (1991), funded in its research and development phase by Artangel and jointly commissioned by the Arnolfini in Bristol and the London International Festival of Theatre, Khan drew on this carnival experience. Working alongside a team of artists, including Zaidi and choreographer, percussionist and educator H. Patten, Khan constructed a cross-cultural, cross-disciplinary 'mas camp' with more than 300 participants (from playback singer Jayachandran to local Bharat Natyam and canoeing groups) in the two cities. Giant costumes, red and green sculptures supported by cranes, Islamic music and celebratory dance combined to tell the story of the martyrdom of the brothers Hussein and Hasan. The piece played to more than 8,000 people on the docks in central Bristol and in London's Paddington Basin in the months of June and July, and earned a Time Out London Dance and Performance Award.

Further collaborations between Khan, who became known as a 'spectacularist', and Zaidi followed soon after. These included the Notting Hill Carnival band projects *Some Kine Ah Wave* (1991) and *Before Columbus* (1992), led by Khan, and the *Colours of Asia* mixed-arts festival, which was curated by Zaidi at the Black Art Gallery, Islington and the Tom Allen Centre, Newham (1992). A number of collaborating visual artists (Nina Edge, Mazhar Hussain, Sasha Kelly and Betty Vaughan Richards) from *Flying Costumes, Floating Tombs* continued to work with the pair on some of these projects.

From street to stage: *Moti Roti, Puttli Chunni*

An afternoon of dance pieces had been staged at Theatre Royal Stratford East as part of the *Colours of Asia* festival. Khan and Zaidi were impressed with the level of commitment that the Theatre Royal had to developing new audiences, and approached Philip Hedley, the Artistic Director, again when it came to *Moti Roti, Puttli Chunni*[7] (1993):

> I was interested in the work of Philip Hedley, Artistic Director of Theatre Royal Stratford East because he was very focused on audience development and had built an audience that was clearly not the kind of audience that other venues had. It seemed that the way Theatre Royal approached marketing and audience development was as important as their actual productions, and I thought that they would be a good fit for our own aspirations for this project.[8]

Moving off the street and into the theatre might seem like a strange decision for a pair of artists interested in participation and inclusion, but Khan had become a little frustrated with the lack of development of carnival as a form. 'When *Flying Costumes, Floating Tombs* was seen by people, they only saw it as this exotic performance ... There was very little emotional engagement, or a kind of engagement when people could have said more than yes it was very colourful and very spectacular.'[9] Performed in English, Hindi and Urdu, and often referred to as a 'film project' rather than a piece of theatre, *Moti Roti, Puttli Chunni* drew on the popularity of the Bollywood musical form, 'recreating in minute detail all of those effects like tracking shots and close ups and the kind of interplay between screen and stage'.[10] Yet, whilst preserving the visual impact of the previous carnival-inspired work through the sets, costumes and choreography, Khan and Zaidi took a bold step by moving into the theatre building: 'I'd made this piece kind of innocently, because I'm trained in visual art but I wanted to make a film on stage, using all the identity of Indian movies, because they are really rich.'[11] The learning curve was quite steep, particularly when it came to writing the dramatic text: 'We'd actually put a whole piece together and then realised that we couldn't write it ... The reality was that we were learning what writers do.'[12] In addition to the Theatre Royal's commitment to audience development, the casting of Pakistani film star Laila Khan and Nitish Bharadwaj, who had played Krishna in the television serialisation of the *Mahabharat*,[13] meant that 'a huge audience turned up to this project wherever it showed'.[14]

The production was directed and designed by Khan with Zaidi. The screenplay was by Diane Esguerra, who had collaborated with Khan on *Images of Purdah*, an early work for the National Review of Live Art at the Riverside Studios in 1987. Music was once again provided by Gavin O'Shea, working with Pete Harmon, and the choreography was conceived by Monisha Patil-Bharadwaj. In addition to Khan and Bharadwaj, the original performers were Ajay Chhabra, Shobna Gulati, Mamta Kaash, Kaleem Janjua, Pravesh Kumar, Jamila Massey, Nayesh Radia and Nina Wadia. Produced by Gill Lloyd for Artsadmin, the work was co-commissioned by the Theatre Royal and London International Festival of Theatre, and received additional funding from the Baring Foundation, the Hamlyn Foundation, International Initiatives, Arts Council of Britain and the London Arts Board.

After its five-week run at the Theatre Royal from 19 June to 17 July 1993, for which it won a Time Out London Dance and Performance Award, and an appearance at Festival Hamburg '93, *Moti Roti, Puttli Chunni* went on tour in mid-1994 with a revised cast comprising Mina Anwar, Monisha Bharadwaj, Nitish Bharadwaj, Kaleem, Pravesh Kumar and Jamila Massey. During that time it played in short runs of between three and five days at Greenwich Theatre in London and the Harbourfront Centre in Toronto in April 1994; the New Athenaeum Theatre in Glasgow, Haymarket Theatre in Leicester, and Birmingham Repertory Theatre in May; and The Dance House in Manchester in early June.

1995: a year of contrasting contexts

1995 demonstrated **motiroti**'s flexibility as an organisation, choosing different contexts and modes of audience engagement as appropriate to each new project they undertook:

The pieces that I make are either incredibly tiny, or delicate, or small, or one-to-one, or big huge things that are over-scale in a way, and I kind of like that difference ... I'm as interested in a small conversation as I am fireworks across cities, because I think all of them engage with the urban society in very, very different ways, and potentially very exciting ways.[15]

Maa (1995) saw the company develop its practice further within the mainstream theatre context. Commissioned for a week's run as part of the Barclays New Stages Festival at the Royal Court Theatre in London from 13 to 17 June 1995, with additional funding from the Arts Council of Great Britain's New Collaborations Fund, the production's programme shows how the roles for the project were formalised in quite traditional theatre terms. Khan is credited as director, Zaidi as designer and Ashish Kotak as writer (except for the Urdu/Trinidadian dialogue, which is credited to Zaidi and Khan). Kotak, who was not trained in theatre either, but rather in journalism and film-making, was brought in to sidestep some of the writing problems that had occurred during the writing of *Moti Roti, Puttli Chunni*. He developed the initial dramatic structure of the piece, but after five drafts he ended up writing the spoken dialogue as well. Khan had hoped that Kotak's background would make him more likely to collaborate with other project participants. But the very short rehearsal process at Toynbee Hall (the home to Artsadmin, **moti**roti's producers at the time) meant that most narrative decisions were made in advance of any work in the studio.[16]

I don't mind it being perceived as a play because in some way it helps in our attempts to attract a more culturally mixed audience. Barclays [New Stages] itself will bring in a live art audience but they will probably hate it. They might feel this is just a straight play with a few nice costumes thrown in. Fundamentally it does have a linear narrative that people answer back to—they do have roles ... [the important issue is] access to the work, not the theatricality or live artiness of it.[17]

The programme notes for *Maa* emphasised how the production had picked up, both in form and content, where *Moti Roti, Puttli Chunni* left off two years before:

Maa has been in gestation for about two years, following the success of *Moti Roti, Puttli Chunni* in 1993. Artistically we have hoped to create a piece of theatre that is a complex fusion of not only artforms, but current cultural debate. This piece of the project is the second part of an epic, in which we trace eight generations of women, starting with the life of courtesans in India in the 1850s, through to a life of indentureship of Indians in Trinidad in the early 20th century, through to Sadhana's existance in Britain in the late 1990s—including the dilemma of her second generation son, Ricky—the only son for eight generations.[18]

Other key credits for *Maa* include Jo Martin (assistant director); Sumant Jayakrishnan (assistant designer); Keith Waithe, Gavin O'Shea and Pete Harman (music and sound); Shobna Gulati (choreography); Darrel Butlin (scratch animation films); Masquerade 2000 (carnival costumes); Siddiqua Akhtar, Raji James, Mamta Kaash, Laila Khan, Nicholas Khan, Sakuntala Ramanee and Vivek Trivedi (performers).

In contrast to *Maa*, *Wigs of Wonderment* (also 1995), originally commissioned by the Institute of Contemporary Arts in London as part of the 'Mirage: Enigmas of Race, Difference and Desire' season, sat firmly within the live art context, as Khan acknowledges.

It is a live piece—set in a deviant beauty salon, run by artists and performers with a photographic installation, and an intriguing ambience. In a one-to-one relationship with the performers, the audience is invited to examine the way they look and feel about themselves, whilst the portraits of black Britons illuminate dark corners of the space. The piece uses a walk-through installation highlighting skin lightening and hair straightening products. There is an interactive salon with wigs, hair, nail and face accessories to try, and most importantly a head massage, using hair oils and perfumes. In the piece there are seven performers, five women, two men, and one cross dresser, some of whom are second generation black British.[19]

An immersive installation of African and Asian transformative cosmetic products; a hair make-over from a black beautician; a head massage from Asian men dressed in hairy clothes; intimate conversations and stories; visual, sonic and olfactory experiences combined to form a 'gentle probing of identity construction which cuts beyond categories of ethnicity and colour and exposes the cultural assumptions that accrue to such basic "facts" as hair and skin'.[20] Previous collaborators O'Shea and Edge joined Khan and Zaidi on the project; the original ICA cast comprised Sharon Martin, Tammy Harwood, Nick Khan, Sumant Jayakrishnan.

Wigs of Wonderment was reworked for a number of particular contexts over the subsequent four years: Kannonhallen in Copenhagen (1996), Union Chapel in Islington as part of the Windrush Celebrations (1998), Old Ikon Gallery in Birmingham as part of Queerfest99 (1999) and DeBeweeging Festival in Antwerp (1999). Funding was provided by Copenhagen City of Culture, Black Theatre Co-operative, Fierce Earth and DeBeweeging Festival respectively. An interactive CD-ROM adapted from the live work was funded by the London Arts Board and published by the Live Art Development Agency in 2003.

1995 also saw *The Seed The Root*, directed by Zaidi, a series of series of culturally challenging, carefully positioned installations and mini-performances playing with representations of the masculine and the feminine, inserted into the landscape and communities of Brick Lane and Spitalfields in the East End of London. The installations were present in the cityscape for a month, and the guided tours for fifteen to twenty people at a time (led by Shobna Gulati, Nick Khan and Jo Martin) took place over two days. Notably, the tour included a stop for 'off menu', 'authentic' Bangladeshi food amid 'suggestive' photographs of papaya and aubergine: 'Where I work best is with intimacy, and not necessarily with the spectacular … Food is a great connector.'[21]

Years of stabilisation and growth

In order to support the increasing range and quantity of **moti**roti's output, Khan and Zaidi decided to formalise its structure. In December 1996 the company incorporated, and in January 1997 became a registered charity. The initial members of the board of directors were Rose Fenton, Behroze Gandhy, Mohammed Khan, Rosalind Price and Catherine Ugwu.[22] Karla Barnacle-Best, who had been producing with London Bubble, became the company's administrator.

Khan was still employing the spirit of the mas camp when he was appointed as designer of the opening ceremony for the Millennium Dome at the start of 2000. Working on an even larger scale, as part of the *Celebration Commonwealth* project **moti**roti worked with around 4,000 artists and participants to stage the Jubilee Parade on 4 June.[23] Rather than the simple and reductive display of national dress of former Empire Parades, the company was interested in 'looking at the Commonwealth as a place of interchange … So, with New Zealand, we invited a number of Māori performers over to work with schools in the East End and transfer those skills.'[24]

Alladeen

> Social networking, the Bebo-Facebook generation, how people will find out about things, how people will engage with things, is going to be increasingly more important, and I think people are going to be looking for very, very local experiences in very far away places.[25]

Over the years of activity, both Khan and Zaidi became annoyed that **moti**roti was 'often seen as an "Indian" or "Asian" company and having played within and beyond those cultural genres we felt that it was time to play out "cultural fluidity" on an international stage'.[26] *Alladeen* (2003) provided an opportunity to explore these concerns.

Marianne Weems, the artistic director of The Builders Association from New York, had seen *Moti Roti, Puttli Chunni* in 1993 when she toured to London as dramaturg with the Wooster Group. Likewise, Khan and Zaidi had seen The Builders Association's production of *Jet Lag* in 2000 when it came to the Barbican. Both companies had been knitting film and live performance together for years and there was 'mutual respect and fascination for each other's work'.[27]

During their initial discussions, an article on Indian call centres was published in the New York Times which 'highlighted the plight of detachment/displacement that media can create',[28] and Weems, Khan and Zaidi embarked on two research trips to Bangalore. They immersed themselves in the training process, in which operators were given common American/UK forenames, bombarded with American/UK cultural references and trained to imitate American/UK speech patterns.

After two years of intense artistic discussions, research, major fundraising, negotiation with co-producers, workshops, and experimentation with participating artists and rehearsal, the work made it into the theatre. The performance component of the project is succinctly summarised by Weems:

> By drawing on fragments of the story of Aladdin, the street urchin who goes from a pauper to a prince in *The Arabian Nights*, *Alladeen* operates on two levels. It situates spectators in a call center in India, where performers portray phone operators, but actors and audiences are also in a porous space where threads from the myth of Aladdin occasionally bleed through. *Alladeen* explores how people function as "global souls" caught up in circuits of technology and how our voices and images travel—and morph—from one culture to another.[29]

The trio wanted to access an audience beyond the normal theatre-going public, in particular 'a younger, more digitally inclined audience'.[30] As such, the project comprised three interrelated parts: a live multimedia performance element, a music video that was seen on MTV Asia, and an interactive website.[31] The live performance was itself complex:

> On a split screen (a large screen the width of the stage is raised above the playing space) the actors below become part of a composite image, much like a computer screen with many windows open, which blends footage from actual call center operators with projections of contemporary cultural images, such as characters from the popular TV series, *Friends*.[32]

The key performance credits are Penny Andrews (UK producer); Kim

Whitener (executive producer); Marianne Weems (director); Keith Khan and Ali Zaidi (design); Christopher Kondek (video); Dan Dobson (sound); Jennifer Tipton (lighting); Martha Baer (text); Norman Frisch (dramaturg); Rizwan Mirza, David Pence, Heaven Phillips, Tanya Selvaratnam, Jasmine Simhalan and Jeff Webster (performers). The music video was directed by Ali Zaidi, with additional video by Peter Norman, sound by Dan Dobson and original music by Shri (Shrikanth Sriram). The website was directed by Ali Zaidi and conceived by Keith Khan, Marianne Weems and Ali Zaidi.

Alladeen was co-produced by Arts International, Barbican BITE:03, Le Maillon in Strasburg, Romaeuropa Festival 03 and Melbourne International Arts Festival, and co-commissioned by Wexner Center for the Arts in Columbus, Museums of Contemporary Art in Chicago, Walker Art Center in Minneapolis, REDCAT in Los Angeles and the MIST Residency Program at The Kitchen in New York. The UK funders were the British Council, Arts Council England, Connecting Flights, PRS Foundation for New Music and the Asian Music Circuit.

Opening at the Wexner Center for the Arts in Columbus on 4 April 2003 and closing on 14 May 2005 at John F. Kennedy Center in Washington, *Alladeen* toured widely across the USA. It was also shown internationally at Singapore Arts Festival, Barbican BITE:03 in the UK, La Ferme du Buisson in France, Romaeuropa Festival 03 in Italy, Warwick Arts Centre in the UK, Contact Theatre in the UK, Tramway in the UK, Bogotá International Theatre Festival in Colombia, Bergen International Theatre Festival in Norway, Bonn Biennale in Germany, Melbourne International Arts Festival in Australia, Belfast Festival in Northern Ireland and Highlights Festival in Canada.

> In certain cities in North America it had massive audiences, like Chicago has a really switched on Asian community, all of whom were there, and the UK doesn't. We did a publicly funded tour in the UK, but the audience base was very, very thin, because that idea of visual theatre in a literary culture doesn't really exist.[33]

Recent developments

In 2004, the year that *Alladeen* won a New York OBIE award for Outstanding Production, Khan chose to leave **moti**roti and take up the post of chief executive of Rich Mix, a new multi-artform venue in Shoreditch established 'to create and celebrate work from BAME [Black, Asian and Minority Ethnic] and marginalised communities'.[34] In developing the vision for the organisation (which opened in Spring 2006), Khan was keen to establish new models of artist support and audience development based on experimentation and collaboration: 'I created it as a house of process. Rich

Mix has become a place where you can see work as it's being made and see artists trying things out.'[35]

In April 2006 Khan was appointed as a National Council Member (Practising Artist) for Arts Council England, and in June of the same year he left Rich Mix to become Head of Culture for the 2012 Olympic Games and Paralympic Games.

> I took the job, and I've purposefully stopped making work, because I really did feel that as an artist I've reached as far as I could go ... I've got involved with the Olympics because I really do want to see big change in society, and I want to see a better reflection of the cultures around us that isn't just necessarily hierarchical or arts top-down, but much more embracing of the energies of cultural forces that are around us.[36]

The commitment of the London Organising Committee for the Olympic Games to the Cultural Olympiad was questioned when Khan's contract was not renewed at the end of 2008.

When Khan left **moti**roti in 2004 Zaidi become the sole artistic director. A new role of learning director was created, and filled by Janice Galloway, who had been a projects co-ordinator and producer for the British Council: 'Artistic production and learning are part of the same process, which is achieved through the collaborative participation of artists, key cultural institutions, audiences, communities and organisations.'[37] One such project that demonstrates this commitment is *Priceless* (2006), which Zaidi conceived and developed with key collaborators Daniel Saul (video) and Poulomi Desai (sound and music).

> Serpentine Gallery commissioned **moti**roti to use as a canvas the entire Exhibition Road ... Home to major museums: Natural History Museum, Victoria and Albert Museum, the Science Museum, and other Royal institutions ... Curators selected objects/ideas priceless to their institutions that were used as triggers for "road shows"/live events, by inviting people into these institutions.[38]

As ever, though, **moti**roti continued to work on a variety of scales and across different media and cultural contexts. *Cooked With Love* (2004), commissioned by Laura Godfrey-Isaacs for home live art,[39] was a banquet of forty-five dishes cooked by Zaidi with forty-five ingredients for forty-five guests to celebrate the forty-fifth wedding anniversary of his parents. The event incorporated a slide show, small rituals and autobiographical reminiscences, after which 'the food was presented and so the people became the performers'.[40] There have been two more recent iterations: *Cooking with Love* (LiteSide Festival, Amsterdam, 2007) and *Journeys of Love and More*

Love (Napoli Teatro Festival Italia, 2009). *Light it!* (2006) and *Harvest it!* (2007), by contrast, also produced by home live art and **moti**roti, were autumn festivals created alongside large teams of artists and community collaborators/participants, for Myatt's Fields Park, Camberwell, in London.

> Festivals, both secular and religious, from many different cultures were brought together for *Light it!* from Diwali (literally "festival of lights"), Eid and the Jewish Channukah (also known as the "festival of lights") to the more secular Halloween, Guy Fawkes and the Mexican Day of the Dead. These events point out the similarity between communities as opposed to their differences.[41]

At the time of writing, **moti**roti's main focus is the major project *360°: Britain India Pakistan* (2007–2010). This three-year project continues to explore the core themes that have been present in the company's work from *Flying Costumes, Floating Tombs*, right through to *Alladeen* and *Priceless*: those of multiple perspectives, of displacement, of the familiar and the unfamiliar: 'If you've got twenty artists from each of the countries ... giving their interpretation of what home means to them, and what identity means to them in the twenty-first century, then the result is chaos. From that chaos, you would take out your own meaning, I would take out my own meaning. That feels to me much more in sympathy with how I am, with how my life is, with how I view the world.'[42]

In the wake of **moti**roti follows a host of third-generation individual live artists, such as George Chakravarthi, Jiva Parthipan, Rajni Shah, Qasim Riza Shaheen and Harminder Singh Judge. These artists share, in common with Khan and Zaidi, a desire to work across forms and contexts, depending on the needs of any given project, and many are multi-skilled, internet-savvy polymaths, who combine the roles of artist, producer, educator, researcher and archivist.

14

On the Making of *Mr Quiver*

Rajni Shah

This essay charts the development of the four-hour performance installation *Mr Quiver* from its conception in the early 2000s to its final performance as part of the British Asian theatre conference at the University of Exeter on 12 April 2008. It is primarily a personal reflection on the journey I took as director and performer, making what started as a short autobiographical solo and grew organically over the years into something much longer and more complex. I shall use this space to trace ideas, situations and connections that I feel were significant in the hope of shedding a small ray of light on the experience of making such a piece at such a time, including where it sits at the time of writing, December 2008.

Dreams

It began with a show I directed in Atlanta, GA (USA) in 2001, called *The Most Unlikely People Confess to their Dream*. Each of five people, a mix of artists and non-artists, worked for two months with someone else in the group, learning about the other person's life and their vision of the world. They then each made a solo for the other person, an expression of the other one's dream. It was an ambitious idea and an incredibly challenging process, but it was also compelling and humbling. At the end of the run, I wanted to give them all something to say 'thank you', something that would honour their courage and openness. So I made a short solo of my own dream and performed it after the audience had left on the last night. All I can remember is that I sang wildly and poured water over my head. But I know this was the start.

Identity from the outside

It took a few years before I technically started making what was to become *Mr Quiver*. But somewhere in my mind, I had already begun: collecting pertinent images, noting thoughts, trying to evaluate what it might be that would define a solo about 'me'. I walked my life looking for clues and finding them, as one does, all over. Alongside these inner daydreams, two events strike me as particularly significant. They occurred to me as markers of a moment in time, parallel comments on the over-defined and misunderstood experience of being an immigrant.

1. In May 2003 artists from all over England performed at an Arts Council England event in Manchester: the decibel x.trax performing arts showcase. It was one of the first big decibel events and was designed to redress the imbalance in presenting opportunities for artists of colour in the UK. I attended as a delegate and spent a lot of time talking to artists, presenters and promoters about what the event meant to them. By the time I left the showcase, I understood something I had never fully understood before: that most people from the art world saw me as Asian before they saw me as an artist, a director or a performer.

2. In November 2003 I visited my family in India. It had been more than twelve years since I had last visited, and this was my first visit as

12. Rajni Shah, family photograph, November 2003, Haldwani, India.
(Photograph: O.P. Sah)

an adult. I was there to attend an uncle's wedding. The day after the wedding, my new aunty-in-law took great delight in dressing me up in her bridal outfit. My husband was dressed in my uncle's wedding outfit, and we took family photos. I stood in the middle of the photo, posing as a version of myself in a parallel universe: the me who was not European; the me who understood the language, traditions and country of my parents' birth; a person I could and would never be. Everyone was delighted.

There are maps, lying on our bodies, lighting us and carving our routes across the earth. And inside our bodies we also carry them: maps of our history and our travels, maps of our influences and memories, maps of kindnesses and hurt and breath—and we carry them knowing so or not knowing so.

Queen Elizabeth I

The two events threw me into the game. I knew I had to pursue the idea of making a solo based on outside assumptions about my own cultural identity. In the following year I made a successful application to Chisenhale Dance Space's Artists' Programme to lead a workshop called *the body as culturally diverse artefact*. In April 2004, along with participants Sam Lim, Persis Jade Maravala and Colin Poole, I spent a week exploring what it felt like to be brown in the UK arts scene at that moment in time. We talked, dressed up, argued, danced and finally made a public presentation that invited controversial discussion. And it was during this workshop that, in spite of the influence of decibel and my visit to India, I found the image that struck me as most relevant and immediate was that of Queen Elizabeth I of England.

This is a part of the process that I will never be able to explain rationally. I knew I didn't want to make a 'historical' piece as such; I've never been very interested in so-called historical accuracy. But I've always been compelled by images and references that people can read easily, even (especially) images that are somewhat clichéd—clear enough for an audience to claim, but open enough to leave room for play. So when I looked for a starting point, something onto which I could tether these first ideas for a new show, it was the image of Elizabeth I that came into my mind. Along with Elizabeth came notions of history, self-conscious fashioning of public image, the body as land and the idea of 'England'. Then along with England came the English National Anthem, *God Save the Queen*. This was my earliest material.

13. Rajni Shah,
Mr Quiver (in progress),
January 2005, Chelsea
Theatre London.
(Photograph:
Theron Schmidt)

Writing

Texts come from all over. At some point I started writing monologues. I would keep a notebook by my bed. Every morning, in the moment when I was waking up, I'd read what was already written and write one word more. After 120 days, I had the following raw material to work with:

> *Elizabeth, I struggle with the telling of things further from the truth. I struggle with the telling of it. For today I am bitter, hostile, standing hostile. Forgetting nothing, I wait for no-one except my vulnerable self. Take majesty, take calm, take forgiveness. I battle endlessly for you. Without fear, holding, who does ever stage such a languid fight as she who settles? I am weeping gloriana. Ktch. Drip drip. Buy what you can. Carry only what you mark in my presence. Mark my presence, for without it you will be gone. But never destroy me or your world, never give. While birds may be always, I have finished. I cannot go on. Today is the day that I finish. Thank you.*

This and other similar exercises provided me with material straight from the heart, uncluttered by inhibitions of writing for the stage. I could then forge more polished material from these raw spaces, sometimes using translations between languages as another filter before arriving at the material I needed. Later, I added text from emails I had written to lovers and friends, from historical speeches that Elizabeth I delivered, and from current news items to make the final textual material of the piece. The writing became a pool of raw material from which all the monologues in the show were written. In keeping with the themes of the piece, the writing bled across personas and encouraged multiple readings of the same texts, each time reshaped by the ever-unfolding contexts in which we presented them.

Costume

After the Chisenhale workshop, I started to work with a costume designer I knew, Lucille Acevedo-Jones. This was the beginning of a long and fruitful relationship. Her dad is from Venezuela and she grew up there, speaking Spanish; my parents are both from India but I have never lived there or spoken any of their languages. We talked about our opposite dilemmas: no-one ever understood the extent to which she did not feel English, and no-one ever understood the extent to which I did not feel Indian. Our stumbling connections with our supposed homelands brought us closer to each other and complicated the process in a fruitful way. We continue to work together to this day, our ideas meshing and progressing without boundaries. Each item of costume in our collaborative work is inseparable from the ideas of the piece and the visual design of the entire space. Every costume is developed over the lifespan of the piece; just as the written, vocal and movement material, it is continually adapted to open up new questions, reveal new ideas and interact more intricately with the other elements of performance. The costumes become open-ended, full of questions, part of a journey.

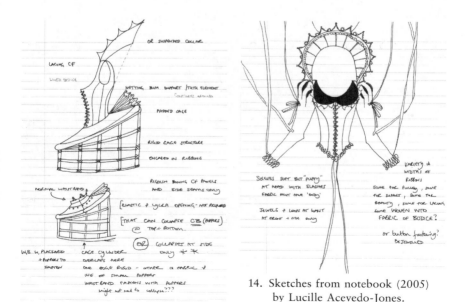

14. Sketches from notebook (2005) by Lucille Acevedo-Jones.

Indian bride

Although Elizabeth was developed first, we always had in mind two central images: Queen Elizabeth I and a traditional-looking Indian bridal figure. The latter was, of course, influenced by my 2003 visit to India. Where Elizabeth had come to represent ideals of country, female power and the body as symbol, the bride came to represent ideals of heterosexual romance, desire and humility. These gave us two fixed points around which we could anchor less stable material; material that was about movement and change, about shifting borders and malleable interpretations of identity.

Before making costumes and writing material, Lucille and I had many conversations about research strategies and authenticity. I had initially thought about taking lessons in Indian dance and vocal technique, and we had considered undertaking detailed research into regional variations in Indian wedding traditions and costumes. But when we started working, we realised that such authenticity would in fact be deeply inappropriate. We realised that our central images had to be based on cultural assumptions, clichés and medleys of popular images; this was part of the DNA of the piece. It was definitely about authenticity, but it was a questioning of what that means, not a validation through historically or culturally accurate representation. The allure of the recognisable had to be a layer that led to other questions. So we created a bride based on our prior knowledge, learned

15. Rajni Shah, *Mr Quiver*, June 2005, Camden People's Theatre London.
(Photograph: Chiara Contrino)

stereotypes, and the fabrics we were able to find around London; and, as with Elizabeth, we knowingly created a figure that was a manipulation of popular images so that she could act as a gateway to other dialogues. We wanted to use familiarity as a threshold to a place where we could uproot, unsettle and reconfigure the very thing we had created.

There is no jewel, be it of never so rich a price, which I set before this jewel: I mean your love. For I would venture my life for you, for your good and safety. And I would lie down in surrender to fulfil my promises to you. But never destroy me or your world, mark my presence in your hearts and in this land. For without it you will be gone. And I want, very soon, to make the choice to have our love achieving each time. Each time, when you have each sad right, each time when each raw unreal claim is made to my body, each time when each cold denied claim is made to my land. I love you, in some state, and the borders are breaking …

Mr Quiver

'Who is Mr Quiver?'
I was asked this question many times during the development of the show, and would never answer, perhaps because Mr Quiver stands for so many slippery and elusive concepts that I found it impossible to summarise. I eventually created a fake interview as part of the soundtrack, where I play both interviewer and interviewee and pose this very question to myself. The interview was designed to be slightly humorous but simultaneously to touch on some important themes of the piece. All the questions are very blunt, and the answers very earnest. Below is an extract from the response to the Mr Quiver question as it would have been heard in the soundtrack:
    Well, I think Mr Quiver is someone different for all of us. For me Mr Quiver represents a kind of super-ego, or alter-ego, those parts of my personality that I have no control over, those things that have shaped me that are so much bigger than me and tie into things like the land, to my history, my family history … They're parts of our identities that we haven't chosen … In a sense it's quite a, a dark concept, it's the dark side of a lot of those ideas, of something, something we can't quite grasp … And it ties into these, these vast concepts really of land and of time …
    The concept of Mr Quiver is intricately tied up with the core concepts of the entire performance and its structure. It is an attempt to expose the borders in borderlessness, the inequalities in human rights, the power of history and geography to shape us all whether we admit their presence or not. It is an admission that whilst I might claim to be free and liberal, not buying into any kind of classification or stereotype, I am in fact on some

level deeply boundaried, surrounded by frontiers, invisible and visible, from my past and its geography.

Sometimes we trip over our own boundaries, we crumble our own illusion. This is constantly happening in *Mr Quiver*. It is as if we are kicking at our own beliefs, constantly reasserting that they are fictional and delicate and real all at once.

If Mr Quiver is a person, he is constantly falling in and out of being.

We make so much effort to construct identities, to provide ourselves with shells that we can live in: routines, houses, communities, ways of being. And Mr Quiver is the thing that goes on forever, the fear of eternity, of the land, of the past where everything bleeds together.

Are you a fish?

Sorry, am I ... a fish?

No, I said are you English? Where is your home now?

Shifting formats

2005	Chisenhale Dance Space, London	Ten minutes, anthem, Elizabethan-style dress
	Camden People's Theatre, London	Ten minutes, anthem, Elizabethan-style dress, modified
	ROAR, Chelsea Theatre, London	Twenty minutes, anthem, salt map, costume attached with ribbons, Elizabeth, falling lightbulb
	Sprint 2005, Camden People's Theatre, London	One hour, salt maps, ribbons, Indian bride, Elizabeth, falling bulbs, two other performers, soundtrack, staged get-out
	Hackney Empire, London	Two two-hour improvisations using all material including get-out/de-rig in front of audience
2006	South Hill Park, Bracknell	Test of new and redeveloped material for four-hour performance installation including fully developed sequence of salt maps, two CD soundtrack, microphones, development of bride costume, interaction with audience

National Review of Live Art, Glasgow	Four hours, full performance installation developed with three performers—part improvised and tailored for every subsequent venue—added cushions for audience comfort
Fresh festival, Hastings and Southampton	
2007 Sensitive Skin, Nottingham	
Nuffield Theatre, Lancaster	
2008 The Bluecoat, Liverpool	
British Asian theatre conference, Exeter	

Mr Quiver began life as an experimental piece of theatre using the solo form. Developed through low-budget platform events, it was premiered as part of the Sprint festival at Camden People's Theatre in 2005 as an hour-long show. It later became a four-hour performance installation, and after a period of development at South Hill Park in 2006, funded by Arts Council England, Lucille and I started working with a third performer and collaborator: lighting designer Cis O'Boyle. Following this development period we were invited to present it at the National Review of Live Art and various other UK venues.

The initial hour-long performance incorporated many of the core elements that remained in the show, but adhered to the conventional theatrical format of a static, seated audience watching an end-on, staged performance. For the first section of the performance I was dressed as Queen Elizabeth and surrounded by a salt map of England. I delivered several monologues and invited the audience to sing 'God Save the Queen'. Once this image had been established and broken down (through the use of falling light bulbs, audio interruptions, sweeping of salt and the costume falling from its initial hanging position), I moved into the Indian bride costume. This second image was similarly established and then broken down, and I ended the formal part of the show coming out of costume and dressing in simple working clothes. Throughout the final moments of the show, Lucille and I worked with the venue technicians to clean the space and reset the lights in preparation for the next performance. Audience were free to leave during this 'get-out' section but many remained either through devotion or decorum.

You could say that the shift in format came by chance, or that the show was always meant to become durational. In 2005 we were given a slot in a new festival at the Hackney Empire in London. Although not ideal for

16. Rajni Shah and Lucille Acevedo-Jones, *Mr Quiver*, September 2006,
St-Mary-in-the-Castle, Hastings. (Photograph: Theron Schmidt)

various reasons, this was an opportunity to showcase the piece so I accepted
it. But I later realised that it would be impossible to re-create the show in
its existing form within the allotted get-in time of only a few hours. So I
decided to let it spill. We took apart the show and each made a list of our
tasks: sweep salt, lower bodice, make salt map, play track two, sing national
anthem, monologue one, converse with audience, monologue two and so
on. Each person got to do what they wanted when they wanted, interacting
freely with each other and with the audience, with the exception of a few
key rules: everybody had to stand and sing during the national anthem;
everybody had to be still while I performed the monologues; we would
respond to each other non-verbally in performance; and we had to begin at
4pm and end at 9pm with an hour's interval at 6pm.

It was as much a surprise to me as anyone else that the new format
worked so well. It was liberating to know that at any moment the audience
in the room were those who chose to be there; some would pop in and out,
or poke their heads around the door to take in the visuals and then leave
again; others would stay for hours, some falling asleep and awakening
within the space. And from a performance perspective, it was also a hugely
positive experience. Instead of pouring our effort into remembering what
we were supposed to do at any given moment, we were able to give priority
to what would be most effective, responding immediately to the changes
in light, sound and dynamic brought by each new tide of audience. As a
performer I was able to be fully present in the performance space, embracing

the natural fatigue that set in over the four hours and the different levels of awareness that were present as the performance evolved.

In its final version *Mr Quiver* toured as a four-hour, durational performance installation at which audiences could wander in and out, staying for as long or as little as they wished and walking around the space to view the piece from various angles. It was performed by costume designer Lucille Acevedo-Jones, lighting designer Cis O'Boyle, and myself, Rajni Shah. We worked together using light, sound, salt, costume and performance to shift the space over the duration of the piece, responding within a set structure to the patterns of movement and energy created by the audience. The show contained many of the same elements as the initial one-hour version, but instead of being set within a script we used them within an improvised structure. This resulted in a series of performative loops that wove in and out of synchronisation throughout the performance, and which were framed by the overarching four-hour structure (see appendix).

Reflections on translation, overspill and instinct

There were flashes of knowing what it needed to be from the start. That it needed to be about borders and definitions. That it needed to be highly theatrical, and knowingly so. That it needed to reference my own cultural dilemmas but reach out to all those who feel displaced by borders and alienated by the idea of a national history. And that it needed to move. It needed to be a piece that could in its very structure embody that fluidity that is at the heart of my sense of identity and power, but which gains so little recognition because of its non-quantifiable nature. Even before the performance structure shifted this piece was pulling at the leash, demanding to take itself beyond its own boundaries by falling in and out of the performance moment and presenting the get-out in front of the audience, challenging the definition of what constituted 'on-stage' and what 'off-stage'. The bathos was there early on too: the idea that there should be moments of great beauty intertwined inseparably with excruciating embarrassment; moments of nationalism that would verge on one side to stirring the heart and on the other to disgust, rejection. I wanted to explore our Western need to contain, and our desperate fear and shame of over-spilling given categories, overstepping the boundaries. In particular, I wanted to explore how this applies to immigrants and women.

I have already mentioned using translation as a creative tool when writing material. I would like now to address how the notion of translation is present in the creative structure of this performance installation. In many ways, *Mr Quiver* was made from a collage of languages and cultural misunderstandings. I myself sang in a mix of found and made-up languages in the performance, desperately trying to find some way to communicate to the passive and sometimes exiting audience; I used snippets of language

I might have overheard as well as sounds from languages that I did not properly understand, making a collage from my experiences in Europe, India and the US and drawing on a kind of collective general awareness that is ever-present in our two-dimensional, culture-saturated twenty-first century.

Our languages as artists were also challenged. Cis, the lighting designer, was always aware of the light and sound in the space, looking for and creating patterns that she found intriguing and beautiful, responding to the room and audience positions. Lucille, costume- and set-designer, paid great attention to detail, ensuring the costumes were always returned to a proper state, repairing broken salt maps, arranging ribbons, sewing, and meticulously packing everything into three suitcases during the last hour. I moved between and within, breaking the patterns as they were set up, entering and exiting identities in an exhausting, exhilarating series of attempts to communicate something worthwhile in such a rapidly shifting space. My presence veered between pathetic and bathetic, beautiful and ridiculous, desperate and laughable, as I repeatedly tried on the same costumes and used the same words to try and communicate something new. Opening up to the influences around us, we became temporary receptacles of received ideas, of opinions and readings that passed through us. We became like landmarks. And because each of us had such different priorities during the performance, our trajectories criss-crossed and clashed constantly. At every moment I was having to re-evaluate the performance space and reconfigure my next move in the context of an unstable landscape.

This is how we were constantly falling into being, allowing it all to be fluid by counting on this one solid truth: everything changes. And so the idea of translation goes beyond a simple or unidirectional action. It is a complex, trembling quiver of presence; it is the only way we can begin to face the shocking, overwhelming complexity of humanity. Within this type of performance I have found a space where I can confront the real emotions of this world, sit with them, let them tremble through my body. It is because they are being given and received by the audience and performers around me. I am held. And I am falling.

Things falling: light, salt and movement

It's funny how falling can mean so many things. This translates into performance too. *Mr Quiver* had lights, bodies, costumes, salt, all falling into the space and creating a small rupture in the continuum, adjusting the direction of the pattern and rhythm a little. Each time something fell, an opening was created; something would come to be, and something would disappear. The costumes could be reconfigured endlessly, falling apart in different ways and being painstakingly stitched back together every time. The soundtrack, on two simultaneous CDs, was played repeatedly in different overlapping configurations. And every time I found myself emotionally attached to an idea (for example, I might plan to wait for the end of a piece of music and then run into the space, tearing myself out of one of the costumes), something else would happen (for example, Lucille would strip me of my costume, or Cis would cut the music and turn off all the lights). This constant reordering of objects and events was what gave the show an edge. Lucille, Cis and I are different enough that even when we had worked together for years we still found ourselves surprised by each other's decisions. We had to remain alert and responsive to the entire space, and we had to give in to the surprise and dismay of each moment as we performed. This was an integral part of the piece, as crucial as the more formal elements of soundtracks, costumes, monologues and lights.

Then and now: how the work progressed and where it took us

It is hard critically to assess the success of a piece like *Mr Quiver*, which is by design constantly shifting and reordering itself to fit the landscape. It certainly felt like a piece of work that lived through a lifetime, and was affected by our own lives during that time. The beauty of such a long development period was that we each in our own way became very familiar with each other and the material. The performance itself gave us a space within which we could place both our emotional relationship with the material of the piece and also our history, knowledge and judgement as artists. At every venue, we hung the costumes in a new configuration that best reflected that particular context. Each time it was performed, it became a window on that moment, a sliver of time and space.

It feels to me that during the lifespan of this piece the world has become more connected and less engaged. The increased potential for communication that new technology continues to offer has brought with it a far greater fear of our fellow human beings, and a far greater need to categorise each other. We are overwhelmed by our planet, and we are paralyzed by our understanding. The ways in which this is manifest may have changed since we first performed *Mr Quiver*, but I still feel an urgency around many of the questions it raised. In 2006 when we began to tour the show in its final version, it became clear to me that *Mr Quiver* needed to be one in a series of performance installations, each providing a space where one could contemplate the state of the world and our place within it.

Mr Quiver has now become the first in a trilogy of performance installations, with an overarching intent to deconstruct mythologies around national identity and race. In December 2008, we completed the second in the trilogy, a two-and-a-half-hour performance installation ending in a shared meal and exploring the everyday mythologies generated by the word 'America'. *Dinner with America* would tour until the end of 2009 before making way for the next and final piece in the trilogy, *Glorious*. Each piece is born of a moment in time, and goes to rest when it has exhausted its cycle.

Appendix

Mr Quiver: A story about Queen Elizabeth I, a traditional Indian bride, about the relationships we have to the land we live on, and the theatres we all invent ...

The following is an outline of actions that provided a guiding structure for the final performance installation, and within which the three of us (lighting designer, costume designer and performer) could improvise. For more on *Mr Quiver* and the trilogy please visit www.rajnishah.com.

2008
First hour

Track one: mix
Rajni dressing as bride
Salt labels for each pile of costume
Cis and Lucille unroll bride fabric
R to bride
Bride hands music
Bride monologue
Bulb and light change for Elizabeth (E)
Let down E fabric
R+L dress E
Cis begins map of England
opening music or other quiet music
L brings R E wig
Cis brings mic
Sound: lipsynch mono
Bulb swings into space, lit
R walks backwards
music runs into quiet Elizabeth track
Anthem
R walks forward to mic
Mic on for anthem

Second hour

R as bride again
Salt patterns emerge (mehndi patterns and maps)

Audience interaction—give them ribbons to hold, ask them to choose music etc
Bulb falls
Start to mix and play with music

Third hour

No full resets of costumes
Salt into small piles
Bulbs start to come down and move on floor level
Lots of audience involvement
Lots of sound (any track except interview)—build up
Some interruptions—house lights on, change space, go back into performance

Fourth Hour: first half

De-rig slowly (leave low general light for packing)
Everything on floor including lightbulbs, unplugged
Some sound (not interview)
Can consult with each other

Fourth Hour: second half

Salt map of England and place candles at cities
Packing things into suitcases
No sound
We are silent (no talking)
Final state: all light candles, adjust other lighting, play bare interview, leave space with suitcases

Notes

Introduction

1. *British South Asian Theatres: A Documented History*, eds Graham Ley and Sarah Dadswell (Exeter: University of Exeter Press, 2011). Both books are products of the academic research project conducted at the University of Exeter from 2004 to 2009, funded by the Arts and Humanities Research Council.
2. The 'sector' is the term used by the Arts Council to designate those companies who would be embraced by the term 'black and minority ethnic'.
3. Of these two theoretical terms, diaspora asserts the existence of a dual sense of identity or 'home' in its subjects, while postcolonial explicitly marks the break from a colonial past. So Avtar Brah explored the meanings of diaspora in *Cartographies of Diaspora: Contesting Identities* (London: Routledge, 1996), while Nasreen Ali, Virinder Kalra and S. Sayyid as editors placed their emphasis on the latter term in *A Postcolonial People: South Asians in Britain* (London: Hurst, 2006).
4. *Alternatives within the Mainstream: British Black and Asian Theatres*, ed. Dimple Godiwala (Newcastle: Cambridge Scholars Press, 2004); *Staging New Britain: Aspects of Black and South Asian British Theatre Practice*, eds Geoffrey Davis and Anne Fuchs (Brussels: Peter Lang, 2006); Gabriele Griffin, *Contemporary Black and Asian Women Playwrights in Britain* (Cambridge: Cambridge University Press, 2003). Dimple Godiwala also edited a selection from her collection in a special issue of *Studies in Theatre and Performance* 26.1 (2006), pp. 3–97.
5. 'Tara Arts and Tamasha: Producing Asian Performance—Two Approaches', in *Alternatives within the Mainstream*, ed. Godiwala, pp. 174–200.
6. The most valuable contribution to the documentation of British Asian performance in *Staging New Britain* came from Vayu Naidu, with her reflections as a practitioner on the background to her story-telling production South: 'Vayu Naidu's Company's South: New Directions in Theatre of Storytelling', in *Staging New Britain*, eds Davis and Fuchs, pp. 141–54. Her account of her own practice there is extended by the essay from her director Chris Banfield published here in our collection.
7. For example, Susheila Nasta, *Home Truths: Fictions of the South Asian Diaspora in Britain* (Basingstoke: Palgrave, 2002); a longer view, with attention falling largely on leading figures in periods before the contemporary, was published by C.L. Innes, *A History of Black and Asian Writing in Britain, 1700–2000* (Cambridge: Cambridge University Press, 2002).

8. Colin Chambers, *Black and Asian Theatre in Britain: A History* (London: Routledge, 2011); Dominic Hingorani, *British Asian Theatre: Dramaturgy, Process and Performance* (Basingstoke: Palgrave, 2010).

9. We have previously edited a shorter collection of essays, arising directly from the conference 'British Asian Theatre: Past and Present' held at Exeter in 2008, for a special issue of the journal *South Asian Popular Culture* 7.3 (2009), which extends the range of concerns here and adds a North American perspective.

10. Naseem Khan, *The Arts Britain Ignores: The Arts of Ethnic Minorities in Britain* (London: Community Relations Commission, 1976).

11. Khan's essay might be read alongside the excellent, concise history provided by Raminder Kaur and Alda Terracciano, 'South Asian/BrAsian Performing Arts', in *A Postcolonial People*, eds Ali, Kalra and Sayyid, pp. 343–57.

1 *Naseem Khan*—British Asian Theatre: The Long Road to Now, and the Barriers in-between

1. Address given by the Home Secretary, the Rt Hon Roy Jenkins MP, on 23 May 1966 to a meeting of the Voluntary Liaison Committees, National Council for Commonwealth Immigrants, London.

2. Naseem Khan, *The Arts Britain Ignores: The Arts of Ethnic Minorities in Britain* (London: Community Relations Commission, 1976). The research was funded by the Arts Council of Great Britain, Calouste Gulbenkian Foundation and Community Relations Commission.

3. Britain was not alone in inappropriate pigeonholing. The Californian Arts Council in the 1990s was still terming the celebrated Indian sarod player Ustad Ali Akbar Khan an 'Ethnic folk musician'.

4. I no longer have a record of the names of the short-lived Punjabi theatre groups in Birmingham at that time.

5. Dark and Light Theatre Company, formed by Frank Cousins in 1970 and based in Longfield Hall, Knatchbull Road, Brixton, London SE5; it ended in 1977.

6. *Behzti (Dishonour)*, by Gurpreet Kaur Bhatti, was a controversial play featuring murder, rape and incest in a Sikh temple. Its opening at the Birmingham Rep in December 2004 was marked by violent demonstrators by some local Sikhs, and led to both the withdrawal of the play and debates over freedom of speech that still continue.

7. Iniva—International Institute of Visual Arts—was established in 1994 to address an imbalance in the representation of culturally diverse artists, curators and writers.

8. See the essay by Alda Terraciano, 'Mainstreaming African, Asian and Caribbean Theatre: The Experiments of the Black Theatre Forum', in *Alternatives within the Mainstream: British Black and Asian Theatre*, ed. Dimple Godiwala (Newcastle: Cambridge Scholars Press, 2006), pp. 22–60, and the section on Asian Cooperative Theatre in *British South Asian Theatres: A Documented History*, eds Graham Ley and Sarah Dadswell (Exeter: University of Exeter Press, 2011), pp. 87–103.

9. LIFT was formed by Rose de Wend Fenton and Lucy Neal in 1981 (see Fenton and Neal, 'The Turning World: Stories from London International Festival of Theatre', Calouste Gulbenkian Foundation, 2005). Partnerships included: USA's 'YOU—the City' with Arts Admin (1989); Ghana Dance Ensemble and London's Carnival Costume Club (1993); and Nigerian director Chuck Mike

working with British actors on a version of Chinua Achebe's *Things Fall Apart* (1997).

10. Reported on in Tony Bennett, *Differing Diversities: Cultural Policy and Cultural Diversity* (Brussels: Council of Europe, 2001).

11. Jasbir Jain, 'The New Parochialism: Homeland in the Writing of the Indian Diaspora', in *In Diaspora: Theories, Histories, Texts*, ed. Makarand Paranjape (New Delhi: Indialog, 2001), pp. 79–93.

12. Edgar's introduction to his *Playing with Fire*, performed at the Royal National Theatre (London: Nick Hern, 2005).

13. Naseem Khan, *The Road to Interculturalism: Tracking the Arts in a Changing World* (London: Comedia, 2006).

14. Khan, *The Road to Interculturalism*; Peter Badejo is a Nigerian dancer-choreographer invited to Britain in 1987 by LIFT; he then remained and formed his own company, Badejo Arts.

15. ITC's Fast Track scheme started in 1997; 'Gain' (Governance, Access, Inclusion, Networking) is a board development programme first started in 2004 and now administered by ITC; Arts Council England's Eclipse black and Asian initiative grew out of its BRIT (Black Regional Theatre) circuit: it ran from 2001 and included board development, commissioning, venues consortia, training and touring; ACE's Sustained Theatre grew out of the 2005 'Whose Theatre?' enquiry, chaired by Professor Lola Young, into Black and Asian theatre and led to recommendations on areas that include archiving and internationalism; it can be followed up via www.sustainedtheatre.org.uk.

16. Arts Council England's Decibel initiative aimed to 'raise the voice of African, Asian and Caribbean artists' in Britain. A complex multi-disciplinary arts programme, it included showcases, bursaries, publications, debates, awards and exhibitions, and ran from 2003 to 2008.

17. Escapade took place indoors and outdoors at London's South Bank Centre on 1 and 2 August 2003.

18. Tara Arts productions at the National Theatre are as follows: *Tartuffe*, Cottesloe Theatre, National Theatre (RNT), January 1990, and international tour; *Little Clay Cart*, Cottesloe Theatre, RNT, May 1991; *Cyrano*, co-production with the RNT, October 1995.

2 Colin Chambers—Images on Stage: A Historical Survey of South Asians in British Theatre before 1975

1. 'The Oriental in Elizabethan Drama', *Modern Philology*, 12.7 (January 1915), pp. 423–47.

2. *The Campaign* was first produced in Dublin; Covent Garden is given as its first English venue.

3. For the examples given, see Greg Dening, *Mr Bligh's Bad Language: Passion, Power and Theatre on the Bounty* (Cambridge: Cambridge University Press, 1992), pp. 269–76; Laura J. Rosenthal, '"Infamous Commerce": Transracial Prostitution in the South Seas and Back', in *Monstrous Dreams of Reason: Body, Self, and Other in the Enlightenment*, eds Laura J. Rosenthal and Mita Choudhury (London: Associated University Press, 2002), pp. 189–208; Kathleen Wilson, *The Island Race: Englishness, Empire and Gender in the Eighteenth Century* (London: Routledge, 2003), pp. 163–70; Gillian Russell, 'An "Entertainment of Oddities": Fashionable Sociability and the Pacific in the 1770's, in *A New*

Imperial History: Culture, Identity and Modernity in Britain and the Empire, 1660–1840, ed. Kathleen Wilson (Cambridge: Cambridge University Press, 2004), pp. 48–70; Daniel O'Quinn, *Staging Governance: Theatrical Imperialism in London, 1770–1800* (Baltimore: Johns Hopkins University Press, 2005), pp. 74–114; O'Quinn, 'Theatre and Empire', in *The Cambridge Companion to British Theatre, 1730–1830*, eds Jane Moody and Daniel O'Quinn (Cambridge: Cambridge University Press, 2007), pp. 233–46.

4. O'Quinn, *Staging Governance*, p. 281.

5. O'Quinn, *Staging Governance*, pp. 14–29, and 'Theatre and Empire', p. 236.

6. There are different spellings for *Sakuntala* (e.g. *Sacontala, Sakoontala, Shakuntala*), as there are for most transliterated names. See Dorothy Matilda Figueira, *Translating the Orient: The Reception of Śākuntala in Nineteenth-century Europe* (New York: State University of New York Press, 1991), for versions of *Sakuntala* in different art forms. See Said's *Orientalism* (London: Routledge and Kegan Paul, 1978), which has provoked much continuing debate about western representations of the Other.

7. See Michael H. Fisher, *Counterflows to Colonialism: Indian Travellers and Settlers in Britain 1600–1857* (Delhi: Permanet Books, 2004), p. 383.

8. David Worrall, *Harlequin Empire: Race, Ethnicity and the Drama of the Popular Entertainment* (London: Pickering & Chatto, 2007), pp. 94–101.

9. Heidi J. Holder, 'Other Londoners: Race and Class in Plays of Nineteenth-century London Life', in *Imagined Londons*, ed. Pamela K. Gilbert (New York: SUNY Press, 2002), pp. 31–44.

10. Holder, 'Other Londoners', p. 43.

11. Holder, 'Other Londoners', p. 38.

12. Worrall, *Harlequin Empire* (pp. 94–101), gives a more sympathetic reading than O'Quinn of the widespread Tipu dramatic phenomenon, which involved many theatres over several decades (*Staging Governance*, pp. 321–40).

13. For example, *Kermuh Kareena, or the Fall of Delhi* (Anon., 1857), C.A. Somerset's *The Storming and Capture of Delhi* (1857), and Dion Boucicault's *Jessie Brown; or, the Relief of Lucknow* (1862 in London).

14. Edward Ziter, *The Orient on the Victorian Stage* (Cambridge: Cambridge University Press, 2003), p. 10.

15. See Brendan Gregory, 'Staging British India', in *Acts of Supremacy: British Empire and the Stage, 1790–1930*, ed. J.S. Bratton et al. (Manchester: Manchester University Press, 1991), pp. 152–53. According to Annie E. Coombes, *Reinventing Africa, Museums, Material Culture and Popular Imagination in Late Victorian and Edwardian England* (New Haven and London: Yale University Press, 1994), p. 254, n. 5, Kiraly was the central figure behind the organisation of the majority of the major colonial exhibitions of this period.

16. Shompa Lahiri, *Indians in Britain: Anglo-Indian Encounters, Race and Identity, 1880–1930* (London: Frank Cass, 2000), p. 83.

17. Girish Karnad, 'The Inter-relationship between British and Indian Theatre: An Historical Perspective' (keynote speech given at the British Asian Theatre Conference, 'British Asian Theatre: From Past to Present', University of Exeter, April 2008).

18. Claire Pamment, '"Police of Pig and Sheep": Representations of the White Sahib and the Psyche of Theatre Censorship' (paper given at the Exeter British Asian Theatre Conference, April 2008). This paper was later published in *South Asian Popular Culture*, 7:3 (2009), pp. 233–45.

19. *The Times*, 21 December 1885.
20. Details from William Poel, 'Hindu Drama on the English Stage', *Asiatic Quarterly Review*, n.s. 1 (April 1913), pp. 319–31, from which all subsequent Poel quotations are taken; and Robert Speaight, *William Poel and the Elizabethan Revival* (London: Heinemann, 1954), p. 147.
21. *The Times*, 4 July 1899.
22. *The Times*, 13 February 1912. S.C. Bose is probably Sarat Chandra Bose (b. 1889) rather than his younger brother, the future independence leader Subhas Chandra Bose (b. 1897), who would have been only just fifteen at the time.
23. Also mentioned in the *Era Annual 1913*, p. 128, which suggests that the cast included white British performers playing Indian roles alongside Indian performers.
24. *The Times*, 15 April 1912.
25. According to the *Era Annual 1914*, p. 80, Cosmopolis was founded in 1910 as the Foreign Literary Society for those interested in the cultures of foreign countries, and in 1912 established a dramatic section called the Foreign Theatre Society.
26. *The Times*, 22 July 1912, wrongly attributes the translation to a leading Sanskrit scholar, E.J. Rapson, who had been involved in the project but who wrote to Poel to complain of the association. Poel thought a French version by Bergaigne the best. A translation of this by Harinath De, Head of the Imperial Library, Calcutta and noted linguist, was cut short when he died (in 1911) having completed only two of the seven acts. Poel used a large part of that, and F.W. Hubbock of Trinity translated Bergaigne's verses for the remaining acts. The prose used was modified from Sir William Jones's 1789 version, as in the 1899 production. See also William Poel Collection, Department of Special Collections, MS. 31, Kenneth Spencer Research Library, University of Kansas Libraries.
27. Poel, 'Hindu Drama', pp. 327–28; *The Times*, 26 February 1912 and 2 March 1912. R.T.H. Griffith's verse translation of Kalidasa's *Kumarsambhava* as *The Birth of the War-God* first appeared in English in 1853. Poel says all the cast were women and children whereas *The Times* agrees at first but in its second reference says 'almost entirely'. The first *Times* reference also says the programme included tableaux illustrating the *Rubaiyat* of Omar Khayyam. A letter to *The Times* (28 February 1912) from the organisers of the performance says 'We Indian ladies have promoted it entirely ourselves' and gives the subtitle as *The Coming of the Prince*.
28. The material on Das Gupta is drawn from a number of sources: reviews of and announcements about individual productions in *The Times*, the *Stage*; J.P. Wearing, *The London Stage: A Calendar of Plays and Players, 1900–1909, 1910–1919* and *1920–1929* (New Jersey: The Scarecrow Press, 1981 and 1982); details given in the published edition of Kalidasa's *Sakuntala* (London: Macmillan, 1920); Poel, 'Hindu Drama', p. 327; *New York Times*, 1 July 1922; Marcus Braybrooke, 'A Wider Vision: A History of the World Congress of Faiths, 1936–1996' http://www.religion-online.org/showchapter. asp?title=3378&C=2771.
29. *The Times*, 9 December 1912. According to the *Era Annual 1914*, p. 95, *The Maharani of Arakan* was also produced by the Bushey Repertory Theatre in November 1913.
30. *The Times*, 28 October 1916. Francis Griffiths had published a version of *The*

Hero and the Nymph by Sri Ananda Acharya in or before 1913. Other English versions had appeared since 1830, published in both India and England, but no records of productions in Britain have been found.

31. The Committee was chaired by Bhupendra Nath Basu (who became Vice-Chancellor of Calcutta University), and, with Das Gupta as honorary secretary, included the Rt. Hon. Lord Sinha K.C., Sir Prabashanka Pattani, Mr and Mrs Sen, and Jamnadas Dwarkadas.

32. The published version (Macmillan, 1920) makes it clear that this fragment of the original was prepared solely for presenting to an English audience (p. viii). Laurence Binyon writes (p. viii): 'Fidelity to what is universal in Kalidasa has been sought for, rather than the reproduction of exotic beauties.' Das Gupta adds (p. xi): 'He [Kalidasa] is of all countries and of all ages, and his work is the inheritance of mankind.'

33. *The Times*, 15 November 1919.

34. *The Abbey* company had performed *The Post Office* in Dublin and London (at the Court) in 1913. The claim concerning the five short plays is carried in *The Times*, 26 July 1920.

35. Details taken from her autobiography, *India Calling: The Memories of Cornelia Sorabji* (London: Nisbet, 1934), pp. 46–47; and Richard Sorabji, *Opening Doors: The Untold Story of Cornelia Sorabji, Reformer, Lawyer and Champion of Women's Rights in India* (London and New York: I.B. Tauris, 2010), pp. 105–8.

36. *The Times*, 30 June 1924. Pran Nevile, *The Tribune*, Chandigarh, India, 18 September 2010, says Himansunath Rai founded the company in India and brought it to London, and that the production played in Manchester, Liverpool and other British cities before being invited to France, Italy and Egypt.

37. *Era*, 21 June 1922; *Sunday Times*, 11 June 1922; *The Times*, 7 June 1922; *Stage*, 22 June 1922.

38. Details of the production and the company garnered from *The Times*: 7 June ('diction remarkably good'), 3, 20 and 31 July, and 7 August 1922; the *Stage*, 25 May and 22 June 1922.

39. See *The Times*, 30 June and 8 July 1924; the *Stage*, 26 June, 10, 24 and 31 July 1924.

40. The *Stage*, 1 May 1924.

41. See Shompa Lahiri, 'From Empire to Decolonisation, 1901–1947', in *A South-Asian History of Britain: Four Centuries of Peoples from the Indian Sub-continent*, ed. Michael H. Fisher (Oxford: Greenwood World, 2007), p. 143, and Brinda, *Maharani: The Story of an Indian Princess* (New York: Henry Holt, 1953), pp. 216–17.

42. This, and subsequent quotations, from Marie Seton, 'English Theatre of the Left', *New Theatre* (December 1934), p. 21.

43. See Mohammed Elias, *Aubrey Menen* (*Kerala Writers in English*, 7, Madras: Macmillan India, 1985); Seton, 'English Theatre of the Left'; and Andre van Gyseghem, 'British Theatre in the Thirties: An Autobiographical Record', in *Culture and Crisis in Britain in the 30s*, ed. Jon Clark et al. (London: Lawrence and Wishart, 1979), p. 211. Menon writes of his life, his homosexuality and his philosophy in *The Space Within the Heart* (London: Hamish Hamilton, 1970). His book *Rama Retold* (London: Chatto and Windus, 1954) was banned in India. His novel *SheLa* (London: Hamish Hamilton, 1963) was also a play.

44. *The Times*, 11 August 1937.

45. *The Times*, 1 March 1938.

46. Mayura (a.k.a. Mayura Vincent) was an Indian dancer who appeared on BBC TV in the late 1930s and at the Arts in 1937 in a Tibetan fairy tale, *Djroazanmo*, by Ernest Berk, presented by the Mask Theatre (with Ay Lien Tai in the cast). See *The Times*, 13 October 1937.

47. See Colin Chambers, *The Story of Unity Theatre* (London: Lawrence and Wishart, 1989), p. 236.

48. Naseem Khan, *The Arts Britain Ignores: The Arts of Ethnic Minorities in Britain* (London: Community Relations Commission, 1976): Bangladeshis, pp. 13–22; Indians, pp. 53–77; Pakistanis, pp. 80–89.

49. *The Times*, 6 April 1960.

50. According to Human Rights Watch, 'The Security Situation Immediately after the Fall of Basra' (http://www.hrw.org/node/12320/section/4), the term Ali Baba is also used by American troops and, ironically, by Iraqis of foreign troops they find or suspect are looting.

3 *Susan Croft*—Bridging Divides: the Emergence Theatre of Bilingual Theatre in Tower Hamlets in the 1980s

1. David Mazower, *Yiddish Theatre in London* (London: The Jewish Museum, 1996), p. 19.

2. Naseem Khan, *The Arts Britain Ignores: the Arts of Ethnic Minorities in Britain* (London: Community Relations Commission, 1976), pp. 14–15.

3. The current Barbican Theatre in the Barbican Centre opened in 1982, with construction beginning in 1971. The Victoria and Albert Museum Theatre Collections have no record of an earlier theatre of that name. It is unclear to what venue Rehman is referring.

4. *Times Educational Supplement*, 23 February 1973: press cutting in Tower Hamlets Local History Library (THLHL).

5. It was located near the Curtain Road, site of Burbage's original 1576 Curtain Theatre. Khan gives its location as Whitechapel (*The Arts Britain Ignores*, p. 20).

6. *East London Advertiser*, 19 July 1974 (press cutting in the THLHL).

7. Report: *The Changing East End 1960–1990: A brief personal impression*, paper submitted to the Asian Theatre research project by Norman Goodman. After teaching at Daneford School from 1960–84, Norman became Education Officer at the Half Moon YPT.

8. Later called the Kobi Nazrul Centre for some years.

9. They also campaigned in 1974 for the GLC to reverse its decision to lease the old Wilton's Music Hall building to Island Records, and allow the Half Moon to take it over as a theatre for the East End: *Times Literary Supplement*, 5 July 1974 (press cutting in THLHL).

10. This company bears no relationship to Wherehouse La MaMa, the London arm of Ellen Stewart's New York-based La Mama theatre set up by Beth Porter and Peter Reid.

11. See file on Performance, THLHL.

12. Edgar was covering similar territory to his play *Destiny*, which was staged by the RSC in 1976.

13. The theatre initially took over a former Methodist Chapel as performance space, but began development of a large new breezeblock building on the site

behind. The failure, at a time of Arts Council cuts, to find adequate funds for this new development led to a scenario in which the company's revenue grant was servicing the building debt, and so to the eventual bankruptcy of the parent company. The building is now a very large pub.

14. 'The Bangladeshi Community' document, hand-dated 1981 in the THLHL. This anonymous document appears to have been commissioned for and circulated by TEEF!'s management.

15. Khan, *The Arts Britain Ignores*, p. 15.

16. By Dilip Hiro, directed by Michele Frankel. Dhirendra, however, felt that it was 'a disaster' … 'A video fantasy about a young Bangladeshi boy growing up in the East End, with some projected images on video. … Dilip was not the right person to write that show, because he was again very first-generation, and the sort of Bollywood element he brought was really bad Bollywood.' Interview with Dhirendra and Harmage Singh Kalirai, by Sarah Dadswell and Susan Croft, 29 April 2007. *Raj*, originally devised in 1982 by Leeds Playhouse TIE, was widely produced across the young people's theatre movement, and subsequently published (London: Amber Lane Press, 1984).

17. Interview with Dhirendra and Singh Kalirai, 29 April 2007.

18. Originally an associate director, Steve Harris's role crossed over the main company and the YPT. His advocacy of the importance of the YPT's work brought about the appointment of Deborah Bestwick as Director of the YPT.

19. Earlier shows drawing on the experience of local communities included an adaptation of a story 'Chudb' by former local schoolteacher and activist Chris Searle. Searle became the centre of a media storm, and attempts were made to sack him after he compiled *Classrooms of Resistance* (London: Writers and Readers Publishing Co-operative, 1975), an anthology of stories and poems by his pupils at St John Cass School, Stepney. He went on to publish *An Exclusive Education: Race, Class and Exclusion in British Schools* (London: Lawrence and Wishart, 2001) and other works.

20. Funded by ILEA.

21. Interview with Norman Goodman, by Dominic Rai, Graham Ley and Sarah Dadswell, Brady Centre, 2 August 2005.

22. Susan Croft, 'Black Women Playwrights in Britain', in *British and Irish Women Dramatists since 1958*, eds Trevor M. Griffiths and Margaret Llewellyn-Jones (Milton Keynes: Open University Press, 1993), pp. 97–98.

23. *A Meeting of Mother Tongues*, pp. 13–17.

24. NPT, of which I was then Director, responded to the challenge through its establishment of 'Tell Me a Story: An Exchange of Stories, An Exchange of Languages', a series of workshops aimed at local Asian writers on working with bilingualism and alternative storytelling-based theatrical traditions.

25. Dodgson founded the Royal Court's International Programme and continues to be its Director.

26. Deborah Bestwick, 'The Development of Bilingual Theatre by the Half Moon Young People's Theatre' (undated), Half Moon YPT archive, digitised as part of the East London Theatre Archive: http://www.elta-project.org/browse. html?recordId=609, p. 2.

27. Interview with Norman Goodman, 2 August 2005.

28. Deborah Bestwick, 'The Development of Bilingual Theatre', p. 2.

29. I was at the time Chair of the HMYPT, having been invited in my capacity as Director of the New Playwrights' Trust.

30. It continues today in the HMYPT's bilingual work using British Sign Language and English see http://www.halfmoon.org.uk/index.html.

31. Bestwick, 'The Development of Bilingual Theatre', p. 3.

32. Guillermo Gomez-Pena, *The New World Border: Prophecies, Poems, & Loqueras for the End of the Century* (San Francisco: City Lights, 1996), and *Dangerous Border Crossers* (London: Routledge, 2000). See also Coco Fusco, *English is Broken Here: Notes on Cultural Fusion in the Americas* (New York: The New Press, 1995).

33. Quoted by Maya Jaggi in Keynote Address, 'From Writing Back to Rewriting Britain', additional paper distributed with *Whose Heritage? The Impact of Cultural Diversity on Britain's Living Heritage* (Report of National Conference at G-Mex, Manchester, 1–3 November, 1999).

4 *Rukhsana Ahmad*—Experiments in Theatre from the Margins: Text, Performance and New Writers

1. For an account of this and later productions by Kali Theatre Company, including *Black Shalwar*, see the section on Kali in *British South Asian Theatres: A Documented History*, eds Graham Ley and Sarah Dadswell (Exeter: University of Exeter Press, 2011).

2. Dr Ranjana Ash is a teacher and writer who founded SALS (South Asian Literature Society) and was for several years, a foremost campaigner for South Asian literature and artists.

3. *Guardian*, 29 October 2008.

5 *Christiane Schlote*—Dramatising Refuge(e)s: Rukhsana Ahmad's *Song for a Sanctuary* and Tanika Gupta's *Sanctuary*

1. C. Brothers, 'Migrants Held in Shadows', *The Herald Tribune*, 31 December 2007, pp. 1, 3 (p. 1).

2. Thomas Roma and Henry Louis Gates, *Sanctuary* (Washington, DC: The Johns Hopkins University Press, 2002), p. ix.

3. J. Charles Cox, *The Sanctuaries and Sanctuary Seekers of Mediaeval England* (Whitefish: George Allen & Sons, 1911; repr. Kessinger Publishing, 2005), p. 2.

4. For a discussion of my use of the term 'British Asian theatre' see Christiane Schlote, 'Either for Tragedy, Comedy, History or Musical Unlimited: Women Playwrights in British South Asian Theatre', in *Staging New Britain: Aspects of Black and South Asian British Theatre Practice*, eds Geoffrey V. Davis and Anne Fuchs (Brussels: Peter Lang, 2006), pp. 65–85.

5. There are numerous fiction and non-fiction books bearing the title *Sanctuary*. In one of Agatha Christie's short stories, also entitled 'Sanctuary', where Christie, likewise, plays with the ambiguity of the concept, we find the following definition: 'Sanctuary in Roman and Greek temples applied to the *cella* in which stood the statue of a god. The Latin word for altar *ara* also means protection. ... In three hundred and ninety-nine AD the right of sanctuary in Christian churches was finally and definitely recognised'. Agatha Christie, 'Sanctuary', in *The Complete Miss Marple Short Stories* (London: The Folio Society, 2003), p. 259; emphasis in original.

6. Liisa H. Malkki, 'Refugees and Exile: From "Refugee Studies" to the National

Order of Things', *Annual Review of Anthropology*, 24 (1995), pp. 495–523 (p. 497).

7. Malkki, 'Refugees and Exile', pp. 497–99.

8. Giorgio Agamben, *Means Without End. Notes on Politics* (Minneapolis: University of Minnesota Press, 2000), p. 38; emphasis in original.

9. Liisa H. Malkki, 'Speechless Emissaries: Refugees, Humanitarianism, and Dehistoricization', *Cultural Anthropology*, 11.3 (1996), pp. 377–404 (p. 378).

10. Stephen Dobson, *Cultures of Exile and the Experience of Refugeeness* (Bern: Peter Lang, 2004), pp. 23–24.

11. *Refugees and the Transformation of Societies: Agency, Policies, Ethics and Politics*, eds Philomena Essed, Georg Frerks and Joke Schrijvers (Oxford: Berghahn Books, 2004), p. 3.

12. *Refugees and the Transformation of Societies*, eds Essed, Frerks and Schrijvers, p. 4.

13. See the UNHRC website at: http://www.unhcr.org/pages/49c3646c36b.html.

14. *Refugees and the Transformation of Societies*, eds Essed, Frerks and Schrijvers, p. 4.

15. Roland Robertson, quoted in *Living the Global City: Globalization as a Local Process*, ed. John Eade (London: Routledge, 1997), p. 4.

16. *Refugees and the Transformation of Societies*, eds Essed, Frerks and Schrijvers, p. 2.

17. Malkki, 'Refugees and Exile', p. 495.

18. Avtar Brah, *Cartographies of Diaspora: Contesting Identities* (London: Routledge, 1996), p. 209; emphasis in original.

19. Sallie Westwood and Annie Phizacklea, *Trans-Nationalism and the Politics of Belonging* (London: Routledge, 2000), p. 116.

20. Malkki, 'Refugees and Exile', p. 501.

21. Malkki, 'Refugees and Exile', pp. 506–7.

22. Malkki, 'Refugees and Exile', p. 511.

23. Malkki, 'Refugees and Exile', pp. 508–9.

24. Interview with Christiane Scholte, London, 14 April 1999. For detailed background information on Balwant Kaur's case see Gabriele Griffin, *Contemporary Black and Asian Women Playwrights in Britain* (Cambridge: Cambridge University Press, 2003), pp. 149–50.

25. Griffin, *Contemporary Black and Asian Women Playwrights in Britain*, p. 150.

26. Rukhsana Ahmad, *Song for a Sanctuary*, in *Six Plays by Black and Asian Women Writers*, ed. Kadija George (London: Aurora Metro Press, 1993), pp. 159–86 (p. 166).

27. Ahmad, *Song for a Sanctuary*, p. 160.

28. Ahmad, *Song for a Sanctuary*, p. 160.

29. Ahmad, *Song for a Sanctuary*, p. 161.

30. Griffin, *Contemporary Black and Asian Women Playwrights in Britain*, p. 151.

31. Griffin, *Contemporary Black and Asian Women Playwrights in Britain*, p. 156.

32. Ahmad, *Song for a Sanctuary*, pp. 182–83.

33. Ahmad, *Song for a Sanctuary*, p. 174. Dobson explains that not only do discourses 'provide the opportunity to delimit refugees from each other (the Vietnamese refugee from the Iranian and so on)' but also that there are 'degrees of inclusion, exclusion, and at times simultaneous inclusionary exclusions, all depending on the particular discourse and its relation to other discourses.' (Dobson, *Cultures of Exile*, p. 28).

34. Griffin, *Contemporary Black and Asian Women Playwrights in Britain*, p. 154.

35. In general, however, Rajinder very much believes in divine providence: 'It doesn't mean you can't make any choices ... just that ... the circumstances in which you have to make them are often beyond your control. Like birth, or death' (Ahmad, *Song for a Sanctuary*, p. 174).

36. Ruth Krulfeld and Jeffery MacDonald regard the representation of refugees as powerless victims as 'a distortion of the reality of their lives' and argue that 'refugees belie concepts of powerlessness through their own actions for self-empowerment'; *Power, Ethics, and Human Rights: Anthropological Studies of Refugee Research and Action*, eds Ruth Krulfeld and Jeffery MacDonald (Lanham: Rowman & Littlefield, 1998), pp. 5–6.

37. Norman Long, *Development Sociology: Actor Perspectives* (London: Routledge, 2001), p. 49.

38. Dobson, *Cultures of Exile*, p. 23.

39. *Refugees and the Transformation of Societies*, eds Essed, Frerks and Schrijvers, pp. 2–3.

40. Malkki, 'Refugees and Exile', p. 509.

41. Griffin, *Contemporary Black and Asian Women Playwrights in Britain*, pp. 152–53.

42. Ahmad, *Song for a Sanctuary*, p. 171.

43. Shamita Das Dasgupta, 'Introduction' in *A Patchwork Shawl: Chronicles of South Asian Women in America*, ed. Shamita Das Dasgupta (New Brunswick, NJ: Rutgers University Press, 1998), pp. 1–17 (pp. 5–6; emphasis in original).

44. Anannya Bhattacharjee, 'The Habit of Ex-Nomination' in *A Patchwork Shawl: Chronicles of South Asian Women in America* (New Brunswick, NJ: Rutgers University Press, 1998), pp. 163–85 (p. 172).

45. May Joseph, *Nomadic Identities: The Performance of Citizenship* (Minneapolis: University of Minnesota Press, 1999), p. 116.

46. Malkki, 'Refugees and Exile', p. 509.

47. S. Kossew, 'A Violent State: Truth and Reconciliation in Gillian Slovo's *Red Dust* (2000) and Jann Turner's *Southern Cross* (2002)', in *Violence and Transgression in World Minority Literatures*, eds Rüdiger Ahrens et al. (Heidelberg: Winter, 2005), pp. 305–18 (p. 307).

48. Griffin, *Contemporary Black and Asian Women Playwrights in Britain*, p. 50.

49. Ahmad, *Song for a Sanctuary*, p. 159.

50. Craig Tapping, 'South Asia Writes North America: Prose Fictions and Autobiographies from the Indian Diaspora', in *Reading the Literatures of Asian America*, eds S. Geok-Lin Lim and A. Ling (Philadelphia: Temple University Press, 1992), pp. 285–301 (pp. 295–96).

51. Griffin, *Contemporary Black and Asian Women Playwrights in Britain*, p. 225. Many thanks are owed to Amrit Wilson for kindly providing me with her play *Survivors*.

52. Jatinder Verma, 'The Impact of Cultural Diversity on the Performing Arts in the UK Today', in *New Stages. Conference at Norsk Kulturråd*, ed. Shanti Brahmachari, February 2001 available: http://www.kulturrad.no/sitefiles/1/fou/notater37-58/notat44.pdf.

53. Griffin, *Contemporary Black and Asian Women Playwrights in Britain*, pp. 20 and 158.

54. Joseph, *Nomadic Identities*, p. 117.

55. Kathleen Starck, '"They Call Me an "Asian Writer" as Well". Tanika Gupta's

Sanctuary, Skeleton and *Inside Out*', in *Alternatives within the Mainstream: British Black and Asian Theatres*, ed. Dimple Godiwala (Newcastle: Cambridge Scholars Press, 2006), pp. 347–62 (p. 349).

56. Tanika Gupta, *Sanctuary* (London: Oberon Books, 2002), p. 73; emphasis in original.

57. Tanika Gupta, 'An Advocate for Change. Tanika Gupta in Conversation with Caridad Svich', in *Trans-Global Readings*, ed. Caridad Svich (Manchester: Manchester University Press, 2004), pp. 99–103 (p. 102).

58. Gupta, *Sanctuary*, p. 69.

59. Michael Billington, 'Sanctuary', *Guardian*, 31 July 2002 http://www.guardian.co.uk/stage/2002/jul/31/theatre.artsfeatures3.

60. See also Jacqueline Mosselson, who argues that the 'refugee, at least in transit, represents the state of statelessness. ... a candidate for insignia of a "postnational" world' in *Roots & Routes. Bosnian Adolescent Refugees in New York City* (Bern: Peter Lang, 2006), p. xxxii.

61. Billington, 'Sanctuary'.

62. Griffin, *Contemporary Black and Asian Women Playwrights in Britain*, p. 228.

63. Starck, '"They Call Me an "Asian Writer" as Well"', p. 350. As Starck (350) notes, the biblical allusions also continue in the image of the characters being driven out of their 'Paradise', as Kabir explains in Scene 5: 'I have made this my garden of paradise ... It's going to be flooded. It's going to be a swimming pool' (Gupta, *Sanctuary*, p. 71).

64. For a similar use and deconstruction of an enclosed garden setting see Ayub Khan-Din's play *Last Dance at Dum Dum* (1999) about a group of elderly Anglo-Indian citizens in Calcutta.

65. In his play *Fish Men* (2005), about 'chess hustlers' in New York's Washington Square Park, the Puerto Rican American playwright Candido Tirado uses a similar set of characters who represent different genocides, including a young Guatemalan programmer, a retired Cherokee construction worker, an old Jewish man and African American and Ukrainian chess hustlers.

66. Gupta, *Sanctuary*, p. 29. A comparison of Margaret and the character of Maude in Caryl Churchill's *Cloud Nine* (1979) may be interesting here.

67. Gupta, *Sanctuary*, p. 30.

68. Gupta, *Sanctuary*, p. 23.

69. Gupta, *Sanctuary*, pp. 92–93.

70. Gupta, *Sanctuary*, p. 112.

71. Gupta, *Sanctuary*, pp. 106 and 112; emphasis in original. Griffin further reads the fact that the killing takes place in the graveyard, a place which 'contains the remains, both of the colonial empires and of the church as an institution', as a comment that 'state institutions cannot and do not protect the individual': Griffin, *Contemporary Black and Asian Women Playwrights in Britain*, p. 230.

72. Gupta, *Sanctuary*, p. 81.

73. Mosselson, *Roots & Routes*, p. xxviii.

74. Mosselson, *Roots & Routes*, pp. xxx–xxxi.

75. Hannah Arendt quoted in Malkki, 'Refugees and Exile', p. 502.

76. Gupta, *Sanctuary*, p. 104.

77. Gupta, *Sanctuary*, p. 92. Earlier, as part of a project for kids called 'Twenty-four hours in the life of a garden', Sebastian had already installed a camera with a timer mechanism in the garden, of which Michael is frightened (pp. 31, 40).

78. The relation between photos, memory, refugees and their past history is also dramatised in Wertenbaker's *Credible Witness* (2001) and, marginally, in Wilson's *Survivors* (1999).

79. Malkki, 'Speechless Emissaries', p. 390.

80. For an analysis of refugeeness and displacement in *In This World*, see D. Farrier, 'The Journey Is the Film Is the Journey: Michael Winterbottom's *In This World*', *Research in Drama Education*, 13.2 (2008), pp. 223–32.

81. Doreen Massey, *Space, Place, and Gender* (Minneapolis: University of Minnesota Press, 1994), p. 11.

82. Malkki, 'Refugees and Exile', p. 509.

6 *Chris Banfield*—Directing Storytelling Performance and Storytelling Theatre

1. For Vayu Naidu's own eloquent account of practice referred to here, as well as wide-ranging reflections on British Asian Theatre, see Vayu Naidu, 'Call-response: Migration as Metaphor in Theatre', *Contemporary Theatre Review*, 19.2 (2009), pp. 227–32.

2. Vayu Naidu Company's mission statement reads: 'The mission of the Vayu Naidu Company is to champion the direct experience of Storytelling. The company also produces Storytelling events for cross generational/cultural participation, sometimes exploring multidisciplinary art forms, sometimes as "pure" performance storytelling. Replication of successes and expansion of partnerships and exploration for the long term is at the heart of the company's ethos. VNC curates programmes for specific events as well as having small scale touring work "in repertoire" which can tour both nationally and internationally. VNC is also a training and developing organisation that supports Vayu Naidu in her creative development as an artist in theatre and performance. VNC also enables learning and participation especially by young people or those with educational, physical, health, social or cultural special needs, and aims to provide skills training for young, developing, and experienced storytellers.'

3. The first performance of *Nine Nights: Stories from the Rāmāyana* was given at Leicester Haymarket Studio Theatre on Thursday 7 October 1999, with design by Jenny Campbell, performers: Vayu Naidu (storyteller), Colin Seddon (music). The first performance of *South* was given at the Gulbenkian Theatre, Canterbury on 1 May 2003, with design by Marsha Roddy, lighting design by Dee Ashworth, performers: Magdalen Gorringe (*bharatanatyam* dance), Vayu Naidu (storyteller), Lia Prentaki (contemporary dance), Orphy Robinson (music), Shane Shambhu (*bharatanatyam* dance). The first performance of *Mistaken ... Annie Besant in India*, by Rukhsana Ahmad, was given on 25 April 2007 at the Yvonne Arnaud Theatre, Guildford, with design by Marsha Roddy and lighting design by Mark Dymock, performers: Rosalind Stockwell (Annie Besant), Vayu Naidu (storyteller), Ruby Sahota (Sidra), Narinder Samra (Krishnamurti), Ranjit Krishnamma (Narayaniah, Governor, Yogi), Rohit Gokani (Gandhi, Judge Jessel, Man).

4. Michael Wilson, *Storytelling and Theatre* (Basingstoke: Palgrave Macmillan, 2006), p. 142.

5. Clive Barker gives a useful summary of Littlewood's work in *Twentieth-century Actor Training*, ed. Alison Hodge (London: Routledge, 2000), pp. 113–28.

6. Farley Richmond supports a view that while the *Nātyaśāstra*, the ancient classical Sanskrit text on dramaturgy from which the theory of *rasa* is drawn,

was initially applied to theatre performance, 'subsequently it was borrowed and applied to dramatic literature and expanded to include other forms of Sanskrit literature and other performing arts, as well': Farley Richmond, 'Characteristics of Sanskrit Theatre and Drama', in *Indian Theatre: Traditions of Performance*, eds Farley P. Richmond, Darius L. Swann and Phillip B. Zarrilli (Honolulu: University of Hawaii Press, 1990), pp. 25–85 (p. 80). Outlining *rasa* as sentiment and identifying its theory as directly linked to explaining how aesthetic experience is perceived by the spectator of Sanskrit theatre, he continues, '*Nātyaśāstra* divides human experience into eight basic sentiments: erotic, comic, pathetic, furious, heroic, terrible, odious, and marvelous. It is these which the spectators savor in various permutations and combinations as they observe the work in performance. And yet to give focus to the experience, just as a meal has a dominant flavor, one sentiment should dominate all others in the total context of the performance' (p. 81).

7. *Bharatanatyam* is one of the principal Classical Indian dance forms of south India. Traditionally a solo dance art performed by Hindu temple dancers, its practice was revived in the late nineteenth century.

8. In the performative context of Classical Indian dance-drama forms such as *kathakali, mudrās* are hand gestures that are acquired through many years of a dancer's training and practice and which carry codified, symbolic significance according to the traditions laid down in the *Nātyaśāstra*.

9. The first performance of *Mistaken ... Annie Besant in India* in India was given at Senate Hall, University of Allahabad on 30 November 2007. I acknowledge with gratitude the support of Vice-Chancellor Professor Rajen Harshe and Professor Mukherjee of the English Department in making this possible. The play was subsequently performed at the Habitat Theatre, Delhi on 2 December and at the Museum Theatre, Chennai as part of Prakriti Foundation Park's New Festival on 5 December. I'm grateful for the support of Festival Organiser, Ranvir Shah in facilitating this. The tour could not have happened without the financial support of Tani Dhamija and Copper Beech (UK) Limited, to whom grateful thanks are also due. During the tour the cast was unchanged, apart from Hari Sajjan, who took the parts of Gandhi, Judge Jessel and Man.

10. I would like to thank James Barber, Director and Chief Executive of Guildford's Yvonne Arnaud Theatre, and its General Manager Brian Kirk for their support for the production.

11. Vayu Naidu has advanced the view that the Arts Council England funding decision was based more on the play's content rather than deficiencies in its form: Naidu 'Call-response Migration', p. 232.

7 *Claire Cochrane*—Engaging the Audience: A Comparative Analysis of Developmental Strategies in Birmingham and Leicester since the 1990s

1. For a more detailed account of Birmingham Rep's record in developing opportunities for Black British and British Asian artists and audiences see Claire Cochrane '"A Local Habitation and a Name": The Development of Black and Asian Theatre in Birmingham since the 1970s', *Alternatives within the Mainstream British Black and Asian Theatres*, ed. Dimple Godiwala (Newcastle: Cambridge Scholars Press, 2006), pp. 153–73.

2. Leicester Haymarket Theatre is now closed and has been replaced since late 2008 with Curve Theatre. This essay looks at the record at the Haymarket.

3. Claire Cochrane, *Birmingham Rep: A City's Theatre 1962–2002* (Birmingham: Sir Barry Jackson Trust, 2003), pp. 196–98.

4. 'Theatre to Close Temporarily', BBC News, 20 May 2003, http://news.bbc.co.uk/1/hi/england/leicestershire/3043339.stm; see also Geoffrey Davis, '"Once You Open Doors, You Have to Walk through Them." An Interview with Kully Thiarai', in *Staging New Britain: Aspects of South Asian British Theatre Practice*, eds Geoffrey V. Davis and Anne Fuchs (Brussels: Peter Lang, 2006), pp. 293–307 (p. 301).

5. Leicester Theatre Trust Limited, Annual Report for the year ended 6 April 2003, pp. 1–20 (p. 2).

6. Cochrane, *Birmingham Rep*, pp. 198–99.

7. Pervaiz Khan, letter in response to Michael Billington's review of *The Ramayana* in the *Guardian*, 26 October 2000.

8. The detailed account of *Bali—The Sacrifice* is taken from J. Wilson Associates, *Evaluation Report: Leicester Haymarket Theatre—'Arts Connect' New Audiences* (Arts Council of England, September 2002). All the Arts Council England commissioned reports cited in this essay may be accessed at http://www.takingpartinthearts.com/content.php?content=1113.

9. J. Wilson Associates, *Audiences for the Leicester Haymarket Theatre: A Future-scoping Report* (Arts Council of England, September, 2002).

10. In an interview with Sarah Dadswell on 19 August 2006 in Bangalore, Girish Karnad recorded his regret that he had not written a new play for Leicester rather than permitting a revival of *Bali* which he felt 'went over the heads of the audience'. The casting of Naseeruddin Shah had been made to rehabilitate the actor's reputation in England following the disastrous reception of his performance as Cyrano de Bergerac in the Tara Arts National Theatre production in 1995.

11. Quoted in Cochrane, '"A Local Habitation and a Name"', p. 154.

12. Dipak Joshi, interview with the author, 7 July 2008. 'Roots' was an Arts Council England and BBC English Regions cultural-diversity project which ran as a pilot scheme with BBC East Midlands.

13. Cochrane, *Birmingham Rep*, p. 198.

14. J. Wilson Associates, *Evaluation Report: Leicester Haymarket Theatre*.

15. Joanna Herbert, *Negotiating Boundaries in the City: Migration, Ethnicity, and Gender in Britain* (Aldershot: Ashgate, 2008), pp. vii, 26.

16. Cochrane, '"A Local Habitation and a Name"', p. 162.

17. Claire Cochrane, 'Theatre and the Urban Space: The Case of Birmingham Rep', *New Theatre Quarterly*, 62 (May 2000), pp. 137–47.

18. Cochrane, *Birmingham Rep*, pp. 45–57.

19. John Blackmore, 'The Haymarket Theatre, Leicester', in *Making Space for Theatre: British Architecture and Theatre since 1958*, eds R. Mulryne and M. Shewring (Stratford-Upon-Avon: Mulryne and Shewring, 1995), p. 70.

20. The main auditorium of Birmingham Rep originally seated 901; following refurbishments in 1999 the capacity was reduced to 824.

21. Reports include Qnun Ltd, *Asian Caribbean and African Arts Strategy for West Midlands Arts Board* (Birmingham: West Midlands Arts, 1992); Harris Research Centre, *Black and Asian Attitudes to the Arts in Birmingham* (London: Arts Council of England, 1993); Helen Jermyn and Philip Desai, *Arts—What's in a Word? Ethnic Minorities in Britain* (London: Arts Council of England, 2000).

22. Tahir Abbas, *Muslims in Birmingham, UK*, Background paper for the University

of Oxford Centre on Migration Policy and Society, 2006, http://www.compas. ox.ac.uk/publications/papers/Birmingham%20Background%20Paper%200206. pdf [accessed 15 April 2009].

23. As reported by Youth Arts Worker Jonathan Cochrane in 1998.

24. Herbert, *Negotiating Boundaries in the City*, pp. 21–22.

25. Vayu Naidu, telephone interview with Claire Cochrane, 27 July 2008.

26. For example, Harris Research Centre, *Black and Asian Attitudes to the Arts in Birmingham*, p. 10.

27. Vayu Naidu, telephone interview with Cochrane.

28. This was picked up in J. Wilson Associates, *Evaluation Report: Leicester Haymarket Theatre*.

29. Herbert, *Negotiating Boundaries in the City*, p. 133.

30. Suman Buchar, interview with Claire Cochrane, 5 August 2008.

31. Vayu Naidu, telephone interview with Cochrane.

32. Vayu Naidu, 'Vayu Naidu Company's South: New Directions in Theatre of Storytelling', in *Staging New Britain: Aspects of Black and South Asian British Theatre Practice*, eds Geoffrey V. Davis and Anne Fuchs (Brussels: Peter Lang, 2006), pp. 141–54 (p. 147).

33. Tamasha's productions at the Rep in this period are discussed in the section on Tamasha in *British South Asian Theatres: A Documented History*, eds Graham Ley and Sarah Dadswell (Exeter: University of Exeter Press, 2011).

34. For a more comprehensive picture of Suman Bhuchar's evolving marketing strategies for Tamasha, see her essay 'The Marketing of Commercial and Subsidised Theatre to British Asian Audiences: *Bombay Dreams* (2002) and Tamasha's *Fourteen Songs, Two Weddings and a Funeral* (1998 and 2001)' in this book.

35. For a more detailed account of Tamasha's productions in the wider context of Birmingham Rep's programming policy see Cochrane, *Birmingham Rep*, pp. 172–206.

36. Liz Gilbey, 'Where East Meets West', *The Stage*, 30 November 2000.

37. 'Oration for Parminder Nagra by Professor Gordon Campbell', 11 July 2007, University of Leicester eBulletin, http://www2.le.ac.uk/ebulletin/news/2000–2009/2007/07/nparticle.2007–07–16.2017932467 [accessed 15 April 2009].

38. Details of produced and presented plays and other events in the Leicester Haymarket seasons 1993–2007 are taken from brochures held in the Record Office for Leicestershire, Leicester & Rutland.

39. Naidu, 'Vayu Naidu Company's South', pp. 146–47.

40. Naidu, 'Vayu Naidu Company's South', p. 149.

41. Naidu, 'Vayu Naidu Company's South', pp. 148–49.

42. Timeri N. Murari, 'The Square Circle (Theatre)', http://www.timerimurari. com/theatre.htm. The original film of *The Square Circle* made in India and directed by Amol Palekar, won the *Time* magazine award for the best film of 1996. However, Palekar subverted Murari's original narrative by having the transvestite character killed at the end. The Haymarket commission gave Murari the opportunity to restore the ending where Lakshmi/Laksham and Sita fall in love.

43. Murari, 'The Square Circle (Theatre)'.

44. Murari, 'The Square Circle (Theatre)'.

45. The relationship between Tamasha and the Rep effectively ended with the new artistic policy introduced by Jonathan Church and Stuart Rogers.

46. Opening stage directions in Amber Lone, *Deadeye* (London: Oberon, 2006), p. 13.

47. Scene locations in Gurpreet Kaur Bhatti, *Behsharam (Shameless)* (London: Oberon, 2001).

48. The personal threats associated with the events surrounding *Behzti* have made it difficult to establish the facts surrounding the way the crisis developed. However, the unpublished account 'An Actor's Personal View from Onstage', written by Madhav Sharma who played Mr Sandhu, and the interview given by Shelley King, who played Balbir, to Sarah Dadswell on 20 April 2006 have helped to clarify what happened. Details of the set and stage action are based on the author's experience of the play in performance on Wednesday 15 December 2004. See Claire Cochrane's letter published in the *Guardian* on 30 December 2004, http://www.guardian.co.uk/world/2004/dec/30/religion.uk.

49. Sampad was also condemned by critics of *Behzti* for involvement in the production.

50. The Giani of the welcoming Gurdwara spoke about the hypocrisy of many 'suit wallahs' and tied Madhav Sharma's turban, which the actor wore in performance: Sharma, unpublished essay.

51. Anthony Frost, 'Drama in the Age of *Kalyug*: *Behzti* and Sikh Self-Censorship', in *Alternatives within the Mainstream: British Black and Asian Theatres*, ed. Dimple Godiwala (Newcastle: Cambridge Scholars Press, 2006), pp. 203–25 (p. 213).

52. Gurpreet Kaur Bhatti, '"This Warrior Is Fighting on. I Am Proud to Be a Sikh, and My Play Is Both Respectful to Sikhism and Honest"', *Guardian*, 13 January 2005. Also in conversation with Cochrane, 30 September 2008.

53. Cochrane, '"A Local Habitation and a Name"', p. 154.

54. Details of these problems were discussed by Shelley King in her interview in 2006.

55. *Samachar* is Hindi for news.

56. J. Wilson Associates, *Evaluation Report: Leicester Haymarket Theatre*, pp. 5–8.

57. J. Wilson Associates, *Evaluation Report: Leicester Haymarket Theatre*, p. 14.

58. For a description of Curve Theatre go to Alfred Hickling, 'Leicester's Curve Is a Theatre without Secrets', *Guardian*, 15 September 2008. Kully Thiarai's resignation was announced in *The Stage* on 3 April 2007.

59. Anon, 'Asian Recruits Reflect Leicester's Ethnic Mix', *The Stage*, 28 June 2001.

60. *The Eclipse Report: Developing Strategies to Combat Racism in the Theatre* (London: Arts Council of England, 2001).

61. Davis, 'Once You Open Doors', p. 304.

62. J. Wilson Associates, *Audiences for the Leicester Haymarket Theatre*, p. 8.

63. The complete account of Joshi's work on *Bollywood Jane* may be found online: http://www.cultivate-em.org.uk/uploads/case_studies/450c44b4a472d0f1dd5fc7eab0178c20.doc.

64. Leicester Partnership, *Diverse City A Vision for Cultural Life in Leicester*, Cultural Strategy Partnership Annual Review, December 2004.

65. Davis, 'Once You Open Doors', p. 303.

66. Davis, 'Once You Open Doors', pp. 297–99.

67. Bhikhu C. Parekh, *The Future of Multi-Ethnic Britain: Report of the Commission on the Future of Multi-Ethnic Britain* (London: Profile Books, 2000), p. 35.

68. Audience data supplied in conversation with Vicky Price, Marketing and Communications Officer, and Selene Burn, Community Engagement Officer.
69. Selene Burn, email response to Claire Cochrane's questions, 18 August 2008.
70. Interview with Amanda Holden, formerly Associate Producer at Birmingham Rep, 6 November 2008.

8 *Victoria Sams*—Patriarchy and Its Discontents: The 'Kitchen-Sink Drama' of Tamasha Theatre Company

1. Kristine Landon-Smith, 'Spotlight: Asian Theatre', *Independent*, January 16, 2004. Retrieved from the Tamasha website, http://www.tamasha.org.uk/strictly-dandia-article/.
2. In this respect, Tamasha is similar to another company founded by women in 1989, Talawa Theatre Company, which is still run by one of its founders, Yvonne Brewster, and continues to actively commission and develop new writing for the theatre (particularly through its festival of new work, Zebra Crossings).
3. Landon-Smith, telephone interview, 15 September 2008.
4. Interviews with Khan-Din, on the other hand, do mention his childhood home and the Northern realist plays and films as strong influences on the play, noting that many critics overlook such influences and stamp Khan-Din as 'the next Hanif Kureishi', which is a label Khan-Din finds misleading. For more from Khan-Din on his work and its reception, see Harriet Lane, 'I Speak English, Not Urdu ...', *Observer*, 31 October 1999, Arts Section, p. 6; Simon Hattenstone and Lyn Gardner, 'What Country, Friend, Is This?' *Guardian*, 29 January, 1997, p. 12.
5. Keith Bruce, 'Balti Kings', *Herald*, 20 January 2000, p. 17.
6. Frances Spalding, 'Edward Middleditch (1923–87). London, Serpentine Gallery', *The Burlington Magazine*, 130, 1021, Special issue on Twentieth-Century Art (April 1988), pp. 310–11.
7. Arnold Wesker, 'Living-room Revolt', *Guardian*, 26 January 2008.
8. The following books contain brief to lengthy deconstructions of scholarly and popular accounts of postwar British drama: Dominic Shellard, *British Theatre Since the War* (New Haven and London: Yale University Press, 1999); Dan Rebellato, *1956 and All That: The Making of Modern British Drama* (London and New York: Routledge, 1999); and Stephen Lacey, *British Realist Drama: The New Wave in Its Context 1956–1965* (London and New York: Routledge, 1995).
9. Ayub Khan-Din, Introduction, *East Is East* (London: FilmFour Books/MacMillan, 1999), pp. i–ix.
10. See Michael Billington, 'Curryoke Night: *Balti Kings*', *Guardian*, 15 January 2000; Sarah Hemming, 'Sizzling Kitchen-sink Drama Is Hot Stuff', *Financial Times*, 19 January 2000; Benedict Nightingale, '*Balti Kings*', *The Times*, 17 January 2000; and Maeve Walsh, '*Balti Kings*', *Independent*, 16 January 2000.
11. See, for instance, Michael Billington, 'East Is Best', *Guardian*, 25 November 1996; Charles Spencer, 'Rich Mix of Culture and Comedy', *Daily Telegraph*, 25 November 1996; and John Peter, 'Crossed Countries', *Sunday Times*, 1 December 1996.
12. See, in particular: Hattenstone and Gardner, 'What Country ...'; and Khan-Din, *East Is East* (1999), p. ix; on depersonalising his writing, p. xii.
13. Terry Grimley, 'Home Grown Variety Is the Spice of Life: Curry Wars in

Birmingham's Balti Belt Have Provided the Subject for the Latest Show from an Award-winning Team', *Birmingham Post*, 17 December 1999, p. 14.

14. Dominic Hingorani analyses Tamasha's realist approach to their set design and other elements, with an emphasis on *House of the Sun* and *East Is East*, in his essay 'Tara Arts and Tamasha: Producing Asian Performance—Two Approaches', in *Alternatives Within the Mainstream: British Black and Asian Theatres*, ed. Dimple Godiwala (Newcastle: Cambridge Scholars Press, 2006), pp. 174–200.

15. Khan-Din, *East Is East* (London: Nick Hern Books, 1997), p. 60.

16. Khan-Din, *East is East* (1999), p. ix.

17. Mentioned briefly in programme introduction to *Balti Kings*, and confirmed in a telephone interview with Kristine Landon-Smith, 15 September 2008.

18. Khan-Din, *East Is East* (1999), pp. ix–x.

19. Khan-Din, *East Is East* (1997), p. 30.

20. Khan-Din, *East Is East* (1997), p. 65.

21. Khan-Din, *East Is East* (1997), p. 36.

22. Patricia Schroeder, *The Feminist Possibilities of Dramatic Realism* (Madison, NJ: Farleigh Dickinson University Press, 1996), p. 26. Schroeder's book examines American feminist realism from the 1910s to the 1960s, but her use of feminist critiques of realism as a basis for analysing its feminist potential is useful in considering the ways British realist drama illustrates both the pitfalls and the potential. For an excellent analysis of both in post-war British Drama, see Michelene Wandor, *Postwar British Drama: Looking Back in Gender* (London: Routledge, 2001).

23. Arnold Wesker, *Volume Two: The Kitchen and Other Plays* (London: Penguin Books, 1960; this collection repr. 1976), p. 9.

24. I would like to thank the Research and Development Committee at Dickinson College for the travel grant that made the research for this essay possible. I am grateful for the insights and help of all the participants in the British Asian Theatre Conference in Exeter, April 2008, and especially for the thoughtful feedback of Graham Ley and Sarah Dadswell. My thanks also to Kristine Landon-Smith and the staff at Tamasha Theatre Company for their responses to my many questions.

9 *Suman Bhuchar*—The Marketing of Commercial and Subsidised Theatre to British Asian Audiences: Tamasha's *Fourteen Songs, Two Weddings and a Funeral* (1998 and 2001) and *Bombay Dreams* (2002)

1. I am using the term 'Asian' here to refer to people of Indian, Pakistani, Bangladeshi origin who live in the UK and those whose heritage originates from the Indian sub-continent.

2. I am making this claim as there is no contemporary British Asian musical in the West End by a commercial producer at this point. There were four Black Theatre Seasons (1983, 1985, 1986 and 1987) at the Arts Theatre, London, which have included Asian productions. For a detailed discussion of the Black Theatre Seasons, see Alda Terracciano, 'Mainstreaming African, Asian and Caribbean Theatre: The Experiments of the Black Theatre Forum', in *Alternatives within the Mainstream: British Black and Asian Theatres*, ed. Dimple Godiwala (Newcastle: Cambridge Scholars Press, 2006), pp. 22–50. See also note 17, below.

3. For an account of the back-story to the production of *Untouchable*, and of

the productions by Tamasha leading up to *Fourteen Songs*, see the section on Tamasha in *British South Asian Theatres: A Documented History*, eds Graham Ley and Sarah Dadswell (Exeter: University of Exeter Press, 2011).

4. Sudha and I had been interested in the arts for a long time and had attended the regular drama sessions held by Tara Arts at the Millan Centre in Tooting Bec, London, in the 1980s, and acted in their shows. Sudha become a professional actor for Tara during this time.

5. Second-generation Asians is a self-styled nomenclature adopted by the children of immigrants to the UK during the 1970s and 1980s, irrespective of whether they were British-born or not.

6. *Untouchable* toured to Phoenix Arts, Leicester, 9–10 January 1990; Green Room, Manchester, 11–13 January; Derby Community Arts Centre, 16–18 January; and Octagon Theatre, Bolton, 19–20 January, www.tamasha.org.uk.

7. Sudha Bhuchar, 'The Tamasha Method', *Prompt* (Journal of The Theatrical Management Association), 19 (November 1999), pp. 9–10.

8. 'As Tamasha believe in a naturalistic way of working, the Company spent a great deal of time meeting and interviewing the Sindhi community in London and later went to Bombay for further research. The results of this, together with the use of "Bombay Speak" give the play a very authentic feel.' Marketing letter, 21 February 1991.

9. February 1991, and in my personal files.

10. Hardish Virk, interviewed by Sarah Dadswell, Jerri Daboo and Graham Ley, Exeter, 26 February 2008.

11. According to Box Office India website, the film grossed the equivalent of £1.6 million in the UK. www.boxofficeindia.com.

12. The music of the original film was re-scored by music director, Barrie Bignold, for the production as the pre-recorded film music was not suitable to be used in a live production.

13. Translated as 'Take the Shoes and Give Me the Money', the song illustrates an Indian wedding custom in which the girl's side try to steal the groom's shoes, and his relatives have to ensure that does not happen or pay a forfeit to the girls to retrieve them. In the film and the play this is the moment when Prem and Nisha feel a mutual attraction.

14. Kristine Landon-Smith, programme to *Fourteen Songs, Two Weddings, and a Funeral*, 1998.

15. He later appeared as lead Akash in *Bombay Dreams*.

16. *East Is East* had travelled to all these three venues in its initial small-scale tour in 1996, and became an instant hit from its first performance at the Rep Studio on 8 October 1996. In addition to the huge Asian audience, it had significant cross-over appeal.

17. The revival of *East Is East* ran from 5 February to 8 March 1997 at the Theatre Royal Stratford East, and from 26 March to 19 April at the Royal Court Downstairs (in its temporary home at the Duke of York's Theatre, St Martin's Lane, whilst the Sloane Square venue was being refurbished), chalking up over 100 performances and becoming the first British Asian play in the West End.

18. At the time Barclays plc was the UK's principal Sponsor of Regional Theatre. Launched in 1995, Barclays Stage Partners was a six-year £4.5 million sponsorship scheme from Barclays plc and Arts Council England designed to generate new opportunities for theatre organisations to work together and produce high-quality drama for the benefit of audiences nationwide.

19. *Evening Standard*, 2 December 1998.
20. John Peter, *Sunday Times*, 15 November, 1998.
21. A chain of cinemas that has been programming Bollywood films regularly since 1997.
22. This is anecdotal evidence from conversations and letters sent to the office, and also occurred on *Bombay Dreams*.
23. Charles Spencer, 'Bollywood Lends Hilarity to a Tale of Love', *Daily Telegraph*, 20 February 2001.
24. The 'book' refers to the story and dialogue of the show in a musical.
25. Later in 2009 A.R. Rahman composed music for the film *Slumdog Millionaire*, which won seven BAFTAs (including Best Music) and Oscars (including two for him) in 2009.
26. From the publicity postcard issued six months before the show opened, in my personal files.
27. Interview by Suman Bhuchar with A.R. Rahman, February 2008.
28. From the publicity postcard issued six months before the show opened, in my personal files.
29. It must be noted that Andrew Lloyd Webber was at pains to stress that he was the 'producer' of the show, to prevent any misconception occurring.
30. From the Really Useful Group website: www.reallyuseful.com.
31. Robert Gore Langston, *Daily Express*, 20 June 2002, reporting on the 'First Night'; his full review 'Indian Summer', appeared in the *Daily Express* on 21 June 2002.
32. Georgina Brown, 'Hooray for This Bite of Spicy Bollywood', *Mail on Sunday*, 23 June 2002.
33. Alastair Macaulay, 'Dreams Meet Reality', *Financial Times*, 21 June 2002.
34. Michael Billington, 'Deliriously Dotty Bollywood', *Guardian*, 20 June 2002.
35. Apollo Theatre, Victoria website: www.apollovictoria.co.uk.
36. Hardish Virk interviewed by Dadswell, Daboo and Ley, 2008.
37. None of these programmes usually includes the book or lyrics to the show.
38. In the subsidised theatre sector the print distribution would focus on limited outlets depending on the show, target audience and budget, whereas for a West End show the print distribution circuit is much larger.
39. Meaning the third sex, or transgender.
40. A catchy film song composed by A.R. Rahman for the Telegu film, *Mudhalavan* (1999), and its Hindi remake: *Nayak: The Real Hero* (2001), both directed by S. Shankar.
41. From the film *Dil Se* (1998), also composed by A.R. Rahman.
42. The first preview of the show was on 31 May 2002.
43. 231/2 days of Bollywood ran from 3 to 26 May 2002 and represented a major celebration of Bollywood film-culture in the UK.
44. A BFI, UK-wide celebration of cinema cultures from India, Pakistan, Bangladesh, Sri Lanka and British Asian work.
45. This was in connection with the new set of gates being created at the top of Constitution Hill, from the approach of Duke of Wellington Place, to mark the contribution and sacrifice made in the First and Second World Wars by five million volunteers from the Indian sub-continent, Africa and the Caribbean. The Gates were officially opened on 6 November 2002 by the Queen.
46. He was the director of *Lagaan*.
47. Interview by Suman Bhuchar with Richard Pulford in April 2008.

48. Summary of research findings for West End Theatre Audience Report, published by SOLT/TMA in September 2004, from research survey conducted by MORI at forty-five performances (forty-four different productions) between 13 March 2003 and 9 February 2004. The total number of responses to the surveys was 6,615, a response rate of 33 per cent. Note that *Bombay Dreams* was also running until 16 June 2004, and so would have been included in this survey.

49. I am thinking here of the Arts Council's initiatives in this area, including Naseem Khan's report on British Asian Theatre (1994); 'Black Regional Initiative in Theatre', a key strategic fund aimed creating more equitable Black and Asian Theatre in England (2000); the Eclipse Conference (12–13 June 2001) and Report (April 2002).

10 *Jerri Daboo*—Mixing with the Mainstream: Transgressing the Identity of Place

1. Tim Cresswell, *In Place/Out of Place: Geography, Ideology, and Transgression* (Minneapolis and London: University of Minnesota Press, 1996), p. 149.

2. The term 'British Asian' is problematic in itself, as 'Asian' is a homogeneous term for a wide range of countries and cultures. For the purpose of this essay, 'Asian' and 'British Asian' refers to those originating from, or descendants of migrants from, the Indian subcontinent.

3. Christopher Innes, 'West End', in *The Cambridge Guide to Theatre*, ed. Martin Banham (Cambridge: Cambridge University Press, 1998), pp. 1194–55 (p. 1194).

4. Kay Anderson, 'Introduction', in *Cultural Geographies*, eds Kay Anderson and Fay Gale (South Melbourne: Longman, 1999), p. 8.

5. Claire Dwyer, 'Veiled Meanings: Young British Muslim Women and the Negotiation of Differences', *Gender, Place and Culture*, 6.1 (1999), pp. 5–26 (p. 6).

6. Sarah Radcliffe, 'Frontiers and Popular Nationhood: Geographies of Identity in the 1995 Ecuador–Peru Border Dispute', *Political Geography*, 17.3 (1998), pp. 273–93 (p. 290).

7. Cresswell, *In Place/Out of Place*, p. 8.

8. Cresswell, *In Place/Out of Place*, p. 26.

9. Geoffrey Davis, 'Introduction', in *Staging New Britain: Aspects of Black and South Asian British Theatre Practice*, eds Geoffrey Davis and Anne Fuchs (Brussels: Peter Lang, 2006), pp. 15–34 (p. 24).

10. Tanika Gupta, '20 Questions with … Tanika Gupta', *What's on Stage*, 21 January 2008, http://www.whatsonstage.com/index.php?pg=207&story=E8821 200679850.

11. Anderson, 'Introduction', p. 7.

12. For further information on this programme, see the final report at: http://www.takingpartinthearts.com/content.php?content=1021.

13. Quoted in Claire Cochrane, '"A Local Habitation and a Name": the Development of Black and Asian Theatre in Birmingham since the 1970s', in *Alternatives within the Mainstream: British Black and Asian Theatres*, ed. Dimple Godiwala (Newcastle: Cambridge Scholars Press, 2006), pp. 153–73 (p. 154).

14. Hardish Virk, Interview with Jerri Daboo, University of Exeter, 26 February 2008.

15. By 'negative', I mean non-existent, blank or empty.

16. Virk, 2008.

17. Virk, 2008.

18. *Eclipse Report: Developing Strategies to Combat Racism in Theatre*, Arts Council of England, East Midlands Arts Board, Theatrical Management Association, Nottingham Playhouse, 2001, http://www.artscouncil.org.uk/media/uploads/documents/publications/307.doc, p. 52.

19. Anderson, 'Introduction', p. 8.

20. Cochrane, '"A Local Habitation and a Name"', p. 157.

21. Virk, 2008.

22. Jigna Desai, *Beyond Bollywood: the Cultural Politics of South Asian Diasporic Film* (London: Routledge: 2004), p. 74.

23. Arjun Appadurai, *Modernity at Large* (Minneapolis: University of Minnesota Press, 1996), pp. 6, 49.

24. Dominic Rai, 'Exile: Forty Years in the West Midlands', http://www.manmela.org.uk/theatrecontent.html.

25. Anderson, 'Introduction', p. 8.

26. Virk, 2008.

27. For further discussion of this production, see Jerri Daboo, 'One under the Sun: Globalization, Culture and Utopia in *Bombay Dreams*', *Contemporary Theatre Review*, 15.3 (2005), pp. 330–37.

28. Rachel Dwyer, 'Bollywood Cinema and the UK', in the programme for *Rafta, Rafta ...*, produced by the Royal National Theatre, London, 2007.

29. Anuradha Kapur, 'Intra-cultural Performance Training and British Asian Collaborations', paper delivered at the conference 'British Asian Theatre: from Past to Present', University of Exeter, April 2008.

30. Girish Karnad, comments made following a talk by Naseem Khan at the conference 'British Asian Theatre: from Past to Present', University of Exeter, April 2008.

31. Michael Billington, '*Rafta, Rafta ...*', *Guardian*, 27 April 2007, http://www.guardian.co.uk/stage/2007/apr/27/theatre2.

32. Girish Karnad, 'The Inter-relationship between British and Indian Theatre, an Historical Perspective', keynote speech given at the conference 'British Asian Theatre: from Past to Present', University of Exeter, April 2008.

33. Kristine Landon-Smith, 'The Real Reason for the Boom in Multicultural Theatre', *Guardian* website, The Blog: Theatre and the Performing Arts, 23 May 2007, http://www.guardian.co.uk/stage/theatreblog/2007/may/23/thereal reasonfortheboomi.

34. Maddy Costa, 'Saint Nick', *Guardian*, 22 March 2004, http://www.guardian.co.uk/stage/2004/mar/22/theatre2.

35. Deirdre Osborne, 'The State of the Nation: Contemporary Black British Theatre and the Staging of the UK', in *Alternatives within the Mainstream: British Black and Asian Theatres*, ed. Dimple Godiwala (Newcastle: Cambridge Scholars Press, 2006), pp. 82–100 (p. 83).

36. Jatinder Verma, 'Asian Arts in the 21st Century', http://www.tara-arts.com/#/archive/articles_archive/asian_arts_in_the_21st_century.

37. Cochrane, '"A Local Habitation and a Name"', p. 154.

38. Shelley King, Interview with Jerri Daboo, London, 27 October 2008.

39. http://www.tamasha.org.uk/fourteen-songs/.

40. Kapur, 'Intra-cultural Performance Training and British Asian Collaborations'.

41. Cresswell, *In Place/Out of Place*, p. 26.

42. Jerri Daboo, 'One under the Sun'.

43. Virk, 2008.
44. Cresswell, *In Place/Out of Place*, p. 175.
45. David Farr, Programme note for *The Ramayana*, Lyric Theatre Hammersmith.
46. Jatinder Verma, 'Towards Cultural Literacy: 30 Years of Tara', http://www.tara-arts.com/#/archive/articles_archive/towards_cultural_literacy.

11 *Giovanna Buonanno*—Between Page and Stage: Meera Syal in British Asian Culture

1. Meera Syal, 'Finding My Voice', in *Passion: Discourses on Blackwomen's Creativity*, ed. M. Sulter (London: Urban Fox Press, 1990), pp. 57–61 (p. 57).
2. Syal, 'Finding My Voice', p. 59.
3. Akin Ojumu, 'All About Meera', *Observer Review*, 16 June 2002 http://observer.guardian.co.uk/comment/story/0,6903,738309,00.html.
4. A reminder of the increasingly important role assigned to the visualization of British Asian gendered subjectivities is offered by Amrit Wilson in her most recent study, where, among the various crucial questions concerning the social role of South Asian women in Britain, the author addresses precisely the question of representation and voices her discontent over the still largely stereotyped images that are available to reflect them, underlining the importance of 'contesting misrepresentation' on film and in the media. See Amrit Wilson, *Dreams, Questions, Struggles: South Asian Women in Britain* (London: Pluto Press, 2006), pp. 128–38. Interestingly enough, cultural and media representations of Asian womanhood were not discussed in Wilson's earlier, groundbreaking work *Finding a Voice: Asian Women in Britain* (London: Virago, 1978).
5. Raminder Kaur and Alda Terracciano, 'SouthAsian/BrAsian Performing Arts', in *A Postcolonial People: South Asians in Britain*, eds Nasreen Ali, Virander Kalra and S.H. Sayyid (London: Hurst and Co., 2006), pp. 343–57 (p. 353).
6. Ranasinha has noted that 'the financial support for minority art by the Greater London Council and the British Film Institute led to the creation of several Black and Asian theatre and film collectives', while the creation of Channel 4 in 1982 'which funded Kureishi's *My Beautiful Laundrette* and Syal's first feature films *A Nice Arrangement* and *Bhaji on the Beach*' represented a decisive moment in providing institutional funding for minority art. See Ruvani Ranasinha, *South Asian Writers in Twentieth-Century Britain: Culture in Translation* (Oxford: Clarendon Press, 2006), p. 266. Terracciano has amply documented the vitality of black and Asian theatres in the 1980s by retracing the history of the Black Theatre Forum, a collective of several companies that were active in the 1980s to 1990. See Alda Terracciano, 'Mainstreaming African, Asian and Caribbean Theatre: The Experiments of the Black Theatre Forum', in *Alternatives within the Mainstream: British Black and Asian Theatre*, ed. Dimple Godiwala (Newcastle: Cambridge Scholars Press, 2006), pp. 22–60.
7. Meenakshi Ponnuswami, 'Citizenship and Gender in Asian-British Performance', in *Feminist Futures? Theatre, Performance, Theory*, eds Elaine Aston and Geraldine Harris (Basingstoke: Palgrave Macmillan, 2006), pp. 34–55 (p. 34).
8. *Companion to Contemporary Black British Culture*, ed. Alison Donnell (London and New York: Routledge, 2002), p. xiii.
9. Meera Syal, *Life Isn't All Ha Ha Hee Hee* (London: Doubleday, 1999), p. 40.
10. Syal, *Life Isn't ...*, pp. 44–45.
11. Meera Syal, 'Last Laugh' in *Cultural Breakthrough*, published by VSO, 2003.

Available at http://www.vso.org.uk/Images/culturalbreakthrough_essays_tcm 8-2848.pdf (para. 1 of 17). [accessed 10 March 2008].

12. For the representative value assigned to black and Asian artists who are all too often taken to stand for a whole community see in particular Kobena Mercer, 'Black Art and the Burden of Representation', *Third Text*, 10.4 (1990), pp. 61–78. Stuart Hall has notably explored the link between identity and representation, pointing out that 'identity … is never complete, always in process and always constituted within, not outside representation': see Stuart Hall, 'Cultural Identity and Diaspora', in *Identity: Community, Culture, Difference*, ed. J. Rutherford (London: Lawrence & Wishart, 1990), pp. 222–37 (p. 222).

13. Interview with Syal in Alison Oddey, *Performing Women: Stand-ups, Strumpets and Itinerants* (Basingstoke: Palgrave Macmillan, 1999), p. 57.

14. Syal, 'Last Laugh', p. 17.

15. For Asian Cooperative Theatre, see the section in *British South Asian Theatres: A Documented History*, eds Graham Ley and Sarah Dadswell (Exeter: University of Exeter Press, 2011).

16. Interview with Syal in Carol Woddis, 'A Question of Perception', *Plays and Players*, March 1990, pp. 14–16 (p. 16).

17. Jatinder Verma, 'Cultural Transformations', in *Contemporary British Theatre*, ed. Theodore Shank (London: Macmillan, 1994), pp. 55–61 (p. 55).

18. Syal, 'Finding My Voice', p. 59.

19. Pratibha Parmar, 'Womanvoice, Womanvision. South Asian Women and Film', Rungh. A South Asian Quarterly of Culture, Comment and Criticism, 1, 1–2 (1991), pp. 16–19 (p. 18).

20. Meera Syal, *Anita and Me* (London: Flamingo, 1997; 1st edn, 1996), p. 150.

21. See Roger Bromley, *Narratives for a New Belonging: Diasporic Cultural Fictions* (Edinburgh: Edinburgh University Press, 2000); in particular chapter VI: 'Britain's Children Without a Home', pp. 142–68.

22. Syal, *Anita and Me*, p. 65.

23. Syal, *Anita and Me*, p. 146.

24. Syal, *Anita and Me*, pp. 165–66.

25. Syal, *Anita and Me*, p. 166.

26. See in particular Jim Pines, *Black and White in Colour: Black People in British Television since 1936* (London: BFI, 1992) and Sarita Malik, *Representing Black Britain: Black and Asian Images on Television* (Sage: London, 2002).

27. Woddis, 'A Question of Perception', p. 15.

28. See Malik, *Representing Black Britain*, pp. 99–100.

29. Salman Rushdie, *Imaginary Homelands* (London: Granta, 1991), p. 87.

30. Judith Butler, *Gender Trouble* (London: Routledge, 1990), p. 25.

31. Syal, *Anita and Me*, p. 10.

32. Syal, *Life Isn't …*, pp. 142–43.

33. *Goodness Gracious Me* was pioneered by a live sketch show called *Peter Sellers Is Dead* which was performed in the Riverside Studios in Hammersmith, West London, in 1995 by the four young actors Sanjeev Bhaskar, Kulvinder Ghir, Meera Syal and Nina Wadia for an audience of largely family and friends. This live performance offered a blueprint for what was to become the first British Asian sketch show. The original title chosen for the pilot show referred to Peter Sellers's famous interpretation of the clumsy Indian in Blake Edwards's 1968 film *The Party* and suggested that the time for humorous representations of

Indian people on film and television by white comedians was over. The show eventually hit mainstream radio and television and became *Goodness Gracious Me*, broadcast first as a hugely successful Radio 4 comedy programme in 1996 and then two years later turned into an even more successful BBC2 TV comedy series which ran until 2001.

34. Anon., 'Mirth of a Nation', *Guardian*, 20 February 1999 http://www.guardian.co.uk/Archive/Article/0,4273,3824542,00.html (para. 34 of 37).
35. Syal, *Life Isn't ...*, p. 109.
36. Malik, *Representing Black Britain*, p. 103.
37. Among a number of articles testifying to the mixed reception of the show see in particular Anon., 'Mirth of a Nation'.
38. Graham Huggan, *The Postcolonial Exotic: Marketing the Margins* (London: Routledge, 2001), p. vii.
39. Huggan, *The Postcolonial Exotic*, p. xii.
40. Huggan, *The Postcolonial Exotic*, p. xii.
41. Interview with Meera Syal, *Parkinson*, ITV1, 23 June 2007.
42. Charles Spencer, 'Laughter Laced With Warmth', *Daily Telegraph*, 27 April 2007.
43. Tarquin Hall, 'Review of *Rafta, Rafta ...*', *Sunday Times*, 29 April 2007.
44. Huggan, *The Postcolonial Exotic*, p. xii.
45. Syal, 'Finding My Voice', p. 59.

12 *Chandrika Patel*—Imagine, *Indiaah* ... on the British Stage: Exploring Tara's 'Binglish' and Tamasha's Brechtian Approaches

1. AUT [Online] http://www.tamasha.org.uk/about/.
2. Both Tara and Tamasha are currently a part of the 'Sector', a section of the Arts Council associated with the funding of African, Caribbean, South Asian and East Asian arts. Their role is defined as the representation of 'cultural diversity': see the editors' introduction to *Staging New Britain: Aspects of Black and South Asian British Theatre Practice*, eds Geoffrey Davis and Anne Fuchs (Brussels: Peter Lang, 2006), p. 1.
3. AUT [Online] http://www.tara-arts.com/#/about_tara.
4. Leela Gandhi, *Postcolonial Theory: A Critical Introduction* (Edinburgh: Edinburgh University Press, 1998), pp. 131–32.
5. Alda Terracciano, 'South Asian Diaspora Theatre in Britain' [Online] http://www.salidaa.org.uk/salidaa/site/Collections?mode=catalogue&adlib_id=900000006 [accessed 22 July 2008]. The Salidaa archive is now kept at Brunel University, with details of access given at http://www.brunel.ac.uk/services/library/research/special-collections/salidaa.
6. Aijaz Ahmed, *In Theory: Classes, Nations, Literatures* (Oxford: Oxford University Press, 1992), p. 85.
7. Ahmed, *In Theory: Classes, Nations, Literatures*, p. 86.
8. Avtar Brah, *Cartographies of Diaspora: Contesting Identities* (London and New York: Routledge, 1996), p. 183.
9. Brah, *Cartographies of Diaspora*, p. 16.
10. Brah, *Cartographies of Diaspora*, p. 209.
11. Brah, *Cartographies of Diaspora*, p. 210.
12. AUT [Online] http://www.tamasha.org.uk/about/.
13. Quoted in Dominic Hingorani, 'Tara Arts and Tamasha: Producing Asian

Performances—Two Approaches', in *Alternatives within the Mainstream: British Black and Asian Theatres*, ed. Dimple Godiwala (Newcastle: Cambridge Scholars Press, 2006), pp. 174–200 (p. 190).

14. Jigna Desai, *Beyond Bollywood: The Cultural Politics of South Asian Diasporic Film* (London: Routledge, 2004), p. 8.

15. Farley Richmond, 'Suggestions for Directors of Sanskrit Plays', in *Sanskrit Drama in Performance*, eds Rachel Van M. Baumer and James R. Brandon (Honolulu: The University Press of Hawaii, 1981), pp. 74–109 (p. 81).

16. Adya Rangacharya, *The Natyasastra: English Translation with Critical Notes* (New Delhi: Munshiram Manoharlal Publishers, 1981), p. 115.

17. Rangacharya, *The Natyasastra*, p. 78.

18. Rangacharya, *The Natyasastra*, pp. 85–86.

19. Rangacharya, *The Natyasastra*, p. 138.

20. Graham Ley, 'Aristotle's Poetics, Bharatmuni's *Natyasastra* and Zeami's Treatises: Theory as Discourse', *Asian Theatre Journal*, 7.2 (2000), pp. 191–214 (p. 195).

21. The idea of a 'competent spectator' appears to be implicit in the notion of *abhinaya* that is amplified in the twenty-seventh chapter, which describes an ideal spectator being an expert in all the varieties of *natya*: Rangacharya, *The Natyasastra*, p. 215.

22. Colin Counsell, *Signs of Performance: An Introduction to Twentieth-Century Theatre* (London and New York: Routledge, 1996), p. 99.

23. Counsell, *Signs of Performance*, p. 101.

24. Philip Auslander, *From Acting to Performance: Essays in Modernism and Postmodernism* (London and New York: Routledge: 1997), p. 36.

25. Graham Ley, *From Mimesis to Interculturalism: Readings in Theatrical Theory before and after 'Modernism'* (Exeter: University of Exeter Press, 1999), p. 272.

26. John Fiske, *Introduction to Communication Studies* (London and New York: Routledge, 1990), p. 42.

27. Roland Barthes, 'Myth', in *Performance Analysis*, eds Colin Counsell and Laurie Wolf (London and New York: Routledge, 2001), pp. 12–16 (p. 12).

28. Clifford Geertz, 'Deep Play: Notes on the Balinese Cockfight', in *Performance Analysis*, eds Counsell and Wolf, pp. 222–28 (p. 225).

29. This quotation from Jatinder Verma, the artistic director of Tara Arts, was found in the marketing flyer of the play. AUT [Online] http://redhotcurry.com/entertainment/theatre/marriageoffigaro.htm [accessed 10 January 2008].

30. Graham Ley, 'Theatre of Migration and the Search for a Multicultural Aesthetic: Twenty Years of Tara Arts', *New Theatre Quarterly*, 52 (1997), pp. 349–71 (p. 355).

31. Kapila Vatsyayan, *Traditional Indian Theatre: Multiple Streams* (New Delhi: National Book Trust, 1980), p. 152.

32. Vatsyayan, *Traditional Indian Theatre*, p. 146.

33. Tarla Mehta, *Sanskrit Play Production in Ancient India* (New Delhi: Motilal Banarasidass Publishers Private Ltd, 1999), p. 189.

34. '*Margi* covers forms that are in the *shastras* and therefore have a scientific basis', while '*Desi* applies to modes that are light and entertaining and of appeal to the commonality': Mohan Khokar, *Traditions of Indian Classical Dance* (New Delhi: Clarion Books, 1979), p. 58.

35. Vatsyayan, *Traditional Indian Theatre*, p. 153.

36. Vatsyayan, *Traditional Indian Theatre*, p. 192.

37. Desai, *Beyond Bollywood*, p. 8.

38. Ley, 'Theatre of Migration', p. 355.

39. Geertz, 'Deep Play', p. 225.

40. The roots of the *tawa'if* (courtesan) tradition, in which women danced and sang for the Muslim nobility, can be traced in the Moghul period. In a contemporary context, Kali Theatre's production *Bells* (2005), written by Yasmin Whittaker-Khan, explored the existence of *tawa'if* culture (more popularly known as *mujra* culture) in Britain.

41. Rangacharya, *The Natyasastra*, p. 115.

42. 'Hindu–Muslim' synergy is a term Michael Wood uses in the BBC series *The Story of India* (2008), in reference to a particular period of 'Indian' history that was 'culturally hybrid' in nature and not defined by faith, before the divisions introduced by the British colonisers in the nineteenth century.

43. Hingorani, 'Tara Arts and Tamasha', pp. 178–81.

44. Bertolt Brecht, *Brecht on Theatre: The Development of an Aesthetic*, ed. and trans. John Willett (London: Methuen, 1964), p. 200.

45. Vatsyayan, *Traditional Indian Theatre*, p. 176.

46. Brecht, *Brecht on Theatre*, p. 196.

47. Sue Mayes, interview with Chandrika Patel, 22 June 2007.

48. Mayes, 2007.

49. Stuart Wood's *Mahabharata*, a dance-theatre created from Draupadi's perspective, employed a voice coach for its Sanskrit/Hindi/English dialogues delivered by its large multi-cultural cast. The author watched a performance at the Sadlers Wells theatre on 27 April 2007.

50. Helen Gilbert, 'Performing Ethnicity: Orality', in *Performance Analysis*, eds Counsell and Wolf (London and New York: Routledge, 2001), pp. 116–24 (p. 121).

51. Sudha Bhuchar and Kristine Landon-Smith, *A Fine Balance*, based on the novel by Rohinton Mistry (London: Methuen, 2007), p. 4.

52. Bhuchar and Landon-Smith, *A Fine Balance*, p. 4.

53. Bhuchar and Landon-Smith, *A Fine Balance*, p. 63.

54. Two examples would be *'jeena yaha, marna yaha, us ke siva jana kahaa'* ('We have to live here and die here, where else is there to go'), and *'babul ki duaen leti jaa'* ('Take the good wishes of father before you leave home'), a song contextualised at the end of a wedding when a daughter prepares to leave her home and go to the house of her in-laws.

55. Counsell, *Signs of Performance*, p. 101.

56. Bhuchar and Landon-Smith, *A Fine Balance*, p. 60.

57. Abdul JanMohamed, 'Performing Ethnicity: The Other', in *Performance Analysis*, eds Counsell and Wolf (London and New York: Routledge), pp. 97–103 (p. 100).

58. JanMohamed, 'Performing Ethnicity', p. 100.

59. T. Abeysekere, 'Review of Kiran Desai's *The Inheritance of Loss*', *Confluence*, 6.5 (2007), p. 9.

60. JanMohamed, 'Performing Ethnicity', p. 99.

61. JanMohamed, 'Performing Ethnicity', p. 99.

62. In *Strictly Dandia* (2005), Tamasha's hybrid script (English mixed with Gujarati words and phrases) highlighted the inter-caste tensions between Gujarati sub-castes and between Hindu-Gujaratis and Muslims through plot

and verbatim dialogues. It was based on research carried out in north London during the *Navratri* festival, celebrated in schools and community halls.

63. AUT [Online] http://www.tara-arts.com/#/archive/articles_archive/asian_theatre_in_britain.

64. AUT [Online] http://www.tara-arts.com/#/archive/articles_archive/asian_theatre_in_britain.

65. Susan Bennett, 'Watching Another: Viewing Theatre: Questions for Audience Reception and Cross-Cultural Performance', in *New Approaches to Theatre Studies and Performance Analysis, Papers Presented at the Colston Symposium, Bristol, 21–23 March 1997*, ed. Gunther Berghaus (Tubingen: Max Niemeyer Verlag, 2001), pp. 175–87 (p. 176).

66. Barthes cited in Bennett, 'Watching Another', p. 176.

67. Chandrika Patel, 'The Taste of British South Asian Performance', PhD thesis (Exeter: University of Exeter, 2008), p. 247.

68. Colin Counsell, 'Signs of Performance', in *The Routledge Reader in Politics and Performance*, eds Lizbeth Goodman and Jane De Gay (London and New York: Routledge, 2000), pp. 202–7 (p. 204).

69. In her keynote presentation, 'Asian Theatre—Paradise Lost or Paradise Regained', given at the 'British Asian Theatre: from Past to Present' conference in 2008, Naseem Khan used the phrase to refer to certain kinds of Asian theatres.

70. Patel, 'The Taste of British South Asian Performance', p. 248.

71. Naseem Khan, 'New Audience and Diversity', 2005 [online]: http://www.taking partinthearts.com/content.php?content=1039.

13 *Stephen Hodge*—British Asian Live Art: motiroti

1. L. Keidan and D. Brine, 'Live Art in London', *PAJ: A Journal of Performance and Art*, 81 (2005), pp. 74–82 (p. 74).

2. Extensive documentation of the company's history can be found in the Future Histories 'Black Performance and Carnival Archive' (part of the National Archives). Public access to the archive is currently at **moti**roti's London office: 1 Whitehorse Yard, 78 Liverpool Road, London N1 0QD.

3. A. Zaidi, unpublished interview with S. Hodge, **moti**roti office, London, 10 July 2009.

4. Naseem Khan, 'The Art of the Magician: The Work of Keith Khan', in *A Split Second of Paradise: Live Art, Installation and Performance*, eds N. Childs and J. Walwin (London: Rivers Oram Press, 1998), pp. 136–51 (p. 136).

5. Naseem Khan, 'The Art of the Magician', p. 142.

6. All quotations from Zaidi interviewed by Hodge, July 2009.

7. Translated on the production's publicity as 'Thick Bread, Thin Veils'.

8. Keith Khan, 'Making Smaller', in *Programme Notes: Case Studies for Locating Experimental Theatre* (London: Live Art Development Agency, 2007), pp. 94–103 (p. 96).

9. Zaidi interviewed by Hodge, July 2009.

10. Khan, 'Making Smaller', p. 97.

11. Khan, *Leading Voices*.

12. Keith Khan in R. Ben-Tovim, 'Writing for Performance: Three Contrasting Approaches', in *Writing Live: An Investigation of the Relationship Between Writing and Live Art*, ed. J. Deeney (London: New Playwrights Trust, 1998), pp. 51–83 (p. 55).

13. Produced by B.R. Chopra, its ninety-four episodes were broadcast on BBC2 in 1990–91.
14. Khan, *Leading Voices*.
15. Khan, *Leading Voices*.
16. See Ben-Tovim, 'Writing for Performance' for a detailed account of the development of the *Maa* script.
17. Keith Khan in Ben-Tovim, 'Writing for Performance', p. 75.
18. motiroti, programme for *Maa* (1995).
19. Keith Khan, 'Cultural Morphing', in *British Studies Now*, 9 (1997), pp. 16–17 (p. 16).
20. D. Rowe, 'Cultural Crossings: Performing Race and Transgender in the Work of moti roti', in *Art History*, 26:3 (2003), pp. 456–73 (p. 464).
21. Zaidi interviewed by Hodge, July 2009.
22. Julia Rowntree joined the board in 1998; John Simms in 2002; Ravinder Gill and Katy Khan in 2003; Guy Briggs, Jennifer Edwards and Kate Mayne in 2008. Catherine Ugwu left in 1998; Mohammed Khan in 2003; Rosalind Price in 2004; Behroze Gandhy and Ravinder Gill in 2008.
23. The event was commissioned for the Queen's Golden Jubilee in 2002 by the Commonwealth Institute, and funded by the Department of Culture, Media and Sport, London Arts and the British Council.
24. Khan, *Leading Voices*.
25. Khan, *Leading Voices*.
26. A. Zaidi in A. Pizzo, 'Identity, Transformation, and Digital Languages: a Conversation with Ali Zaidi', in Noema: *Tecnologie & Società*, Section 47 (2006), p. 2.
27. A. Zaidi in Pizzo, 'Identity, Transformation, and Digital Languages', p. 1.
28. A. Zaidi in Pizzo, 'Identity, Transformation, and Digital Languages', p. 2.
29. Marianne Weems, 'I Dream of Global Genies', *American Theatre*, 20:10 (2003), pp. 24–28 (p. 24).
30. Weems, 'I Dream of Global Genies', p. 26.
31. http://www.alladeen.com/.
32. J. Parker-Starbuck, 'Global Friends: The Builders Association at BAM', *PAJ: A Journal of Performance and Art*, 77 (2004), pp. 96–102 (p. 97).
33. Khan, *Leading Voices*.
34. Rich Mix, *Rich Mix Mission*, http://www.richmix.org.uk/about/about-us/.
35. Khan, 'Making Smaller', p. 101.
36. Khan, *Leading Voices*.
37. motiroti, *History*, http://www.motiroti.com/work/company/moti-history.php [accessed 21 January 2009].
38. A. Zaidi in Pizzo, 'Identity, Transformation, and Digital Languages', p. 6.
39. A live art production company based in the private house of the artist Laura Godfrey-Isaacs in Camberwell, London.
40. A. Zaidi in Pizzo, 'Identity, Transformation, and Digital Languages', p. 10.
41. motiroti, *motiroti corporate brochure* (London: motiroti, 2008), p. 12.
42. Zaidi, interviewed by Hodge, July 2009, talking about *60x60 Secs*, the first *360°* project.

Bibliography

A Meeting of Mother Tongues: Bilingualism, Theatre and Schools (London: ILEA, 1986).

A Nice Arrangement, dir. G. Chadha (Film Four, 1990).

Abbas, Tahir, *Muslims in Birmingham, UK*, Background paper for the University of Oxford Centre on Migration Policy and Society (2006), available: http://www.compas.ox.ac.uk/publications/papers/Birmingham%20Background%20Paper%200206.pdf [accessed 15 April 2009].

Abeysekere, T., 'Review of Kiran Desai's *The Inheritance of Loss*', *Confluence*, 6.5 (2007).

Agamben, Giorgio, *Means without End: Notes on Politics* (Minneapolis: University of Minnesota Press, 2000).

Ahmad, Rukhsana, *Mistaken ... Annie Besant in India* (London: Aurora Metro Publications, 2007).

Ahmad, Rukhsana, *Song for a Sanctuary*, in *Six Plays by Black and Asian Women Writers*, ed. Kadija George (London: Aurora Metro Press, 1993), pp. 159–86.

Ahmed, Aijaz, *In Theory: Classes, Nations, Literatures* (Oxford: Oxford University Press, 1992).

Ali, Nasreen, Virinder Kalra and S. Sayyid, eds, *A Postcolonial People: South Asians in Britain* (London: Hurst, 2006).

Anderson, Kay, 'Introduction', in *Cultural Geographies*, ed. Kay Anderson and Fay Gale (South Melbourne: Longman, 1999).

Anon., 'Mirth of a Nation', *Guardian*, 20 February 1999, available: http://www.guardian.co.uk/Archive/Article/0,4273,3824542,00.html.

Appadurai, Arjun, *Modernity at Large* (Minneapolis: University of Minnesota Press, 1996).

Auslander, Philip, *From Acting to Performance: Essays in Modernism and Postmodernism* (London and New York: Routledge, 1997).

Barker, Clive, 'Joan Littlewood', in *Twentieth-century Actor Training*, ed. Alison Hodge (London: Routledge, 2000), pp. 113–28.

Barthes, Roland, 'Myth', in *Performance Analysis*, ed. Colin Counsell and Laurie Wolf (London and New York: Routledge, 2001), pp. 12–16.

Bennett, Susan, 'Watching Another: Viewing Theatre: Questions for Audience Reception and Cross-Cultural Performance', in *New Approaches to Theatre*

Studies and Performance Analysis, Papers Presented at the Colston Symposium, Bristol, 21–23 March 1997, ed. Gunther Berghaus (Tubingen: Max Niemeyer Verlag, 2001), pp. 175–87.

Bennett, Tony, *Differing Diversities: Cultural Policy and Cultural Diversity* (Brussels: Council of Europe, 2001).

Ben-Tovim, R., 'Writing for Performance: Three Contrasting Approaches', in *Writing Live: An Investigation of the Relationship Between Writing and Live Art*, ed. J. Deeney (London: New Playwrights Trust, 1998), pp. 51–83.

Bestwick, Deborah, 'The Development of Bilingual Theatre by the Half Moon Young People's Theatre' (undated), Half Moon YPT archive, available: http://www.elta-project.org/browse.html?recordId=609.

Bhaji on the Beach, dir. Guirinder Chadha (Channel Four, 1993).

Bhattacharjee, Annanya, 'The Habit of Ex-Nomination', in *A Patchwork Shawl: Chronicles of South Asian Women in America* (New Brunswick, NJ: Rutgers University Press, 1998), pp. 163–185.

Bhatti, Gurpreet Kaur, *Behsharam (Shameless)* (London: Oberon, 2001).

Bhatti, Gurpreet Kaur, *Behzti (Dishonour)* (London: Oberon, 2004).

Bhatti, Gurpreet Kaur, '"This Warrior Is Fighting on. I Am Proud to Be a Sikh, and My Play Is Both Respectful to Sikhism and Honest"', *Guardian*, 13 January 2005.

Bhuchar, Suman, 'The Tamasha Method', *Prompt* (Journal of the Theatrical Management Association), 19 (November 1999), pp. 9–10.

Billington, Michael, 'Curryoke Night: *Balti Kings*', *Guardian*, 15 January 2000.

Billington, Michael, 'Deliriously Dotty Bollywood', *Guardian*, 20 June 2002.

Billington, Michael, 'East Is Best', *Guardian*, 25 November 1996.

Billington, Michael, '*Rafta, Rafta …*', *Guardian*, 27 April 2007, available: http://www.guardian.co.uk/stage/2007/apr/27/theatre2.

Billington, Michael, 'Sanctuary', *Guardian*, 31 July 2002, available: http://www.guardian.co.uk/stage/2002/jul/31/theatre.artsfeatures3.

Blackmore, John, 'The Haymarket Theatre, Leicester', in *Making Space for Theatre: British Architecture and Theatre since 1958*, eds R. Mulryne and M. Shewring (Stratford-upon-Avon: Mulryne and Shewring Ltd, 1995), p. 70.

Brah, Avtar, *Cartographies of Diaspora: Contesting Identities* (London: Routledge, 1996).

Brahmachari, Sita, *In Conversation*, an evaluation report commissioned by Tamasha and the Arts Council England. 9 January 2006. Retrieved from the Tamasha Theatre Company website: http://www.tamasha.org.uk/about/resources/in-conversation/.

Braybrooke, Marcus, 'A Wider Vision: A History of the World Congress of Faiths, 1936–1996', available: http://www.religion-online.org/showchapter.asp?title=3378&C=2771.

Brecht, Bertolt, *Brecht on Theatre: The Development of an Aesthetic*, ed. and trans. John Willett (London: Methuen, 1964).

Brinda, *Maharani: The Story of an Indian Princess* (New York: Henry Holt, 1953).

Bromley, Roger, *Narratives for a New Belonging: Diasporic Cultural Fictions* (Edinburgh: Edinburgh University Press, 2000).

Brothers, C., 'Migrants Held in Shadows', *The Herald Tribune*, 31 December 2007, pp. 1, 3.

Brown, Georgina, 'Hooray for This Bite of Spicy Bollywood', *Mail on Sunday*, 23 June 2002.

Bruce, Keith, 'Balti Kings', *Herald* (Glasgow), 20 January 2000, p. 17.

Butler, Judith, *Gender Trouble* (London: Routledge, 1990).

Cavendish, Dominic, 'Theatre: A Force to be Reckoned With', *Independent*, 21 October 1998.

Chambers, Colin, *The Story of Unity Theatre* (London: Lawrence and Wishart, 1989).

Chambers, Colin, *Black and Asian Theatre in Britain: A History* (London: Routledge, 2011)

Christie, Agatha, 'Sanctuary', in *The Complete Miss Marple Short Stories* (London: The Folio Society, 2003).

Cochrane, Claire, '"A Local Habitation and a Name": The Development of Black and Asian Theatre in Birmingham since in the 1970s', in *Alternatives within the Mainstream: British Black and Asian Theatres*, ed. Dimple Godiwala (Newcastle: Cambridge Scholars Press, 2006), pp. 153–73.

Cochrane, Claire, *Birmingham Rep: A City's Theatre 1962–2002* (Birmingham: Sir Barry Jackson Trust, 2003).

Cochrane, Claire, 'Theatre and Urban Space: The Case of Birmingham Rep', *New Theatre Quarterly*, 62 (May 2000), pp. 137–47.

Coombes, Annie E., *Reinventing Africa, Museums, Material Culture and Popular Imagination in Late Victorian and Edwardian England* (New Haven and London: Yale University Press, 1994).

Costa, Maddy, 'Saint Nick', *Guardian*, 22 March 2004, available: http://www.guardian.co.uk/stage/2004/mar/22/theatre2.

Counsell, Colin, 'Signs of Performance', in *The Routledge Reader in Politics & Performance*, eds Lizbeth Goodman and Jane De Gay (London and New York: Routledge, 2000), pp. 202–7.

Counsell, Colin, *Signs of Performance: An Introduction to Twentieth-Century Theatre* (London and New York: Routledge, 1996).

Cox, J. Charles, *The Sanctuaries and Sanctuary Seekers of Mediaeval England* (Whitefish: George Allen & Sons, 1911; repr. Kessinger Publishing, 2005).

Cresswell, Tim, *In Place/Out of Place: Geography, Ideology, and Transgression* (Minneapolis and London: University of Minnesota Press, 1996).

Croft, Susan, 'Black Women Playwrights in Britain', in *British and Irish Women Dramatists since 1958*, eds Trevor M. Griffiths and Margaret Llewellyn-Jones (Milton Keynes: Open University Press, 1993).

Cultivate, *Roots at Leicester Haymarket*, added 29 February 2008, available: http://www.cultivate-em.org.uk/resources/casestudies/11/roots-at-leicester-haymarket-theatre.

Daboo, Jerri, 'One under the Sun: Globalization, Culture and Utopia in *Bombay Dreams*', *Contemporary Theatre Review*, 15.3 (2005), pp. 330–37.

Dasgupta, Shamita D., 'Introduction', in *A Patchwork Shawl: Chronicles of South Asian Women in America*, ed. S.D. Dasgupta (New Brunswick, NJ: Rutgers University Press, 1998), pp. 1–17.

Davis, Geoffrey, 'Introduction', in *Staging New Britain: Aspects of Black and South Asian British Theatre Practice*, eds Geoffrey Davis and Anne Fuchs (Brussels: Peter Lang, 2006), pp. 15–34.

Davis, Geoffrey, '"Once You Open Doors, You Have to Walk Through Them". An Interview with Kully Thiarai', in *Staging New Britain Aspects of Black and South Asian British Theatre Practice*, eds Geoffrey Davis and Anne Fuchs (Brussels: Peter Lang, 2006), pp. 293–307.

Davis, Geoffrey V. and Anne Fuchs, eds, *Staging New Britain: Aspects of Black and South Asian British Theatre Practice* (Brussels: Peter Lang, 2006).

Dening, Greg, *Mr Bligh's Bad Language: Passion, Power and Theatre on the Bounty* (Cambridge: Cambridge University Press, 1992).

Desai, Jigna, *Beyond Bollywood: The Cultural Politics of South Asian Diasporic Film* (London: Routledge, 2004).

Dobson, Stephen, *Cultures of Exile and the Experience of Refugeeness* (Bern: Peter Lang, 2004).

Donnell, Alison, ed., *Companion to Contemporary Black British Culture* (London and New York: Routledge, 2002).

Dwyer, Claire, 'Veiled Meanings: Young British Muslim Women and the Negotiation of Differences', *Gender, Place and Culture*, 6.1 (1999), pp. 5–26.

Dwyer, Rachel, 'Bollywood Cinema and the UK', in the programme for *Rafta, Rafta ...*, produced by the Royal National Theatre, London, 2007.

Eade, John, ed., *Living the Global City: Globalization as a Local Process* (London: Routledge, 1997).

Eclipse Report: Developing Strategies to Combat Racism in Theatre, Arts Council of England, 2001, http://www.artscouncil.org.uk/media/uploads/documents/publications/307.doc.

Edgar, David, *Destiny* (London: Eyre Methuen, 1976).

Edgar, David, *Playing with Fire* (London: Nick Hern, 2005).

Elias, Mohammed, *Aubrey Menen* (*Kerala Writers in English*, 7, Madras: Macmillan India, 1985).

Essed, Philomena, Georg Frerks and Joke Schrijvers, eds, *Refugees and the Transformation of Societies: Agency, Policies, Ethics and Politics* (Oxford: Berghahn Books, 2004).

Farr, David, Programme note for *The Ramayana*, Lyric Theatre Hammersmith.

Farrier, D., 'The Journey is the Film is the Journey: Michael Winterbottom's *In This World*', *Research in Drama Education*, 13.2 (2008), pp. 223–32.

Figueira, Dorothy Matilda, *Translating the Orient: The Reception of Śākuntala in Nineteenth-Century Europe* (New York: SUNY Press, 1991).

Fisher, Michael H., *Counterflows to Colonialism: Indian Travellers and Settlers in Britain 1600–1857* (Delhi: Permanent Books, 2004).

Fiske, John, *Introduction to Communication Studies* (London and New York: Routledge, 1990).

Frost, Anthony, 'Drama in the Age of *Kalyug*: *Behzti* and Sikh Self-Censorship', in *Alternatives within the Mainstream: British Black and Asian Theatres*, ed. Dimple Godiwala (Newcastle: Cambridge Scholars Press, 2006), pp. 203–25.

Fuchs, Ann, 'Looking at New British Heritage: Tamasha Theatre Company', in *Staging New Britain: Aspects of Black and South Asian British Theatre Practice*, eds Geoffrey Davis and Ann Fuchs (Brussels, Peter Lang, 2006), pp. 127–39.

Gandhi, Leela, *Postcolonial Theory: A Critical Introduction* (Edinburgh: Edinburgh University Press, 1998).

Geertz, Clifford, 'Deep Play: Notes on the Balinese Cockfight', in *Performance Analysis*, eds Colin Counsell and Laurie Wolf (London and New York: Routledge, 2001), pp. 222–28.

George, Kadija, ed., *Six Plays by Black and Asian Women Writers* (London: Aurora Metro Press, 1993).

Gilbert, Helen, 'Performing Ethnicity: Orality', in *Performance Analysis*, eds Colin Counsell and Laurie Wolf (London & New York: Routledge, 2001), pp. 116–24.

Gilbey, Liz, 'Where East Meets West', *Stage*, 30 November 2000.

Godiwala, Dimple, ed., *Alternatives within the Mainstream: British Black and Asian Theatres* (Newcastle: Cambridge Scholars Press, 2004).

Goodness Gracious Me (BBC 2, 1998–2001).

Gregory, Brendan, 'Staging British India', in *Acts of Supremacy: British Empire and the Stage, 1790–1930*, eds J.S. Bratton et al. (Manchester: Manchester University Press, 1991).

Griffin, Gabriele, *Contemporary Black and Asian Women Playwrights in Britain* (Cambridge: Cambridge University Press, 2003).

Grimley, Terry, 'Home Grown Variety Is the Spice of Life: Curry Wars in Birmingham's Balti Belt Have Provided the Subject for the Latest Show from an Award-winning Team', *Birmingham Post*, 17 December 1999, p. 14.

Gupta, Tanika, '20 Questions with … Tanika Gupta', *What's on Stage*, 21 January 2008, available: http://www.whatsonstage.com/index.php?pg=207& story=E8821200679850.

Gupta, Tanika, 'An Advocate for Change: Tanika Gupta in Conversation with Caridad Svich', in *Trans-Global Readings*, ed. Caruidad Svich (Manchester: Manchester University Press, 2004), pp. 99–103.

Gupta, Tanika, *Sanctuary* (London: Oberon Books, 2002).

Hall, Stuart, 'Cultural Identity and Diaspora', in *Identity: Community, Culture, Difference*, ed. J. Rutherford (London: Lawrence & Wishart, 1990), pp. 222–37.

Hall, Tarquin, 'Review of Rafta, Rafta …', *Sunday Times*, 29 April 2007.

Harris Research Centre, *Black and Asian Attitudes to the Arts in Birmingham* (London: Arts Council of England, 1993).

Hattenstone, Simon and Lyn Gardner, 'What Country, Friend, Is This?', *Guardian*, 29 January 1997, p. 12.

Hemming, Sarah, 'Sizzling Kitchen-sink Drama Is Hot Stuff', *Financial Times*, 19 January 2000.

Herbert, Joanna, *Negotiating Boundaries in the City, Migration, Ethnicity, and Gender in Britain* (Aldershot: Ashgate, 2008).

Hickling, Alfred, 'Leicester's Curve Is a Theatre without Secrets', *Guardian*, 15 September 2008.

Hingorani, Dominic, *British Asian Theatre: Dramaturgy, Process and Performance* (Basingstoke: Palgrave, 2010).

Hingorani, Dominic, 'Tara Arts and Tamasha: Producing Asian Performances—Two Approaches', in *Alternatives within the Mainstream: Black & Asian British Theatres*, ed. Dimple Godiwala (Newcastle: Cambridge Scholars Press, 2006), pp. 174–200.

Hodge, Alison, ed., *Twentieth-century Actor Training* (London: Routledge, 2000).

Holder, Heidi J., 'Other Londoners: Race and Class in Plays of Nineteenth-Century London Life', in *Imagined Londons*, ed. Pamela K. Gilbert (New York: SUNY Press, 2002).

Huggan, Graham, *The Post-colonial Exotic: Marketing the Margins* (London: Routledge, 2001).

Human Rights Watch, 'The Security Situation Immediately after the Fall of Basra', available: http://www.hrw.org/node/12320/section/4.

Innes, Christopher, 'West End', in *The Cambridge Guide to Theatre*, ed. Martin Banham (Cambridge: Cambridge University Press, 1998), pp. 1194–95.

Innes, C.L., *A History of Black and Asian Writing in Britain, 1700–2000* (Cambridge: Cambridge University Press, 2002).

Jaggi, Maya, 'From Writing Back to Rewriting Britain', additional paper distributed with *Whose Heritage? The Impact of Cultural Diversity on Britain's Living Heritage* (Report of National Conference at G-Mex, Manchester, 1–3 November, 1999).

Jain, Jasbir, 'The New Parochialism: Homeland in the Writing of the Indian Diaspora', in *In Diaspora: Theories, Histories, Texts*, ed. Makarand Paranjape (New Delhi: Indialog, 2001), pp. 79–93.

JanMohamed, Abdul, 'Performing Ethnicity: The Other', in *Performance Analysis*, eds Colin Counsell and Laurie Wolf (London and NewYork: Routledge), pp. 97–103.

Jermyn, Helen and Philip Desai, *Arts—What's in a Word? Ethnic Minorities in Britain* (London: Arts Council of England, 2000).

Joseph, May, *Nomadic Identities: The Performance of Citizenship* (Minneapolis: University of Minnesota Press, 1999).

Kalidasa, *Sakuntala* (London: Macmillan, 1920).

Kapur, Anuradha, 'Intra-cultural Performance Training and British Asian Collaborations', paper delivered at the conference, 'British Asian Theatre: from Past to Present', University of Exeter, April 2008.

Karnad, Girish, comments made following talk by Naseem Khan at the conference 'British Asian Theatre: from Past to Present', University of Exeter, April 2008.

Karnad, Girish, 'The Inter-relationship between British and Indian Theatre: An Historical Perspective', keynote speech given at the conference, 'British Asian Theatre: From Past to Present', University of Exeter, April 2008.

Katyal, Anjum, 'Tamasha: An Asian Voice in British Theatre,' *The Seagull Theatre Quarterly*, 23 (September 1999), pp. 68–83.

Kaur, Raminder and Alda Terracciano, 'SouthAsian/BrAsian Performing Arts', in *A Postcolonial People: South Asians in Britain*, eds Nasreem Ali, Virinder Kalra, and S.H. Sayyid (London: Hurst and Co., 2006), pp. 343–57.

Keidan, L., and D. Brine, 'Live Art in London', *Performing Arts Journal*, 81 (2005), pp. 74–82.

Khan, Keith, 'Cultural Morphing', *British Studies Now*, 9 (1997), pp. 16–17.

Khan, Keith, *Leading Voices: Cultural Diversity and the Art of Making Creative Cities* (Sydney: Australia Council for the Arts, 19 March 2008), downloaded as MP3 file from: http://www.australiacouncil.gov.au/news/news_items/leading_voices_audio on 15 December 2008.

Khan, Keith, 'Making Smaller', in *Programme Notes: Case Studies for Locating Experimental Theatre* (London: Live Art Development Agency, 2007), pp. 94–103.

Khan, Naseem, 'The Art of the Magician: The Work of Keith Khan', in *A Split Second of Paradise: Live Art, Installation and Performance*, eds N. Childs and J. Walwin (London: Rivers Oram Press, 1998), pp. 136–51.

Khan, Naseem, *The Arts Britain Ignores: The Arts of Ethnic Minorities in Britain* (London: Community Relations Commission, 1976).

Khan, Naseem, 'New Audience and Diversity', 2005 [online] http://www.taking partinthe arts.com/content.php?content=1039.

Khan, Naseem, 'The Public-going Theatre: Community and "Ethnic" Theatre', in *Dreams and Deconstructions: Alternative Theatre in Britain*, ed. Sandy Craig (Derbyshire: Amber Lane, 1980), pp. 59–75.

Khan, Naseem, *The Road to Interculturalism: Tracking the Arts in a Changing World* (London: Comedia, 2006).

Khan-Din, Ayub, *East Is East* (London: Film Four Books/MacMillan, 1999).

Khan-Din, Ayub, *East Is East* (London: Nick Hern Books, 1997).

Khan-Din, Ayub, *Last Dance at Dum Dum* (London: Nick Hern Books, 1999).

Khokar, Mohan, *Traditions of Indian Classical Dance* (New Delhi: Clarion Books, 1979)

King, Shelley, Interview with Jerri Daboo, London, 27 October 2008.

Kossew, S., 'A Violent State: Truth and Reconciliation in Gillian Slovo's *Red Dust* (2000) and Jann Turner's *Southern Cross* (2002)', in *Violence and Transgression in World Minority Literatures*, eds Rudiger Ahrens et al. (Heidelberg: Winter, 2005), pp. 305–18.

Krulfeld, Ruth M. and Jeffery L. MacDonald, eds, *Power, Ethics, and Human Rights: Anthropological Studies of Refugee Research and Action* (Lanham: Rowman & Littlefield, 1998).

Lacey, Stephen, *British Realist Drama: The New Wave in Its Context* (London and New York: Routledge, 1995).

Lahiri, Shompa, 'From Empire to Decolonisation, 1901–1947', in *A South-Asian History of Britain: Four Centuries of Peoples from the Indian Sub-continent*, ed. Michael H. Fisher (Oxford: Greenwood World, 2007).

Lahiri, Shompa, *Indians in Britain: Anglo-Indian Encounters, Race and Identity, 1880–1930* (London: Frank Cass, 2000).

Landon-Smith, Kristin, 'The Real Reason for the Boom in Multicultural Theatre', *Guardian* website, The Blog: Theatre and the Performing Arts, 23 May 2007, http://www.guardian.co.uk/stage/theatreblog/2007/may/23/therealreasonfortheboomi.

Landon-Smith, Kristine, 'Spotlight: Asian Theatre', *Independent*, 16 January 2004.

Lane, Harriet, 'I Speak English, Not Urdu ...', *Observer*, 31 October 1999, Arts Section, p. 6.

Langston, Robert Gore, 'Indian Summer', *Daily Express*, 21 June 2002.

Leicester Partnership, *Diverse City: A Vision for Cultural Life in Leicester*, Cultural Strategy Partnership Annual Review, December 2004.

Ley, Graham, 'Aristotle's Poetics, Bharatmuni's *Natyasastra* and Zeami's Treatises: Theory as Discourse', *Asian Theatre Journal*, 7.2 (2000), pp. 191–214.

Ley, Graham, *From Mimesis to Interculturalism: Readings in Theatrical Theory before and after 'Modernism'* (Exeter: University of Exeter Press, 1999).

Ley, Graham, 'Theatre of Migration and the Search for a Multicultural Aesthetic: Twenty Years of Tara Arts', *New Theatre Quarterly*, 52 (1997), pp. 349–71.

Ley, Graham and Sarah Dadswell, eds, *British South Asian Theatres: A Documented History* (Exeter: University of Exeter Press, 2011).

Lone, Amber, *Deadeye* (London: Oberon, 2006).

Long, Norman, *Development Sociology: Actor Perspectives* (London: Routledge, 2001).

Macaulay, Alistair, 'Dreams Meet Reality', *Financial Times*, 21 June 2002

Malik, Sarita, *Representing Black Britain: Black and Asian Images on Television* (London: Sage, 2002).

Malkki, Liisa H., 'Refugees and Exile: From "Refugee Studies" to the National Order of Things', *Annual Review of Anthropology*, 24 (1995), pp. 495–523.

Malkki, Liisa H., 'Speechless Emissaries: Refugees, Humanitarianism, and Dehistoricization', *Cultural Anthropology*, 11.3 (1996), pp. 377–404.

Massey, Doreen, *Space, Place, and Gender* (Minneapolis: University of Minnesota Press, 1994).

Mazower, David, *Yiddish Theatre in London* (London: The Jewish Museum, 1996).

Mehta, Tarla, *Sanskrit Play Production in Ancient India* (New Delhi: Motilal Banarasidass Publishers Private Ltd, 1999).

Mercer, Kobena, 'Black Art and the Burden of Representation', *Third Text*, 10.4 (1990), pp. 61–78.

Mosselson, Jacqueline, *Roots & Routes. Bosnian Adolescent Refugees in New York City* (Bern: Peter Lang, 2006).

Murari, Timeri, 'The Square Circle (Theatre)', available http://timerimurari.com/theatre.htm.

Naidu, Vayu, 'Call-response: Migration as Metaphor in Theatre', *Contemporary Theatre Review*, 19.2 (2009), pp. 227–32.

Naidu, Vayu, 'Vayu Naidu Company's South: New Directions in Theatre of Storytelling', in *Staging New Britain: Aspects of South Asian British Theatre Practice*, eds Geoffrey Davis and Anne Fuchs (Brussels: Peter Lang, 2006), pp. 141–54.

Nasta, Susheila, ed., *Home Truths: Fictions of the South Asian Diaspora in Britain* (Basingstoke: Palgrave, 2002).

Nightingale, Benedict, '*Balti Kings*', *The Times*, 17 January 2000.

Oddey, Alison, *Performing Women: Stand-ups, Strumpets and Itinerants* (Basingstoke: Palgrave Macmillan, 1990).

Ojumu, Akin, 'All About Meera', *Observer Review*, 16 June 2002, available: http://observer.guardian.co.uk/comment/story/0,6903,738309,00.html.

O'Quinn, Daniel, *Staging Governance: Theatrical Imperialism in London, 1770–1800* (Baltimore: Johns Hopkins University Press, 2005).

O'Quinn, Daniel, 'Theatre and Empire', in *The Cambridge Companion to British Theatre, 1730–1830*, eds Jane Moody and Daniel O'Quinn (Cambridge: Cambridge University Press, 2007).

Osborne, Deidre, 'The State of the Nation: Contemporary Black British Theatre and the Staging of the UK', in *Alternatives within the Mainstream: British Black and Asian Theatres*, ed. Dimple Godiwala (Newcastle: Cambridge Scholars Press, 2006), pp. 82–100.

Pamment, Claire, '"Police of Pig and Sheep": Representations of the White Sahib and the Psyche of Theatre Censorship', paper given at the conference, 'British Asian Theatre: From Past to Present', University of Exeter, April 2008.

Parekh, Bhikhu, *The Future of Multi-Ethnic Britain: Report of the Commission on the Future of Multi-Ethnic Britain* (London: Profile Books, 2000).

Parker-Starbuck, J., 'Global Friends: The Builders Association at BAM', *PAJ: A Journal of Performance and Art*, 77 (2004), pp. 96–102.

Parmar, Pratibha, 'Womanvoice, Womanvision: South Asian Women and Film', *Rungh. A South Asian Quarterly of Culture, Comment and Criticism*, 1, 1–2 (1991), pp. 16–19.

Patel, Chandrika, 'The Taste of British South Asian Performance', PhD thesis (Exeter: University of Exeter, 2008).

Peter, John, 'Crossed Countries', *The Times*, 1 December 1996.

Pines, Jim, *Black and White in Colour: Black People in British Television since 1936* (London: BFI, 1992).

Pizzo, A., 'Identity, Transformation, and Digital Languages: a Conversation with Ali Zaidi', *Noema: Tecnologie & Società*, Section 47 (2006), p. 2.

Poel, William, 'Hindu Drama on the English Stage', *Asiatic Quarterly Review*, n.s. 1 (April 1913), pp. 319–31.

Ponnuswami, Meenakshi, 'Citizenship and Gender in Asian-British Performance', in *Feminist Futures? Theatre, Performance, Theory*, eds Elaine Aston and Geraldine Harris (Basingstoke: Palgrave Macmillan, 2006), pp. 34–55.

Qnun Ltd, *Asian Caribbean and African Arts Strategy for West Midlands Arts Board* (Birmingham: West Midlands Arts, 1992).

Radcliffe, Sarah, 'Frontiers and Popular Nationhood: Geographies of Identity in the 1995 Ecuador–Peru Border Dispute', *Political Geography*, 17.3 (1998), pp. 273–93.

Rai, Domonic, 'Exile: Forty Years in the West Midlands', available: http://www.manmela.org.uk/theatrecontent.html.

Ranasinha, Ruvani, *South Asian Writers in Twentieth-Century Britain: Culture in Translation* (Oxford: Clarendon Press, 2006).

Rangacharya, Adya, *The Natyasastra: English Translation with Critical Notes* (New Delhi: Munshiram Manoharlal Publishers, 1981).

Rebellato, Dan, *1956 and All That: The Making of Modern British Drama* (London and New York: Routledge, 1999).

Richmond, Farley, 'Suggestions for Directors of Sanskrit Plays', in *Sanskrit Drama in Performance*, eds Rachel Van M. Baumer and James R. Brandon (Honolulu: The University Press of Hawaii, 1981), pp. 74–109.

Richmond, Farley P., 'Characteristics of Sanskrit Theatre and Drama', in *Indian Theatre: Traditions of Performance*, eds Farley P. Richmond, Darius L. Swann and Phillip B. Zarrilli (Honolulu: University of Hawaii Press, 1990), pp. 25–85.

Roma, Thomas and Henry L. Gates, *Sanctuary* (Washington, DC: The Johns Hopkins University Press, 2002).

Rosenthal, Laura J., '"Infamous Commerce": Transracial Prostitution in the South Seas and Back', in *Monstrous Dreams of Reason: Body, Self, and Other in the Enlightenment*, eds Laura J. Rosenthal and Mita Choudhury (London: Associated University Press, 2002).

Rowe, D., 'Cultural Crossings: Performing Race and Transgender in the Work of moti roti', *Art History*, 26.3 (2003), pp. 456–73.

Rushdie, Salman, *Imaginary Homelands* (London: Granta, 1991).

Russell, Gillian, 'An "Entertainment of Oddities": Fashionable Sociability and the Pacific in the 1770s', in *A New Imperial History: Culture, Identity and Modernity in Britain and the Empire, 1660–1840*, ed. Kathleen Wilson (Cambridge: Cambridge University Press, 2004).

Said, Edward, *Orientalism* (London: Routledge and Kegan Paul, 1978).

Schlote, Christiane, 'Either for Tragedy, Comedy, History or Musical Unlimited: Women Playwrights in British South Asian Theatre', in *Staging New Britain: Aspects of Black and South Asian British Theatre Practice*, eds Geoffrey Davis and Anne Fuchs (Brussels: Peter Lang, 2006), pp. 65–85.

Schroeder, Patricia, *The Feminist Possibilities of Dramatic Realism* (Madison, NJ: Farleigh Dickinson University Press, 1996).

Searle, Chris, *An Exclusive Education: Race, Class and Exclusion in British Schools* (London: Lawrence and Wishart, 2001).

Seton, Marie, 'English Theatre of the Left', *New Theatre* (December 1934), p. 21.

Shellard, Dominic, *British Theatre since the War* (New Haven and London: Yale University Press, 1999).

Sorabji, Cornelia, *India Calling: The Memories of Cornelia Sorabji* (London: Nisbet, 1934).

Spalding, Frances, 'Edward Middleditch (1923–1987): London, Serpentine Gallery', *The Burlington Magazine*, 130, 1021, Special Issue on Twentieth-Century Art (April 1988), pp. 310–11.

Speaight, Robert, *William Poel and the Elizabethan Revival* (London: Heinemann, 1954).

Spencer, Charles, 'Bollywood Lends Hilarity to a Tale of Love', *Daily Telegraph*, 20 February 2001.

Spencer, Charles, 'Laughter Laced With Warmth', *Daily Telegraph*, 27 April 2007.

Spencer, Charles, 'Rich Mix of Culture and Comedy,' *Daily Telegraph*, 25 November 1996.

Starck, Kathleen, '"They Call Me an 'Asian Writer' as Well". Tanika Gupta's *Sanctuary*, *Skeleton* and *Inside Out*', in *Alternatives Within the Mainstream. British Black and Asian Theatres*, ed. Dimple Godiwala (Newcastle upon Tyne: Cambridge Scholars Press, 2006), pp. 347–62.

Syal, Meera, *Anita and Me* (London: Flamingo, 1997; 1st edn, 1996).

Syal, Meera, 'Finding My Voice', in *Passion: Discourses on Blackwomen's Creativity*, ed. M. Sulter (London: Urban Fox Press, 1990), pp. 57–61. Reprinted in *Writing Black Britain 1948–1998: An Interdisciplinary Anthology*, ed. J. Procter (Manchester, New York: Manchester University Press, 2000), pp. 252–56.

Syal, Meera, 'Last Laugh', in *Cultural Breakthrough*, published by VSO, 2003, available: http://www.vso.org.uk/Images/culturalbreakthrough_essays_tcm8-2848.pdf [accessed 10 March 2008].

Syal, Meera, *Life Isn't All Ha Ha Hee Hee* (London: Doubleday, 1999).

Syal, Meera, *My Sister Wife*, in *Six Plays by Black and Asian Women Writers*, ed. Kadija George (London: Aurora Metro Press, 1993).

Tapping, Craig, 'South Asia Writes North America: Prose Fictions and Autobiographies from the Indian Diaspora', in *Reading the Literatures of Asian America*, eds S. Geok-Lin Lim and A. Ling (Philadelphia: Temple University Press, 1992), pp. 285–301.

Terracciano, Alda, 'Mainstreaming African, Asian and Caribbean Theatre: The Experiments of the Black Theatre Forum', in *Alternatives within the Mainstream. British Black and Asian Theatres*, ed. Dimple Godiwala (Newcastle: Cambridge Scholars Press, 2006), pp. 22–60.

The Kumars at no. 42 (BBC2, 2002–2006).

Tirado, C., *Fish Men* (unpublished manuscript, 2005).

van Gyseghem, Andre, 'British Theatre in the Thirties: An Autobiographical Record', in *Culture and Crisis in Britain in the 30s*, eds Jon Clark et al. (London: Lawrence and Wishart, 1979).

Vatsyayan, Kapila, *Traditional Indian Theatre: Multiple Streams* (New Delhi: National Book Trust, 1980).

Verma, Jatinder, 'Asian Arts in the 21st Century', http://www.tara-arts.com/#/archive/articles_archive/asian_arts_in_the_21st_century.

Verma, Jatinder, 'Asian Theatre in Britain', available from: http://www.tara-arts.com/#/archive/articles_archive/asian_theatre_in_britain.

Verma, Jatinder, '"Binglishing" the Stage: a Generation of Asian Theatre in Britain', in *Theatre Matters: Performance and Culture on the World Stage*, eds Richard Boon and Jane Plastow (Cambridge: Cambridge Press, 1998), pp. 126–34.

Verma, Jatinder, 'The Challenge of Binglish: Analysing Multicultural Productions', in *Analysing Performance: A Critical Reader*, ed. Patrick Campbell (Manchester: Manchester University Press, 1996), pp. 193–203.

Verma, Jatinder, 'Cultural Transformations', in *Contemporary British Theatre*, ed. Theodore Shank (London: Macmillan, 1994), pp. 55–61.

Verma, Jatinder, 'The Impact of Cultural Diversity on the Performing Arts in the UK Today', in *New Stages: Conference at Norsk Kulturråd*, ed. S. Brahmachari, February 2001, available: http://www.kulturrad.no/sitefiles/1/fou/notater37-58/notat44.pdf.

Verma, Jatinder, 'The Shape of a Heart', in *Alternatives within the Mainstream: British Black and Asian Theatres*, ed. Dimple Godiwala (Newcastle: Cambridge Scholars Press, 2006), pp. 383–89.

Verma, Jatinder, 'Towards Cultural Literacy: 30 Years of Tara', http://www.tara-arts.com/#/archive/articles_archive/towards_cultural_literacy.

Virk, Hardish, Interview with Jerri Daboo, Sarah Dadswell and Graham Ley, Exeter, 26 February 2008.

Walsh, Maeve, '*Balti Kings*', *Independent*, 16 January 2000.

Wandor, Michelene, *Post-War British Drama: Looking Back in Gender* (London and New York: Routledge, 2001).

Wann, Louis, 'The Oriental in Elizabethan Drama', *Modern Philology*, 12.7 (January 1915), pp. 423–47.

Wearing, J.P., *The London Stage: A Calendar of Plays and Players, 1900–1909, 1910–1919* and *1920–1929* (New Jersey: The Scarecrow Press, 1981 and 1982).

Weems, Marianne, 'I Dream of Global Genies', *American Theatre*, 20.10 (2003), pp. 24–28.

Wertenbaker, Timberlake, *Credible Witness* (London: Faber and Faber, 2001).

Wesker, Arnold, 'Living-room Revolt', *Guardian*, 26 January 2008.

Wesker, Arnold, *Volume Two: The Kitchen and Other Plays* (London: Penguin Books, 1960; this collection repr. 1976).

Westwood, Sally and Annie Phizacklea, *Trans-Nationalism and the Politics of Belonging* (London: Routledge, 2000).

Williams, Raymond, *The Politics of Modernism* (London and New York: Verso, 1989; repr. Verso, 2007).

Wilson, Amrit, *Dreams, Questions, Struggles: South Asian Women in Britain* (London: Pluto Press, 2006).

Wilson, Amrit, *Finding a Voice: Asian Women in Britain* (London: Virago, 1978).

Wilson, Amrit, *Survivors* (unpublished manuscript, 1999).

Wilson, J. Associates, *Audiences for the Leicester Haymarket Theatre: A future-scoping report* (Arts Council of England, September, 2002), available from: http://www.takingpartinthearts.com/content.php?content=1113.

Wilson, J. Associates, *Evaluation Report: Leicester Haymarket Theatre—'Arts Connect' New Audiences* (Arts Council of England, September, 2002), available from: http://www.takingpartinthearts.com/content.php?content=1113.

Wilson, Kathleen, *The Island Race: Englishness, Empire and Gender in the Eighteenth Century* (London: Routledge, 2003).

Wilson, Michael, *Storytelling and Theatre* (Basingstoke: Palgrave Macmillan, 2006).

Woddis, Carol. 'A Question of Perception', *Plays and Players* (March 1990), pp. 14–16.

Worrall, David, *Harlequin Empire: Race, Ethnicity and the Drama of the Popular Entertainment* (London: Pickering & Chatto, 2007).

Zaidi, Ali, interview with Stephen Hodge, London, July 2009.

Ziter, Edward, *The Orient on the Victorian Stage* (Cambridge: Cambridge University Press, 2003).

Index